CROWN
OF
BLOOD

The Deadly Inheritance Of
Lady Jane Grey

NICOLA TALLIS

Michael O'Mara Books Limited

This paperback edition first published in 2017

First published in Great Britain in 2016 by
Michael O'Mara Books Limited
9 Lion Yard
Tremadoc Road
London SW4 7NQ

Copyright © Nicola Tallis 2016, 2017

All rights reserved. You may not copy, store, distribute, transmit, reproduce or
otherwise make available this publication (or any part of it) in any form, or by
any means (electronic, digital, optical, mechanical, photocopying, recording or
otherwise), without prior written permission of the publisher. Any person who
does any unauthorized act in relation to this publication may be liable to criminal
prosecution and civil claims for damages.

A CIP catalogue record for this book is available from the British Library.

Papers used by Michael O'Mara Books Limited are natural, recyclable products
made from wood grown in sustainable forests. The manufacturing processes
conform to the environmental regulations of the country of origin.

ISBN: 978-1-78243-867-0 in paperback print format
ISBN: 978-1-78243-672-0 in ebook format

1 2 3 4 5 6 7 8 9 10

www.mombooks.com

Cover design by Claire Cater
Typeset by Ed Pickford
Cover image: Peter Barritt/SuperStock

Printed and bound by CPI Group (UK) Ltd, Croydon, CR0 4YY

This book is, in many ways, a story about cousins,
and thus I've chosen to dedicate it to mine.
For the brightest star in the sky,
Alan William Robertson
(1985–2005)

CONTENTS

LIST OF ILLUSTRATIONS

Mary Tudor and Charles Brandon, Duke and Duchess of Suffolk, Jan Gossaert, c. 1516 (© His Grace the Duke of Bedford and the Trustees of the Bedford Estates, from the Woburn Abbey Collection).

Tomb of Frances Brandon, Duchess of Suffolk, St Edmund's Chapel, Westminster Abbey (© Dean and Chapter of Westminster).

Lady Katherine Grey, Levina Teerlinc, c. 1555-60 (© Victoria and Albert Museum, London).

Lady Mary Grey, Hans Eworth, sixteenth century (by kind permission of the Chequers Trust; photo © Mark Fiennes / Bridgeman Images).

Engraving of John Aylmer, Unknown Artist, eighteenth century (© National Portrait Gallery, London).

Bradgate Park (© Andrew Tongue).

Henry VIII, Unknown Artist, c. 1545 (© National Portrait Gallery, London).

Edward VI, by Workshop associated with Master John, c. 1547 (© National Portrait Gallery, London).

Mary I, Antonio Moro, 1554 (© Prado, Madrid, Spain / Bridgeman Images).

Elizabeth I when Princess, at the age of about thirteen, Guillaume Scrots, c. 1546 (Royal Collection Trust © Her Majesty Queen Elizabeth II, 2015 / Bridgeman Images).

King Edward VI and the Pope by Unknown Artist c.1575 (© National Portrait Gallery, London).

Katherine Parr, attributed to Master John, c. 1544 (© National Portrait Gallery, London).

Sir Thomas Seymour, Unknown Artist, sixteenth century (© National Portrait Gallery, London).

Sudeley Castle, Gloucestershire (© Nigel Schermuly on behalf of Sudeley Castle).

Engraving of Durham Place, English School, nineteenth century (Private Collection © Look and Learn / Bridgeman Images).

Engraving of Syon House from R. Ackermann's 'Repository of Arts', John Gendall, 1823 (Private Collection / The Stapleton Collection / Bridgeman Images).

'My Devise for the Succession' Inner Temple Library, Petyt MS. 538.47, folio 317 (by kind permission of The Masters of the Bench of the Inner Temple).

Framlingham Castle, Suffolk (© Sean Milligan).

The Great Hall, Guildhall (© Mike Booth / Alamy).

The White Tower, Tower of London (© Nicola Tallis).

Queen's House, Tower of London (© Nicola Tallis).

'Jane' Carving in the Beauchamp Tower, Tower of London (© Nicola Tallis).

Jane's signature as queen, 1553, MS328, ff.36-40 (by kind permission of the Warden and Scholars of New College, Oxford).

Dudley Carving in the Beauchamp Tower, Tower of London (© Nicola Tallis).

Lady Jane Grey's Prayer Book (© The British Library Board).

The Execution of Lady Jane Grey, Paul Delaroche, 1833 (© National Gallery, London, England; photo by VCG Wilson / Corbis via Getty Images).

THE HOUSE OF TUDOR

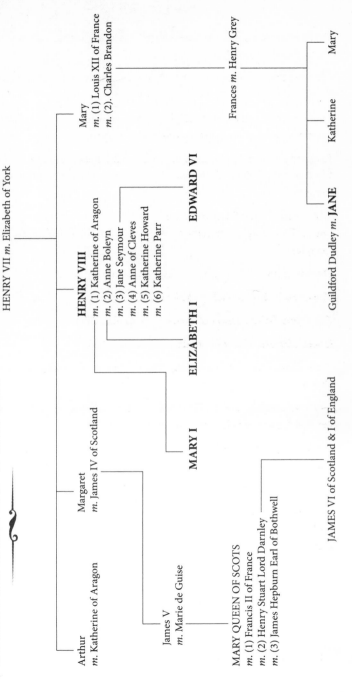

HENRY VII *m.* Elizabeth of York

Arthur
m. Katherine of Aragon

Margaret
m. James IV of Scotland

Mary
m. (1) Louis XII of France
m. (2). Charles Brandon

HENRY VIII
m. (1) Katherine of Aragon
m. (2) Anne Boleyn
m. (3) Jane Seymour
m. (4) Anne of Cleves
m. (5) Katherine Howard
m. (6) Katherine Parr

Frances *m.* Henry Grey

James V
m. Marie de Guise

MARY I   **ELIZABETH I**   **EDWARD VI**

MARY QUEEN OF SCOTS
m. (1) Francis II of France
m. (2) Henry Stuart Lord Darnley
m. (3) James Hepburn Earl of Bothwell

JAMES VI of Scotland & I of England

Guildford Dudley *m.* **JANE**   Katherine   Mary

THE HOUSE OF SUFFOLK

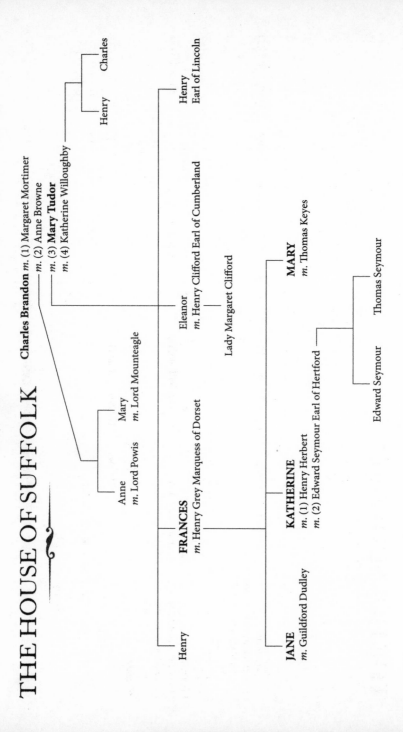

Charles Brandon *m.* (1) Margaret Mortimer
m. (2) Anne Browne
m. (3) **Mary Tudor**
m. (4) Katherine Willoughby

Henry

Charles

Henry
Earl of Lincoln

Eleanor
m. Henry Clifford Earl of Cumberland

Lady Margaret Clifford

Anne
m. Lord Powis

Mary
m. Lord Mounteagle

Henry

FRANCES
m. Henry Grey Marquess of Dorset

JANE
m. Guildford Dudley

KATHERINE
m. (1) Henry Herbert
m. (2) Edward Seymour Earl of Hertford

MARY
m. Thomas Keyes

Edward Seymour

Thomas Seymour

THE HOUSE OF GREY

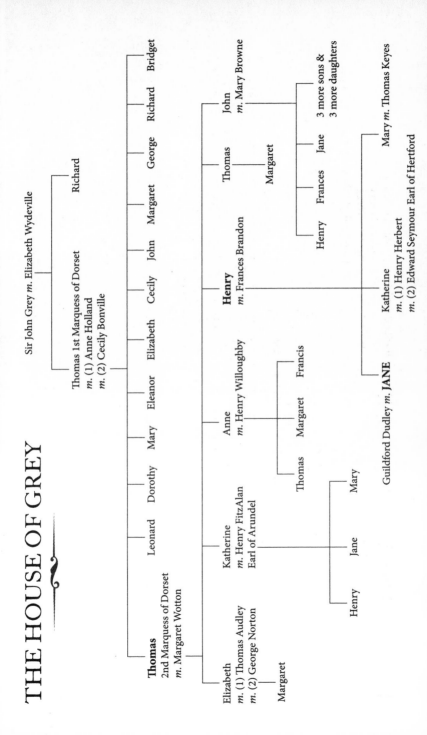

TIMELINE

1533–4	Henry Grey marries Frances Brandon
1536	Lady Jane Grey is born
October 1536	The Pilgrimage of Grace breaks out in Lincolnshire
12 October 1537	Prince Edward is born
1540	Lady Katherine Grey is born
1544	Third Act of Succession passed in Parliament
1545	Lady Mary Grey is born
30 December 1546	Henry VIII makes his final will
28 January 1547	Henry VIII dies, succeeded by Edward VI
February 1547	Jane becomes Sir Thomas Seymour's ward
May 1547	Thomas Seymour marries Katherine Parr
June 1548	Jane travels to Sudeley Castle
30 August 1548	Katherine Parr gives birth to a daughter at Sudeley
5 September 1548	Katherine Parr dies
7 September 1548	Jane is Chief Mourner at Katherine's funeral
Mid-September 1548	Jane travels home to Bradgate Park
October 1548	Jane returns to Seymour Place
17 January 1549	Thomas Seymour is arrested
21 January 1549	The Act of Uniformity is passed in Parliament
20 March 1549	Thomas Seymour is executed

11 October 1549	Lord Protector Somerset is arrested
November 1549	Jane visits the Lady Mary at Beaulieu
December 1549–January 1550	Jane celebrates Christmas with her family at Tilty
June 1550	Roger Ascham visits Bradgate Park
11 October 1551	Henry Grey is created Duke of Suffolk
November 1551	Jane joins the welcome party for Marie de Guise
22 January 1552	Lord Protector Somerset is executed
25 May 1553	Jane is married to Guildford Dudley
June 1553	'My Devise for the Succession' is signed
6 July 1553	Edward VI dies and Lady Jane Grey becomes queen
10 July 1553	Jane is openly proclaimed Queen of England
19 July 1553	Jane is deposed and Mary is proclaimed queen
18 August 1553	Mary I makes a proclamation about religion
22 August 1553	The Duke of Northumberland is executed
5 October 1553	The Act of Repeal is passed in Parliament
13 November 1553	Jane is tried and condemned at Guildhall
January 1554	Negotiations for Mary's marriage are concluded
February 1554	The Wyatt Rebellion ends in failure
12 February 1554	Jane and Guildford are executed

AUTHOR'S NOTE

I HAVE SPENT many an hour strenuously transcribing material for this book, and have taken great pleasure in reading the delightful sixteenth-century hands in which it appears. For the sake of clarity and continuity, however, I have chosen to modernize all of the spelling and punctuation from the books and documents I have consulted, in order to allow the narrative to flow more easily for the reader.

On the occasions that I have referred to money, readers will notice that I have stated the contemporary amount followed by the modern-day equivalent in parentheses. All conversions were done according to the National Archives Currency Convertor (www.nationalarchives.gov.uk/currency), and are approximate values. Please also be aware that they may be subject to change.

During the period in which this book is set, the Julian calendar was in use in England, under which the year turned on 25 March. For clarity, however, the Gregorian calendar that remains in use today, and under which the year turns on 1 January, has been used instead. Interestingly, despite the dominance of the Julian calendar, the annual celebration of New Year, which was one of the great occasions for festivities during the Tudor year, also fell on 1 January.

INTRODUCTION

MEMORIES OF LADY Jane Grey conjure up a life of sadness and injustice: a young lady sacrificed through the actions of ambitious power-players in the complex world of sixteenth-century politics. And there is no doubt that Jane was a victim, but that is only part of the story. Jane was, in fact, a spirited girl who demonstrated character, passion, talent and strength, and deserves to be remembered as such. She was precocious and intelligent, and could also be wilful on occasion, with an acute sense of her own abilities. Jane was also incredibly pious, and her Protestant zeal developed to the point of fanaticism. Moreover, it is certainly possible to argue that she had many of the ingredients necessary in a successful monarch. During her short term as queen, she demonstrated that she was capable of making strategic decisions and of asserting her authority – from the day of her proclamation on 10 July 1553, she showed that she had ample potential to wield the power behind the crown before it was snatched away from her with alarming speed. Furthermore, her numerous other admirable qualities that were showcased throughout the course of her short life support this: she had dignity, integrity and displayed bravery by defending herself against powerful men in an age when women were expected to be wholly obedient. While Jane was undoubtedly used and forced into a queenship she did not want, such qualities reveal that she had strength of character and will, and was capable of asserting them, often to the surprise and disturbance of those who sought to wield power through her. There are those who would argue that, having reigned for so brief a period and having never been crowned, Jane should not be classified as a monarch, but I would dispute this. To those who do acknowledge her as such, Jane is often referred to as 'the Nine Days Queen', but this too is incorrect. She was, albeit for a short time, acknowledged as queen by the Council of the realm through the machinations of Edward VI from the moment of his death on 6 July. As the contemporary martyrologist John Foxe later remembered, 'When King Edward was dead, this Jane was established in the kingdom by the Nobles consent.'[1] The news that Jane was queen, however, was not made public until 10 July, when she was conducted to the Tower of London and a proclamation was issued in her name, supported by the lords of the Council, which is where the 'Nine Days' comes from. Once again, Foxe remarked that Jane was 'published Queen by proclamation at London, and in other Cities where was any great resort, and was there so taken and named'.[2] Jane was made queen and proclaimed queen, and the fact that she was referred to as such by many of her contemporaries is perhaps the most revealing evidence that this was indeed how she was regarded. For thirteen days, therefore, Jane was Queen of England, but only nine of these days were conducted openly with public knowledge of Jane's exalted status. In the immediate aftermath of Edward's death, Jane was given four days to prepare herself for the challenge that lay ahead, a task that she faced with dignity. It is true that Jane was not crowned, but neither were Edward V and Edward VIII, and Jane certainly deserves recognition on a par with both. Therefore, in writing Jane's story, I do so very much with the belief that she was, and should be remembered as, Queen Jane.

The sources for Jane's life are scant, and at times are absent altogether. For example, none of her contemporaries remarked on the precise date or place of her birth, and neither do we know anything of her childhood with certainty. By the same token, none of Jane's contemporaries left a description of her physical appearance – the account accredited to the Genoese merchant Battista Spinola, in which she was described as being 'very short and thin, but prettily shaped and graceful', has been proven to be fraudulent.[3] Unsurprisingly, most of the surviving sources relate to the events of 1553, and for that reason they vary in terms of their quality and reliability. One of the most important and indeed detailed accounts is *The Chronicle of Queen Jane*, a contemporary narrative of the events of 1553 and 1554 that was first published in the nineteenth century. Some of the pages of the manuscript are sadly missing, but it is nevertheless comprehensive. Although the author left no name and has never been conclusively identified, he is generally believed to have been one Rowland Lea, a gentleman who worked in the royal mint at the Tower of London, and probably resided there too.[4] Lea was evidently a man of some standing, for not only did he have access to the Tower but, much to his surprise, on one occasion he dined with Jane herself during her imprisonment. Lea's position ensured that he was well placed to report on the events of which he wrote, and also explains why his narrative often provides details that other accounts lack.

The Tudor antiquarian John Stow also consulted Lea's manuscript, and often quoted heavily from it in his *A Summarie of the Chronicles of England*, an account of the history of England. It is possible that some of his insights also come from parts of Lea's manuscript that are no longer extant, in which case his account should also be taken seriously. Although Stow had a thorough knowledge of London, and in 1598 published his most famous work, *A Survey of London*, his interest was not specifically in Jane, and his account repeated much of what was recorded elsewhere. He was also a Merchant Taylor, and he may have even met Jane, for on one occasion he reported visiting her parents' home at Sheen, the Charterhouse.

Someone who had an advantage over many of his contemporaries was her Italian tutor, Michelangelo Florio. He had a personal relationship with Jane, and was therefore well placed to know the truth of matters. Florio was an Italian Franciscan who later became a leading Protestant and spent time preaching in several cities in the country of his birth. This led to his arrest and imprisonment in Rome in 1548. Managing to escape in 1550, he eventually made his way to England, where he came under the protection of Archbishop Thomas Cranmer and Sir William Cecil. He began preaching in London, a career that was destined to fail. However, he soon found favour with Jane's father, and took up a post as Italian tutor to Jane. Florio was an eyewitness to the events about which he wrote, and was naturally sympathetic to Jane. His narrative, the first biography of Jane's life, is often corroborated by other sources, however, and his placement in the Grey household meant that he had close and regular access to Jane and her family. The accession of Mary I forced Florio into exile abroad, and it was in Strasbourg that he wrote his account in 1561. It was not published until 1607, after his death, for which reason some historians have questioned its reliability. Florio is, however, a crucial source, and one who cannot be overlooked.

In 1563 the martyrologist John Foxe published the first edition of his *Acts and Monuments*, better known as *The Book of Martyrs*. This work was an account of the persecution of Protestants under the Catholic Church during the sixteenth century, all of whom were Foxe's contemporaries. Jane was one of its main characters, cast in the light of Foxe's sympathies as a martyr to the Protestant faith. For this reason and that some of his descriptions of events have been proven to be inaccurate, Foxe must be approached with some caution. But many of his accounts have been corroborated by other sources and he also had access to many of the people who had known Jane – in 1550, for example, he was staying with her step-grandmother, Katherine Willoughby – and so his work remains important and illuminating.

Some of the interesting details of the period come from the Imperial ambassadors, the representatives of the Holy Roman Emperor Charles V, who resided in England. Although they were supporters of Mary I, they, again, had close access to many of those who were involved in Jane's story, and often heard about events at first-hand. Besides that, their job was to report on the events they witnessed as well as the state of affairs in England, and thus they were, for the most part, remarkably accurate and comprehensive. Nonetheless, on occasion they were known to add the odd salacious detail which highlighted the pleasure they sometimes took in the gossip that came to their ears.

There are other Catholic sources that report on Jane's life, one of which comes from the papal envoy, Giovanni Commendone. Commendone produced his version of events, *The Accession, Coronation and Marriage of Mary Tudor*, based on what he saw when he arrived in England on 8 August 1553, shortly after Jane's deposition. He had arrived in England at the behest of Pope Julius III in order to discuss Queen Mary's hopes to return the realm to Catholicism. His sojourn in the country was only of short duration, for he was back in Rome the following month, but during that time he did make strident efforts to try to obtain material for his narrative. It is unclear precisely where Commendone's information came from, but it can often be corroborated, and his account probably also formed the basis of the later *L'Historia Ecclesiastica della Rivoluzion d'Inghilterra*, published by Fra Girolamo Pollini in 1594.

Another Catholic source comes in the form of the *Vita Mariae Angliae Reginae*, a chronicle composed by Robert Wingfield. Wingfield was a supporter of Mary I, and even played host to her in East Anglia during the summer of 1553. The strong Catholic bias in Wingfield's narrative is evident, and following the death of Edward VI he described Mary as 'the most sacred Princess Mary, the next, true and undoubted heir to the kingdom'.[5] In spite of this, Wingfield was also closely connected to Jane's family, and he was indeed sympathetic to them. He was the son and heir of Sir Humphrey Wingfield of Brantham, a cousin of Jane's maternal grandfather, Charles Brandon. Sir Humphrey even resided in Brandon's household during the childhood of Jane's mother, Frances. Thus the two would have known one another, and Frances in turn would have come to know Robert. Although Robert was in a good position to know of the events of which he wrote, he was not inside the Tower as Rowland Lea was. Some of the details in his account are wrong, and it is evident that he viewed the Duke of Northumberland as the villain of the piece. It is possible that he obtained some of his version of events from Frances, whose will he later witnessed.

Though the accounts vary in their approach, bias and detail, when combined with other sources – including pieces of material culture and sources where we can learn about Jane indirectly – they provide enough to allow us to piece together a reasonable picture of Jane's life, her motivations, and how her contemporaries viewed her. There are inevitably gaps in the story, and it is therefore the role of the historian to try to ascertain what may have happened and suggest theories based on a balance of probabilities. I believe, however, that enough remains to allow us to get comparatively close to the real Jane, and to view her as an extraordinary young woman who inspired many of those who knew her.

In the nineteenth century, Edward Baldwin observed that 'the history of Lady Jane Grey is worthy to be written', and in the pages which follow, her story will be carefully examined, using, to my knowledge, a certain collection of material – including an inventory of the jewels that were delivered to her during her brief queenship and documents relating to her trial, among others – that has never previously been incorporated into a published biography.[6] Such evidence will be used to help pick apart the complex threads of Jane's life, thereby unravelling the grim tapestry of her fall, and charting the deadly intrigues that led inexorably to its horrific and searing climax.

Nicola Tallis, London, 2016

PROLOGUE

ON A BITTERLY cold February night, within the thick and gloomy walls of the Tower of London, a young girl, aged just seventeen, awaited her execution on the morrow. From her room she could see the scaffold on which she was to die – she had heard the dull echoes of metal on wood as it had been erected. Perhaps her thoughts turned to the two other queens, Anne Boleyn and Katherine Howard, who had lost their lives in a similarly violent manner on the precise same spot, less than twenty years previously. They too had experienced the terror of imprisonment in the Tower, waiting to hear whether they would receive a last-minute pardon or face the executioner's block.

But Jane was not the only prisoner that night. Little more than eleven miles away in Sheen stood Jane's magnificent family home, the Charterhouse. Inside, her mother Frances, Duchess of Suffolk, awaited a double tragedy, for it was not only her daughter but also her husband, Jane's father, who was imprisoned, awaiting trial and imminent death. Her immediate thoughts, however, were with Jane, the daughter in whom she had invested so many of her hopes and ambitions for future glory.

Also within the Charterhouse that sombre evening were Jane's two younger sisters, Katherine and Mary. Just thirteen and eight years old, the girls must have witnessed their mother's distress, known of their father's absence, and been utterly terrified. There is no way of knowing whether Jane's letter to Katherine, a sober lesson in morality written in a copy of the Greek New Testament, brought her any comfort. Nevertheless, Jane's words are striking: 'As touching my death, rejoice as I do and consider that I shall be delivered of this corruption and put on incorruption.'

At the royal Palace of Whitehall, Jane's cousin Queen Mary, by whose authority Jane had been condemned, waited in anguish at the thought that this poor, tortured young soul, so steadfast in her religious belief – her heresy in the Queen's view – was destined to endure the flames of Hell. The Queen had been merciful at first, doing all that she could to try to save Jane's life, defying her Councillors' most ardent advice. When that had failed, her thoughts had turned to saving Jane's soul, and she had tried to make Jane see reason and embrace the Catholic faith. But Jane had not wavered. Queen Mary, the only person with the power to save her life, was reluctantly resolved: Jane would have to die.

Queen Mary's half-sister, the Lady Elizabeth, in what was almost certainly a pretence intended to keep her away from danger and save her own skin, claimed to be sick at Ashridge, but would have been painfully aware that her young cousin's life was about to come to a sudden and violent end. There were those about the Queen who would be happy to see Elizabeth go the same way. They whispered in the Queen's ear, warning her that Elizabeth was plotting against her, and soon Elizabeth too would find herself languishing within the same walls that had once held Jane prisoner.

Shortly after ten o'clock on the morning of 12 February, Jane was informed that her time had come.

'Lord, into thy hands I commend my spirit,' she cried on the scaffold. And then the axe fell. To Jane, her death signalled immortality and martyrdom; for her mother and her sisters it was a tragic loss; and for Queen Mary it was the necessary removal of a figurehead of conspiracy. For the Lady Elizabeth, Jane's death was utterly terrifying, demonstrating that for one who aspired to wear a crown, the possibility of a violent death was always looming.

CHAPTER 1

A Time to be Born and
a Time to Die

'THERE IS A time to be born and a time to die, and the day of our death is better than the day of our birth.'[1] These poignant words were those of the seventeen-year-old Lady Jane Grey, immortalized for posterity in the pages of the exquisitely decorated prayer book that she treasured until her final moments. It is ironic that this courageous young woman of great intellect and character, whose end is so well documented, began her life in such an obscure manner that the precise circumstances of her birth are lost to us. The only certainty is that simply by right of her blood, Jane was born a potential heir to the English throne; she was a member of the royal family, and, more importantly, she was a Tudor. Her family connections would shape her life, and ultimately determine her fate.

Jane's date of birth has been the subject of debate from almost the moment of her death. Today the debate continues, and the answer has yet to be satisfactorily established. Born into an age in which it was not unusual for such details to go unrecorded, even among the royal family, it is hardly surprising that nobody considered noting the arrival of Jane, who was, after all, one of several girls born into the Tudor family within the past three decades. Jane herself never made any mention of her birthdate, though in several of her surviving letters she referred to 'my youth' and 'my age' and inexperience in order to stress a point.[2] Such a detail may seem trivial, but it is in fact one of the greatest mysteries surrounding

1

Jane's life. Her youth is central to her story, and as such modern historians have hotly debated it.

For many centuries it was believed that Jane was born in October 1537, just days prior to or after the arrival of Henry VIII's longed-for male heir, Prince Edward, whose life would come to be so intricately linked with Jane's own.[3] This theory has long since been disproved beyond dispute, due to the fact that on 15 October her mother, Frances, Marchioness of Dorset, was expected to have attended Prince Edward's christening at Hampton Court Palace, a duty she would have been spared had she either been expecting or recently given birth.[4]

In fact the likeliest date for Jane's birth is in the latter half of 1536.[5] The most convincing evidence comes from a letter written on 29 May 1551 by Jane's tutor John Aylmer, to the Swiss reformer Heinrich Bullinger, in which he noted Jane's age: 'And you are well able to determine, in your wisdom, how useful are the counsels of the aged to guide and direct young persons at her time of life, which is just fourteen.'[6] Much has been made of Aylmer's phrase 'just fourteen', which has been taken as an implication that Jane had only recently turned fourteen. If this was indeed the case then Jane's birth must have taken place in the spring of 1537.[7] However, when Aylmer's remark is read in the proper context of his letter, then the implication of a recent birthday falls away. Aylmer continued to inform Bullinger:

> For at that age, as the comic poet tells us, all people are inclined to follow their own ways, and by the attractiveness of the objects, and the corruption of nature, are more easily carried headlong unto pleasure ... so to these tender minds there should neither be wanting the counsel of the aged, nor the authority of men of grave and influential character.[8]

From this it seems clear that Aylmer was in fact using Jane's age to highlight the difference between the young and the old, stressing an aversion by the young to heed the advice of their elders. It should not therefore be taken as conclusive evidence of Jane's recent birthday.

If Aylmer was correct and Jane was fourteen on 29 May 1551, then a date in the latter half of 1536 seems probable. Certainly, Aylmer was in a good position to know the truth of the matter, as someone who knew Jane well and who could 'look upon [her] with affection as a pupil'.[9] This would also corroborate the claim from Jane's Italian tutor Michelangelo Florio that she was seventeen at the time of her death in February 1554, but in her eighteenth year.[10] The evidence from those who knew Jane all points towards a birthdate in 1536, and though the precise date will never be ascertained with any certainty, the year at least can be settled without further debate.

Disputed with equal vigour is the precise location of Jane's birth. According to tradition she was born within the tranquillity of Bradgate Park, the Leicestershire seat of her father's family. Set in beautiful parkland in which Jane's family once enjoyed excellent hunting, the romantic ruins of the house can still be seen today, a tangible reminder of its grand Tudor past.[11] The ruined tower, still named 'Lady Jane's Tower', once claimed to have hosted the arrival of its famous namesake, while local legend states that Jane was christened in the parish church at nearby Newtown Linford.[12] It is true that Jane passed a great deal of her childhood within the red brick walls of Bradgate, and would have been familiar with its sumptuous and spacious rooms, decorated with expensive tapestries and costly furniture, and its 'fine park' as described by the Tudor scholar and antiquary John Leland, but it is unlikely to have been the setting for her birth.[13] It was not until 1538, shortly before Jane's second birthday, that her parents took up residence at Bradgate, and prior to this her paternal, rather headstrong grandmother Margaret Wotton was firmly installed there, which makes it an unlikely choice.

It is more probable that Jane was born in London, possibly at her father's grand town house, Dorset House, situated on the fashionable Strand in

Westminster.[14] Though at the time of Jane's birth her parents had probably spent little time there as a married couple, the convenience of Dorset House for the royal court which they attended made it a desirable location. London was a popular choice for the births of royal children, and it may have allowed Jane's grandmother, who was in control of Dorset House in the same manner as Bradgate Park, to be close at hand for her birth. Today, the splendid house has long since vanished, swallowed up by the buildings of modern-day Westminster.[15] However, the few surviving descriptions allow us glimpses of the house that was once one of the most magnificent in the capital. Dorset House was situated only a short distance from the royal palaces of Westminster and Whitehall, and was built in the typical Tudor style around a courtyard, and with domed turrets and fashionable red brick. The house was surrounded by elaborate formal gardens that were full of sweet-smelling flowers and medicinal herbs, and the interior was equally grand. There were spacious apartments for the family, including a modern gallery where they could take exercise during bad weather, and a chapel. The glass in the windows was emblazoned with the family coat of arms, proudly proclaiming its ownership. It was a luxurious house that struck awe into passers-by.

The protocol surrounding the births of royal and noble children was strict, and it seems likely that Jane's mother followed the conventions of other high-born women and went into seclusion several weeks prior to the arrival of her child. Preparations for the births of high-born children were well organized and elaborate; the lying-in chamber was carefully prepared with a great four-poster bed hung with luxurious and expensive fabrics of the finest quality, and sometimes a birthing stool was provided, the use of which had become increasingly popular during this period.[16] Often a roaring fire blazed in the grate, and fresh aromatic rushes were strewn on the floor to sweeten the air. In an attempt to ward off evil spirits the room was kept eerily dark, with the windows closed and covered over, and even the keyholes blocked. The walls were covered in costly tapestries, with the only light coming from flickering candles. In such stifling conditions, there was nowhere for fresh air to circulate. These extremes were all precautions that had been in place for centuries, and they had thus become an accepted part of the process of childbirth. The process was also exclusively female, managed by midwives who were often local women with very little training, and even less understanding of the importance of hygiene. Men were strictly forbidden from going anywhere near the birthing chamber, and Jane's father would therefore not have been present at the birth of his daughter, having bidden farewell to her mother as she entered her confinement. Though he was banned from the birthing chamber, one can imagine him close by, pacing the rooms of Dorset House in eager anticipation of the arrival of his first-born child.

Jane was the eldest daughter of Henry Grey, 3rd Marquess of Dorset, 'an illustrious and widely loved nobleman of ancient lineage, but lacking in circumspection', and his wife, Lady Frances Brandon.[17] The couple were among the leading nobility in the realm, and at the time of Jane's birth they had been married for nearly three years. Sadly, no likenesses of Henry Grey survive, and the only authenticated image of Frances is that which adorns her tomb effigy in Westminster Abbey.[18]

On her father's side Frances had little to boast of in the way of lineage, for the success of the Brandon family stemmed purely from loyalty to the Tudor dynasty. Her father, Charles Brandon, came from a humble family of Suffolk origin, and had himself earned his wealth and title of Duke of Suffolk through nothing more than his own merits and his close relationship to the King.[19] However, on her mother's side Frances had the royal blood of the Tudors. Blood that she in turn passed on to her daughter Jane. Frances was the daughter of Henry VIII's younger sister, Mary Tudor – 'a young and beautiful damsel', and the widowed queen of Louis XII of France – who had made a clandestine, scandalous second marriage in 1515, for love, to her brother's jousting partner and lookalike, Charles Brandon.[20] Brandon had also been married before, twice, making his marriage with Mary his third. Despite the fact that her second marriage made her Duchess of Suffolk, for the rest of her life Mary continued to be regally addressed as the French Queen. Her marriage was a happy one that produced four children: two sons and two daughters. Henry was born in 1516, followed by Frances, her parents 'first begotten daughter', and Eleanor.[21] At some time prior to 1522, however, young Henry died, for it was almost certainly in that year that he was replaced in the Suffolk nursery with another son, who was also christened Henry.[22]

Frances was born between two and three in the morning of Wednesday 16 July 1517, at the Palace of Bishop's Hatfield, twenty miles north of London. According to her father's own account, 'she was named Frances, being born on St Francis's day'.[23] Her name may also have been intended as a compliment to the French King, Francis I, with whom the Duke and Duchess were both on friendly terms since Mary's first marriage.[24] Three days after her birth, Frances was christened in the nearby church of St Etheldreda, her godmothers being none other than Mary's sister-in-law, Queen Katherine of Aragon, and her niece the Princess Mary.[25] The Princess was herself only a baby of fifteen months, but she had been named in honour of her aunt, and in time would grow to be close to her cousin and goddaughter.

Frances had passed much of her childhood in the picturesque Suffolk countryside, in the village of Westhorpe that lay just thirteen miles from Bury St Edmunds. The grand Westhorpe Hall, the favoured residence of her parents, dominated the village, and it was here that Frances was raised in the utmost splendour.[26]

Charles Brandon had acquired Westhorpe Hall in 1514, and following his marriage to Mary Tudor, the couple spent vast sums of money on improvements – in fact, Charles later claimed that the costs totalled £12,000 (£3,865,000).[27] Mary in particular seems to have enjoyed spending time there when she was not at court, surrounded by the lush green fields and forests of the Suffolk countryside, and it was here that she chose to establish a household for her children.

A survey taken in 1538 reveals that the house stood in a moat which could be crossed by an elaborate three-arched bridge. The house itself was built partly from stone, and partly from brick covered with black and white chequered plaster. Visitors to Westhorpe Hall were greeted by the sight of a large three-storey gatehouse, while the 'fair stately hall' boasted a life-sized statue of Hercules and the lion – almost certainly a tribute to the Duke of Suffolk's military prowess.[28]

As well as her siblings, Frances also had the company of her two elder half-sisters. Anne and Mary were her father's daughters, born of his second marriage, and were aged ten and seven at the time of her birth.[29] Frances may also have spent some time with her cousin and godmother, the Princess Mary, for in later life the two would become extremely close, and it seems likely that this bond was forged during their youth. Sadly, however, Frances's idyllic childhood was shattered when her mother died shortly before Frances was married, though plans for the wedding had been established during her mother's lifetime and with her approval.[30] After all, Henry Grey, too, had royal connections, albeit of a less prestigious nature than his wife's. Henry was proud of his lineage, and clearly considered himself to be royal, for the German scholar John of Ulm whom Henry had later patronized wrote that he 'is descended from the royal family with which he is very nearly connected'.[31] Ulm also related of Henry that, whether through his marriage or in his own right, 'He told me he had the rank of Prince.'[32]

Henry stemmed from the house of Grey, which could trace its origins back to the Norman Conquest, when it is probable that one of the family's ancestors accompanied William the Conqueror to England from Normandy.[33] The family settled in Leicestershire, but they did not rise to prominence until the fifteenth century, when their claim to nobility came in the form of Henry's great-grandmother, the formidable Elizabeth

Wydeville, queen of Edward IV. Before allying with the King, Elizabeth had been married to Sir John Grey, a Lancastrian knight killed during the Cousins' Wars (later termed the Wars of the Roses) at the Second Battle of St Albans on 17 February 1461. The union produced two sons. It was the eldest of these sons, Thomas, 1st Marquess of Dorset, who was Henry's grandfather.[34] By his wife Cecily Bonville, Thomas in turn had twelve surviving children. It was his eldest son and namesake, Thomas, 2nd Marquess of Dorset, whose second marriage to Margaret Wotton resulted in Henry's birth.[35] Though their marriage was by no means a love match on the same scale as that of the Suffolks', to all appearances it was a happy one which produced six surviving children. Elizabeth, Katherine and Anne were the eldest, followed by Henry, Thomas and John.

Henry was born on 17 January 1517, almost certainly at his father's newly built home, Bradgate Park in Leicestershire. He was named in honour of the King, Henry VIII, and spent the first few years of his life at Bradgate and Astley Castle, his father's Warwickshire estate, under his mother's supervision.[36] Like Charles Brandon, Thomas Grey was in high favour with the King, and this would prove to be extremely beneficial when it came to his son Henry's education.[37] In 1525, through the auspices of his father, Henry was fortunate enough to secure a place in the household of Henry Fitzroy, Duke of Richmond, the illegitimate son of Henry VIII by his mistress Elizabeth (Bessie) Blount.[38] Richmond was two years younger than Henry Grey, and this, coupled with his rank as the son of a marquess, made him an ideal companion for the young boy and was a sign of great favour for the Greys. Known to his intimates as Harry, young Henry spent four years of his childhood in Richmond's household, which was established far away from the court in London, at Sheriff Hutton Castle in Yorkshire.[39] Though parts of the castle were already falling into disrepair at the time of the party's arrival, in 1534 John Leland claimed that he 'saw no house in the North so like a princely lodgings'.[40] The apartments Richmond occupied were lavishly furnished and he lived in great state; as such, Henry too became used to living in palatial surroundings. Henry's place at Sheriff Hutton ensured that he was in close contact with the boy whom many of his contemporaries at one time suspected would be made his father's heir in preference to the King's daughter, Princess Mary. The two boys appear to have been close, and Henry also struck up friendships with other boys who were fortunate enough to be members of Richmond's household. One of these was William Parr, the younger brother of Katherine, future wife of Henry VIII, who would later play a key role in the life of Henry's daughter Jane. It was a friendship that was maintained until the end of their lives.

From London, Richmond's godfather, Cardinal Wolsey, controlled his household, but it was Sir William Parr of Horton who oversaw the everyday running of it.[41] Appointed Chamberlain, it was Sir William's responsibility to ensure that his young charge and his companions received an education befitting their status. Education was of critical importance to Henry's family; his father had certainly been well taught, and Henry enjoyed a splendid education too.[42] Alongside his royal companion, at Sheriff Hutton he was instructed in Latin and Greek, both of which he spoke fluently, as well as the French that was essential for members of the aristocracy. Initially, John Palsgrave, who had formerly been employed to teach Frances's mother French, conducted some of the boys' lessons.[43] Palsgrave, however, found his pupils to be so mischievous that he resigned the following year, to be replaced by Richard Croke.

Henry proved to be incredibly gifted when it came to intellectual pursuits, and an impressed contemporary described him as 'well learned and a great wit'.[44] His interest and enthusiasm for learning continued throughout his life, and in time came to be shared by his eldest daughter, Jane.

Henry remained in Richmond's household at Sheriff Hutton until October 1529, when, with his companion, he returned to London following the break-up of Richmond's household. The reason for the sudden return to London is unclear, but it is possible that the King had become concerned that Richmond was not applying himself wholeheartedly to his lessons, and he was installed primarily in Windsor Castle where his father was better able to monitor his behaviour. Henry was just thirteen years old when, a year later on 10 October 1530, his father died at Bradgate Park.[45] Through his years of unswerving loyal service to the King, Thomas had become a very wealthy man, leaving his eldest son and heir well provided for. Henry now succeeded his father as 3rd Marquess of Dorset, Baron Ferrers of Groby, Baron Harington and Baron Bonville. His father had been eager that his son should continue with his education, and in his will Thomas Grey had left the great sum of twenty pounds a year (£6,400) to Henry's tutor, Robert Brock, until the task was complete.[46] His father's wish was one that Henry seems to have been only too happy to fulfil.

At thirteen, however, Henry was a minor, and he now became a ward of the Crown, unable to receive his full inheritance until his twenty-first birthday. Up to that time it was to be held in keeping by his mother, much to his chagrin. The young teenager now spent most of his time at court, bringing him into close contact with other nobles of the realm. Given his youth, it seems unlikely that he spent much time with such men, or saw much of the monarch. In February 1531, however, he is recorded as having dined with the King and the Dukes of Suffolk and Norfolk.[47] Suffolk may already have had Henry in mind as a potential suitor for his daughter Frances, although if this was the case he did not yet act on it, and for good reason.

As a youngster with little or no firm male guidance, Henry's lack of experience managed to get him into trouble on at least one occasion, leading to his temporary banishment from court. The circumstances are unclear, but the Imperial ambassador Eustace Chapuys, one of the best informed sources of the period, reported to his master the Emperor Charles V that 'the young Marquis [Dorset] has been forbidden to go to Court for some time, because he has been charged with assembling the people of Cornwall and the neighbourhood'.[48] The details of this episode are somewhat baffling, and no other source makes any mention of it. Whatever the truth of the matter, it cannot have posed a serious threat for Henry was forgiven, and his banishment proved to be over within two months. Following his return, though, Chapuys observed that 'he has been allowed to return more to be under vigilance and some kind of arrest than otherwise'.[49] He may have been displaying that rebellious streak that is so common in teenagers; he was also self-indulgent, lazy and incredibly naïve. The English chronicler Raphael Holinshed, who may have known Henry, described him as 'bountiful' and 'very liberal'.[50] Holinshed was an evangelical who may have been educated at Cambridge. If this was the case then it could explain how he became acquainted with Henry and why he was so flattering in his description, for not only was Henry a devoted evangelical, but, as Holinshed explained, Henry was also 'a great favourer of those that were learned', and later patronized several scholars.[51] As he grew older, Henry became fond of hunting and gambling, and would later accrue huge debts that he struggled to pay. The court was the ideal place for him to indulge his vices, and with no male figurehead in his life he ran almost wild. Yet he could also be extremely generous: 'of nature to his friends gentle and courteous', Holinshed said, especially to his servants.[52] This may have been seen as a weakness by some of his contemporaries, for one observed that Henry was 'young, lusty and poor, of great possessions but which are not in his hands, many friends of great power, with little or no experience'.[53] His mother was alarmed by his behaviour, and wrote to the King's chief advisor, Thomas Cromwell, of her desire to attend on her son daily at court, presumably to keep an eye on him. Besides that, Margaret also begged Cromwell himself to intervene: 'whenever you shall see in him any large playing or great usual swearing, or any other demeanour unmeet for him to use, which I fear me shall be very often, I pray you for his father's sake to rebuke him, and if he has any grace, he will be grateful to you when he grows older'.[54] Margaret's letters to Cromwell reveal that the relationship between mother and son was fraught with difficulties, financial issues being a particular bone of contention.[55]

On 24 March 1533, the Duke of Suffolk bought the wardship of the sixteen-year-old Henry without his estates at a cost of four thousand marks.[56] This gave Suffolk the right to arrange Henry's marriage, and he had only one bride in mind: his daughter, Lady Frances Brandon. Suffolk had been considering his daughter's marriage prospects for some time, and probably settled on Henry in 1532.[57] It was a marriage, though, that would cause some scandal, for Henry had been previously betrothed. As part of a double negotiation, it had been agreed that Henry should wed Katherine FitzAlan, the daughter of William FitzAlan, 11th Earl of Arundel and his wife Anne Percy. Arundel's heir, Henry FitzAlan, Lord Maltravers, meanwhile, would be married to Henry's sister, Katherine.[58]

It is unclear exactly when this deal had been brokered – it had almost certainly been engineered with the approval of Henry's father. Henry, however, had other ideas, and under his own auspices he 'refused' Katherine in order to marry Frances – a match that was far superior in prestige.[59] Precisely when his betrothal was broken off is obscure, but it had certainly taken place prior to 16 November 1532, for on that day his mother wrote to Cromwell to complain about the compensation that had to be paid to the Earl, 'whose daughter my son refused'.[60] This amounted to three hundred marks a year until the sum of four thousand marks had been paid, an exorbitant sum. Margaret begged for Cromwell's intercession to help reduce the yearly sum to one hundred marks a year, else 'I shall not be able to marry my poor daughters nor keep my house'.[61] However, there had evidently been some attempt to force Henry to marry Katherine FitzAlan, for in the same letter his mother declared that 'the Earl refused to take my son when the King's grace was contented that he should have had him after his refusal'.[62]

The King had almost certainly intervened because Henry was his ward, though the reason for the Earl's refusal of the match was at this point a matter of pride. Moreover, the nature of the arrangement between Henry and Katherine had been *per verba de praesenti* (in the words of the present), which meant that they had made an agreement to marry (otherwise known as a common-law marriage). This made their betrothal immediately binding, and meant that it could be consummated at once before a later church ceremony in which they were officially married. Such arrangements were common in the sixteenth century, and were taken so seriously that they were enforceable in a church court. This was almost certainly part of the reason why Henry's refusal to marry Katherine caused such outrage, although there is no evidence that the union was consummated, and the case was not taken to a church court.[63] Unsurprisingly, and in spite of the successfully concluded marriage between Henry's sister Katherine and Lord Maltravers, relations with the FitzAlan family were frosty. For Katherine FitzAlan, Henry's refusal of her was an insulting and humiliating snub over which she harboured resentment for some time, and, despite being young and the daughter of a peer of the realm, she would never take a husband.

Frances and Henry may have been formally betrothed following the purchase of his wardship, and it is possible that at the same time her younger sister Eleanor was betrothed to Henry, Lord Clifford, the heir of the Earl of Cumberland. It was common practice to settle the marriage provisions of more than one child at once, and the same arrangement was later put in place for Frances's own daughters. It is probable that Frances and Henry knew one another prior to their betrothal, for their fathers had been friends and colleagues, but it is unlikely that they knew each other well. What is certain is that their marriage did not take place immediately, and there may have been several reasons for this. Henry's mother was greatly concerned about the financial implications of the marriage, as is confirmed in a letter she wrote to Cromwell the following

February. Margaret claimed that 'I wrote to my lord of Suffolk that since it was his pleasure to match my son into honourable blood, if he would see me discharged of my bond for support of my son during his minority, I would consent.'[64] As the instigator of the marriage, Suffolk had therefore agreed to support the couple financially until Henry turned twenty-one and obtained his majority. Keen, though, to protect his interests, he made it clear that should Frances die before the wedding, he ought to be able to retain Henry's wardship, 'to dispose and sell him to my pleasure'.[65]

There may, however, have been an altogether different explanation for the delay in the marriage, which was the declining health of Frances's mother. The Duchess of Suffolk had been ailing for some time, and on 30 March, just days after the purchase of Henry's wardship, she had signed off a letter addressed to Lord Lisle 'in a very shaky hand'.[66] She was in no fit state to organize a wedding, and before her daughter's marriage could take place she died on 25 June at Westhorpe Hall.[67]

AT THE TIME of their marriage, both Henry and Frances were sixteen. The wedding was almost certainly conducted in the latter half of 1533 in the brilliant surroundings of Suffolk Place, the palatial London residence of Frances's father.[68] The precise date is unknown, but a letter written by the Duke of Suffolk to Henry's mother on 28 July makes it clear that the marriage had not yet taken place. All that can be stated with any certainty is that the couple were married before 4 February 1534, the first occasion on which Frances is referred to as Henry's wife in another letter written by Henry's mother.[69] No details of the wedding survive, but it was undoubtedly a lavish affair at which the King himself may have been present.[70] More importantly, the marriage sealed the bonds of alliance between the houses of Suffolk and Dorset that were a crucial part of sixteenth-century networking. In the style of many aristocratic matches, it was a marriage made for politics, not passion.

The marriage of Jane's parents brought Frances Brandon a title – Marchioness of Dorset – but due to her husband's minority it was, for the moment, in name only. Her mother-in-law was still alive, and continued to be styled Marchioness of Dorset despite her status as dowager. During Margaret's lifetime, therefore, Frances was sometimes referred to as 'the Young Marchioness' in order to distinguish her from her mother-in-law, who was often referred to as 'the Old Marchioness'.[71] Frances was one of the most important ladies in the land, and in later years was always listed immediately after the King's daughters in order of precedence in all documents and state reports, as well as being afforded a prominent role in ceremonial occasions at court.

Under Henry's mother's insistence, the Duke of Suffolk had agreed to support the young couple, and it seems that in order to cut costs, in the immediate aftermath of the wedding he had arranged for his daughter to join the household of her mother-in-law, while Henry returned to court where he had spent much of the last three years. In personal terms this must have been a very difficult arrangement: after all, Henry and Frances were a newlywed couple, and to all appearances their marriage was a successful one. It may have been based on politics, but the evidence suggests that it was a happy marriage, if not a love match in the same manner as Frances's parents. Sadly, no letters between the couple survive, but Frances's mother Mary had been the victim of an arranged first marriage, and knew only too well the potentially painful consequences of such a match. As such she would surely have been eager to avoid her daughter being forced into an unhappy marriage. There are numerous examples during this period of unsuccessful arranged marriages, but Frances and Henry were not among them, and lived harmoniously together.[72] However, the evidence strongly suggests that Frances was the dominant partner, and this is also borne out by contemporary reports of Henry's weak character. A seventeenth-century writer claimed that Frances 'was of greater spirits, but one who could accommodate it to the will of her husband', and this does appear to have been the case.[73] Henry seems to have been perfectly happy, at least at the beginning, to be led by his young wife, and to allow her to make important decisions – especially when it came to the welfare of their daughter Jane.

It has often been claimed that two children were born to the couple prior to Jane's birth, a son and a daughter who died in infancy. These assertions, though, are not supported by any contemporary source, and the story seems to originate with the historical writer Agnes Strickland in the nineteenth century.[74] Strickland appears to have misinterpreted a message written much later by Jane to her father shortly before her execution, in which Jane refers to the loss of 'two of your children'.[75] It has often been assumed that the two children in question refer to two earlier children born by Frances, when in fact the two children in question were undoubtedly Jane and her husband, Guildford Dudley. This becomes clear when the phrase is read in the context of the message written in Jane's prayer book, in which she attempts to comfort her father: 'And though it has pleased God to take away two of your children, yet think not, I most humbly beseech your grace, that you have lost them, but trust that we, by leaving this mortal life, have won an immortal life.'[76] No other children were ever referred to by either Frances or any of her contemporaries, which makes their existence unlikely. Moreover, Jane was frequently referred to as the couple's 'first-born daughter'.[77]

Jane's birth would have been a cause of both celebration and disappointment. She was born into a world in which male children were by far the more desirable, but daughters could be useful too. This would become glaringly apparent when the country erupted into joyous celebrations when Jane Seymour gave birth to the King's longed-for male heir, 'the goodly prince' Edward, in the year following Jane's own birth.[78] Any disappointment which Jane's parents might have felt at her sex may have been overshadowed by relief at the fact that the baby was healthy, which boded well for future births. There was every reason to hope for sons.

Unfortunately no details of Jane's christening survive, but it is likely to have taken place roughly three days after her birth.[79] It was almost certainly conducted in a similar manner to that of her mother's, which was performed with the utmost grandeur. According to the account of Frances's father, the Duke of Suffolk:

The road to the church was strewed with rushes; the church porch hung with rich cloth of gold and needlework; the church with arras [a wall hanging made of a rich tapestry fabric] of the history of Holofernes and Hercules; the chancel, with arras of silk and gold; and the altar with rich cloth of tissue, and covered with images, relics, and jewels ... The font was hung with a canopy of crimson satin, powdered with roses, half red and half white, with the sun shining, and fleur de lis gold.[80]

Jane's name was chosen as a compliment to the Queen, Jane Seymour, who was probably also asked to stand as godmother to the child. However, it is highly unlikely that the Queen herself attended Jane's christening; she would instead have sent a representative on her behalf. There is no indication as to who Jane's godfather was, but it would certainly have been someone of high standing. It may have been the King himself, or perhaps his chief advisor, Thomas Cromwell.

Following her birth, Jane would have been given into the immediate care of a wet nurse, whose responsibility it was to suckle her.[81] This was an established practice among royal and noble families – one that had been in use for centuries – as high-born women who breastfed their own children were thought to be unfashionable. The woman appointed for the task would have been carefully chosen and in all likelihood have had previous experience, as well as children of her own who she was feeding at the same time.[82] The name of Jane's wet nurse has not survived, but she was doubtless handpicked by her mother. The wet nurse was responsible for overseeing Jane's everyday care, and remained with her until she was old enough to be weaned. In accordance with customary practice, Jane's nursery staff would have also included several rockers, whose job it was to take turns to rock the infant Jane to sleep in her cradle. Her every need was attended to, the arrangements for which were put in place by her mother. Lady Frances had very little to do with Jane's everyday care, for relatively soon after Jane's birth she was churched. This ceremony of purification traditionally took place forty days after a woman had given birth, and was a necessary part of sixteenth-century ritual that allowed a woman to resume her place in society and her conjugal relationship with her husband. From then on, all responsibility for Jane's care rested with those appointed to nurse her. Though it is by no means certain, it seems possible that Jane's nursery was at least initially established at Dorset House, the likely setting for her birth. Alternatively, the rural Bradgate Park may have been seen as preferable to London.[83]

Jane's arrival in the world was of great significance to her family, for in this tiny girl rested many of her parents' hopes for the future. As the infant Jane lay in her cradle, her parents may already have been making plans for the glittering future that they foresaw for her. She had royal blood in her veins, and they would do all that they could in order to ensure that their ambitions for her were realized. At the time of Jane's birth, both of the King's daughters had been declared illegitimate. Thus, though it was not officially regarded as such, Jane's could be considered the stronger claim to the throne. As Jane grew, so too did her importance, and the pressure her parents put on her to succeed.

CHAPTER 2

Rejoiced All True Hearts

I N 1536 THE London that Jane was born into was one of the most
vibrant and sophisticated cities in Europe, with a rapidly expanding
population of approximately 50,000 people.¹ It was fast becoming a
centre for trade and industry, and art and literature were beginning to
flourish following the development of the printing press by Wynkyn de
Worde, which was established in Fleet Street, transforming the city into
one of the most desirable locations of the Renaissance.² Splendid churches
were scattered across the city, from the imposing Westminster Abbey
where Jane's great-grandparents, Henry VII and Elizabeth of York – who
would later be hailed as founders of the Tudor dynasty – lay entombed in
the magnificent new chapel of Henry's creation, to the great St Paul's
Cathedral with its towering spire towards the east. The city was also
crammed with the beautiful and majestic palaces of the royal family and
the nobility: Dorset House and Suffolk Place, the London residence of
Jane's maternal grandfather, were just two of the fine examples. The streets
were alive and bursting with people pushing their wares on every passer-by;
all sorts of produce, from meat and fish to the finest silks and perfumed
gloves, was available. However, the rapidly expanding population was
beginning to lead to overcrowding, as well as poor sanitation and living
conditions. This resulted in an increase in crime, with thieves lurking in
the shadows of street corners, waiting to pounce on an unfortunate victim
as they tumbled out of the nearest inn or brothel in the Southwark stews. A
contemporary ambassador observed that 'The subjects of this realm are

wont to live in pleasure-seeking and intemperance, haunt taverns and become wholly idle and disorderly', and there was certainly an element of truth in this.[3] Life expectancy hovered between thirty and forty years old, and infant mortality was high. It was not unusual, even among the nobility, for families to have experienced the untimely loss of at least one child or family member, and indeed, there were numerous examples of this within Jane's own family.[4] The streets of the capital were incredibly narrow and in a constant state of congestion, with traffic from horses drawing the litters of the nobility to and from their townhouses, while cats, dogs, chickens and pigs were a common sight. Hordes of people from all walks of life flooded the city's thoroughfares: foreign merchants on business, bedecked in costly outfits displaying the latest European fashions, to beggars who limped through the streets with genuine or false injuries, attempting to extract money from sympathetic passers-by. At the time, London Bridge, crammed with shops and houses, was the only bridge over the river, so many people chose to travel by water, which was infinitely quicker. Boats could be commandeered complete with a boatman for a penny, and the King and many of the nobility maintained their own barges and staff for this purpose. Thousands of swans glided along the Thames, while passengers sailing under London Bridge cannot have failed to notice the Bridge Gate, on which the decomposing severed heads of traitors were displayed in a chilling reminder of the fate of those who dared to cross the monarch.

The capital also served as the backdrop for the splendour of the royal court, which was fast becoming one of the most glittering in Europe, and of which Jane's family was an integral part. At the time of Jane's birth, her great-uncle, Henry VIII, had been on the English throne for twenty-seven years. A 'worthy King' who was 'liberal and handsome', the forty-five-year-old Henry was a commanding presence; the very embodiment of monarchy to his subjects.[5] Only later would he gain notoriety for having six wives and becoming grossly overweight.[6] The events of Henry's reign would prove to be pivotal in shaping Jane and ingraining her religious beliefs. She was born as the cogs of the Reformation in England were starting to turn; initiated by Martin Luther in Germany and spreading to the rest of Europe under the influence of other leading evangelicals, the reformed faith had recently caused England to be divided by Henry's decision to split from the Catholic Church, headed by the Pope in Rome. He had instead established the Church of England with himself at its head, and this was to have profound consequences for both Jane and her family, as well as for the King's subjects. The decision was momentous; not only did it split the country, but as time would reveal, it also shattered Henry's own family, causing great bloodshed. Though in essence the King's personal beliefs remained intrinsically traditional, such a drastic move demonstrated that he was willing to accept the authority of only one man in his realm: his own. Furthermore, as the years passed, the divide between Catholics and reformers, or evangelicals (the term Protestant was not used in England until the 1550s), became ever more apparent.

Henry's break with Rome had been fuelled by his desire to rid himself of his first wife, Katherine of Aragon – a close friend of Jane's maternal grandmother and godmother to her own mother – for her failure to provide him with a living son.[7] By 1527 almost two decades of marriage had produced only one living daughter, Mary, the King's only legitimate heir.[8]

Princess Mary was born on 18 February 1516 at Greenwich Palace. Despite her father's disappointment at her sex, Henry was proud of his daughter, and for the first ten years of her life Mary grew up within the security of a happy family with parents that doted on her. Following the example of her mother, who was a devout and religious woman, Mary would grow to be fervently pious, and remained devoted to the Catholic faith until her dying breath. Conspicuously, when she was two years old she called out her first recorded word: 'Priest!'[9] Proud of her Spanish heritage, Katherine cherished hopes that her daughter would marry into her native country, and her wishes appeared to be granted when in 1521 her nephew, the twenty-two-year-old Holy Roman Emperor Charles V, made an offer of marriage to the five-year-old Mary.[10] Although Mary was too young to be wed, and the marriage was not due to take place until she was twelve years old, Charles travelled to England the following year, where a formal betrothal took place. It was then that Mary met her royal cousin for the first time: he was to be a constant figure in her life, and one whose support and approval she would always seek. The marriage between the two cousins, however, never took place, for unable to wait for Mary to mature, in 1526 Charles married the twenty-three-year-old Isabella of Portugal.

From the outset Katherine of Aragon took an active interest in her daughter's education, ensuring that the curriculum arranged for Mary provided her with a thorough grounding in all subjects. When she was nine years old, Mary and her household were established at Ludlow Castle on the Welsh Marches, and it was here that she was to be instructed in the art of government. Despite the physical distance between mother and daughter, the two remained close; as Mary grew she would demonstrate that she was very much her mother's daughter. When it became clear to Katherine that she would bear her husband no more children, there was no doubt in her mind that Mary, as her husband's only legitimate child, was his natural successor. What was more, Katherine ensured that Mary knew it too. There was, though, virtually no precedent for a female monarch in England, and Henry had no intention of starting one now.

Henry saw Katherine's failure to produce a son to succeed him as God's judgement that his marriage to her was unlawful, on the grounds that she was his dead brother Arthur's widow.[11] Katherine, on the other hand, declared that her first marriage had never been a true one because it had never been consummated. Thus began the most famous separation case in English history, as the King started proceedings to have his marriage to Katherine annulled. What was more, he had already found a replacement: her name was Anne Boleyn.

Anne Boleyn was the daughter of Sir Thomas Boleyn by his wife Elizabeth Howard. Through the auspices of her father, who had a diplomatic post abroad, in 1513 Anne was fortunate enough to secure a place in the household of Margaret of Austria in Brussels, and eventually moved to Paris to serve the French Queen, Claude.[12] While she was in France, Anne had been exposed to ideas of religious reform expressed by the King's sister, Marguerite d'Angoulême; Anne's family – particularly her father – were also supporters of reform. It was not long before Anne had formed her own reformist opinions, opinions that would continue to develop as she began reading books that were banned in England, and that she later encouraged Henry VIII to read too.[13] At the end of 1521 Anne returned to England, and the following year she was serving in Queen Katherine's household, where she eventually caught the King's eye. In 1526 Henry began pursuing Anne, and having fallen passionately in love with her, he resolved to make her his wife. He began by ordering an investigation into the validity of his first marriage, enlisting the help of his chief advisor, Cardinal Wolsey, and appealing to the Pope. The King hoped that his marriage would be annulled, but Katherine refused to comply. She insisted that her marriage to the King was good and valid, a conviction she maintained for the rest of her life. She loved her husband, and was determined not to do anything that might jeopardize her daughter Mary's right to succeed her father. After all, her mother Isabella of Castile had been a queen regnant, and she saw no reason why Mary could not also rule in the same way, an idea that was abhorrent to the King. Katherine was distraught at the breakdown of her marriage and fought tirelessly to save it. Jane's cousin the Princess Mary was also deeply affected by these events, and the stress impacted so badly on her health that it caused her problems for the rest of her life. A Venetian ambassador would later remark that 'Few other women in the world of her rank ever lived more wretchedly.'[14]

At the onset of her parents' marital troubles, Mary's happy family life was shattered. With Katherine refusing to bow to the King's demands,

Mary sided with her mother, thus causing a breach with her father that had terrible personal consequences for her. Katherine, however, had instilled in Mary her right to rule as her father's heir, and had no intention of allowing her to give this up. Public sympathy was with Katherine, who had spent more than two decades in England and was beloved by the people, who also loved her daughter. Anne Boleyn was unpopular, and Chapuys frequently referred to her as 'the Concubine', while Frances's mother, who championed Katherine, once reportedly used 'opprobrious language' about her.[15]

The proceedings for the annulment dragged on unresolved for years, delayed by the fact that since the Emperor Charles V's troops had sacked Rome in 1527 while on campaign in Italy, Pope Clement VII had been imprisoned in the city and was under the Emperor's control. Due to the Emperor's close familial relationship to Katherine, Clement did not dare to offend him, and was therefore unable to deliver a verdict in Henry's favour. Henry and Anne became increasingly frustrated by the delay. Furthermore, Anne perceived that while he did the King's work, Wolsey was no friend to her, so she encouraged the King to order his arrest when the annulment failed to materialize quickly. Wolsey was already a sick man, and on 29 November 1530, he died at Leicester Abbey on his way to imprisonment in the Tower of London. He was replaced in the King's favour by a member of Wolsey's own household, Thomas Cromwell, who was a member of the Privy Council by the end of 1530, and whose rise was swift. Cromwell now took over the supervision of the King's annulment, and for the next ten years would be one of the most powerful men in the kingdom.

Katherine of Aragon, meanwhile, had been banished permanently from court in 1531 to a range of damp and uncomfortable houses, with the Duke of Suffolk having been given the unenviable task of breaking up her household. At the same time, the Princess Mary's support of her mother enraged her father, who banned her from seeing Katherine. This caused both Katherine and Mary great sorrow and distress, and mother and daughter never saw one another again.

With the Pope proving to be less than pliable, the King thus decided to formulate his own church, one with Henry at its head and with the authority to annul his marriage to Katherine. And so it was that in January 1533, Henry and Anne were at last secretly married with the support of Thomas Cranmer, a Boleyn adherent who was consecrated Archbishop of Canterbury in March.[16] On 7 April, Parliament passed the Act of Restraint of Appeals, which challenged the Pope's jurisdiction and emphasized the King's authority as the Supreme Head of the Church of England. Cromwell drafted the Act, and, significantly, it forbade all appeals to Rome. This meant that Archbishop Cranmer could make a pronouncement on the state of the King's marriage in England, and it was clear what was afoot. Five days after the Act was passed, Anne appeared in public as queen for the first time, and on 23 May, having summoned an ecclesiastical court in Dunstable, Cranmer declared the King's marriage to Katherine to have been null and void. This meant that Mary, estranged from her father, was now disinherited. It was a state of affairs that neither Katherine nor Mary accepted, and until the day she died Katherine would continue to declare that she was the King's lawful wife.

Five days later, the King's marriage to Anne was affirmed to be lawful. By this time Anne was pregnant with the King's child, a child that was confidently expected to be a boy. On 1 June she was crowned in Westminster Abbey, with Jane's father being afforded the great honour of bearing the sceptre.[17] His future wife was nowhere to be seen, for, like her mother, Lady Frances disliked Anne Boleyn and had no intention of attending her coronation.

The King's annulment had important political consequences for Jane's family, consequences that would in turn impact on Jane. Until the birth of Anne Boleyn's child, the declaration of the Princess Mary as illegitimate meant that Jane's mother, Frances, was now superior in status to her cousin by law. Just short of her sixteenth birthday, Frances was now closer to the throne than the King's own daughter.

~

THE HIGH HOPES for the outcome of Anne Boleyn's pregnancy were dashed when on 7 September, between three and four o'clock in the afternoon, she gave birth to 'a fair lady'.[18] The King was bitterly disappointed, but put on a brave face and was hopeful that sons would soon follow. Once again Henry Grey played an important role in the baby's christening, which took place on 10 September in the Church of the Observant Friars at Greenwich. Henry carried the ceremonial salt, while his mother was granted the honour of becoming the child's godmother. The little girl, named Elizabeth, now officially became the King's heir, confirmed in Parliament by the Act of Succession on 23 March 1534. The effect that Elizabeth's birth had on her half-sister Mary was profound. As a result of her parents' annulment and the Act of Succession, she had been officially deprived of the title of Princess, and was instead styled the Lady Mary. Furthermore, shortly after Elizabeth's birth, Mary's household was dissolved, and she was sent to join the household of her infant half-sister, which was established at Hatfield. Despite the unpleasant circumstances in which she now found herself, Mary soon became fond of Elizabeth, but while at Hatfield she frequently fell ill, most likely as a result of the stress she had suffered, for she continued to refuse to acknowledge her parents' divorce or her own illegitimacy.

During the years of estrangement from her father it is unlikely that Mary saw much of her cousin Frances. Prior to the disbanding of her household, Mary's accounts for the beginning of 1533 reveal that she did, however, spend time with Henry Grey and his family. Despite their apparent loyalty to Anne Boleyn, they had evidently managed to retain good relations with Mary, for not only was Henry's sister Katherine, Lady Maltravers, a member of Mary's household, but Mary's accounts demonstrate that Henry and his mother came to dine with her at Otford in June.[19]

By this time plans for his marriage to Frances were well underway, and it is certainly possible that Henry discussed these with Mary, who would have taken a keen interest in her cousin's impending wedding.

On the same day as Elizabeth's birth, Jane's grandfather the Duke of Suffolk, recently widowed by the death of his royal wife, married again. His bride was his fourteen-year-old ward, Katherine Willoughby, who had been betrothed to his young son Henry.[20] Although remarrying soon after the death of a spouse was not considered to be unusual in the sixteenth century, the marriage did cause some comment in court circles. On 3 September, the amused Imperial ambassador, Chapuys, wrote to inform his master the Emperor Charles V:

> *On Sunday next the Duke of Suffolk will be married to the daughter of a Spanish lady named Lady Willoughby. She was promised to his son, but he is only ten years old; and although it is not worth writing to you Majesty, the novelty of the case made me mention it. The Duke will have done a service to the ladies who can point to his example when they are reproached, as is usual, with marrying again immediately after the death of their husbands.*[21]

Despite the age difference (Suffolk was almost fifty), the marriage was a happy one. The new Duchess was described as 'virtuous, wise and discreet', and was popular at court.[22] Even the King was fond of her. In addition, the marriage produced two sons, Henry and Charles.[23] This was of particular importance to Suffolk, as in 1534 his only surviving son by the French Queen, Henry, died.[24]

⸺⸺⸺◦⸺⸺⸺

ON 7 JANUARY 1536 Katherine of Aragon died at the age of fifty at Kimbolton Castle. Though Mary's reaction to her death is not recorded, she fell ill shortly afterwards, and given the close bond she had shared with her mother her grief may be easily imagined. At court meanwhile, Chapuys recorded that 'you could not conceive the joy that the King and those who favour this concubinage [Anne Boleyn] have shown at the death of the good Queen, especially the Earl of Wiltshire and his son [Anne's father and brother], who said it was a pity the Princess [Mary] did not keep company with her'.[25] Anne's triumph would, however, prove to be short-lived.

Though he was at last married to Anne, the King's love for her had quickly waned. On 29 January 1536, the same day as the funeral of her recently deceased rival, Anne miscarried of a child – certainly the second, and possibly even the third that she had suffered – which had all the appearances of being male. The King's patience was exhausted, and by the beginning of May, Anne found herself imprisoned in the Tower of London on trumped-up charges of adultery and incest with her own brother. There was to be no mercy, and following the swift annulment of their marriage which saw Anne's daughter Elizabeth, like Mary before her, declared illegitimate and deprived of her title, the King ordered Anne's execution within the confines of the Tower on 19 May. She was replaced just eleven days later with one of her own ladies, Jane Seymour, whom the almost forty-five-year-old Henry married on 30 May. Jane was a more popular choice than the controversial Anne had been, and Sir John Russell, a gentleman of the court who was a friend of the King's and had been Anne's enemy, wasted no time in relating that through his attachment to Jane, the King 'hath come out of hell into heaven, for the gentleness in this, and the cursedness and the unhappiness in the other'.[26] Where Anne had been insufferably arrogant and was prone to outbursts of temper, managing to alienate even her own supporters, Jane showed herself to be placid and submissive.[27] In short, while Anne's behaviour demonstrated that she was highly unsuited to queenship, Jane proved to have all the qualities expected of a consort. But the outward show of obedience masked a steely determination.

During her lifetime, Jane Grey's grandmother, the French Queen, had made no secret of her dislike for Anne Boleyn. Despite the role her father had played in her coronation and his show of loyalty, Jane's parents may have been relieved at her removal. They probably also approved of Queen Jane, for shortly after her marriage Jane resolved to do all that she could to achieve a reconciliation between her husband and his eldest daughter, Mary. It was clear that this could not be achieved until Mary made a formal submission to her father, acknowledging that her parents' marriage had been invalid and that she herself was a bastard. Mary, like her mother, had denied this for years, much to the detriment of her health. But her mother was now dead, and craving her father's love and worn down by emotional stress and anxiety, she finally capitulated. On 13 June, Mary signed all of the articles given to her, which at a stroke defied everything she had previously fought for. She never forgave herself for what she saw as an act of treachery against her mother, but her submission immediately improved her situation. After writing loving letters to her father and stepmother, on 6 July Mary was reunited with the King and his new queen privately at a house in Hackney. Henry was now only too happy to play the role of the doting father and showered her with gifts, while Jane gave her stepdaughter a beautiful diamond ring. Mary was thrilled at this seemingly perfect reconciliation, and the common people, who had always been fond of her, were pleased at the improvement in her treatment; however, Queen Jane's interest did not extend to the King's other daughter, the two-year-old Elizabeth, who had been banished to the Palace of Hatfield and was out of favour following the execution of her mother.

Queen Jane's efforts to restore Mary were only successful in personal terms. On 4 July the King had passed the Second Succession Act in Parliament, which barred both of his daughters from inheriting the throne. The Act stated that, instead, any children the King had by his 'most dear and entirely beloved wife Queen Jane' should succeed him.[28] Should he fail to produce any further children by Jane or subsequent queens, Henry could appoint any heir he chose. At this time, however, he declined to do so, lest the person named should 'take great heart and courage and by presumption fall to inobedience and rebellion'.[29] Shortly afterwards, on 23 July at St James's Palace, the King's illegitimate son the Duke of Richmond, Henry Grey's childhood friend, died of a pulmonary infection at the age of seventeen. There were many at court who believed that the King intended Richmond to succeed him, and for that reason his death was initially kept a secret in order to avoid anxiety over the succession. The young Duke's body was smuggled out of London in a wagon covered with straw, and buried by arrangement of the Duke of Norfolk.[30] Once again, the stigma of illegitimacy that attached itself to the King's daughters meant that Lady Frances, her sister Lady Eleanor and their children were technically superior in status to their royal cousins – though they were not mentioned in the Second Succession Act, their legitimacy had not been questioned. From the beginning, Jane was intimately connected with both Mary and Elizabeth, and as she grew she would discover that her fate lay intertwined with theirs, all by chance of the royal blood they shared.

Shortly after the restoration of good relations between father and daughter, the King was confronted by one of the greatest threats of his reign. Henry VIII's decision to split from Rome and establish the Church of England with himself at its head had set the wheels of religious reform in motion, and in 1536 the Ten Articles were introduced. Probably set out by Cranmer, the Articles were a formulary for the new church, and set out moderate doctrinal and ceremonial changes. Perhaps more disturbing was the fact that in the same year, reform had led to the dissolution of many of the religious houses in England, whose treasure had found its way straight into the royal coffers and those of the nobility. As a result, many monks and nuns had been forced into poverty, and could only watch as the buildings they had once lived in were ransacked and destroyed. There were many who felt that the King had taken his religious reforms too far and, in a violent demonstration of outrage, on 2 October, the first riot in the rebellion known as the Pilgrimage of Grace broke out in the town of Louth in Lincolnshire. The rebellion spread rapidly through the northern counties of England, with its ranks growing each day and marching under a banner of the Five Wounds of Christ. By the time the rebellion reached York, the rebels had taken as their leader a barrister named Robert Aske, and soon the rebel army began marching south to lay their complaints before the King. The Dorsets would not have felt much sympathy for the rebels, for they were champions of religious reform. They had also profited greatly from the dissolution of the monasteries, for Henry had been granted sixteen estates in his home county of Leicestershire, and certainly had no wish to hand these back. However, they were no doubt appalled and afraid when word reached them that Lady Frances's sister, Eleanor, now married to Henry Clifford, had become directly and dangerously involved.[31]

Members of the northern nobility, many of them under duress, had joined the rebels on the march south, but Lady Clifford's husband and her father-in-law, the Earl of Cumberland, were among those who resisted. Realizing that this might put them in danger from the rebels, they fortified their castle at Skipton in Yorkshire in preparation for a possible siege. Soon afterwards, however, Lady Clifford's husband journeyed north to Carlisle to defend the city against the rebels, leaving his wife in the safekeeping of his father. Fearing for Lady Clifford's safety if she were to remain at Skipton, her father-in-law sent her, together with her baby son and two of his daughters, to his estate at Bolton Abbey, where he believed they would be safe.[32] On 22 October Skipton Castle came under siege, and 'finding the castle impregnable', the rebels, discovering that Lady Clifford was ensconced in Bolton Abbey just ten miles from Skipton, forced their way into the Abbey and took Lady Clifford, her son and her sisters-in-law hostage.[33] Lady Clifford was terrified, and in great fear for her own life and that of her child. The evidence suggests that she was treated with appalling severity by her captors. Before long her father-in-law received a message informing him of what had happened, and warning him that unless he surrendered Skipton Castle, Lady Clifford, her baby and the Earl's daughters would be placed in the front line of the besiegers of the castle 'to violate and enforce them with knaves, unto my Lord's great discomfort'.[34] This was a disgraceful way to treat the King's niece, and the outraged Earl set out to rescue his family. Travelling to Bolton, Cumberland bravely entered the rebels' camp with 'none but the vicar of Skipton, a groom of the stable and a boy'.[35] The negotiations were concluded by none other than Robert Aske's brother, Christopher, who later gave an account of what had happened, and who probably realized that the consequences would be grave indeed if any harm came to Lady Clifford. As a result, Lady Clifford was allowed to leave Bolton, and her relief at being reunited with her father-in-law must have been profound. Together with her son and sisters-in-law, she returned to Skipton Castle that same evening. Cumberland's bravery was commendable, and demonstrates the high regard in which he held his daughter-in-law, of whom he seems to have been genuinely fond. After a five-day siege the rebels abandoned Skipton having failed to take it, much to the relief of the Earl and his family.[36] The Duke of Suffolk, however, was alarmed when he heard of the danger his daughter had been in, and wrote anxiously to Cumberland, 'I heartily pray you my lord in eschewing any further danger or peril ye will send her unto me hither if ye think ye may so do by any surety possible, and here I trust she shall be out of danger.'[37] There is no record of Eleanor making any such journey to be with her father, but the Duke's letter does demonstrate that he was a genuinely loving father, who doubtless felt equally protective of Frances.

While the dramatic events of the Clifford family were being played out, the Duke of Norfolk had ridden north in order to suppress the rebellion, accompanied by Jane's father Henry. This was Henry's first military experience, and it soon became clear that it was a task to which he was completely unsuited. It is possible that the King's decision to send him north was a test of his mettle, or had perhaps been Suffolk's suggestion in order to give his son-in-law an opportunity to shine. In either instance, they were to be disappointed, for Henry did not distinguish himself and had no taste for military action. Frances must have been concerned for her husband's safety as she waited anxiously for news of the rebellion. Like the rest of the court, she must also have been jubilant to learn that Norfolk had successfully disbanded the rebels, following a number of false promises made to them on the authorization of the King. Norfolk and Henry returned to London in time to celebrate Christmas, which the court held at Greenwich Palace.

Having received a formal pardon from the King on 8 December, Robert Aske spent the Christmas of 1536 at court as the King's guest. Though Henry may have visited during the celebrations, Frances was almost certainly absent, probably on account of her baby daughter. The King's show of friendship towards Aske was all a great pretence. This became clear shortly after New Year 1537, when in February a resurgence in the rebellion, this time led by Sir Francis Bigod (and frequently called Bigod's Rebellion), gave the King the excuse he needed to send Norfolk north once more to deal with the rebels.[38] This time Henry did not accompany him, for which Henry must have been grateful. After suppressing the rebellion once and for all, Norfolk set about punishing those involved, many of whom, Sir Francis Bigod included, were hanged as an example to other potential rebels.[39] Though Aske had not sanctioned the second rebellion, it gave the King a convenient reason to rid himself of the former dissident. Aske was captured, and having been condemned for high treason was sentenced to a grisly end. On 12 July he was hung in chains over the gates of York and left to die, his fate serving as a gruesome warning to any who dared to contemplate rebelling against the King.

AT THE BEGINNING of April, news of a more exciting nature was announced: after almost a year of marriage, Queen Jane was pregnant with her first child. The kingdom rejoiced at the news, and throughout London bonfires were lit, and free wine was distributed to the people by way of celebration. Prayers were offered up in churches for the Queen's safe delivery, and both the King and Queen were in high spirits. All of the doctors employed were confident that the child would be a boy.

Hampton Court Palace had been chosen as the setting for the birth of the royal child, and at the beginning of September the court moved there to await its arrival. The Queen officially withdrew to her chambers on 16 September to await the birth, attended by the Lady Mary. When her labour pains began on 9 October it became clear that the birth was not going to be an easy one. Finally, after three long days and nights, at two o'clock in the morning of 12 October, Queen Jane gave birth to a healthy prince. The King was utterly elated, and the Queen was able to write a proud letter to the Council announcing the Prince's birth, declaring triumphantly that 'we be delivered and brought in childbed of a prince, conceived in most lawful matrimony between my lord the king's majesty and us'.[40] The child was named Edward after his great-grandfather Edward IV, and Lord Lisle's informant John Husee related that the Prince's birth 'has more rejoiced all true hearts than anything done this forty years'.[41] Jane's paternal grandmother, Margaret Wotton, also took the opportunity to write to the King, congratulating him on 'the most joyful news that has come to England these many years of the birth of a prince'.[42] The King's joy was, however, of short duration, for not long after the Prince's delivery, Queen Jane fell dangerously ill. It soon became clear that she was not going to survive, and the Duke of Norfolk wrote to urge Thomas Cromwell, then absent from court, 'to be here tomorrow early to comfort our good master, for as for our mistress there is no likelihood of her life, the more pity'.[43]

Norfolk's prediction was sadly true, and on 24 October, twelve days after providing her husband with a male heir, Queen Jane died of puerperal fever. The King was devastated. In a letter to the French King Francis I, Henry wrote that 'Divine Providence has mingled my joy with the bitterness of the death of her who brought me this happiness', and retired 'to a solitary place to pass his sorrows'.[44] Jane's mother was among the women who joined the funeral party as the Queen was laid to rest in St George's Chapel at Windsor Castle, in 'the presence of many pensive hearts'.[45]

Meanwhile, the birth of Prince Edward was of the utmost significance for the country: after many years of waiting, their king had at last produced a legitimate male heir to succeed him. The male heir was to become an important figure in the life of Lady Jane Grey, and as the two cousins grew they would have much in common. As infants in the cradle, however, for the moment these events were of little matter, and the politics of the Tudor court in London seemed a world away.

CHAPTER 3

Anyone More Deserving of Respect

F IVE MILES TO the north-west of the city of Leicester lies Charnwood Forest. Within the seclusion of the forest, surrounded by acres of peaceful and beautiful parkland, the magnificent Bradgate Park dominated the scenery. Built of fashionable and expensive red brick, the house was two storeys high, structured around three sides of a central courtyard, and was around two hundred feet in length. Visitors to Bradgate were greeted by the sight of an imposing gatehouse, typical of Tudor architecture, flanked by two ornamental towers and decorative chimneys.[1] At the beginning of 1538 this splendid house, one of the first stately homes in England, became the main seat of Jane's parents, and it was here, in the heart of the countryside, that Jane was raised. She was a Tudor who, though distant from the court in London, knew what it was to be royal.

The land at Bradgate had been acquired in 1490 by Jane's great grandfather, the 1st Marquess, and he began to build a new and sumptuous residence that would shortly supersede Astley Castle as the family's main home.[2] Most of the building work, however, was the enthusiastic endeavour of Jane's grandfather, and it was one of the first houses in England that was built as a family residence rather than as a fortress for defensive purposes. The family also had other assets on the estate, which included slate quarries and a lake, beyond which lay the forest of Chartley.

At the beginning of 1538 Jane's father turned twenty-one. It was a highly significant moment, for he had at last reached his majority, and he was now legally entitled to take control of all of his estates and the financial responsibilities that came with them. This was doubtless a great relief to both Henry and his wife, who for the first time in their marriage now had financial independence. Along with their young daughter Jane, they were finally able to move into Bradgate Park, and they wasted no time in doing so, forcing Henry's mother to leave. Unsurprisingly, this caused a great deal of friction in the relationship between mother and son, and Margaret, in great distress, wrote to Cromwell: 'in the honour of Our Lord's passion, my lord, I beseech you to be my good lord and consider me, a poor widow, how unkindly and extremely I am handled by my son Marquess'.[3] She claimed that Henry would not even permit her to take her personal belongings from her former home, and begged for Cromwell's intercession. She also pleaded ill health, writing pitifully that her 'sickness and continual aches and pains' meant that her days were numbered, and that it would not be long before all she owned became Henry's in any case.[4] It seems unlikely that Margaret's petition to Cromwell did her much good; she had no option but to leave, and from then on spent much of her time as the guest of Sir Richard Clement at Ightham Mote.[5] Though the relationship between Margaret and her son did later improve, such harmony was not destined to last. As usual, financial issues were at the root of the problem, and by the time that Margaret died in 1541, it seems improbable that the rift between the two was fully healed.[6] This evident discord between mother and son certainly paints Henry in a bad light, though how far Frances was responsible for influencing his behaviour is impossible to say. After several years of being in a marriage which brought her no financial independence or home of her own, Frances was understandably elated to now have both of these things, and must have been eager to establish her authority as mistress of her own household at the splendid Bradgate.

The exterior of Bradgate was an impressive sight, but the interior was equally striking. It boasted a fine hall, eighty feet long with large bay windows, with a musician's gallery at one end and a dais at the other, which formed the central point for the bustling household. There was also a chapel, which, as Jane grew, she attended daily with her parents to hear the family chaplain, James Haddon, speak from the pulpit of 'the demolition and over-throw of the idols, and the weakening and downfall of idolatry'.[7] The rooms used by Jane and her family were located in the east wing of the house, and included a fashionable gallery used for indoor exercise and games, while behind the closed doors of their apartments Jane's parents were known to enjoy gambling at cards and dice. This drew the disapproval of their chaplain who disdainfully observed: 'In the houses of our men of rank there are practiced not only such recreations as refresh both the body and mind after a moderate and godly manner, but such also as occasion sloth, and beget idleness and ungodliness: of this kind are games of cards and dice.'[8] Throughout the house, which was decorated with the finest expensive tapestries, Jane's family motto, *A Ma Puissance* (According To My Power), supported by two ermined unicorns, armed, crested and hooped with gold, proudly proclaimed Bradgate's ownership. There were also impressive kitchens and a bakery, rendering the household entirely self-sufficient, and quarters for the servants, of which there were many. In 1530 Bradgate housed around three hundred servants, a number that would have been at least equalled if not increased by the time that Jane took up residence with her parents.[9]

In addition to the interior comforts, Bradgate enjoyed beautiful scented gardens, laid out in the modern, formal style of a parterre that was so popular at the time. Surrounded by a magnificent park that stretched for six miles, it provided excellent hunting, another hobby of which Jane's parents were particularly fond, and in which Jane herself may have participated on occasion. It was an idyllic spot, and though she was yet to reach her second birthday at the time she took up residence, Bradgate provided the ideal backdrop for Jane's development.

AT NEW YEAR 1540, Jane's mother presented the King with a gift of 'a linen and two collars, the turrets gilt', while Henry offered a brace of greyhounds.[10] In return Henry received a gilt glass with a gold cover, while Frances was given a gold cup with a gold cover, a lavish gift which highlighted her status as the King's niece.[11] She appears to have shared a good relationship with her uncle, and when that same month Henry VIII married the German Princess, Anne of Cleves, Jane's parents were prominent among the wedding guests at Greenwich Palace. So repelled was the King by Anne's person, however, that by the beginning of July he had divorced her, and on 28 July he married one of her ladies, Katherine Howard.[12] In true courtier style, it was in honour of the King's fifth wife that Jane's sister, probably born in August, was named.[13] Five years later in 1545 another daughter named Mary, perhaps as a compliment to Jane's grandmother and her royal cousin, completed the Grey family.[14] The sisters were all raised at Bradgate, and here Jane could play, learn and enjoy the company of her two siblings, though they were both strikingly different from Jane; or Jane, perhaps, was different from them.

As the Grey sisters grew, the variances in their characters became increasingly apparent, with their interests branching out in contrasting directions. Katherine was the beauty of the family, with golden hair, blue eyes and delicate features. She adored animals, and at Bradgate could indulge her love for them with an array of pets that she enjoyed playing with.[15] Their father also owned a tamed bear and licensed theatricals that Katherine probably took great delight in watching.[16] Jane, though, appears to have had little time for such frivolities, and therefore Katherine was forced to look to their youngest sister, Mary, for a playmate. There was something slightly unusual about Mary, for as she grew, it became clear that she had a spinal deformity that made her appear hunchbacked. She was also small, and in later years was cruelly described by the Spanish ambassador as 'little, crooked-backed and very ugly'.[17] However, the later suggestion that 'Mary's birth amounted to a disaster' is a gross exaggeration, for besides the unkind comments of the ambassador, Mary's condition drew no other comment from her contemporaries.[18] Mary was not hidden away by her parents as she might have been had her condition been severe, but instead benefited from the same education that her sisters were receiving, and travelled with her family. That her parents also later arranged for her betrothal confirms that whatever condition she may have suffered from was not considered serious enough to exclude her from the marital market. But Mary was no great beauty like her sister Katherine; neither was she a scholar like Jane. Sadly, as the three sisters grew, Mary appeared almost to fade into the background.

The lack of a son was probably a source of great disappointment to Jane's parents. Frances and Henry had three daughters, and at this point it is interesting to consider that there were gaps of four and five years between each of their births. This may simply have been by chance, but it is equally possible that Frances may have experienced miscarriages and even stillbirths of which no record survives. However, it may also be indicative of several other things. It may highlight a rift in the Dorsets' marriage, although there is no contemporary evidence that points towards any marital discord between them. Indeed, it may be no reflection on their marriage, and could be attributed to the possibility that the couple spent large periods of time away from one another, although this too is unlikely given what we know of their recorded movements. There are other possibilities: the couple may have experienced difficulties when it came to conception; perhaps on Frances's side, or Henry could have experienced problems when it came to sexual performance. It could even have been that Henry had a low sex drive. He was never noted as being promiscuous in an age when many of his contemporaries were, and certainly had no known mistresses. This may be a reflection of the fact that he was happily married, but it is possible that it points to something more. It is notable that Mary was the couple's last child, despite a further nine years of marriage following her birth, and that, following Frances's second marriage, it took her but a few months to conceive.[19]

ROYAL AND NOBLE children had a daily routine that was strictly adhered to, and Jane and her sisters would have been no different. After rising early, at around seven o'clock, they would begin the day with prayers. This was followed by breakfast at eight o'clock, which consisted mainly of bread, meat and weak ale – the water in sixteenth-century England not being considered safe to drink. The main meal of the day was dinner, which the family conducted within their private apartments. As the century progressed, there was an increasing desire for privacy, and the family would only have dined publicly in great state on special occasions. Dinner was usually held between ten and eleven in the morning and sometimes lasted for several hours. Many dishes were served over several courses, primarily made up of various types of meat, the main constituent in the Tudor diet. Beef, lamb, chicken, swan, pigeon, pork, rabbit, goose and capon were popular choices, all served in a variety of sauces. During Lent, when meat was banned, various fish dishes, such as herring, salt cod, salmon and carp, were served instead. In addition, there was freshly baked bread from the Bradgate bakehouse, and a few vegetables. These dishes were followed by the sweet course, which consisted of a whole array of delightful treats including fruit pies and elaborate constructions made of marchpane.

Following dinner, the Grey children spent the greater part of their day engaged in lessons, leaving them with little time for play. Supper was usually held at around five o'clock, and was lighter and more informal than dinner. More prayers before bed followed, and Jane and her sisters probably retired for the evening at around nine o'clock. When her parents were at home, Jane received a daily blessing from them, and this is likely to have been one of the few times she saw her parents on any one day.

As was usual in the case of noble families, the Grey girls would have seen very little of their parents, who were often engaged in other activities. The daily routine they followed was a strict one, but they were treated with all of the deference and respect due to children of the royal blood. Their parents were very conscious of their status, and were determined that they ought to be brought up in as virtuous a manner as possible. On a later occasion Henry thanked the theologian Heinrich Bullinger, to whom Jane had been writing, for exhorting her 'to a true faith in Christ, the study of the scriptures, purity of manners, and innocence of life; and I earnestly request you to continue these exhortations as frequently as possible', demonstrating the importance that these qualities in his daughters held for him.[20]

From the start the girls were raised as evangelicals, as were their cousins, the Lady Elizabeth and Prince Edward. Though Jane's parents had both been born Catholics, they too were in favour of religious reform, with Henry being the more zealous of the pair. As the Grey sisters grew, this was a faith that Jane would become increasingly fanatical about. The family were, for the moment, in the minority. In June 1539 Parliament had passed the Act of Six Articles, which effectively undid many of the reforms that been previously passed, in essence returning the country to Catholicism in all save papal supremacy. The King had realized that the country was not yet ready for radical religious change, and the Act was therefore an attempt to find a middle ground between Catholicism and reform. It was a balancing act, and one that would remain Henry's policy until the end of his reign.

LIFE AT BRADGATE Park was conducted in a similar way to life at the royal court. Jane's parents were nothing if not sociable, and there were often visitors. In the summer of 1550 Lady Frances wrote to the Earl of Shrewsbury with a request that he might send her a stag, for 'divers of my friends' whom 'I have cause to gratify with venison this summer'.[21] Frances could be generous to her friends, and doubtless played the role of hostess to perfection. Henry's brothers, Thomas and John, frequently visited Bradgate, and her aunt Anne Willoughby and her family, who resided at Middleton Hall in Warwickshire and Wollaton in Nottinghamshire, also visited. Frances's stepmother, Katherine Willoughby, though only recorded as staying on one occasion, was almost certainly a regular visitor, as was Elizabeth Brooke, who later married Henry's childhood friend, William Parr.[22] Presumably Jane would have come to know her uncles well. Later they were both to become dangerously entangled in her story. Similarly, Katherine Willoughby shared Jane's religious enthusiasm for reform, and appears to have taken an interest in Jane and her sisters, while Elizabeth Brooke was subsequently believed to have been the instigator of Jane's marriage.[23]

Given what we know of later family occasions, it seems likely that Jane spent time with other relations on her father's side too, for the Grey family appear to have been close. Certainly on occasion Jane visited family members with her parents. During the Christmas celebrations of 1549, the family took the opportunity to visit Jane's paternal aunt Elizabeth, Lady Audley, at her home of Audley House in Saffron Walden.[24] Lord Audley died in 1544, and shortly before the visit Lady Audley had remarried, taking as her second husband Sir George Norton. Also living at Audley House was Lady Audley's only surviving child by her first husband, Margaret, who was of an age with Jane's sister Katherine, and the two girls appear to have shared a bond.[25]

Whether the closeness of Jane's paternal family also extended to her mother's family is uncertain; they were, for the most part, fond of one another, but there is no evidence that this led to physical visits.[26] Even without visitors the family would not have lacked for company, for both of Jane's parents had a vast retinue of attendants with whom Jane would have been familiar. In 1545, Lady Frances welcomed a new addition to her household at Bradgate in the form of Elizabeth Hardwick, better known to history as the formidable Bess of Hardwick. During the reign of Elizabeth I, through four increasingly prestigious marriages Bess would become one of the richest women in England and the builder of some of the great Elizabethan prodigy houses.[27] Bess's first husband, Robert Barlow, had died at the end of 1544, and the following year Bess joined Frances's household as a waiting gentlewoman. The two women quickly became close, Bess also becoming fond of Jane and her sisters.[28] It was almost certainly through her place in the Grey household that Bess met her second husband, Sir William Cavendish, and at two o'clock in the morning of 20 August 1547, the Dorsets hosted the couple's wedding at Bradgate.[29] The celebrations lasted for a further two days, and though Jane's parents were hardly in a position to afford such lavish hospitality, that they did so is further evidence of their generosity. Bess then left Frances's service, but they remained on good terms. When Bess gave birth to her first child, a daughter, the following year, she was named Frances as a compliment to Bess's former employer, who was also asked to play the part of senior godmother to the child together with Katherine Willoughby.[30]

AT BRADGATE, THE Dorsets hunted regularly in the park, which was well stocked with deer, enjoyed hawking and indulged their passion for gambling, while their daughters were left under the supervision of their household staff. Occasionally they also visited the royal court, but as Henry held no office under the King his presence was by no means a necessity, and for the most part they remained in the country. However, the luxurious lifestyle the family led came at a price, and Henry and Frances, unable to get a grip on their financial affairs, were constantly living beyond their means, resulting in large debts.[31]

Outside of their estate, as the highest-ranking peers in the neighbourhood, the couple were admired in Leicestershire, and paid occasional
visits to the city of Leicester. Here they were often presented with gifts,
primarily consisting of fruit and wine, such as the time recorded in the
town books of Leicester when a payment of two shillings and sixpence
(£40) was made 'for strawberries and wine, for my lady's grace', a gift
from the mayoress and her sisters.[32] On another occasion, four shillings
(£60) was paid to the apothecary 'for making a gallon of hippocras [a
sweet, spiced wine], that was given to my lady's grace, by mistress
mayoress and her sisters, the wives of the aldermen of Leicester, who
gave, besides wafers, apples, pears, and walnuts at the same time'.[33] Food
was expensive, and as such it was therefore a highly respectable choice
of gift. As she grew older, Jane may well have accompanied her parents
on occasion – she is known to have paid a visit to Leicester in 1548.

While her parents enjoyed their leisure pursuits and paraded themselves through the neighbourhood, their daughter Jane passed the early
years of her childhood in relative obscurity. However, around the time of
her fifth birthday, she began a journey that she quickly discovered would
alter her whole outlook on life: her formal education.

The fact that the Dorsets had no son did not diminish their ambitions; if anything it appears to have heightened them. They were acutely
conscious of the royal status of their three daughters, and had decided
to ensure that they received the best education money could buy. In
the past, women's learning had been limited, even frowned upon, but
times were changing. The world around them was becoming increasingly
more cultured, and a good education was considered to be of the utmost
importance. Both of Jane's cousins, the Ladies Mary and Elizabeth, were
well educated, and if Jane was to make her mark on the world it was
essential for her to match them. Elizabeth in particular drew the admiration of her contemporaries, one of whom observed that her 'mind is
considered no less excellent than her person'.[34]

Having enjoyed an excellent education himself, learning was something that Jane's father Henry was particularly passionate about, and he was eager for his daughters to follow his example. So highly esteemed was he for his intellect and devotion to religious reform that the Swiss reformer Heinrich Bullinger chose to dedicate his fifth *Decades* to 'the most illustrious prince and lord Henry Grey'.[35] The book was a religious work, and the dedication gave Henry much delight: 'For the book for which you have published under the auspices of my name, I return you, not only for my own sake, but for that of the whole church of Christ, the thanks I ought.'[36] It was little wonder, therefore, that Henry's expectations of his daughters were so high. Little is known of Frances's education, but as the daughter of the former French Queen she is likely to have received a good grounding in all of the traditional subjects. Her letters reveal an elegant hand, but the fact that none of her contemporaries made any reference to her intellect suggests that she was not remarkable for her scholarly abilities.

When Jane's first lessons began, it was not long before she discovered that she enjoyed them. Initially she was instructed in the basics: she was taught to read and write, possibly with some input from her mother, probably learning the letters of the alphabet by means of a hornbook (a primer containing the letters, often mounted on wood or sometimes horn). Most importantly, she learned to commit to heart and recite the Lord's Prayer in English. When she had mastered these essential skills, Jane's curriculum began to develop, along with her enthusiasm. The seeds had been sown, and her love of learning quickly blossomed. Her relationship with education was one that would continue to progress throughout her life, becoming ever stronger and providing Jane with a great source of fulfilment.

The man initially charged with teaching Jane was one of her father's chaplains, Dr Thomas Harding.[37] He was not the main influence in her life, however, and she would later bitterly berate Harding for his conversion to Catholicism. Jane's eagerness for learning was bolstered by the fact that her primary tutor proved to be one of the most important people in her life. The relationship that Jane shared with John Aylmer only increased her desire for knowledge, and she was at her happiest when in his company.

John Aylmer, 'a young man singularly well learned both in the Latin and Greek tongue', was the protégé of Jane's father, who would later be consecrated Bishop of London.[38] Born in around 1520, his splendid education at Cambridge had been paid for by Henry. When Aylmer completed his studies, in around 1541, his patron invited him to join his household at Bradgate as his chaplain and the tutor of his daughters. Though Aylmer made no comment on the intellectual abilities of Jane's younger sisters when they were old enough to begin their lessons, he was singularly impressed with Jane, 'whom God has thought fit to adorn with so many excellent gifts', and within no time the two had formed a bond cemented by their shared academic interests.[39] Jane flourished under Aylmer's thorough and careful guidance, and Jane's parents were delighted. As Aylmer himself related:

It has always indeed been my disposition not only to set the highest esteem upon all kinds of learning, but to regard with the greatest affection those who cultivate and profess it. For I well know how brutish this life of ours would be, were not the understanding of mankind cultivated by useful learning and liberal pursuits.[40]

He encouraged Jane as far as was possible, and she was eager not to disappoint. As Jane grew, so did her enthusiasm for religious reform, and as her father and Aylmer were keen advocates, they all became part of a circle whose friendship was bonded by religion.

The curriculum followed by Jane and her sisters was in many ways similar to that which was likely to have been prescribed for her mother,

Frances, in her girlhood. Giovanni Bruto, a sixteenth-century writer on the subject of educating young women, believed that it was of the greatest importance that girls

> *shall learn not only all manner of fine needlework ... but whatsoever belongeth to the distaff, spindle and weaving, which must not be thought unfit for the honour and estate wherein she was born ... and which is more, to the end that becoming a mistress she shall look into the duties and offices of domestical servants, and see how they sweep and make clean the chambers, hall and other places, make ready dinner, dressing up the cellar and buttery, and that she be not proud that she should disdain to be present ... at all household works.*[41]

The girls were, therefore, instructed in all of the traditional accomplishments that were thought to be fitting for ladies of high rank: the etiquette that was necessary to become a successful courtier, how to sew neatly, how to dance elegantly, and how to play their musical instruments. Jane's maternal grandmother, the French Queen, had enjoyed dancing, and a contemporary had observed that her 'deportment in dancing is as pleasing as you would desire', but Jane's skills appear to have lain elsewhere.[42] Music was an integral part of everyday life at Bradgate; the musicians employed by Jane's parents could be heard throughout the day and into the evening, strumming their instruments to the appreciation of the household. Jane was particularly fond of music, and she spent a great deal of time practising with her lute.[43]

The Grey girls were also taught to read and write, and were instructed in languages and history. It was here that Jane particularly excelled: 'Jane was very versed in Greek as well as Latin letters and was also very learned in matters of the Bible.'[44] She also learned Italian under the tutelage of Michelangelo Florio, who dedicated one of his two Italian grammar books,

48

Regole de la lingua thoscana, to her.[45] Jane also learned French, and was believed to have an understanding of several other languages. According to Sir Thomas Chaloner, a Cambridge scholar who may have known Jane and wrote an elegy about her following her death, 'If you were to number her languages, this one lady spoke eight.'[46]

As Jane grew, so too did her scholarly abilities. She quickly demonstrated that when it came to learning, she was gifted. Not only did she excel in her lessons, but she enjoyed them, and found great pleasure in the pages of books. Moreover, with no friends of her own age at Bradgate with whom she could play, books filled the void, and in many ways became a kind of silent companion for Jane. Her enthusiasm and delight in learning new things were evident, and drew admiration from many of her contemporaries, not least of all her tutor.

While her sisters played, chasing their dogs through the gardens of Bradgate, Jane could inevitably be found perusing the pages of books. Florio claimed that Jane was the most learned and religious youth in the kingdom, and on one occasion, the visiting German scholar John of Ulm, another whom Jane's father had financially supported through his education at Oxford, even remembered that she had been busy translating a piece on marriage from Latin to Greek as a New Year's gift for her father.[47] Ulm was part of the Reformist circle in which Henry played a prominent role, and though he was naturally respectful to his patron, he did not exaggerate Jane's talents. Her choice of gift gave Jane the opportunity to showcase her progress and her skills as a linguist. In this Jane was not entirely unique, for her cousin the Lady Elizabeth, herself an expert linguist, also made gifts of translations in her own hand. On one occasion Elizabeth presented her stepmother Katherine Parr, who Jane later came to know well, with her English translation of Marguerite d'Angoulême's poem, *The Glasse of the Synnefull Soule*, beautifully bound and embroidered.[48] Nevertheless, Jane's talent was still extraordinary for a girl of her time, and Ulm wrote admiringly that

'For my own part I do not think there ever lived anyone more deserving of respect than this young lady.'[49] Jane was grateful, thankful even, for the opportunity that her parents had bestowed upon her. As she grew, her education would continue to be an integral part of her life; it was her comfort, and she would prove to be more than worthy of the praise heaped upon her.

CHAPTER 4

The Imperial Crown

W HILE JANE WAS undergoing the rigours of her education within the peaceful serenity of Bradgate Park, elsewhere in England the political climate of sixteenth-century England was undergoing significant changes – changes that would be of the utmost consequence to Jane. In February 1542, when Jane was still a small child, Queen Katherine Howard was executed on charges of adultery. She was replaced a year later by the twice-widowed Katherine Parr, whom Henry VIII married on 12 July 1543. The sister of Henry Grey's childhood companion William, the thirty-year-old Katherine was sensible, mature and intelligent. She also proved to be a loving and considerate stepmother to the King's three children, whom she brought to court and ensured were given some semblance of a happy, family life enjoying their father's favour. Not only had Katherine restored domestic stability, but the King also had great faith in her abilities, for it was to her that he chose to entrust the safekeeping of his realm when he decided to invade France on a quest for military glory in 1544.

Before he left England to embark on the campaign, however, the King's thoughts had turned to his heirs. It was with this in mind that the Act of Succession had been passed, lest any harm should come to the King during his absence. This momentous Act, the third of that name created by Henry, had been passed in Parliament on 7 February, and stipulated in exact terms the King's heirs. Naturally, the first of these was the King's only son, Prince Edward. Should Edward die childless, the throne was to pass first to any children the King might have with Katherine Parr. If Katherine should fail to produce a child then the King decreed that the throne was to be inherited by his eldest daughter, Mary, who he now legally restored to her place in the succession. Mary was to be followed by any heirs of her body, and then by Henry's younger daughter, Elizabeth, whose right was also restored, and any children she might produce. Despite their restoration as heirs to the throne, in all probability Henry never envisaged that either of his daughters would actually inherit. This is further implied by the fact that Mary and Elizabeth were not legitimated, and legally remained bastards. Though both daughters now enjoyed their father's favour in personal terms, Henry sincerely believed that his marriages to their mothers were invalid, and in such circumstances there was no question of legitimating them. The matter of Mary and Elizabeth's legitimacy was quite simply ignored. Little did Henry realize that by doing this he had made his daughters vulnerable, as future events would reveal. No mention was made of any other heirs, in all probability because, as with his daughters, Henry never envisaged the need at this time.

With all thoughts of the succession settled, in July the King departed for France, leaving Queen Katherine behind as Regent. Katherine proved to be an effective regent, and amply demonstrated that a woman could rule, and rule well – lessons that were not lost on her contemporaries, particularly her stepdaughter Elizabeth. Meanwhile, most of the nobility accompanied the King on his journey, including Jane's father. Having shown a complete lack of interest or ability in military affairs, Henry's chagrin at having to participate may have been exacerbated by the fact that he had also contributed sixty men on horseback and 290 footmen for the campaign, stretching his already tight resources to the limit.[1] When the King's army successfully captured Boulogne on 14 September, the victory was in no way thanks to Henry's efforts, and he would have been glad to be able to return to England and his family at the end of the month.

In the immediate aftermath of Boulogne, life at Bradgate began to resume its normal course. But the world that Jane had been born into was continuing to evolve. On 22 August 1545, her maternal grandfather, Charles Brandon, died at Guildford Castle while the court was enjoying its summer progress. For some time the Duke of Suffolk had been suffering from dropsy, gout and rheumatism, but his final illness seems to have been of a different nature and was of short duration.[2] In his will, the Duke left his daughters Frances and Eleanor £200 (£61,000) worth of plate each, which bore the ducal arms, as well as jewellery and other household items.[3] This may have helped to alleviate the perilous finances of Jane's parents, although Frances was surely deeply saddened by the loss of her father. Despite Brandon leaving instructions that he should be buried quietly in Lincolnshire, the King, devastated by the death of his lifelong companion, insisted that he should be buried in St George's Chapel within Windsor Castle.[4] Suffolk's death meant that Jane's half-uncle, Henry Brandon, who was just short of his tenth birthday and probably less than a year older than Jane herself, succeeded to the dukedom of Suffolk. As young Henry was still a minor who had been sharing some of Prince Edward's lessons, Jane's father assumed the role of unofficial head of the family. He proved to be a poor substitute for his father-in-law.

A LITTLE OVER a year after Suffolk's death, within the Palace of Whitehall in the final days of the year 1546, the atmosphere was tense. It was fast becoming clear that Henry VIII was gravely ill, and that his thirty-eight-year reign was coming to an end. Aware that death was approaching, the King, on 30 December, dictated his will. Six marriages had produced just three legitimate children, two girls and a boy. It is probable that the terms of the will were based on an earlier one which has not survived, but which was almost certainly made two years previously to coincide with the Act of Succession in 1544.

In 1544 Henry had felt no need to look any further than his three children when it came to ordering the succession. But at the end of 1546 as he lay dying, the need to nominate further heirs seemed sensible. His marriage to Katherine Parr had produced no children; thus, in the new will the King reiterated that Prince Edward was to be his undoubted successor, followed by his two daughters who remained legally illegitimate, and any heirs that they might produce. The King's thoughts then turned to the alternatives should none of his children have heirs of their own. First, the Scottish line of Henry's elder sister Queen Margaret, who had been married to James IV, was cut out, in all likelihood because the King had no desire to see the Scots ruling England. By doing this, Henry thereby excluded both Margaret's granddaughter, the young Mary, Queen of Scots, whom he envisaged would be later married to his son, and his niece, Margaret, Countess of Lennox, the product of Margaret's second marriage.[5] Instead, the King nominated the heirs of his younger sister Mary, Duchess of Suffolk and one-time Queen of France, probably because of their English origin. In this case, the first heir would naturally have been Mary's eldest surviving child, Lady Frances, Jane's mother. Interestingly, however, Henry decreed that if all three of his children were to die childless, then 'the imperial crown ... shall wholly remain and come to the heirs of the body of the Lady Frances our niece, eldest daughter to our late sister the French queen, lawfully begotton'.[6] At a stroke, Frances was completely overlooked in favour of her daughters. Moreover, should Lady Jane Grey and her sisters as Frances's heirs also die childless, then by the terms of the will the throne was to pass to the heirs of Frances's younger sister, Eleanor, of whom only a daughter, Lady Margaret Clifford, survived. Both of the King's nieces, Frances and Eleanor, had been barred from ever becoming queens of England, and it is difficult to find a satisfactory explanation for this.

The reasons behind Henry VIII's exclusion of his nieces have been much debated, and there is still no certain answer. After all, there is no evidence to suggest that the King's relationship with Frances and Eleanor was anything other than amicable, even fond.[7] There are two possible explanations that ought to be considered, each of which being equally likely. First, Henry had every reason to believe that at least one of his children would produce children of their own, which would thus secure the immediate future of the succession. His decision to exclude the Scottish line and instead look to the heirs of his sister Mary was always a precaution should his direct line fail to produce heirs. In 1546, Frances and Eleanor (at twenty-nine and twenty-seven years old respectively) were still of an age where they could bear male heirs. Thus, if Frances or Eleanor were to produce sons then they would, in any case, naturally take precedence over their mothers in the succession, and the King certainly may have envisaged this happening. Henry had gone to great lengths in order to produce a male heir, and was determined that a woman should not succeed to the English throne if it could be avoided. In Eleanor's case, there was no opportunity for this to transpire, as she tragically died less than a year after the King made his will.[8]

Alternatively, it is possible that Henry realized that should Frances succeed, ultimate power would be invested in her husband, Henry Grey. The King does not appear to have had a high opinion of Henry Grey, who was never awarded any form of office throughout his reign, in all probability due to his failure to demonstrate any initiative or particular skill.[9] Similarly, in the provision the King made for the appointment of the Council of his young son after his death, Henry was conspicuous by his absence – a startlingly clear sign given his status. It was perhaps this that forced the King to overlook Frances, coupled with the fact that he probably never imagined that it would ever be necessary to consider either of his nieces as possible heirs.

———

AT TWO O'CLOCK in the morning of 28 January 1547, squeezing the hand of his Archbishop of Canterbury, Thomas Cranmer, Henry VIII drew his final breath and 'passed from this life'.[10] With his death, his nine-year-old son, Edward, now became the sixth king of England to bear that name, and he had big shoes to fill. The late King had provided for the government of the realm while Edward was a minor, and by the terms of his will a Regency Council was established, the members of which had been appointed by Henry VIII prior to his death. Most of these members were committed reformers, the faith in which the young King had been raised, and which he would make steadfast attempts to impose upon his country. Poignantly, however, Jane's father had been excluded, and it is an insult that he cannot have failed to have noticed. At the head of the Council was Edward's maternal uncle, Edward Seymour, Earl of Hertford, 'a dry, sour, opinionated man'.[11] Hertford moved quickly in order to establish himself as Lord Protector of the realm, though he was 'simply appointed first of the Councillors by the testament of the late King', and in February he was created Duke of Somerset, while his younger brother, Thomas, a man of 'high courage', was made Baron Seymour of Sudeley and Lord High Admiral.[12] Somerset was one of those that the Imperial ambassador Chapuys described as 'stirrers of heresy', due to their commitment to the religious reform of which Jane was so zealous.[13] Both he and his younger brother would later become intimately linked with Jane and her family. In order to hold on to the reins of power Somerset needed as big a base of supporters as possible, and set about trying to secure the loyalty of as many of the lords as he could, including Henry Grey. After all, Henry's eldest daughter Jane was now third in line to the throne, and that was something for which Henry could not be ignored.

Not only was Henry afforded an important role in the coronation of Edward VI, which took place on 20 February in Westminster Abbey, but on 23 May, after years of waiting and several nominations, he was finally admitted to the Order of the Garter.[14] Founded in 1348 by Edward III, the Order was the highest order of chivalry (and still is) in England, dedicated to the patron saint St George. Admittance was solely by appointment of the monarch; therefore, Henry's selection to join many of his friends and colleagues was a singular honour and an indication of potential favour in the future. His copy of the Statutes of the Order of the Garter, known as the Suffolk Garter Book, still survives in the Royal Collection complete with his signature.[15] The book set out all of the rules and regulations which, as Knights of the Garter, members were expected to obey. It was a triumphant moment.

Despite the establishment of the Church of England during the late reign, Henry VIII's religious views had still been relatively conservative, and in essence he had remained a Catholic. When Henry was on his death-bed and beyond speech, Archbishop Cranmer had asked the King for some indication that he died in the true faith of Christ, and Henry, 'holding him with his hand, did wring his hand in his as hard as he could', and this was taken as affirmation.[16] Following the execution of Anne Boleyn, Henry had found some of the ideas of the Reformist movement increasingly distasteful and deplored their radicalism. However, there had been many in England who were becoming progressively interested in reform and whose views leant towards evangelicalism, and thus Henry's court had divided into two parties: the conservatives – with men such as the Duke of Norfolk and Stephen Gardiner, Bishop of Winchester, who were adherents of Catholicism – and the Reformist camp, with Archbishop Cranmer and Edward Seymour at its core.

It was not safe to express evangelical views openly at this time or even ideas that bordered on evangelicalism. In June 1546, a Lincolnshire woman named Anne Askew was put to the rack at the Tower, the Lord Chancellor Sir Thomas Wriothesley turning the handles of this terrifying instrument himself. She was suspected of having discussed her radical religious beliefs with ladies in the Queen's household, and even the Queen herself, but even at the height of her agony as her limbs were stretched, Anne refused to admit to this and would give no names. The following month, Anne was burned at the stake at Smithfield as a heretic.

Like the Dorsets, Katherine Parr was a member of the Reformist camp, to her peril during the reign of her late husband.[17] Though they were no doubt appalled when they heard of the shocking end of Anne Askew, they wisely kept their opinions to themselves. Jane also probably learned of Askew's story, and may have admired her strength of conviction; it was one that she too, in time, would come to display.

With the onset of the new reign, however, the tide had very much turned in favour of the reformers, and Edward VI showed none of the hesitation of his father. With the support of his trusted Archbishop of Canterbury, Thomas Cranmer, the young King began introducing a series of religious reforms that revolutionized the English church, placing it firmly in the realms of the Protestant movement that was growing on the continent. The Act of Six Articles was repealed, and it quickly became clear which direction things were moving in.[18] Jane and her family were surely delighted by such bold moves, and greatly approved of the changes that were taking place. Jane's father, described as 'the thunderbolt and terror of the papists, that is, a fierce and terrible adversary', was foremost among the men at court who actively encouraged these changes.[19] It was little wonder, therefore, that Heinrich Bullinger chose to dedicate the fifth part of his *Decades* to Henry.

Heinrich Bullinger was the successor of Huldrych Zwingli, and the head of the Zurich church. Zwingli was a leading Swiss reformer who used his influence to transform the city of Zurich into one of the leading Protestant centres on the continent. In 1523 Zwingli produced his 'Sixty-Seven Articles': points that detailed his beliefs on a range of religious issues. All of these were based on the reading of the Bible, which was central to his work, and which he believed was the word of God that could not be superseded by any human power. The Bible, in Zwingli's opinion, set out all of the conditions that people should live their lives by, and soon the 'Sixty-Seven Articles' became Zurich's official doctrine. The areas surrounding Zurich, though, were unconvinced by Zwingli's views, and remained adherents to Catholicism. The result was a religious war, initially launched in 1529. During the second campaign of 1531, Zwingli was killed at the Battle of Kepel, leaving his son-in-law, Bullinger, to continue his work. It was Bullinger who was responsible for spreading the ideas of Zwinglianism across Europe, from where they eventually came to reach England. Bullinger also wrote a number of theological works, the most famous of which was the *Decades*. In the course of his work he struck up correspondences with a number of people who were familiar with Jane, one of whom was her tutor, Master Aylmer.

Jane's father's reputation for piety was well known, and it was probably through the auspices of his protégé John of Ulm that he came to Bullinger's notice. Religion was a subject about which Henry was passionate, as his letter to Bullinger in which he thanked the Swiss theologian for the dedication demonstrated:

I acknowledge the divine goodness towards his church, and, as Paul expresses it, the love of God to man, that he has chosen to adorn and illuminate his church with such lights, as that we who are less enlightened, may follow those guides in the beaten path of true religion, who may both be able, by reason of the gifts they have received from God, and willing, by reason of their affection to their brethren, diligently to point out the way in which we ought to walk.[20]

Henry's household at Bradgate became a haven for those devoted to the cause of reform, and the atmosphere was one in which Jane herself was fully immersed. What was more, she was about to be given just the type of fertile ground and encouragement that she needed in order for her religious views to grow.

CHAPTER 5

A Loving and Kind Father

T HOUGH LADY FRANCES had been excluded from the succession, the Grey sisters had not, and currently stood as third, fourth and fifth in line to the throne. Jane's parents were not the only ones who were conscious of their daughters' status – particularly Jane's. Almost immediately after the death of King Henry, the family was in residence at Dorset House when a visitor arrived, seeking a meeting with Jane's father.

John Harington was an intelligent man, who would later become dangerously entangled in Jane's story.[1] Now around thirty years old, he was in the employ of the Lord Protector's younger brother, Sir Thomas Seymour, the Lord Admiral, to whom he was also a close companion. Harington was well known to Jane's father, and perhaps also to Jane, but on this occasion his visit to Dorset House had a very specific purpose. Following the customary exchange of pleasantries, Harington moved swiftly to the point. As Jane's father remembered it, Harington

> [s]howed me that the admiral was likely to come to great authority and, as the king's uncle, might do me much pleasure, advising me to report to him and enter more into his friendship. He advised me to allow my daughter Jane to be with the admiral, saying he would have her married to the king.[2]

Henry's interest was gauged, and he listened as Harington attempted to flatter him by adding that Jane was 'as handsome a lady as any in England'.[3]

Jane had a place in the line of succession in her own right, but now it appeared that Seymour was offering to help Jane's parents to achieve the most glittering future possible for their eldest daughter: marriage to her cousin King Edward, which would make Jane a queen. There is no way of knowing whether the Dorsets had considered the possibility of a marriage between their daughter and the young King prior to 1547; after all, Henry VIII's hopes of a marriage between his son and Mary, Queen of Scots, had been well known, and Jane and Edward were still incredibly young. If the thought had not already occurred to them, the seed had now most definitely been planted. It seems that Seymour had already discussed his plans with a number of his associates, for Sir William Sharington later recalled that 'he heard the Lord Admiral say that the Lady Jane was a fit marriage for the King'.[4]

The grand promises and flattering words were all very well, but despite his familial relationship to King Edward, Henry could not see that the Admiral was well placed enough to be making any such promises. After all, everyone knew that the real powerhouse at court was his elder brother, the Lord Protector. Turning Harington away from Dorset House, Henry made his feelings clear. But the Admiral, ambitious and forceful, could be incredibly compelling when the occasion called for it. Eager to get his own way, he persevered, and Henry later admitted that 'within a week I went to the admiral's house at Seymour Place where he persuaded me to send for my daughter'.[5] A physically attractive man nearing forty, Seymour knew how to employ all of his charms to achieve his desires. But it was not only his honeyed words that had won Henry round – it was his cash too. In return for allowing Jane to join his household as his ward, Seymour promised Henry a tempting loan of £2,000 (£615,000), 'hearing me complain of debt'.[6] Aware of Henry and Frances's ambitions for their daughters and the high hopes that they had for Jane, the ruthless Seymour cunningly played on their greed in order to draw them into his plans. In the complex system of sixteenth-century networking, it was not unusual for noble children to enter the households of others of a similar social standing in order to complete their education, and to form possible future matrimonial alliances. By agreeing to send Jane into the Admiral's keeping, however, Henry and Frances had, in effect, given him control of their daughter and her future. Well known for their fondness of gambling with money, gambling with their daughter was another matter entirely, and one in which the stakes were infinitely higher.

The ten-year-old Jane remained blissfully ignorant of the intrigue and negotiations that had taken place between her father and the Admiral as she prepared to embark on what she may have viewed as an exciting change. Alternatively, the thought of leaving behind the familiar surroundings of Bradgate Park and her family may have seemed a daunting prospect; after all, Jane had never known anything else. Bidding her parents and younger sisters farewell, in February 1547 she arrived at the palatial Seymour Place on the Strand. Located just a stone's throw from Dorset House, but miles away from Bradgate Park in rural Leicestershire, Seymour Place may have taken some adjustment for Jane. There were no younger sisters competing for attention at Seymour Place; Jane was the only child, for the Admiral was unmarried with no children of his own, and Jane, therefore, was the star attraction. She found that she liked her new guardian, whom she later referred to as 'a loving and kind father', and was easily won over by his charms.[7] But once the initial novelty had worn off, she soon found that life was to continue in very much a similar vein as it had done at home. For here, despite the new surroundings, Jane resumed her studies under the kind supervision of her tutor, Master Aylmer. Given the close relationship between teacher and pupil, Jane probably found his continued presence a comfort, especially as she spent little time with her guardian. The Admiral was busy with other plans of his own – plans that for the moment were shrouded in the utmost secrecy.

The Admiral's thoughts had turned to matrimony. Determined to gain the ultimate prize of a royal wife, after first expressing an interest in King Henry's daughters, he turned his attentions to King Henry's widow. Despite the onset of her third widowhood, the Queen Dowager, Katherine Parr, was an attractive woman of almost thirty-five.[8] Tall, with auburn hair and a sensual nature, she was, moreover, a wealthy woman since the death of her royal husband. On top of that, she had fallen in love with Seymour before her marriage to her royal spouse, and later wrote to him that 'As truly as God is God, my mind was fully bent the other time I was at liberty, to marry you before any man I know.'[9] Now that she was at last free and had an attractive dowry to add to her allure, Seymour began to pursue Katherine with alacrity. Much to her disappointment, Katherine had been afforded no place in the government of her stepson King Edward, and her time, therefore, was all her own. Her feelings towards Seymour had remained unchanged during her marriage to the King, and she actively encouraged his advances. In no time at all Katherine had fallen completely under Seymour's spell. Soon after Jane's arrival at Seymour Place, Katherine and Seymour became lovers. However, Katherine was still in mourning for her late royal husband, adding an element of both danger and excitement as the couple were forced to conduct their relationship in secret. In the dead of night, Seymour began visiting Katherine at her dower manor of Chelsea, a short distance from Seymour Place. Jane would have had no inkling that her guardian had gone, for he always left Chelsea early in the morning before Katherine's household awoke.

The relationship was serious, and probably at some time in May, Katherine and Seymour were married clandestinely. It did not, though, remain secret for long, and the following month news of the marriage became public. It caused complete outrage in many quarters, the Lord Protector being furious at his brother's presumption to take such a wife, in so secret a way. His anger can easily be imagined, for when the Admiral had previously expressed an interest in marrying the Lady Mary, the Lord Protector had told him in no uncertain terms that 'neither of them was born to be king, nor to marry a king's daughter'.[10] Equally, Jane's cousin the Lady Mary greatly disapproved of the match, not least because of the indecent haste with which it had been conducted following her father's death, 'who is as yet very ripe in mine own remembrance'.[11] But the young King Edward, who had always been fond of both his uncle and his stepmother, gave the marriage his blessing, writing to assure Katherine that he believed that Seymour 'is of so good a nature that he will not be troublesome any means unto you'.[12] It seems likely that Jane's parents also approved of the marriage, for it would, in turn, have a profound and positive effect on Jane.

For Jane, the marriage of her guardian and Katherine Parr was an excellent development. While she had undoubtedly met Katherine before, she perhaps greeted her for the first time in her capacity as Seymour's wife in July, when it was observed that Katherine 'went lately to dine at the house of her new husband'.[13] Though Jane remained as Seymour's ward, to her delight she now discovered that she was invited to spend more time with Katherine in her household at Chelsea.[14] Completely adored by her stepchildren and always fond of children herself, though with none of her own, Katherine welcomed Jane with open arms. At Chelsea Jane also had the company of her fourteen-year-old cousin, the Lady Elizabeth, who had recently taken up residence with her stepmother. With the slender build of her mother and the fiery red-gold hair of her father, Elizabeth was developing into an attractive young woman, described as 'comely rather than handsome, but she is tall and well formed, with a good skin, although swarthy; she has fine eyes and above all a beautiful hand of which she makes a display'.[15] Such striking features suggest that Elizabeth was always going to turn heads. Unlike Jane, however, Elizabeth's early years had been far from stable. Before she reached her third birthday, her mother, Anne Boleyn, had been executed and she herself had been declared illegitimate. It was thanks to the love and devotion of her stepmother, Katherine, that she was finally beginning to flourish.

Jane's parents almost certainly received frequent reports of her progress, and must have been delighted by what they heard. They certainly approved of Katherine's influence, and Frances in particular was an admirer of the Queen Dowager's. An inventory taken after her death reveals that she owned a portrait of Katherine, and the two women also shared similar religious beliefs.[16] Lady Frances, however, appears never to have been as enthusiastic about her faith as Katherine, and she certainly never demonstrated devotion in the same manner as the Queen Dowager. In the company of Katherine, who actively encouraged her learning, Jane was positively thriving. Katherine herself had been fortunate enough to receive a high-level of education, and as a result was exceedingly cultured. She also took great care of her appearance, and Jane cannot have failed to notice Katherine's passion for beautiful clothes and shoes, her love of costly jewels, and her penchant for fragrant scents.[17] She was an inspiring example for Jane, as her spirited enthusiasm for learning was something she pursued for the rest of her life, serving to further cement the bond between herself and her husband's ward. She was interested in art, and had commissioned numerous portraits of herself from artists whom she patronized, including a miniature as a keepsake for her husband; she wrote poetry and adored books, and through them was able to indulge and express her radical religious beliefs, for among her accomplishments, Katherine was an author.

In November, at the behest of Jane's step-grandmother Katherine Willoughby, Dowager Duchess of Suffolk, Katherine published her second book, *The Lamentations of a Sinner*, in which she communicated some of the religious views she had been forced to suppress in the last few months of her late husband's life.[18] To the young and impressionable Jane, who must have been as dazzled by Katherine's charms as she was by her learning, this was an incredible achievement. Here was a woman who was not afraid to voice her religious views – to commit them to paper. Would it be possible for Jane to aspire to something similar? She had also been raised in the

65

reformed faith, and witnessing Katherine's devoted passion for her beliefs probably heavily influenced her. Moreover, the fact that Jane's cousin, King Edward, was also an enthusiast of reform gave Jane and Katherine a free rein to talk openly about their religious interests and the religious reforms that the King was keen to promote. While Jane's guardian the Admiral appears to have had little time to dabble in such chat, or interest in doing so, at eleven years old Jane was at a highly impressionable age, and it seems likely that it was at this time that many of her religious beliefs took greater shape under Katherine's influence.

Elizabeth too, though three years older than Jane and at that awkward time of transition from child to adolescent, had much in common with her cousin. Like Jane, Elizabeth was remarkably intelligent, and revelled in her educational pursuits and the praise which she received as a result. A contemporary remarked that 'her intellect and understanding are wonderful', and that she excelled as a linguist.[19] Elizabeth also shared similar religious views to Jane, and Jane would later praise her cousin for her devotion to God. But that was probably where the similarities between the two girls ended. No correspondence between the cousins survives, but Elizabeth's later treatment of Jane's sisters suggests that the relationship between them was never a close one. There may even have been some jealousy on the part of both girls over the other's academic abilities and relationship with the Queen Dowager. However, if this was the case then for the most part it almost certainly stemmed primarily from the 'proud and haughty' Elizabeth's side.[20] Jane's later comments about her cousin indicate not only an element of praise and respect, but perhaps also admiration and awe for a cousin who was slightly older than her. Elizabeth's tutor, Roger Ascham, who may have met Jane before, but certainly became more familiarly acquainted with Jane while at Chelsea, later claimed that Jane's abilities were superior to those of his own pupil. If Elizabeth became aware of this then it understandably probably led to some resentment.

As they had done with Elizabeth, Katherine and Seymour may have indulged Jane, perhaps even spoilt her a little. The letters her parents wrote to Seymour the following year certainly indicate that this may have been the case – much to their dissatisfaction, for it had led to Jane demonstrating some of the rebellious and undesirable behaviour so common in teenagers.

Jane, however, was not a witness to the shocking events that occurred in Katherine's household in the spring of 1548. She appears to have spent much of the first half of the year at Seymour Place, and therefore avoided the troubled situation that saw the Lady Elizabeth banished from Katherine's household in the spring, after a shameful flirtation with the Admiral. Elizabeth's governess, Kate Ashley, later confessed that the Admiral would visit Elizabeth's chamber some mornings, and if the girl were still in bed, he would 'strike her familiarly on the back or on the buttocks'.[21] His inappropriate behaviour towards his wife's stepdaughter continued, and on some occasions Katherine also joined in, passing it off as innocent fun.[22] Before long, though, Katherine became suspicious of her husband and her stepdaughter, and matters came to a head one day when she sought them out and, to her great distress, 'found him holding the Lady Elizabeth in his arms, upon which she fell out with them both'.[23] Things appear to have gone no further, but though Elizabeth later wrote to Katherine that she 'was replete with sorrow to depart from your highness', there was no question of her remaining with Katherine any longer, and perhaps this too exacerbated her coolness towards Jane.[24] By the beginning of the year, Katherine would have known that she was pregnant with her first child. This made the betrayal of her husband and her stepdaughter all the more bitter, and permanently damaged her relationship with both Seymour and Elizabeth, though she chose to stand by her husband. The events were scandalous, and whispers continued some time afterwards about the Admiral's early morning romps with Elizabeth, whispers that it is likely Jane heard.

Jane's parents should have been warned by Seymour's misconduct and removed Jane from his care, but they did no such thing, and Jane remained at Seymour Place. They were still driven by their hopes and ambitions that Seymour would arrange Jane's marriage to the King, and this overrode any other considerations. There is no suggestion, however, that Seymour ever showed any sexual inclination towards Jane, and by all accounts he was a considerate guardian to his young charge. Jane's father later acknowledged that Seymour's 'fatherly affection which you bear her', and 'good mind, concerning her honestly and godly education, is so great, that mine can be no more'.[25]

Despite the disruption caused by Elizabeth's unexpected departure, Jane continued to flourish in the Admiral's household with Katherine for company, remaining blissfully ignorant of the fact that her presence was part of a much bigger plan. She was there for a reason: a pawn in Seymour's dangerous play for power.

CHAPTER 6

A Second Court of Right

A S MAY TURNED to June and the seasonal heat began to intensify, Jane prepared to leave London. It was the summer of 1548, and Jane had been the ward of Sir Thomas Seymour for over a year. She had spent many happy times in company with Seymour's wife, Katherine, and she was eagerly anticipating their upcoming sojourn in the country. At thirty-six, Katherine was heavily pregnant with her first child, and she and her husband had opted to retire from the capital before the summer heat and the diseases that came with it had an opportunity to infiltrate the Seymour household. Taking Jane with them, the couple also left the scandal of the affair with the Lady Elizabeth behind them, travelling to Sudeley Castle, Seymour's idyllic Gloucestershire residence.[1]

Any tensions between the couple were brushed over as they looked forward to the future, which Jane had good reason to feel she was a part of. The peaceful countryside that surrounded Sudeley may have come as a welcome change to Jane, who had been enclosed in the bustle of London for some time. On top of that, Sudeley was a little over seventy miles from Bradgate Park, and the two were certainly on an equal footing in terms of beauty. Sudeley had enjoyed a long and turbulent history before it was granted to Seymour by his nephew King Edward in 1547, and was by that time in a state of disrepair.[2] Once it had been chosen as the location for Katherine's confinement, Seymour had been forced to undertake some hasty building work to make Sudeley fit for occupation, and suitable to accommodate Katherine and her large retinue in the style to which she had become accustomed.[3] For the Admiral this was no trouble, as he 'spared no cost his lady to delight, or to maintain her princely royalty'.[4] The results were luxurious: Katherine had a whole new suite of magnificent rooms, which overlooked beautiful knot gardens arranged in fashionable parterres and the charming fifteenth-century church of St Mary's which lay in the grounds. Coupled with Sudeley's location in the heart of the countryside, this made it an ideal place for Katherine to spend the final months of her pregnancy.

Jane quickly settled into life as Katherine's companion at Sudeley, and her presence was a source of great delight to the Queen Dowager. Given Katherine's love of children and the close relationships she had shared with her stepchildren, it seems probable that she provided Jane with all of the love and encouragement that Jane could have hoped for. In turn, Jane almost certainly reciprocated. By this time, Jane had probably not seen her parents since Christmas, possibly longer, and it may therefore have come as a pleasant surprise to her when towards the end of the summer, her father arrived from Bradgate Park to visit his daughter. In reality, however, it was the Admiral that Henry had come to see. According to Henry's later recollection of the encounter, the visit was part of the Admiral's attempt to obtain Henry's support for his bid for power over the government of the realm. By this time Seymour was completely disenchanted with his brother the Lord Protector and King Edward's Council, and was determined to try to stake his own claim to be the main power behind the throne. Sir John Harington later testified that he had heard the Admiral declare that 'when there hath been two brothers, it hath never been seen that one brother should have all the rule and the other none'.[5] All of the honours he had already been granted were not enough to satisfy him and he wanted more. This was hardly surprising, for soon after the death of Henry VIII the Imperial ambassador had remarked that he thought it 'quite likely that some jealousy or rivalry may arise' between the two brothers.[6] Katherine, too, was on bad terms with the Protector, and particularly disliked his wife, due to the couple's refusal to return her collection of royal jewels that had remained in storage at the Tower since the death of her late husband.[7] Therefore, she added further fuel to the Admiral's quarrel by actively encouraging him in his struggles with his brother. Henry later recalled that during a visit he had made to Seymour Place in December, the Admiral had told him that 'he in no way liked the doings of the lord protector and council'.[8] Seymour's custody of Jane and his promise of her marriage to the King gave him the perfect bargaining tool with the naïve Henry, who he advised to rally as many men as he could in order to support his attempt to free the King from the Protector's control – and into his own. Already the Protector was becoming unpopular, not least with his royal nephew, whom he kept 'very straight'.[9] The Admiral had realized, however, that his brother was unlikely to surrender his power without force, and as Henry later testified, 'he advised me rather to make much of the head yeoman and franklins, especially the ringleaders, for they are best able to persuade the multitude and bring the numbers'.[10]

As Jane's father and her guardian quietly discussed tactics, Jane remained unaware of their dealings and continued to enjoy the company of Katherine and her retinue. Katherine's 'house was termed "a second court" of right, Because there flocked still, nobility', which included a vast company of ladies and gentlemen, many of whom had served her since the days of her queenship.[11] Her physician, Robert Huicke, her chaplain, John Parkhurst, and her almoner, Miles Coverdale, also attended her. The latter two were of particular interest to Jane, for both were well favoured by Katherine for their devotion to religious reform. Parkhurst was also a friend of Jane's tutor Master Aylmer, and Coverdale had been responsible for the first translation of the Bible into English.[12] Katherine also received news and letters from her friends – perhaps her fondness for Jane was heightened by the close friendship she shared with Jane's step-grandmother, Katherine Willoughby – and Jane's cousin, the Lady Mary, also wrote to Katherine with good wishes for her pregnancy: 'I trust to hear good success of your grace's great belly.'[13]

Meanwhile, for the moment, the Admiral's plots behind Sudeley's walls went no further than words. Accompanied by Jane, Seymour bade Henry, her father, farewell as he left Sudeley for home. Seeing his daughter's contentment in the company of the Admiral and Katherine as he waved Jane goodbye, Henry had no idea that he was leaving her in an incredibly vulnerable situation, for circumstances were about to take a drastic turn.

At the end of August Katherine's labour pains began. Perhaps she made use of the cramp rings, thought to aid pregnant women, which were later found among her possessions as she drew on every ounce of her strength to deliver her child safely.[14] On 30 August, within the confines of the magnificent apartments that her husband had recently beautified for her, Katherine gave birth to a healthy child. It was not 'the little knave' that she and her husband had been hoping for, but a little girl, named Mary in honour of Katherine's eldest stepdaughter and Jane's cousin, the Lady Mary.[15] Katherine and the Admiral were thrilled with their daughter, and initially all seemed well. The Lord Protector was among those who wrote to congratulate his brother, for he had heard that Katherine 'hath had an happy hour and, escaping all danger, hath made you father of so pretty a daughter'.[16] But the joyous mood did not last. Shortly after the birth, puerperal fever set in, the same deadly illness that had killed Jane Seymour, King Edward's mother and Jane's godmother. As with her queenly predecessor, Katherine's health deteriorated as she descended into delirium. Though Jane is unlikely to have seen her beloved Katherine in this state, she would have seen Katherine's doctor and her ladies as they hurried in and out of her apartments, desperately trying to save their mistress, while the distress of the Admiral was evident. With no one to comfort or reassure her in the unfamiliar surroundings, it must have been a truly frightening experience for the young Jane. The tension as she waited to hear whether Katherine would recover must have been unbearable, and all that she could do was pray that God would be merciful and spare her life.

The news was not good: Katherine's condition worsened, and between two and three o'clock on the morning of 5 September, the serenity of Sudeley vanished when Katherine slipped away and died. The 'Flower, honor, and ornament of the female sex' was no more.[17] The Admiral, now a widower, was in a torment of affliction and shock, and was unable to see past his own grief to consider Jane's interests. Thus, in the blink of an eye, Jane was deprived of the two people with whom she had spent most of the past eighteen months and who had fulfilled the role of parents; she was in an especially lonely position. She was miles from home, and faced with the task of coming to terms with the loss of the woman to whom she had been devoted, and whose corpse now lay close by. In an epitaph dedicated to his late mistress, Katherine's chaplain John Parkhurst summarized the sombre atmosphere at Sudeley following her death – the atmosphere in which Jane was unhappily enveloped: 'For the departed, we her household flow with watery eyes.'[18] Whatever personal feelings of grief Jane had to contend with, she had been raised as a lady of the royal blood. Though only twelve years old, she now chose to adopt an outward display of admirable dignity that Katherine would have been proud of.

As Katherine's body lay in state in her Privy Chamber, 'cered and chested in lead accordingly', and watched over by the members of her household, preparations for her funeral were underway. According to customary practice, etiquette dictated that Seymour could not attend his wife's funeral, and he remained closeted in the castle to come to terms with his sorrow.[19] The same rules did not apply to Jane.

On the morning of 7 September, two days after Katherine's death, Jane prepared to carry out one final duty for her. The picturesque St Mary's Church in the grounds of Sudeley had been chosen as Katherine's final resting place, and on that morning Jane assumed the role of Chief

Mourner, 'her train borne up by a young lady'.[20] Perhaps the Admiral watched from a window as the vast funeral procession left the castle, the deceased Queen's corpse being 'borne by six gentlemen in black gowns, with their hoods on their heads', and Jane following behind.[21] When Jane and her fellow mourners arrived at the church they saw that the small, fifteenth-century chapel was hung with 'black cloth', which was decorated with escutcheons (a shield or emblem bearing a coat of arms) depicting the late Queen's marriages: 'King Henry VIII and her in pale, under the crown; her own in lozenge, under the crown; also the arms of the Lord Admiral and hers in pale, without crown.'[22] The rails were 'covered with black cloth for the mourners to sit in, with stools and cushions accordingly', and two tapers were placed upon the coffin during the service.[23]

Once the great number of people who made up the mourners and the procession had gathered, the service was able to begin.[24] Much to Jane's approval and in accordance with Katherine's wishes, it was performed in English and according to evangelical rites, the first of its kind to be seen in England. To begin with, 'the whole choir began, and sung certain Psalms in English, and read three lessons. And after the third lesson the mourners, according to their degrees and as it is accustomed, offered into the alms-box.'[25] Leading the service, Miles Coverdale then began his sermon, 'which was very good and godly'.[26] He finished with 'a godly prayer', which 'the whole church answered, and prayed the same with him'.[27] When this was done, 'the corpse was buried, during which time the choir sung Te Deum in English'.[28]

The service having been completed, Jane returned to the castle with her fellow mourners where dinner was served amid an atmosphere of sorrow. Soon after, 'the mourners and the rest that would, returned homeward again. All which aforesaid was done in a morning.'[29] As the mourners departed, Jane was alone. She had performed her duty admirably – her final tribute and farewell to the woman who had, for a short time, fulfilled the role of a mother to her. There was now nothing for her to do but to wait and see where her parents would decide that her future lay. Only one thing was certain: with Katherine gone and the Admiral in a torment of anguish, it seemed that there was nothing left for her at Sudeley.

<hr />

AT BRADGATE PARK, Jane's parents were informed of the death of the Queen Dowager, and received word from the Admiral that he was 'so amazed' by the death of his wife that he had 'small regard either to myself or to my doings'.[30] His first thought was to order the disbandment of Katherine's household, and with that in mind he wrote to the Dorsets and offered 'to send my Lady Jane unto you', to those who 'would be most tender on her'.[31] Jane's parents were alarmed by the fact that their daughter was now 'destitute of such one as should correct her as a mistress, and monish her as a mother', and they immediately accepted Seymour's offer for her return.[32]

Jane was probably relieved to receive the summons home – the summer at Sudeley had begun with such happiness, full of hope and anticipation for the future. But now the castle was tinged with sadness and unhappy reminders of Katherine's death, as she lay entombed in the chapel. One thing that might perhaps have offered Jane some small comfort was the tiny, beautifully decorated prayer book that may have been in her possession at this time.[33] Gorgeously bound with gilt edges, the prayer book contained prayers written in English from *An epitome of the Psalmes*, as translated by Richard Taverner in 1539. Taverner was a lay preacher who had also been responsible for a translation of the Bible, commonly referred to as Taverner's Bible.[34] Inside, exquisitely decorated initials in vibrant colours and gold adorned the pages, all the painstaking work of a professional scribe that would have taken much time to complete. Its size meant that Jane could carry the prayer book with her at all times, and for this reason it may have been intended to hang from a girdle (a belt worn around the waist). It was without doubt an object of high value that had been made to a commission, perhaps as a special gift for Jane.[35] She certainly treated it as such, and she would treasure it for the rest of her life.

As Jane prepared to bid farewell to Sudeley and begin the journey home to Bradgate Park soon after Katherine's funeral, she had good reason to believe that the chapter of her life that she had spent with Katherine and the Admiral was at an end. Now Jane prepared for the next one to begin.

CHAPTER 7

Ruled and Framed
Towards Virtue

A T BRADGATE PARK, Henry and Frances waited expectantly for the return of their daughter. Shortly after their summons, a messenger on horseback rode into the courtyard at Bradgate, but there was no sign of Jane. The message was for Henry, and it came from the Admiral. In the brief period that had elapsed since Katherine's death, Seymour had realized that he had been foolish to relinquish the custody of his precious ward and set about attempting to rectify the situation. His letter, dated 17 September, explained to Henry that his grief at the loss of his wife had clouded his judgement and had caused him to break up her household over-hastily. However, knowing that Jane had not yet left Sudeley, and fearing lest Henry should think it unkind of him to 'rid me of your daughter so soon after the Queen's death', with a clearer head on his shoulders, he now desired to 'keep her, until I shall next speak with your Lordship'.[1] Once more putting his skills with his pen to good use, Seymour reassured Henry that with Katherine gone, his own mother, Lady Margery Seymour, would assume Jane's care. The lady would, he promised, 'be as dear unto her, as though she were her own daughter'.[2] For his own part, he assured Henry that he would continue to be 'her half father and more; and all that are in my house shall be as diligent about her, as yourself would wish accordingly'.[3]

The Admiral's words were as smooth as silk, but on this occasion they were not enough to convince the usually pliable Henry, who was 'fully determined that his daughter, the Lady Jane, should go no more to the Lord Admiral's house'.[4] Though they were no doubt grateful for the interest that both the Admiral and the late Katherine had shown in Jane, Henry and Frances were disappointed that her residence in Seymour's household had brought them no tangible advantage. Despite Seymour's promises, eighteen months in his household had brought Jane no closer to marriage with the King, and with the death of Katherine Parr the Dorsets perceived that the Admiral did not now have enough influence to achieve this. Besides that, they were acutely conscious of the fact that their daughter may have become somewhat spoilt. With Seymour being known for his 'liberality and splendour', Jane had perhaps been overindulged while in the Admiral's care.[5] Aware that the situation required the utmost tact, soon after receiving the Admiral's letter Henry sat down to pen his reply. After acknowledging 'your most friendly affection towards me and her [Jane]', he informed Seymour that 'considering the state of my daughter and her tender years', he deemed it wisest that Jane should return home. She would be committed to 'the governance of her mother; by whom for the fear and duty she oweth her, she shall most easily be ruled and framed towards virtue, which I wish above all things to be most plentiful in her'. Henry was eager for Jane to be raised as a virtuous evangelical maid, and he continued to explain why he felt it was so important for Lady Frances to resume the care of their daughter. Jane, he reasoned,

> *shall hardly rule her self as yet without a guide, lest she should for lack of a bridle, take to much the Head and conceive such opinion of her self, that all such good behaviour as she heretofore hath learned, by the Queen's and your most wholesome instructions, should either altogether be quenched in her, or at the least much diminished.*[6]

Henry evidently felt that Jane needed a positive female influence around her, and who better for the task than her own mother, who surely concurred with her husband's views? He hurried to assure Seymour, however, that he would still consult him on the matter of Jane's marriage, and claimed that he sought only 'in this her young years ... the addressing of her mind to humility, soberness and obedience'.[7]

Though they were Henry's words, the hand of his wife shone through. Henry's reference to Jane's relationship with her mother suggests that it was Lady Frances who had the final say in deciding how Jane was raised. It indicates that Frances's 'waking eye in respecting her [Jane's] demeanour' was attentive and firm, and that Jane's upbringing had been strict while she had been at home.

The rigorous nature of Jane's childhood appears to be confirmed when, on the same day, Frances herself also took the opportunity of writing to the Admiral in support of her husband. Addressing him as her 'good brother', Frances thanked him for his 'gentle offer' and attention to Jane, but tactfully declined to allow her to remain in his custody:

> *trusting nevertheless that, for the good opinion you have in your Sister [Frances], you will be content to charge her with her, who promises you, not only to be ready at all times to account for the ordering of your dear Niece, but also to use your counsel and advice in the bestowing of her, whensoever it shall happen. Wherefore, my good brother, my request shall be, that I may have the oversight of her with your good will, and thereby I shall have occasion to think, that you do trust me in such wise, as is convenient that a sister to be trusted of so loving a brother.[8]*

Though the letters of both of Jane's parents appear to indicate that they positively welcomed Seymour's advice when it came to Jane's future, almost begging for permission to keep their daughter at home, in truth their responses displayed the polished diplomacy in which they were both well versed. Frances was an assertive woman, of stronger character than her husband, and her letter proved that when it came to making decisions about Jane's future, she expected to be consulted. The message was clear: while Jane's parents addressed the Admiral in suitably complimentary words, and claimed that they were ready to do his bidding in terms of Jane's welfare, in truth they had already made up their minds: Jane was to come home.

By the time the Dorsets wrote their letters, Seymour had left Sudeley and Jane in order to attend to business at court in London. He hoped that his letter had been enough to convince Jane's parents to allow her to remain with him, and confidently expected his ward to be at Sudeley when he returned. In his absence, however, Jane's father had arranged for his daughter to travel home.

When Jane arrived at Bradgate towards the end of September, it was the first time she had set eyes on her childhood home in at least eighteen months. The palatial surroundings of Bradgate and the woody Charnwood Forest that encompassed the house had not changed, but her parents quickly discovered that their daughter had. The Jane who had returned to them had altered in her manner. Much to their horror, Jane's parents now detected a spark of insolence, a glimmer of wilfulness, and a flicker of disobedience in her countenance. Their worries, it seems, had been well founded. There was, though, barely any time to address the situation, before yet another messenger arrived.

Once again it came from Seymour, whose determined spirit they had wildly underestimated. When Seymour returned to Sudeley in the last week of September, much to his dismay he discovered that Jane was gone. Rather than abandoning his plans, so confident was he in his persuasive abilities that, paying no attention to the words of Jane's grovelling parents, the Admiral tried again. In his attempt to regain his ward, the Admiral even wrote to Jane herself.[9] At the instigation of her parents, on 1 October Jane sent him a short note in reply that highlighted her gratitude for his kindness towards her:

My duty to your Lordship in most humble wise remembered, with no less thanks for the gentle letters which I received from you. Thinking myself so much bound to your Lordship, for your great goodness towards me from time to time, that I cannot by any means be able to recompense the least part thereof, I purposed to write a few rude lines unto your Lordship, rather as a token to show how much worthier I think your Lordship's goodness than to give worthy thanks for the same; and these my letters shall be to testify unto you that, like as you have become towards me a loving and kind father, so I shall be always most ready to obey your godly monitions and good instructions, as becometh one upon whom you have heaped so many benefits. And thus fearing lest I should trouble your Lordship too much, I most humbly take my leave of your good Lordship.

Your humble servant during my life,

Jane Grey[10]

It was a polite note, and one that echoed the sentiments of her parents.[11] Besides that, it demonstrated Jane's fondness for the Admiral, who had indeed always been kind to her. But Jane herself had no choice as to where her future lay, and as her note revealed, on paper at least, she was obedient to the wishes of those that did.

But the Admiral was not to be dissuaded and it is clear that his determination ultimately had the desired effect, for, worn down by his persistence, Jane's parents finally agreed to a meeting in order to discuss their next move. The day after Jane's note, Frances wrote to assure Seymour that she trusted that matters in regards to Jane's custody would soon be resolved to the satisfaction of all. Addressing Seymour in familiar terms once more as 'Mine own good brother', she proceeded to soothe him:

I have received your most gentle and loving letter, wherein I do perceive your approved goodwill which you bear unto my daughter Jane, for the which I think myself most bounden to you, for that you are so desirous for to have her continue with you. I trust at our next meeting, which, according to your own appointment, shall be shortly, we shall so communicate together as you shall be satisfied, and I contented; and forasmuch as this messenger does make haste away, that I have but little leisure to write, I shall desire you to take these few lines in good part: and thus wishing your health and quietness as my own, and a short dispatch of your business, that I might the sooner see you here, I take my leave of you, my good brother, for this time.[12]

Once again, Frances had taken the lead in asserting her voice when it came to her daughter's upbringing. She flattered the Admiral into believing that she would at least consider returning Jane to his care, though that may not have been her true intention. Her ambitions for Jane had not waned, and aware that she and her husband held the upper hand by having what the Admiral sought, she was determined that any arrangements made would be to their advantage. Jane would have to comply.

Encouraged by Frances's letter and feeling certain of a positive outcome, the Admiral shortly afterwards presented himself at Bradgate Park in person. Determined that he would not leave before he had won back his ward, this time he brought his companion, Sir William Sharington, to help him achieve his goal. Sharington was a shady character, who would later be condemned for embezzling the Bristol Mint.[13] At the time of the meeting he was in his early fifties with a serious face and a long brown beard. He had been well favoured by Henry VIII, and was now closely allied with the Admiral. The Admiral's tactics were simple: while he set to work on persuading Henry to relinquish Jane, Sharington exercised his charms on Frances. This time his plan worked, and by Henry's admission, Seymour 'persuaded me to have her return, renewing his promise for her marriage to the king'.[14] Seymour flattered Henry by telling him that 'if the King's majesty, when he came to age, would marry within the realm, it was as likely he would be there, as in any other place'.[15] It would have been a dazzling prospect for Jane: marriage to the King would make her Queen of England, and would bring unimaginable wealth and influence to her family. However, this time, promises of a royal marriage alone were not enough. Henry and Frances had driven a hard bargain, and though 'After long debate we agreed to her return', the Admiral was obliged to produce £500 (£154,000) of the £2,000 loan he had originally offered to Jane's father.[16] Once again, Seymour's eloquent charms had worked, but at a higher price than he had anticipated. That Seymour fought so hard reveals just how highly he perceived Jane's value. Nevertheless, if his intrigues paid off, the prize would be worth the investment.

Having successfully managed to bribe Jane's parents into returning her, by the end of October Jane was once more in London, installed at Seymour Place with the Admiral's mother Lady Seymour for company. On her journey south she had passed through the city of Leicester, where she had been entertained in the style her rank demanded, and where she was admired by the city folk. She was in no mood for such revelries, however, and was no doubt relieved to reach her destination. It had been an exhausting and disruptive time for Jane, and though she was once more the Admiral's ward, this time it was different. There was no Katherine Parr or Lady Elizabeth to offer her companionship – by comparison, at around seventy years old, Lady Seymour must have seemed impossibly old – while the Admiral's infant daughter, Mary, was no more than a baby.[17] In her youth, Lady Seymour had once been praised for her beauty by the famous poet John Skelton, but to Jane she would have appeared as a grandmotherly figure.[18] As Jane adjusted to the changes within the Seymour household and tried to settle into a routine once more, she was oblivious to the fact that the Admiral was now under pressure to fulfil his promise of her marriage to the King. In the eyes of Jane's parents, words were no longer of use: actions were needed.

The Admiral's behaviour, though, was starting to give cause for concern. Following the death of his wife and the removal of her generally steadying influence, Seymour had become progressively erratic and outspoken in his bid for power. He had even made a failed attempt to pursue a second marriage with Jane's cousin, fifteen-year-old Elizabeth, with whom he had enjoyed a previous flirtation. As the year 1548 drew to a close, it was starting to become glaringly apparent that it was dangerous to be associated with this treacherously impulsive man, who was becoming increasingly reckless and was starting to raise eyebrows at court. For Jane and her family, the risk was greater than most, for Jane's residence in the Admiral's household was clear evidence of their association with him. Incredibly, Jane's parents ignored all of the warning signs and clung to the hope that the Admiral would be true to his word, and achieve the grand promises he had made.

As the New Year of 1549 dawned, however, the Admiral went several steps too far. Having realized that his best chance of achieving real power was through securing the King's person and removing him from the clutches of the Lord Protector, Seymour hatched a daring plan. On the night of 16 January, he attempted to break into the King's apartments at Hampton Court. He had almost made it when 'The alarm was given by the gentleman who sleeps in the King's chamber, who, awakened by the barking of the dog that lies before the King's door, cried out "Help! Murder!"'[19] In a moment of blind panic, the Admiral, carrying a loaded pistol, shot the dog before fleeing the scene. 'Everybody rushed in; but the only thing they found was the lifeless corpse of the dog. Suspicion points to the Admiral.'[20] It was a disastrous mistake, and for Seymour time was up. The following day the King's guards arrived at Seymour Place, and he was arrested. Whether Jane witnessed the Admiral's arrest or any change in his behaviour is open to speculation, but what is certain is that she would have witnessed the ransacking of Seymour Place as the guards searched relentlessly for evidence against him. Also at Seymour Place at the time of the arrest were Jane's father and his younger brother, Sir Thomas Grey, who watched in horror as the Admiral was taken to the Tower. His actions had been treasonous, and his true intentions were about to be revealed.

The Admiral's arrest came as a complete shock to the Dorsets. Finally the penny dropped, and they realized that they needed to disassociate themselves from this dangerous man, and quickly. The Council were beginning to gather evidence against him, and soon discovered that it was more than forthcoming. Eager to exonerate himself for having had any relations with Seymour, Henry offered to testify against his former ally the day after his arrest. His deposition was damning.[21]

With no prompting, Henry revealed the true extent of the Admiral's ambitions. How he had plotted to remove the King from the influence of his brother the Lord Protector, whom 'he did not love', and the conversation they had had in which Seymour had advised him to rally the men on his estates.[22] On the subject of his daughter Jane, Henry claimed that following the death of Katherine Parr, the Admiral 'came to my house himself and was so earnestly in hand with me and my wife that in the end because he would not have no nay, we were contented she should again return to his house'.[23] In other words, the Admiral had bullied them into handing over their eldest daughter until they were unable to refuse.

As the evidence against Seymour mounted, he 'refused persistently to answer any of these charges in the Tower', insisting on his right to a public trial.[24] This was to be denied him, and having been 'condemned almost unanimously' on the 'evidence produced in proof of thirty-one charges brought against him', including that 'he had plotted to kill the Protector', the date was set for his execution.[25] While some of the charges had at least a grain of truth in them, others were undoubtedly imagined. Notably, one of the authentic charges brought against him related directly to Jane: 'that he had planned to ally the King with the daughter of an English nobleman', a charge that was clearly considered to be treasonous in the eyes of the King's Council.[26] Nothing could save him, but he continued to plot until the very end. Seymour spent his final evening in the Tower writing secret notes to the Ladies Mary and Elizabeth, in which he urged them to conspire against the Protector. He sewed these into his shoes, and they were only discovered following his death after his servant made the authorities aware of them. On 20 March, the man who had been Jane's guardian for the past two years was executed on Tower Hill. Though her reaction to his death went unrecorded, it seems likely that Jane, already suffering from the upheaval of the months since the death of Katherine Parr, felt some sadness over the Admiral's loss. But she was among the minority, for there were many who were relieved at his removal, including Bishop Hugh Latimer, the court preacher, who condemned Seymour as 'a wicked man, and the realm is well rid of him'.[27] Perhaps the biggest loser, however, was the six-month-old daughter that the Admiral left behind. Lady Mary Seymour was now an orphan, and at her father's request was sent to live in the household of Jane's step-grandmother, Katherine Willoughby. Jane, who had been with Mary's mother throughout her pregnancy, and had been close by at her birth, probably never saw the child again.[28]

The Admiral's association with Jane's family was well known, and could easily have led to their ruin. Miraculously, they survived unscathed, almost certainly due to Henry's cooperation in providing evidence against his former ally. However, there was also another saving grace – Jane herself. The Admiral was not the only one who was aware that Jane was a great prize in the marital market. He himself had been conscious that there would be many offers for her hand, and had resolved to be the first to exploit this. Shortly before his arrest, the Admiral had confided to his brother-in-law, William Parr, Marquess of Northampton, that 'there would be much ado for Lady Jane', and that 'the protector and [the Duchess of Somerset] would do what they could to obtain her for Lord Hertford'.[29] Sure enough, following the Admiral's execution, a verbal agreement was made between Henry and the Lord Protector, whereby Jane was promised in marriage to the Protector's eldest son, Edward, Earl of Hertford. For Henry, his concurrence was an effective and convenient means of extricating himself from blame in the Admiral's affair, but in reality both he and Frances were still intent on Jane's marriage to the King. They were nothing if not versatile, and were willing to work with anyone in power in order to achieve their ambitions and obtain glory for their daughter. Promises, after all, were easily broken. As it transpired, though, there was no need for them to do anything in order to disentangle themselves.

CHAPTER 8

She Did Never Love Her After

A S THE SCANDAL surrounding the Admiral began to die down, in the weeks following his death life for Jane also started to settle. Her family were beginning to spend an increasing amount of time in London, where Jane's parents could be close to the court. Since the death of Henry VIII their fortunes had taken a drastic upwards turn, and despite the recent scandal, they continued to enjoy the favour of King Edward. Six months after the Admiral's execution, on 23 September the King paid the family a visit at Dorset House. A fine meal was prepared consisting of several sumptuous courses, and it would have been customary for Jane's parents to organize a lavish entertainment to delight their royal visitor. The young King, just a few weeks short of his twelfth birthday, probably also took the opportunity to speak with Jane and her younger sisters, Katherine and Mary. Edward had much in common with Jane, for he too was learned, passionate almost to the point of fanatical when it came to religion, and loved his books. But even against the intellect of the King, Jane stood out as being extraordinary. The martyrologist John Foxe later noted that between 'this young Damsel and king Edward there was little difference in age, though in learning and knowledge of the tongues she was not only equal, but also superior unto him'.[1] Doubtless, as the cousins conversed, Jane's parents watched closely, eagerly looking for signs of affection between them. Jane must have been aware of her parents' hopes for her in regards to a marriage with Edward, but it is impossible to speculate as to what her feelings may have been. Similarly, there is no indication of how Edward felt about his cousin in personal terms, or in regards to a possible marriage. There had once been talk of other marriages for the King: first to Mary, Queen of Scots, and later to the French Princess Elisabeth, but both had come to nothing.[2]

The Dorsets must have been aware by this time that the power of the Lord Protector was beginning to wane, and that there was great opposition in the Council to his rule. Many of his policies were unpopular, and more importantly, his nephew the King was becoming increasingly alienated from him as a result of the Lord Protector continuing to treat him like a small child despite his growth. The King was kept consistently short of money by his uncle, and the Admiral had once remarked that 'he was but a very beggarly King now and had nothing for play or to give to his servants', and had given him money.[3] As the King bade farewell to Jane and her family and returned to the Palace of Whitehall, the Dorsets may have been hopeful that they would soon be freed from their promise to the Lord Protector, and that Jane's marriage to the King could then, at last, become a reality.

As with his brother before him, the Lord Protector's time was running out, and his rule of supremacy was about to come to an end. On 6 October, a fortnight after the King's visit to Dorset House, Edward had retired to bed for the evening at Hampton Court. Shortly afterwards he was disturbed by the Protector, who having heard reports that several of the disgruntled lords were marching to confront him, had decided to remove with Edward to the greater security of Windsor Castle. The King was furious at the disturbance, and complained vehemently: 'Methinks I am in prison.'[4] A few days later, on 11 October, the Protector was toppled by a coup d'état, and he was arrested and sent to the Tower. His career was in shreds, along with any hopes of a marriage he may have envisaged between his son and Jane.

Once again Jane's father followed where others led, and lent his wholehearted support to the coup against the Protector. His motivation for doing so was probably not based on any strong feelings of resentment he harboured against the Protector personally, but rather an attempt to ensure that he was on the winning side. It was likely to have been this that led to his appointment in November as a Privy Councillor. After years of political exclusion during the reign of Henry VIII, it appeared that his ambitions were finally beginning to be realized. However, he did not take his new role particularly seriously, and attended Council meetings infrequently – no doubt a sign of his own laziness. It mattered little, for in reality his presence was merely required to weight the Council in favour of another leader.

With the fall of the Lord Protector, it became clear that a new leader was emerging at court. John Dudley, Earl of Warwick, was the son of Henry VII's hated advisor Edmund Dudley, who had been executed soon after the accession of Henry VIII. Following the death of his father, in 1512 Sir Edward Guildford, a close friend of the King's, purchased John's wardship.[5] John had duly been sent to live in his household, where he was betrothed to Sir Edward's daughter, Jane. The marriage took place in 1525 when John was twenty-one and Jane was sixteen, and was a genuine love match. Under the influence of his father-in-law, John spent much of his time at court, where he rose to prominence under Henry VIII. He gained a reputation as a good soldier, and in 1523 was knighted by Jane's maternal grandfather, the Duke of Suffolk, before being created Viscount Lisle in 1542.[6] At the succession of Edward VI, Dudley had supported the Lord Protector, and had been rewarded with the earldom of Warwick. However, he was clearly ambitious, and did not scruple when it came to engineering the fall of his former patron in order to ensure his own elevation.

WITH THE SUPPORT of Archbishop Cranmer, King Edward had stepped up the intensity of his religious reforms, and while for Jane and her family this was a positive development, for Jane's cousin the Lady Mary, life was about to become extremely difficult. In January 1549, the Act of Uniformity had been passed in Parliament. The Act established Cranmer's Book of Common Prayer, written in English, and other evangelical rites as the official form of worship in England. The Act was controversial, not least because clergy who refused to adopt the Book of Common Prayer could be stiffly punished.[7] Among those who were utterly appalled by the Act was the Lady Mary, who steadfastly refused to adhere to any religion other than Catholicism. Since the death of her father she had spent much of her time away from court at the various palatial estates left to her by Henry VIII, and here she defiantly ordered the Catholic Mass to be celebrated.[8] Her faith was something on which she was not prepared to compromise, but it led to a permanent rift with her half-brother. Edward was incensed by Mary's headstrong determination to refute his authority, and as his reign progressed made increasing and ever more aggressive efforts to encourage her to conform.[9] They were all in vain, and Mary later wrote to her cousin Charles V of her distress that 'Our kingdom is daily approaching nearer to spiritual and material ruin, and matters grow worse day by day.'[10] Mary's devotion to her faith would also soon lead to a breach between herself and her cousin Jane, for although social etiquette and the physical distance between them had ensured that the topic had been avoided thus far, as the Christmas of 1549 approached, Jane's views were about to be aired beyond the bounds of protocol to her cousin.

On the last day of October, the Grey family left Bradgate Park and memories of the recent Seymour scandal behind them, determined to enjoy Christmas as a family. Frances 'and all her train', including her three daughters, travelled south to Essex.[11] The journey was a long one, over a hundred miles, and took several days to accomplish. The winter weather also slowed their progress, for the roads, little more than dirt tracks, were always worse in winter, causing the hooves of the horses that drew the litter carrying Frances and her daughters to sink in the mud. The family doubtless travelled in style, perhaps in a litter that was similar to that which had been owned by Jane's maternal grandmother and was 'covered with cloth of gold embroidered with fleur-de-lys, and carried by two large horses equipped with both saddles and harness, all covered with similar cloth. Inside the litter there are four large cushions covered with cloth of gold, and on the outside this litter is covered with scarlet English cloth.'[12]

At long last the family arrived at their destination: Tilty Abbey. The guesthouse of the former medieval abbey had been leased to Jane's paternal grandmother in 1535 for the use of her son from her first marriage, George Medley.[13] George, Jane's half-uncle, and his wife, Mary, greeted their guests with delight, and Jane and her sisters soon settled into their home for the season amid a host of other family members.[14] In addition to George's five children, Jane's three young cousins the Willoughbys were also present, and though all younger than Jane, they perhaps provided a welcome change of company from her sisters.[15] Thomas, Margaret and Francis Willoughby were the children of Jane's paternal aunt, Anne, by her husband, Sir Henry Willoughby. Tragically, however, just months earlier Sir Henry had been killed while supporting the King in trying to suppress Kett's Rebellion in East Anglia, an uprising that broke out in response to rising living costs, particularly land rental prices. His wife having died the previous year, the result was that his three children were made orphans.[16] Jane's father had immediately assumed responsibility for the eldest child Thomas, who was probably slightly younger than Jane's sister Katherine. For a short time, Thomas had joined Jane and her sisters at Bradgate, before being sent away to continue his education at Cambridge. Margaret and Francis, just five and three years old, had been sent to Tilty Abbey to be cared for by their half-uncle.

Before long, other members of the family began to descend on Tilty, and three days after Jane's arrival, her uncles Thomas and John Grey arrived 'with twenty-one servants from London', and stayed at Tilty for three days before travelling to London.[17] Thomas was unmarried, but it seems probable that John brought his wife, Mary Browne, and his six children to share in the merriment.[18] The family was a close one. Jane's father was fond of his brothers, and Thomas in particular paid regular visits to Bradgate, so Jane would certainly have been extremely familiar with at least one of her uncles. In addition, her uncle John's daughter, Frances, was of a similar age to Jane, so was perhaps able to provide her with some suitable company.[19] On 16 November 'many honest men of the country' dined at Tilty; it was not unusual for the house to be busy.[20] Amid the reunion, Jane joined her mother and sisters on a short trip to visit the Lady Mary at Beaulieu to the north-east of Chelmsford; the same visit that was later recorded in the pages of John Foxe, and which may have had such a momentous impact on the relationship between Jane and her cousin.

Mary had chosen to keep Christmas at her Palace of Beaulieu. Given to her by her father, Beaulieu was a large property that had been beautified by Henry VIII, thus earning its name.[21] Beaulieu was a favourite of Mary's, and in previous years she had spent a great deal of time there. At this festive time of year it was normal for Mary to welcome guests; despite the breach with her half-brother, Henry VIII's daughter Mary was still immensely popular with the English people, many of whom remembered her mother, and she had also managed to retain good relationships with many of those at court.

The former monastery of Tilty was not far from Beaulieu, and after breakfast on 26 November, 'my Lady's Grace [Frances], with Lady Jane, Lady Katherine and Lady Mary repaired to Lady Mary's Grace', accompanied by a retinue of servants to attend them.[22] Mary may have greeted the visit from her cousin Frances and her daughters with particular enthusiasm, for to her sorrow she saw little of her half-brother King Edward, or her half-sister the Lady Elizabeth, who also maintained a separate household.[23]

As Jane and her sisters arrived at the Palace, they rode through the impressive entrance gate that was adorned with the magnificent coat of arms of Henry VIII, and was topped with heraldic stone dragons.[24] Having exchanged pleasantries and words of welcome with Mary, their host, they may also have exchanged gifts. Traditionally, New Year was the main gift-giving event of the year, but Mary's surviving jewel inventories reveal that she had made lavish gifts to Jane's mother and her aunt, Eleanor Clifford, on several occasions.[25] Ever generous, especially to those she loved, Mary had once given Frances a rich gift of 'a pair of beads of crystal trimmed with gold, with a tassel at the end of goldsmith's work', while Jane too had been fortunate enough to receive a gift.[26] Mary had given her a beautiful 'lace for the neck of goldsmith work' containing thirty-two pearls, an elaborate and dazzling present for a girl of Jane's youth, and one which she perhaps may not have fully appreciated.[27]

It was neither the time nor the place to draw attention to the fact that Jane and her family were on the opposing side of the religious fence to Mary. However, Jane's dedication to reform was becoming more fervent each day. According to John Foxe, who recorded the story in his *Acts and Monuments*, she found that during her visit to Beaulieu, an occasion arose when she simply could not let it pass.

Foxe relates that Jane was enjoying a walk through Beaulieu's intricate complex with Lady Anne Wharton, one of Mary's ladies, when their tour took them to the chapel. The chapel was dominated by the beautiful, brightly coloured Flemish stained-glass window commemorating the betrothal of Mary's parents, a poignant reminder of where she came from.[28] As they walked, Lady Wharton paused to curtsey in obeisance towards the altar, on which was hung a gorgeous statue of the Virgin Mary. Lady Wharton's actions towards this most venerable of Catholic symbols left Jane utterly perplexed, for her faith placed far less significance on the mother of Christ.[29] 'Why do you do so? Is the Lady Mary in the chapel?' Jane enquired. 'No, madam,' Lady Wharton replied, 'I make my curtsey to Him that made us all.' Astounded, Jane rudely cried, 'Why, how can He be there that made us all, and the baker made Him?'[30] Her comments were astonishing, not least for their brashness. She had not yet learned the diplomacy that was so well practised by her parents – the crucial requirement of a courtier and those socializing in great circles. At thirteen, Jane's devotion to reform was already profound, and would grow ever more zealous as she matured.

Foxe continues to explain that when the Lady Mary was informed of Jane's shocking outburst in the chapel, she was gravely insulted. Her feelings towards Jane immediately cooled, and it was claimed that 'she did never love her after'.[31] More than that, that she 'esteemed her as the rest of that Christian profession'.[32] It has been suggested that the story could be apocryphal; it is true that Foxe is the only writer who refers to such a tale, and that he makes no mention of his source. It is also true that Foxe was determined to highlight Jane's religious enthusiasm. Nevertheless, the story does sound in keeping with what we know of Jane's character, namely that she was prepared to stand her ground on the subject of her religious beliefs. Although Mary's reported reaction is almost certainly a gross exaggeration, on balance it does seem likely that the story has some basis in fact.

IN DECEMBER, JANE and her family returned to Tilty. By now the Christmas celebrations were beginning to get well underway, and the Medleys had spared no expense. The twelve days of Christmas that started on Christmas Day were celebrated with full splendour, and probably began with the family attending a service at the historic local church of St Mary's, which was next to Tilty Abbey.[33] Back at the house, the festivities would be getting started, with feasting and entertainments for 'divers of the country' on such a scale as to rival those of the royal court.[34] The kitchen staff at Tilty had been busy preparing an array of sumptuous dishes especially for the occasion: roast swan, goose, probably a peacock, cooked and then redressed in its magnificent feathers, and wild boar, the head of which adorned the Christmas table as a centrepiece. The rich aroma of spices filled the air as the family celebrated, perhaps with a wassail cup in the hope of a good production of fruit the following year.[35] A delicious choice of puddings accompanied the main course, including Christmas pudding made from meat, oatmeal and a mixture of spices. Hosted by the Lord of Misrule, who was appointed to oversee all of the entertainments and festivities, the guests were treated to a masque performed by strolling players and actors in the employ of John de Vere, Earl of Oxford. Known as Oxford's Men, the troupe were among the best actors in the country, and had staged performances in London and abroad.[36] The theme of such festive masques was frequently religious, often relating to the story of Christ. Games of Blind Man's Buff were also common, in which the whole family participated amid a wave of giggles as they tried to avoid being tagged by the one blindfolded.[37] When the youngsters retired for the evening, exhausted by the excitement of the day, the adults often indulged in gambling at card games, a pastime of which Jane's parents were particularly fond. During a later Christmas celebration, the family chaplain James Haddon publicly rebuked gambling for money from the pulpit. He had already taken Jane's parents to task for such a vice, and though initially they agreed to abstain, Haddon soon learned that the couple 'have secretly played with their friends in their private apartment'.[38] When Haddon took to the pulpit to preach against gambling, the pointedness of his words would not have been lost on the pair. Unsurprisingly Jane's parents did not appreciate being told what to do in their own household, and, said Haddon, 'they thought it was my duty merely to have admonished them in private'.[39]

A family of Jane's high standing would certainly have enjoyed celebrations on this lavish scale every Christmas, and probably took it in turns to host. For Jane, this year in particular, with the trauma of losing her guardian to the headsman's axe still relatively fresh in her mind, the magnificence of the occasion may have done much to help restore her spirits as she enjoyed the beautiful costumes of the actors, and was entertained in the company of her family.

In addition, the festivities extended to outside of Jane's family circle, for members of the court also began to arrive, and it was observed that great numbers of people 'dined and supped at Tilty'.[40] Jane's parents appear to have been relatively popular among their contemporaries; they still counted Lord and Lady Cavendish among their friends – Lady Cavendish being Frances's former lady, Elizabeth (Bess) Hardwick – as well as the Marquess and Marchioness of Northampton. The revels and entertainments continued over the next twelve days, and must have been overwhelming for the excitable youngsters. As New Year arrived, the customary gifts were exchanged between family members, and Jane's parents had likely arranged for a suitable gift to be sent to King Edward on their behalf. This almost certainly pushed their resources to the limit, however. Despite her parents being among the greatest nobility in the land, their finances were often depleted and they were frequently in debt. This was reflected in the nature of the gifts once given to the Lady Mary. Though she gave generous, costly gifts of jewels, she received only a wrought smock in return.[41]

New Year did not signal the end of the celebrations. Though the festivities reached their peak on 6 January, the Feast of the Epiphany, Jane and her family remained at Tilty until 20 January. Jane's family was nothing if not a social one, and certainly on her father's side the family were close and eager to spend time with one another.[42] Though she must have been exhausted after visiting her family and enjoying the plentiful entertainments, Jane would no doubt have relished the opportunity to mix and socialize with her wider family. After an absence of three months, however, it was at last time to return to the seclusion of the peaceful Leicestershire countryside, and to Bradgate.

CHAPTER 9

I Think Myself in Hell

WHILE THE DORSETS had enjoyed a particularly joyous Christmas, not everyone had been so fortunate. The deposed Lord Protector had spent Christmas languishing in the Tower while John Dudley, Earl of Warwick, well and truly established himself in his place. In January 1550 the Imperial ambassador, Van der Delft, wrote to the Emperor Charles V to inform him of Warwick's increasing influence. Warwick, he said, was 'not merely unstable, but evil and cruel too', although he provided no precise justification for such claims.[1] But Warwick had his supporters, as Van der Delft conceded: 'the Marquis of Northampton, who has two wives, and the Marquis of Dorset, a senseless creature, belong to his crew'.[2] This description of Henry highlights the generally low regard in which his contemporaries held him, as well as his perceived lack of political judgement. By the end of the month, Warwick's power had increased still further, as Van der Delft confirmed: 'the Earl of Warwick's pre-eminence will be established. He is to be Great Master of England, and the Great Master (of the Household) is to be made Lord Treasurer, which was the Protector's office. The Marquis of Northampton will be Lord Chamberlain, the Marquis of Dorset Justice Itinerant of the King's Forests.'[3] Jane's parents were, it seemed, already reaping great benefits, and Henry probably congratulated himself on allying himself with Warwick. In time, King Edward would come to depend on the Earl utterly, and, in turn, Warwick took full advantage.

Shortly afterwards, in February Somerset was released from the Tower. On 14 January he had been formally deprived of his title of Lord Protector, but through the intercession of some of his remaining supporters, he was released and received the King's pardon. Before long he was allowed to resume his place on the King's Council, but there was no mistaking that it was Warwick who was the real power behind the throne now, and Somerset was forced to comply. Thus an uneasy working relationship between the two men was established, although the King made it clear that he disliked his uncle and preferred Warwick. For the moment, political dissension continued to simmer.

ON A WARM summer's day in 1550, Henry and Frances Grey had ridden out into the lush woodland surrounding Bradgate Park, where they were indulging their passion for hunting. In their absence, a visitor arrived at the house. Roger Ascham, the famous scholar and tutor to the Lady Elizabeth, had arrived at Bradgate in order to bid farewell to his wife Alice, who was employed in the Grey household, and his friend John Aylmer. He was departing for a diplomatic post abroad as the secretary of Richard Moryson, the English ambassador at the court of the Emperor Charles V. On discovering that the lord and lady of the house were not at home, Ascham was instead conducted to the most senior member of the household: Lady Jane.

As he entered the hall where Jane sat, Ascham noticed that Jane was absorbed in her book, Plato's *Phaedon Platonis*. Jane was reading the book, written in Greek, 'with as much delight as some gentleman would read a merry tale in Boccaccio's'.[4] Jane's fondness for books had seen her progressing to ever more complex works. She could almost forget who she was and the complexities of her situation in life when she became lost in the challenging pages of Plato, whose work she read for fun.

Ascham was surprised to discover Jane inside on such a beautifully sunny day and reading such an astonishingly advanced book. Once the formalities had been exchanged, he enquired as to why Jane was not outside enjoying the hunt with her parents. Jane replied that 'all their sport in the park is but a shadow to that pleasure that I find in Plato'. She added, 'alas, good folk, they never felt what true pleasure meant'.[5] According to Ascham, what happened next, an account of which he published in his book *The Schoolmaster*, has formed the basis of Frances's reputation as a cruel mother – it is a reputation that has lasted in excess of four hundred years. Feeling at ease in the company of one whom she admired, Jane took this opportunity, Ascham relates, to pour out all of the feelings of hurt and resentment she felt towards her parents. 'I will tell you, and tell you a truth which perchance you will marvel at,' she began:

> *One of the greatest benefits that ever God gave me is that He sent me so sharp and severe parents and so gentle a schoolmaster. For when I am in presence either of father or mother, whether I speak, keep silence, sit, stand, or go, eat, drink, be merry or sad, be sewing, playing, dancing or doing anything else, I must do it, as it were, in such weight, measure, and number, even so perfectly as God made the world, or else I am so sharply taunted, so cruelly threatened, yea, presently sometimes with pinches, nips, and bobs and other ways which I will not name for the honour I bear them, so without measure misordered, that I think myself in hell till time come that I must go to Master Aylmer, who teacheth me so gently, so pleasantly, with such fair allurements to learning, that I think all the time nothing whilst I am with him. And when I am called from him, I fall on weeping because whatsoever I do else but learning is full of grief, trouble, fear, and whole misliking unto me. And thus my book hath been so much my pleasure, and bringeth daily to me more pleasure and more,*

that in respect of it all other pleasures in very deed be but trifles and
troubles unto me.[6]

It was a shocking declaration. Taken at face value, it is certainly damning and compelling evidence of parental cruelty, while Jane's apparent distress is heartbreaking. Though it was not unusual for sixteenth-century children to be subjected to beatings in order to instil discipline, Jane's supposedly heartfelt admission makes harrowing reading.[7] However, when scrutinizing Ascham's story in order to ascertain the truth of the matter, there are several factors that ought to be considered.

Ascham was the only one of Jane's contemporaries who ever made any mention of the physical abuse Jane allegedly suffered at the hands of her parents.[8] Furthermore, he was clearly not overly disturbed by the alleged conversation, as his account was not published until 1570, by which time Jane and her parents were all dead and unable to challenge his claim. During this time Ascham's recollections of the events that had taken place twenty years previously could have altered, though he claimed to have a good memory, stating that 'I remember this talk gladly, both because it is so worthy of memory, and because also it was the last talk that ever I had, and the last time that ever I saw that noble and worthy lady.'[9] This was seemingly the first occasion on which he had ever referred to the Dorsets' violent behaviour, despite the fact that he had made several previous mentions of his visit to Bradgate. In a letter written to Jane several months after his visit, Ascham remarked on how impressed he had been to discover Jane pursuing her studies so diligently. What is more, he added: 'Go on then, most accomplished maiden, to bring honour on your country, happiness on your parents, glory to yourself, credit to your tutor, congratulations to all your friends, and the greatest admiration to all strangers!'[10] This indicates that Ascham believed that Jane's parents were proud of their daughter's abilities and achievements. Perhaps he feared retribution if he published his shocking words during their lifetime.

However, it seems strange that Jane would choose to unburden herself in such a way that would prove to be so damning to her parents. It may be that she did make some form of complaint about them, which Ascham then embellished to highlight his points.

Ascham's version of events was written with a very specific purpose: to highlight the benefits of teaching children through kindness. His example of the nurturing care of Jane's tutor, John Aylmer, provides a great contrast to the harsh cruelty supposedly inflicted by Jane's parents. As Ascham himself stated, he had chosen to relate Jane's example of 'whether love or fear both work more in a child, for virtue and learning' in the hope that it 'may be heard with some pleasure, and followed with more profit'.[11] His motives for damning the Dorsets so publicly are, on a personal level, perplexing. There is no record of any discord between the two parties, further evidence for which is suggested by the Dorsets having employed Ascham's wife. He was almost certainly aware of their desire that their daughter be raised with a strong sense of morality, and may have adjusted this encounter in order to demonstrate his points.

It is perfectly clear that Jane's parents were strict: both of their surviving letters show how important it was to them to raise a daughter who was both modest and virtuous, but this does not mean to say that they physically beat her. They may have agreed with the views of the Spanish humanist scholar Juan Luis Vives, who had been consulted in regards to the education of Jane's cousin Mary, on strict parenting, namely that 'specially the daughters should be handled without cherishing', although this too seems extreme.[12] There is a difference between strict parenting and malicious physical and mental abuse, and in this case it seems possible that the boundaries have become blurred. It would be unfair to condemn Jane's parents on the basis of one source, and one in which there are flaws. Ascham's report is not corroborated elsewhere, and other sources suggest that the opposite is true. Indeed, the following year, John of Ulm, who had been spending time with Jane at Bradgate, related his view that in terms of her family connections Jane should be viewed with the utmost respect, nor was there anyone 'more learned if you consider her age; or more happy, if you consider both'.[13] It is true that the term 'happy' was probably a reference to Jane being fortunate and came from a man who was nothing but complimentary to her family, but as one who knew Jane, Ulm's comment is nevertheless suggestive of a young woman who was enjoying a good life and was viewed with pride.

Ascham's account has undoubtedly contributed to the perception later writers have had of Frances. This, surely, is where the image of the cruel mother originates, a misconception that has persisted to the present day. However, the claims of several writers that Frances was, among other things, 'a harsh, grasping, brutal woman', and 'arrogant and energetic', are not borne out by any contemporary evidence.[14] They are all based on the assertion that Frances was an abusive individual who terrorized her daughter Jane, and this was almost certainly not the case.

Henry and Frances do, in fact, appear to have been proud parents, and Robert Wingfield, who was close to the family, observed that Jane was her father's 'favourite daughter'.[15] They were well aware of Jane's intellectual gifts, and this, coupled with her value within society, led them to have extremely high expectations of her. As James Haddon informed Heinrich Bullinger, Jane 'is so brought up, that there is the greatest hope of her advancement in godliness'.[16] When she did not meet those expectations, or began to demonstrate some of the defiant attitude so typical in teenagers, as appears to have been the case following her return from Thomas Seymour's household, frustration may have led them to sharply rebuke her, and perhaps on occasion even inflict some mild physical punishment. Jane's apparent refusal to go hunting seems to demonstrate that she could be wilful, and as historian Eric Ives has suggested, a typical rebellious teenager.[17] However, if Jane was physically punished for her wilful displays, then no other reliable contemporary source makes any mention of it.

Other sources suggest that Jane shared a close relationship with her parents. Jane, 'whom her father loves as a daughter' according to John Aylmer, probably had more in common with her father, with whom she shared similar intellectual interests, while her sisters seem to have identified more with their mother.[18] This does not mean, though, that Jane did not get along with Frances, and Michelangelo Florio, who was well placed to know the truth of the matter, stated that Jane was close to her mother. Doubts have been expressed about the authenticity of Florio's account, as it was not published until 1607, but these are somewhat countered by the appearance of it having been composed much earlier, perhaps in 1561. As was the case with Ascham, when Florio wrote his account Jane and her parents were dead, so had he wished to malign Jane's parents he could quite easily have done so. His account shows his fondness for Jane and sympathy for her later plight, so had her parents mistreated her he could have comfortably woven this into his narrative. Although he was a member of the Grey household, Florio had no reason to gush over his employers in the same way as John of Ulm; they had been good to him, but he was not one of Henry's protégés. Moreover, Florio's residence in the Grey household meant that he was privy to the everyday occurrences – Ascham was not. In Jane's own accounts of the events of 1553 she made references to wishing to be with her mother, which seems to highlight that she craved her familiar presence and is at odds with the claim that her mother was physically terrorizing her. There is also no evidence that Jane's younger sisters were ever physically abused, and they seem to have shared a close relationship with their mother. Similarly, none of Frances's contemporaries ever remarked on any vicious side to her character, and there is no suggestion that she was unpopular or disliked.

Jane's parents were the consistent figures in her life. They had raised her, and planned meticulously for her future. They had every reason to be proud of her and her academic achievements.

THE FOLLOWING YEAR of 1551 proved to be hugely significant for the Dorsets. It was in the opening months that the family made an almost permanent move from the quiet countryside of Bradgate Park to the hustle and bustle of London, where they installed themselves in Dorset House. The move was necessitated by the fact that Jane's parents were beginning to spend a great deal of their time at court, where they also had lodgings. Henry in particular was being given an increasing amount of responsibility. On 25 February he was named Lord Warden of the Northern Marches, and sent to try to stave off the threat posed by the Scots as a result of the Rough Wooing. This had begun eight years earlier, following Henry VIII's aggressive attempt to pursue a marriage between Prince Edward and the infant Mary, Queen of Scots, and tensions between the two nations were still rife.

The Council had expressed their desire to have a 'man of honour' to fill the role, but Henry's appointment is perplexing.[19] He had little military experience, and had never excelled in this field, as his previous experience in Boulogne had revealed, nor had he shown any willingness to pursue such a role. Nevertheless, in April the Imperial ambassador reported that 'the Marquis of Dorset, who has been appointed the King's lieutenant in the North Country, set out in that direction a short time ago with eighty horse'.[20] By 9 April he had reached Bradgate, probably with his wife and daughters in tow, and it was from here that he wrote to the Secretary of State, William Cecil, who was also a family friend, about an alteration that needed to be made to his warden's patent. One cannot help but feel that he was employing stalling tactics to postpone his departure for the north.

By 2 May, however, Henry was in Berwick where he had the support of three sub-wardens: Lord Ogle, Sir Nicholas Strelley and Lord John Conyers. From here he wrote to Cecil, begging him to intercede with the Council in order to send money with which to pay his garrison: 'I have written for money to relieve the poor garrisons here on their lamentable complaints. I long to hear from you, as they that inhabit hell would gladly hear how they do that be in heaven.'[21] Henry's complaints were understandable, for Berwick was a world away from life at court. Jane, though, who had recently begun a correspondence with the renowned Heinrich Bullinger, wrote proudly to the theologian that her father had 'been summoned by most weighty business in his majesty's service to the remotest parts of Britain'.[22] However honourable the position may have been, Henry continued to complain. Having heard nothing from Cecil in response to his pleas, he wrote again on 18 May, repeating his request for money: 'Pray further my request. I want money, for the soldiers of Berwick garrison are in great want of money. Pray be a means that the Lords may consider their poor estate and long bearing.'[23] Henry's health was also troubling him, and he craved permission to visit Newcastle for a short time, 'where I hope to have my health better'.[24] It is unclear whether his last request was granted, but it seems unlikely as on 7 July he was in Alnwick, still dissatisfied with his role, and disquieted at having received no instructions as to 'how to work in requiting the robberies and murders of the Scots on these frontiers, having no hope for redress by justice'.[25]

While Jane's father was miserably attending to the King's business on the borders, Jane herself was spending the spring at Bradgate, where she continued with her lessons, and her religious ideas developed even further. Aside from the royal court, whose leader King Edward was equally fervent, Bradgate Park had been at the very centre of patronage for evangelical theologians and devotees. Henry Grey actively encouraged and promoted evangelicalism as far as was possible, and he himself frequently conversed with theologians and men of learning. One of these was the gentleman John Banks, a member of his circle who later informed Heinrich Bullinger that Henry was a particular admirer of his work: 'The duke also himself devoted as much time as he could steal from the affairs of the nation, in which he was engaged, to the reading of scripture, and especially to your writings, with the milky eloquence of which he used to say that he was wonderfully delighted.'[26]

With a father who was so impassioned in his religious beliefs, it is unsurprising that Jane appeared to be following so diligently in his footsteps. What was more, Henry's relationship with such prominent men would prove to be extremely beneficial for Jane, for soon it was not only her parents and her tutor who took an interest in her intellectual abilities; she also quickly gained a reputation among some of the leading scholars and advocates of evangelicalism in Europe. The fact that she was spoken about by them, both before and after her death, demonstrates just how remarkable she was. Most prominent among these was Heinrich Bullinger himself. Though she was more than thirty years his junior, Jane began a correspondence with Bullinger that she found most fulfilling. On one occasion she even sent a gift of a pair of gloves to Bullinger's wife, and referred to him as 'the father of learning'.[27] The correspondence almost certainly began in 1551, and Jane was clearly overwhelmed by his attentions to someone 'girlish and unlearned' in 'condescending to write to me, a stranger, and in supplying the necessary instruction for the adornment of my understanding and the improvement of my mind'.[28] Her letters to Bullinger provide one of the few visible signs of affection in Jane's character, and are all the more touching considering that she never met him personally.

It was extraordinary that such a renowned theologian should pay such regard to the teenage daughter of a marquess – even one possessed of royal blood. That Jane had established a correspondence with Bullinger was in itself exceptional, for no other teenage girls of this period are known to have done so, and the fact that Bullinger responded with such enthusiasm demonstrates how impressed he was by her. Furthermore, it highlights Jane's desire to be noticed by men whose religious ideas she admired, and her apparent disinterest in having friends of her own age.

Master Aylmer also approved of Bullinger's interest. On 29 May he wrote to thank the pastor for his flattering attention to his pupil:

For what favour more useful to herself, or gratifying to the marquis,
or acceptable to me, can possibly be afforded her, not only by you, but
also by any other person of equal learning and piety, than that she,
whom her father loves as a daughter, and whom I look upon with
affection as a pupil, may derive such maxims of conduct from your
godly breast, as may assist her towards living well and happily?[29]

Aylmer's admiration for his pupil was clear, and he believed that Bullinger's
encouragement could only enhance Jane's abilities. It was Bullinger whom
Aylmer sought advice from when he grew concerned about the amount
of time Jane was committing to music. Jane already admired the theologian, but now that they were writing to one another Aylmer exhorted
him to 'prescribe to her the length of time she may properly devote to the
study of music. For in this respect also people err beyond measure in this
country, while their whole labour is undertaken, and exertions made, for
the sake of ostentation.'[30] Jane was a committed reformer, and for that
reason Aylmer clearly believed that Bullinger's opinion would carry some
weight in the matter, for he continued, 'there will probably, through your
influence, be some accession to the ranks of virtue'.[31] Aylmer attributed
Jane's interest in music, 'which Plato calls the bait of mischief', to her
youth. But he was concerned that it distracted her from

[t]hose studies which are attended with the praise of virtue. In
proportion therefore as the present age teems with many disorders,
must more careful and discreet physicians be sought for; that the
diligence, and labour, and exertion of excellent men may either
remove or correct such evils as are implanted by the corruption of
nature, and the infirmity of youth.[32]

Shortly after Aylmer's letter the matter was resolved, for Jane appeared to
have settled down and devoted herself to her studies, much to Aylmer's

satisfaction. It was Bullinger, however, whom Aylmer believed should receive the credit: 'You have acted therefore with much kindness in administering to the improvement of this young lady; and if you will proceed in the same course, you will afford great benefit to herself, and gratification to her father.'[33]

Jane must have revelled in the flattery of both her tutor and Bullinger. This is confirmed in the first of her surviving letters to the pastor, dated 12 July 1551.[34] Honoured by Bullinger's recent kind attentions to her, Jane began her letter by thanking him for his interest in her:

I give you, most learned sir, unceasing thanks, and shall do so as long as I live, for I cannot engage to requite the obligation; as I seem to myself quite unable to make a suitable return for such exceeding courtesy, unless indeed you should be of opinion that I return a favour while I retain it in my remembrance.[35]

It was clear that she appreciated his notice and the time that he had taken to converse with her, but more than that, he had struck a chord with her:

Because your writings are of such a character, as that they contain, not mere ordinary topics for amusement, but pious and divine thoughts for instruction, admonition and counsel, on such points especially, as are suited to my age and sex and the dignity of my family.[36]

No doubt encouraged by the stimulating conversations she had enjoyed with Aylmer, John of Ulm and the family chaplain, James Haddon, Jane continued to thank Bullinger for an epistle that he had sent her:

In this epistle, as in every thing else that you have published to the great edification of the Christian commonwealth, you have shown yourself not only a man of exquisite learning and singular

acquirement, but also a skillful, prudent, and godly counsellor; one
who can relish nothing that is not excellent, think nothing that is not
divine, enjoin nothing that is not profitable, and produce nothing
that is not virtuous, pious, and worthy of so reverend a father.

Jane had found a great deal of intellectual stimulation in Bullinger's work, and so in awe of the theologian was she that she could barely contain her enthusiasm, and considered their relationship to be a source of immense inspiration: 'Oh! Happy me, to be possessed of such a friend and so wise a counsellor! And to be connected by the ties of friendship and intimacy with so learned a man, so pious a divine, and so intrepid a champion of true religion!'[37]

Bullinger, however, was not the only theologian whom Jane admired, for her letter continued in praise of the German-born Martin Bucer. Bucer was a leading Protestant churchman, and had been among those continental theologians whose advice was sought in the matter of Henry VIII's separation from Katherine of Aragon. He had written several treatises on religion, and eventually travelled to England where he took up a teaching post at Cambridge. Bucer was also a close friend of Jane's step-grandmother, Katherine Willoughby, and Archbishop Cranmer, under whose auspices he was presented to King Edward in 1549.[38] At the time of Jane's letter, Bucer had recently died in Cambridge, the Latin eulogy at his funeral being given by Walter Haddon, the brother of Jane's family chaplain, James.[39] It seems probable that he had met Jane on at least one occasion, and had been instrumental in her development.[40] Aylmer made a touching remark about him, 'whom when alive we reverenced as a father, and the remembrance of whom, now that he is no more, we most constantly retain as of a messenger of God', and Jane too was fond of him:

On many accounts I consider myself beholden to Almighty God; but
especially for having, after I was bereaved of the pious Bucer, that

*most learned man and holy father, who unweariedly did not cease,
day and night, and to the utmost of his ability, to supply me with
all necessary instructions and directions for my conduct in life; and
who by his excellent advice promoted and encouraged my progress
and advancement in all virtue, godliness, and learning.*[41]

Such warmth certainly indicates that she knew Bucer, and highlights the
gratitude that Jane felt for those who had been an influence in her life.
Most of her admiration, though, was directed towards Bullinger.

For a girl of Jane's age and status, such letters were unusual. Though
her cousin the Lady Elizabeth was undoubtedly learned and earned the
admiration of all of her tutors, there is no record of her conversing with
contemporary theologians, nor is it likely that she did so. Jane was unique.
As she continued her letter in gushing tones, she explained exactly why
the theologian's correspondence with her meant so much:

*If you will consider the motive by which I am actuated, namely, that I
may draw forth from the storehouse of your piety such instruction as
may tend both to direct my conduct, and confirm my faith in Christ
my Saviour, your goodness cannot, and your wisdom will not, allow
you to censure them.*[42]

She wanted to improve her mind, and felt sure that Bullinger's advice
would assist her as she strove hard to be the virtuous evangelical maiden
that her parents were so eager she should become. She seems to have had
some sense of her own abilities, and Bullinger had clearly praised her, as
her response shows:

*I now come to that part of your letter which contains a commendation
of myself, which as I cannot claim, so also I ought not to allow: but
whatever the divine goodness may have bestowed upon me, I ascribe*

solely to himself, as the chief and sole author of any thing in me that
bears any semblance of what is good; and to whom I entreat you,
most accomplished sir, to offer your constant prayers on my behalf,
that he may so direct me and all my actions, that I may not be found
unworthy of his so great goodness.[43]

Jane evidently believed that she had God to thank for her academic gifts,
and that it was to him that she should be thankful. Bullinger had recently
sent Jane and her father a copy of his *Decades*, and this had impacted
greatly on Jane. Her ebullient spirit for evangelicalism shone through as
she thanked the author:

From that little volume of pure and unsophisticated religion, which
you lately sent to my father and myself, I gather daily, as out of
a most beautiful garden, the sweetest flowers. My father also, as
far as his weighty engagements permit, is diligently occupied in
the perusal of it: but whatever advantage either of us may derive
from thence, we are bound to render thanks to you for it, and to
God on your account; for we cannot think it right to receive with
ungrateful minds such and so many truly divine benefits, conferred
by Almighty God through the instrumentality of yourself and those
like you.[44]

The comparison between Bullinger's book and 'a most beautiful
garden' demonstrates how much value Jane placed on the author's
work, and reveals that she was savouring his every word of guidance.
Her letter was remarkable, not only for its length, but also for its
evidently genuine and heartfelt enthusiasm in the cause of religion.
It is even more extraordinary considering that Jane had never met
Bullinger, and she must have realized that it was unlikely she would
ever do so. In spite of that, her words signify that she was comfortable

expressing herself and her views on parchment, and to one who was internationally revered. John of Ulm was not exaggerating when he informed Bullinger that Jane was 'pious and accomplished beyond what can be expressed'.[45] She clearly revelled in the attentions of learned men such as Bullinger, and was determined to strive to make herself worthy of that attention.

Jane's correspondence with Bullinger had sparked something in her, and what was more, she seemed more determined to impress than ever. Unsatisfied with her current programme of studies and intent on learning more, she expressed an interest in learning Hebrew. In this she sought the advice of another of her father's protégés, the visiting John of Ulm.[46] Described by Aylmer as 'that excellent and talented youth', John had arrived at Bradgate in the spring of 1551, having returned from the north whence he had initially accompanied his patron.[47] With barely time to settle in, Jane had eagerly consulted him about how she could best approach learning this new and challenging language. Having passed 'these two days very agreeably with Jane, my lord's daughter, and those excellent and holy persons Aylmer and Haddon', John felt himself ill qualified to comment but eager to help.[48] He immediately wrote to his friend in Zurich, the noteworthy Hebrew scholar, Konrad Pellican, to ask for advice. Writing on the same day as Aylmer's letter to Bullinger, John explained that Jane was '[a] lady who is well versed in Greek and Latin, and who is now especially desirous of studying Hebrew. I have been staying with her these two days: she is inquiring of me the best method of acquiring that language, and cannot easily discover the path which she may pursue with credit and advantage.'[49]

Jane had also taken the time to consult Bullinger on the matter, writing to him that 'as I am now beginning to learn Hebrew, if you will point out some way and method of pursuing this study to the greatest advantage, you will confer on me a very great obligation'.[50] John, however, believed that Bullinger would be more than happy for Pellican to take on the task, 'because all the world is aware of your perfect knowledge of that language'.[51] It was of importance because 'By your acceding to my request, she will be more easily kept in her distinguished course of learning.'[52] As it transpired, both Pellican and Bullinger were delighted to advise Jane, and thanking him for his instruction, Jane told Bullinger that 'I shall pursue that method which you so clearly point out.'[53]

Bullinger corresponded with Jane for two years, sending her advice and conversing with her on the subject of religion. The time span and the intensity of Jane's letters are somewhat misleading, however, for only three letters from Jane to the pastor survive, and these may have been the only ones she wrote.[54] In her third surviving letter, dated 1553, Jane complained that 'I am at a great distance from you, the couriers are few, and news reaches me slowly', a reflection of the fact that methods of delivering letters were unreliable, and could take several months or longer to reach their intended recipient.[55] Nevertheless, she revelled in Bullinger's attention, on one occasion gushing, 'Let me but obtain your indulgence, and I shall consider myself on every account exceedingly indebted to your kindness.'[56]

One of Jane's truly exceptional talents was her memory. As John Banks explained to Bullinger, 'The whole family of the Greys, and Jane especially, derived incredible benefit from your writings. She indeed had not only diligently perused, but also committed to memory, almost all the heads of your sixth Decade.'[57] This was incredibly impressive, particularly given that the sermons that made up Bullinger's *Decades* could be in excess of forty pages long! It is also interesting to note Banks's reference to Jane's 'whole family'. This confirms that it was not just Jane and her father who were reading Bullinger's work, but also her mother. What was more, Banks's comment suggests that Frances found Bullinger's writing to be of interest. She evidently kept herself well informed in matters of religion, but did not display the same energy as her husband or her daughter. At eleven and six, Jane's sisters were still very young and are unlikely to have shown much enthusiasm for such weighty religious works, though they perhaps had sections read to them instead.

ONCE AGAIN JANE'S father had failed to impress in his military role, but rather than attempting to make the best of the situation, he resigned as Lord Warden and returned home to the comforts of the south. On 28 September the King wrote in his journal that 'the Lord Marquis Dorset, grieved much with the disorder of the marches towards Scotland, surrendered the wardenship thereof to bestow it upon whomever I wanted'.[58] Henry's complaints had not gone unnoticed, and it was the last occasion on which he would be given a military role, much to his relief. His post was granted to the Earl of Warwick, whose experience far superseded Henry's.

During Henry's absence, a completely unforeseen occurrence transpired that would ultimately change the Dorsets' fortunes in a way that none of them could have anticipated. Lady Frances's two young half-brothers, Henry, Duke of Suffolk, and Charles, had been attending St John's College, Cambridge, where they had been enrolled since 1549.[59] However, the intense summer heat brought a deadly wave of the sweating sickness to Cambridge, and in fear for their health, the brothers were immediately removed to the village of Buckden in order to avoid the contagion.[60] The sweating sickness was often fatal, and within a few hours of contracting it a previously healthy person could be dead. In spite of their move, though, soon after their arrival at Buckden the two boys, aged fifteen and thirteen, both contracted the sickness and lay dangerously ill. On hearing that her sons were ailing, their mother Katherine Willoughby rushed to Buckden to nurse them, but it was too late. Henry succumbed to the illness and died on 14 July, leaving his younger brother to inherit the dukedom of Suffolk. Sadly, it was destined to be a double tragedy, for in a cruel twist of fate, just half an hour later young Charles died too.[61]

Their mother was devastated at losing her two children in such tragic and rapid circumstances. Four months after their death, she expressed her grief in a letter written to Sir William Cecil, in which she exclaimed, 'truly I take this [God's] last (and to the first sight most sharp and bitter) punishment not for the least of his benefits, in as much as I have never been so well taught by any other before to know his power, his love, and mercy, my own wickedness, and that wretched state that without him I should endure here'.[62] King Edward was also saddened by the death of young Henry, who had been one of his childhood companions, and the Imperial ambassador reported that 'He remains almost in hiding, and the French lords saw little of him. The reason seems to be the shock and surprise he received at the news of the Duke of Suffolk's death; for the King loved him dearly.'[63] The boys' deaths signalled the end of the male branch of the Brandon family, and the extinction of the dukedom of Suffolk. For Jane's family, therein lay an opportunity, and one that was soon to be seized.

Having returned from the north, Jane's father was soon back in London. At court, the influence of the Earl of Warwick was continuing to grow, and for the fallen Somerset there seemed no hope of restoration. For Jane's parents, however, this was of little concern, for less than three months after the deaths of the Brandon brothers the King, perhaps in a demonstration of affection for Jane's family, gave his permission for the Suffolk title to pass through the female line. Thus, the rightful heiress was Lady Frances, Jane's mother. On 11 October in a glittering ceremony at Hampton Court, Jane's father was created Duke of Suffolk in right of his wife, while alongside him Warwick was elevated to the dukedom of Northumberland. At a stroke, Jane was now the daughter of a royal Duke and Duchess. Despite Henry's political incompetence, Northumberland still needed him on side in order to retain his hold on power at court, and doubtless played on Henry's greed and ambition just as Thomas Seymour had done before. The relationship between Northumberland and the Suffolks was destined to have devastating consequences.

CHAPTER 10

Godly Instruction

I N THE AFTERMATH of the events at Beaulieu, little appears to have passed between Jane and her cousin, the Lady Mary. Jane had continued in her zealous enthusiasm for religious reform, while Mary remained staunchly Catholic. Insulted though she may have been by Jane's apparent outburst in her chapel, Mary did her best to try to restore good relations between herself and her cousin. After all, Jane was still a young girl lacking in experience. A further opportunity for Mary to demonstrate her kindness to Jane presented itself in November 1551, shortly after the ennoblement of Jane's father.

The occasion was the visit of the Dowager Queen of Scots, Marie de Guise, who had arrived in London following a visit to France. She had been visiting her young daughter, Mary, Queen of Scots, who was being raised at the French court as the future bride of Henri II's heir. In her daughter's absence, Marie had been appointed Regent of Scotland, and had chosen to break her return journey in England. To her delight, she was welcomed to London with a lavish display of royal hospitality amid 'great cheer'.[1] Jane's family were among the welcome party that consisted of a 'great train of noblemen, gentlemen, and ladies'.[2] Moreover, at fifteen Jane was considered old enough to be an integral part of King Edward's attempt to dazzle his guest with the magnificence of the English royal court and family. This may have been one of a series of appearances Jane made at court, for Roger Ascham later observed that 'at court I was very friendly with her, and she wrote learned letters to me'.[3] Ascham's comment must refer to the period before he left for his secretarial post abroad in 1550, the last occasion on which he saw Jane at Bradgate, and indicates that Jane was perhaps already familiar with the trappings and social etiquette that revolved around life at court.[4] The Scottish Queen Dowager's reception, however, was almost certainly Jane's first experience of a ceremonial occasion, and one in which she may not have taken much pleasure given that the fervently Catholic Queen Dowager's religious opinions were so different from her own.

Though the Lady Mary had been invited, she had declined to attend the court on this occasion. By this time relations between Mary and her half-brother the King had drastically deteriorated over her continued defiance of his laws regarding religion. So much so that several of her chaplains had been summoned by the King, who 'cast them into prison'.[5] Edward's religious reforms were becoming increasingly radical, encouraged by Archbishop Cranmer. Mary, therefore, had chosen to avoid a situation that might lead to a bitter confrontation between the siblings, and wisely stayed away. Nevertheless, when she heard that Jane would be attending, she decided to send her cousin a gift. Herself excessively fond of fine clothes, Mary's generosity came to the fore once again when she opted to send Jane some 'goodly apparel of tinsel, cloth of gold, and velvet, laid on with parchment lace of gold', in order that she should be magnificently attired.[6] Mary realized that lavish array meant everything on occasions such as this, and would have assumed that the teenage Jane would appreciate such a gesture. Jane had certainly expressed a great interest in clothes, so much so that it drew concern from her tutor, Master Aylmer, who urged Jane's idol Heinrich Bullinger to write to instruct her

[a]s to what embellishment and adornment of person is becoming in young women professing godliness. In treating upon this subject, you may bring forward the example of our king's sister, the princess Elizabeth goes clad in every respect as becomes a young maiden; and

yet no one is induced by the example of so illustrious a lady, and in so much gospel light, to lay aside, much less look down upon, gold, jewels, and braidings of the hair. They hear preachers declaim against these things, but yet no one amends her life.[7]

Though Elizabeth did not converse with learned theologians, she nevertheless ensured that she met with their approval by means of her sober appearance. Upon receiving Mary's costly gift, however, rather than expressing gratitude, Jane was perplexed. 'What shall I do with it?' she asked her lady as she opened the parcel.[8] 'Marry, wear it, to be sure,' came the astonished response.[9] It appears, though, that Jane had taken the advice sent to her by Bullinger to heart, and had chosen to follow the example of her cousin the Lady Elizabeth. It was a choice of which Aylmer would have approved, for he later wrote of Elizabeth that he was 'sure that her maidenly apparel which she used in king Edward's time made the noblemen's wives and daughters ashamed to be dressed and painted like peacocks'.[10] It now appeared that Jane too was determined to be seen as a sober evangelical maiden, who favoured plain black and white dress. The showy dress provided a stark contrast to this image, but rather than politely accepting the gift, once again Jane seized the opportunity to make a point. Replying to her lady's comments that she should wear the gorgeous dress, she resolutely replied, 'Nay, that were a shame to follow my Lady Mary against God's word, and leave my Lady Elizabeth, which followeth God's word.'[11] Jane's parents were horrified when their daughter's discourtesy was reported to them, and insisted that Jane wear the clothes, much to her distaste.[12] Not only was her fervency becoming greater, but she was also becoming increasingly intolerant of those whose religious views were at odds with her own.

When the royal party arrived at the Palace of Westminster, Jane arrayed in her dazzling new dress, the young King was waiting to greet them. He received Marie 'in most honourable and gracious fashion', and when they sat down to dine at 'a splendid banquet', the young King recorded the proceedings in his journal.[13] He wrote that the Queen Dowager 'dined under the same cloth of estate at my left hand. At her rearward dined my cousin Frances and my cousin Margaret [Lennox].'[14] It was a lavish occasion during which the King remembered that 'we were served by two services of servers, cupbearers, carvers and gentlemen', and 'there were two cupboards brought in, one of gold four tiers high, another of solid silver six tiers high'.[15]

The Suffolks stayed in London for the remainder of the year, having opted to spend Christmas in the capital. On 1 December, Henry was among the twenty-seven lords who were present at the trial of the fallen Duke of Somerset, who had once more been arrested following a suspected attempt to oust Northumberland from power. Somerset was found guilty of felony, and imprisoned in the Tower under sentence of death.

ON 22 JANUARY 1552, according to the young King's own account, 'the duke of Somerset had his head cut off upon Tower Hill between eight and nine o'clock in the morning'.[16] The year had already begun with violence, and the Duke of Northumberland was now the undisputed authority in the land.

Somerset's death brought Jane's family a new home, the Charterhouse at Sheen. The Charterhouse had once been a priory, founded by Henry V in 1414 for the use of Carthusian monks. It had remained thus until the reign of Henry VIII, who had dissolved the priory in 1539. The following year it was granted to Somerset, then Earl of Hertford. Interestingly, it was to the Charterhouse that the body of the Scottish King, James IV, was brought for burial in 1513 following the Battle of Flodden. The Tudor historian and antiquarian John Stow later made the astonishing claim that 'in the reign of King Edward the Sixth Henry Grey then Duke of

Suffolk there keeping house, I have been showed the same body (as was affirmed) so lapped in lead thrown into an old waste room, amongst old timber, stone, lead, and other rubble'.[17] With the acquisition of a luxurious new property, the Suffolks practically abandoned Dorset House as their London residence and relocated to the Charterhouse. According to historian Hester Chapman, on one occasion when the family were enjoying their new home they received some uninvited guests. Following the dissolution of the priory, some of the monks who were distressed at being driven out of their former home contrived to force the Suffolks out. They waited until the Duke and Duchess were walking in one of the galleries and there, from an opening in one of the walls, appeared a hand brandishing a blood-stained axe. Jane's parents were apparently unfazed by this bizarre spectacle, and continued their walk. Though it is an entertaining story, it is completely apocryphal.[18]

With the ennoblement of Jane's father, the family had also come into possession of Suffolk Place near Charing Cross, but like Dorset House, it appears to have been used but rarely.[19]

BY THE SUMMER, Jane had returned to Bradgate Park, perhaps to avoid the unhealthy contagion that the summer heat often brought to the capital. However, rather than taking the opportunity to enjoy some leisure time, instead she took up her pen in order to reply to her most recent letter from Bullinger. Each day she tirelessly attempted to live by the guidance she received from Bullinger and others in order to live up to the high expectations that others had of her, and indeed that she had of herself.[20] Her letters have the tone of a girl who was eager to please the adults whom she held in such high regard, and who dominated her everyday life: her parents, Aylmer, and of course, Bullinger.

By now, Jane had also attracted the admiration of another who shared her intellectual interests. Lady Mildred Cecil was herself a distinguished scholar believed to be on a par with Jane, and took a particular interest in translating Greek texts.[21] Alongside Jane and the Lady Elizabeth, Roger Ascham praised Mildred for her ability, and he claimed that she 'speaks and understands Greek about as well as English'.[22] Mildred was married to Sir William Cecil, King Edward's Secretary of State and Northumberland's man, who Jane's parents knew well from court, and who Jane was probably also on friendly terms with.[23] She must therefore have been delighted when she received the gift of a book from Lady Cecil, with an encouraging note.[24] Addressing Jane as 'My most Dear and Noble Lady', Mildred wrote:

Although I am conversant with many of the writers and theologists of old, yet of no one has the perusal been more pleasing and agreeable to me, than of Basil the Great, excelling all the Bishops of his time, both in the greatness of his birth, the extent of his condition and the glowing zeal of his holiness. To you then so worthy, both in consideration of your noble birth, and on account of your learning and holiness, I thought, the perusal of so rational and holy and noble a man and theologian could be very fitting; for it will raise the soul, grovelling below and set on earthly things, to God the Almighty and the remembrance of heavenly things. With these words then of Basil the Great, I present you, a gift, if the ink and paper be considered, small and trifling, but if you consider the profit, more valuable than gold and precious stones, and a token of my great affection for you – Hoping that the perusal of these words will be no less agreeable and delightful to you than they have been to me throughout my youth – and so imploring for you and your body, health and happiness and all prosperity, I bid you farewell.[25]

The tone of the letter is suggestive of a close relationship between Mildred and Jane, although there is no further evidence for this. Though only ten years Jane's senior, Mildred was already renowned for her ability to translate texts, undoubtedly earning her Jane's admiration. Perhaps Jane felt a similar sense of warmth towards Mildred as she had done for Katherine Parr; she would have been flattered by Mildred's kind and complimentary words, and even more elated with the book that she sent.[26] The text to which Mildred referred was a sermon written by the early Greek bishop Basil the Great that she had translated.[27] Doubtless Mildred felt that the words of this worthy man would prove to have a positive influence on Jane; Basil was revered for having led a saintly life as a renowned theologian who fought for his religious beliefs while staying afloat in the world of politics.[28] Mildred could not have known that, in time, the example of Basil would come to have more relevance in Jane's life than she could ever have anticipated.

With Jane having earned the respect and esteem of so many of her contemporaries through her own merits, it is easy to understand why her parents pinned all of their hopes on her. In a world in which women were considered to be far inferior to their male counterparts, the praise heaped upon Jane was the very greatest of compliments, and this cannot have failed to encourage the young girl's confidence as she grew. Jane's learning was one of the few consistent factors in her life, and one to which she clung for comfort when events spiralled out of her control.

JANE'S RETURN TO Bradgate may have been of relatively short duration, for in August her mother fell ill at the Charterhouse. The nature of her malady soon became dangerously apparent: the sweating sickness. The illness which had killed both of Frances's half-brothers had been particularly savage over the past two years; John Stow had observed that in just one week of the previous year, the number of people who had died of the sickness in London alone totalled 806.[29] Henry was at court when he heard of his wife's sickness, and immediately departed for the Charterhouse to be by Frances's side. On 26 August he wrote to Cecil, explaining that his departure had been caused by the news of Frances's illness.

I never saw a more sicker creature in my life than she is. She hath three diseases. The first is a hot burning ague, that doth hold her twenty-four hours, the other is the stopping of the spleen, the third is hypochondriac passion. These three being enclosed in one body, it is to be feared that death must needs follow.[30]

Henry was deeply agitated by Frances's poor state, and signed off his letter 'by your most assured and loving cousin, who, I assure you, is not a little troubled'.[31] His concern for his wife is touching, and the household at the Charterhouse must have been an anxious one as both Henry and his daughters waited to see whether Frances would survive. His letter confirms that her condition was so serious that she was not expected to live, and it must therefore have come as a great relief when, contrary to expectations, Frances recovered. She was fortunate, as a high proportion of sweating sickness victims did not survive. It is possible that Jane herself had also suffered with the sweat, as in February she reported that she had recently fortunately 'recovered from a severe and dangerous illness'.[32] Sadly for Jane, this was not the last time that she would fall sick.

The Suffolk family almost certainly remained at the Charterhouse for the rest of the year while Frances regained her strength. They were evidently there on 8 November, for on that day Henry wrote to Cecil requesting a licence for one of his servants to travel to Flanders. The King, meanwhile, was celebrating the Christmas season at Greenwich, little knowing that he would never see another: the year 1553 would be his last. Jane too can have had no idea that the coming year would signal the most momentous of her life, and that she would not survive the consequences.

CHAPTER 11

A Comely, Virtuous and Goodly Gentleman

As the year 1553 began, Edward 'fell sick of a cough, which grievously increased'.[1] Jane's parents were in frequent attendance at Edward's court, and given their familial proximity to the King, must have been among the first to hear the hushed whispers of the King's illness.[2] Edward had, in fact, been ill for some time, but on this occasion it was not long before it became clear that his cough was developing into something infinitely more serious.[3] The fifteen-year-old King, whose reign had started with such anticipation, was 'almost wasted away with a long and lingering disease', and was facing the possibility of an early death.[4]

The contemporary chronicler Robert Wingfield later observed that 'his endowments of intellect were so much more outstanding and admirable than his good looks that not without reason might the English reproach the fates for being unjust and utterly envious in carrying off a future leader of such promise'.[5] Throughout his short reign, Edward, who had been 'tall and of a healthy constitution for a boy in middle youth', had diligently advanced the Reformation that his father had begun in England, and by 1553, though the cogs were still turning, England had become a primarily Protestant country.[6] Gone were the Mass, the images in churches, and altars. All services were now conducted in English, and priests were allowed to marry.[7] Edward's work in the cause of religion, however, was very much unfinished, and his Protestant nation was still in its infancy. Nevertheless, Edward's achievements had, in the eyes of some of his admiring contemporaries, already been impressive. His tutor, the learned John Cheke, wrote that same year to Heinrich Bullinger, praising Edward's achievements. Though Edward was 'debilitated by long illness', Cheke commended him for he

[h]as accomplished at this early period of his life more numerous and important objects, than others have been able to do when their age was more settled and matured. He has repealed the act of the six articles; he has removed images from the churches; he has overthrown idolatry; he has abolished the mass, and destroyed almost every kind of superstition.[8]

With Edward having made such significant and positive changes towards creating a stable haven for Protestantism in the space of just six years, his Councillors were fearful as to what would happen if he were to die. He had not married, and thus, by the terms of Henry VIII's will, the next in line to the throne was Edward's half-sister, the Lady Mary. And there was no doubt that, should she inherit, the religious changes implemented by Edward would be quickly undone, and all of his efforts wasted.

Relations between the two siblings were strained over matters of religion, and had been increasingly so over the course of Edward's reign. Despite this, as the new year began, their differences were temporarily put to one side. Mary had decided to visit her half-brother, and on 10 January, Jane's mother, Duchess Frances, was among the ladies of the court who escorted her cousin Mary from the Priory of St John in Clerkenwell to the Palace of Westminster for her visit. All went smoothly, and the following month Mary returned. As she arrived at the Palace of Whitehall, she was 'honourably received and entertained with greater magnificence'.[9] However, at the time of her coming the King was so unwell, having been 'attacked by a fever caused by a chill he had caught', that he was unable to receive her, and it was three days before the siblings finally met.[10] The meeting took place in the King's bedchamber with Jane's parents and other members of the court in attendance, hardly the most private of settings. 'The King received her very kindly and graciously, and entertained her with small talk, making no mention of matters of religion.'[11] Mary, however, was distressed by her brother's deteriorating state, which was glaringly obvious. With little time to dwell further upon it, she bade her half-brother farewell, and when she withdrew 'she was again accompanied by several gentlemen and ladies, and notably by the Duchesses of Suffolk and Northumberland'.[12] Perhaps, conscious of Edward's poor health, Mary perceived that it would not be long until she herself became queen. She would have been wary of the Duke of Northumberland, however, who 'governs with absolute authority' and who exerted an alarming amount of influence over the young King.[13] Nevertheless, it was during this visit that the Imperial ambassador observed that the Duke of Northumberland, and several members of the Council 'did duty and obeisance to her as if she had been Queen of England', so it must have appeared to Mary that they were preparing themselves for her succession.[14] Unbeknown to her, the King's physicians had just diagnosed his illness as consumption. In addition, as 'the disease was lethal', the physicians 'considered he might live until September'.[15]

For Northumberland, whose position of power was entirely dependent upon Edward, whom he had encouraged in his programme of radical religious change, this news of the King's health was disastrous. Though Edward's physicians were in constant attendance, everyone, both at court and in London, knew that his condition was serious, and the Imperial ambassador reported that he was 'very weak'.[16] Northumberland realized that should Edward die and Mary succeed, he would undoubtedly be ousted from power. Mary utterly loathed the Duke and bitterly resented the level of control he levied over the young King. As Edward's health began to decline at an alarming rate, certainly by March, though probably before, Northumberland had decided to hatch a plan whereby both the Lady Mary and the Lady Elizabeth were excluded from the succession. Mary's adherence to the Catholic faith was well known, and should she succeed not only would Northumberland be removed, but she would also surely attempt to return England to Catholicism. That still left Elizabeth, but Northumberland realized that it was impossible to cut out Mary without removing Elizabeth too. After all, their father had declared both sisters bastards, and though they had both been restored to his favour and the succession in his will, the Acts of Parliament that had disinherited them had never been overturned. Although a Protestant, Elizabeth was unlikely to be any more pliable than Mary, and at nineteen, could not be relied upon to look to Northumberland for guidance. The Imperial ambassador later reported that 'they are not too particular about her, and reasons for excluding her from the succession might easily be found'.[17] The Duke needed an alternative successor who would rely on him, and could ensure his own continued power. He did not have far to look.

At the end of April, Edward left Whitehall for the healthier air of Greenwich Palace. He was still extremely ill, and the Imperial ambassador observed that 'there seems to be no improvement in his condition, and he has only shown himself once, in the gardens, the day after his arrival'.[18] His symptoms were becoming worse, and the ambassador had been reliably informed that 'the King is undoubtedly becoming weaker as time passes, and wasting away. The matter he ejects from his mouth is sometimes coloured a greenish yellow and black, sometimes pink, like the colour of blood.'[19] It was becoming evident that the King's days were numbered, but Northumberland, playing for time in order to put his plan into action, was determined to keep up a pretence that the King would recover. He sent regular reports of Edward's health to Mary and Elizabeth, both of whom were greatly concerned by what they had heard. But despite their best efforts, both sisters had been forbidden from visiting him. Nevertheless, Northumberland's feigned reports to Mary were worthy of comment from the Imperial ambassador, who duly noted that 'This all seems to point to his desire to conciliate the said Lady and earn her favour.'[20] Little did he know that Northumberland had no intention of attempting to win Mary's favour: indeed, his plan was far more daring.

NORTHUMBERLAND WAS 'AN ambitious man', and he had been contemplating the future.[21] For the first time since William of Normandy had conquered England by right of his sword in 1066, all of the potential heirs to the throne were female. In this extraordinary situation, Northumberland's plan was simple: the Lady Mary and the Lady Elizabeth, first and second in line to the throne according to the terms of Henry VIII's will, would both be excluded on the grounds of their illegitimacy, and Lady Jane Grey, currently third in line to the throne, would become Edward VI's successor. Furthermore, he had engineered another strategy in order to bolster his own power. In April the Imperial ambassador had learned that 'during the last few days', the Duke 'has found means to ally and bind his son, my Lord Guildford, to the Duke of Suffolk's eldest daughter'.[22] Guildford was Northumberland's fourth surviving son, but as his three elder brothers were all married, he was the best that his father had to offer. Northumberland had realized that a marriage between his son and the as yet unmarried Jane would put him in an extremely powerful position, and one in which he would be able to control the young queen, herself only a year older than King Edward. It was a plan that the Duke had probably been considering for some time, but it is unclear exactly when he informed Jane's parents of his scheme to make Jane the King's heir. Their support was crucial to the plan's success. Blinded by promises of 'proverbial mountains of gold' and a glittering future for Jane and his family, Jane's father Henry appeared ready to comply with Northumberland.[23] According to Robert Wingfield, who was well placed to know the truth of the matter, 'the timid and trustful duke therefore hoped to gain a scarcely imaginable haul of immense wealth and greater honour of his house from this match, and readily followed Northumberland's wishes'.[24] Having enjoyed little prestige during the reign of Henry VIII, Henry's fortunes had taken a dramatic turn for the better under Edward VI, and he was naturally eager for this to continue. Like the young King, Henry was an enthusiastic advocate of Protestantism, and realized that this would be destroyed should Mary come to power. Ultimately, ambition and greed overtook him, and he threw in his lot with Northumberland. But there was still a long way to go.

The first mention of a marriage between Jane and Guildford had been in late April 1553. Despite the belief that the initiative had come from Guildford's father, the Duke of Northumberland, it in fact appears to have originated elsewhere.[25] Following his arrest, Northumberland would claim that 'the marriage had been pushed forward by the Earl of Pembroke', later adding that others, including the Marquess of Northampton and Jane's father, were also keen for the marriage to take place.[26] William Cecil, husband of Jane's friend Mildred and later chief advisor to her cousin Elizabeth, is said to have believed that Northampton's wife, the friend of Jane's parents, was 'then the greatest doer', and the Marchioness certainly appears to have played some part in it.[27] Wherever the impetus came from, the 'marriage was arranged by the Duke not by chance but with a very precise purpose', and Northumberland was now forced to begin implementing his plans for the succession with rapidity due to the sudden decline in King Edward's health.[28] By 28 April the young couple were betrothed, 'with the consent and approval of the King and his Council'.[29] Northumberland was delighted to secure a royal bride for his son, while Jane's father Henry 'was easily led and persuaded', but there were those who were less than enthusiastic.[30] Duchess Frances was unsurprisingly 'vigorously opposed to it; but her womanly scruples were of little avail against opponents of such might and power'.[31] For at least the last six years, almost certainly longer, Frances had been cherishing hopes that her eldest daughter would marry King Edward and thus become Queen of England. So certain had she been that the marriage would one day transpire that it appears that those around her believed it too. John of Ulm once wrote that Jane 'is to be married, as I hear, to the king'.[32] With Jane's betrothal to Guildford, Frances's hopes of a royal marriage for her daughter had now been permanently crushed. Instead she would be forced to watch as Jane, whose veins flowed with royal blood, was married to one of the younger sons of a duke; a devastatingly poor substitute. Little wonder then that 'the Duchess of Suffolk, and her entourage were not convinced'.[33]

There may also have been another, more significant reason for Frances's disapproval; she may have been opposed to Northumberland's plan to make Jane King Edward's successor. Frances was certainly ambitious for her daughter, but she had always anticipated that Jane would achieve these ambitions through her marriage to Edward, and thus become his consort. She may never have considered the possibility of overlooking her cousin the Lady Mary, to whom she was close, and the Lady Elizabeth, in Jane's favour, and the idea could well have appalled her. Also, Frances was not stupid, and she realized that Northumberland's plan was both risky and dangerous. A queen regnant in England was virtually unprecedented, and by contrast to the King's daughters, who were hugely popular, Jane was effectively unknown to the English people, which significantly increased the risk.[34] She had never lived at court as the Ladies Mary and Elizabeth had done, neither had she been raised with any expectations of becoming queen in her own right. If Frances did indeed disapprove of Northumberland's plans, it would certainly explain some of her later behaviour. She may well have feared for her daughter's well-being at this time, but for the moment, overruled by ambitious men, there was little that she could do: she was certainly no match for Northumberland.

Frances was dismayed by Jane's impending marriage, but it was nothing

compared to how Jane felt. Though she had been raised in the knowledge that it was a woman's duty to marry, she had also been raised with
expectations of grandeur. Thus, when she was told that she was to marry
Guildford – a fourth son – Jane, 'strongly deprecating such marriage', did
not bother to hide her contempt.[35] Perhaps a semblance of her defiant
attitude still remained from her time in the late Admiral's household,
where her upbringing had been more relaxed, but Jane's parents were
horrified by her behaviour in voicing her objections to the marriage.
Though Frances was also unhappy, like Jane she knew that she had no
choice but to comply. Therefore, 'by the insistence of her Mother, and
the threats of her Father', Jane was forced to accept what she could not
change.[36] Nevertheless, the choice of Guildford Dudley must have come
as a bitter disappointment.

Guildford, 'a comely, virtuous and goodly gentleman', was maybe a
year older than Jane.[37] Named after his maternal grandfather, Sir Edward
Guildford, he had grown up within the security of a close and happy
family. He was likely raised at his father's Midlands estate, Dudley Castle,
the family's London town house of Ely Place, and, later, at the once-royal
stronghold of Warwick Castle, where he would have been surrounded by
his brothers and sisters.[38] Guildford's parents were loving and considerate, taking an unusual level of interest in the welfare of their children.
In a letter written by their father to Guildford's elder brother John, their
mother Jane added the postscript: 'your loving mother that wishes you
health daily'.[39] Like his betrothed, Guildford had also been brought up
as an adherent to the Protestant faith, and had almost certainly received
a grand education that matched that of his elder brothers, as befitted
the son of an aristocrat.[40] It is difficult to ascertain whether he took the
same avid interest in learning as Jane; none of his contemporaries ever
referred to him as a scholar, but that is not to say that he was not learned.
Clearly an attractive youth, he was also prone to petulant outbursts, so
typical of teenagers, when he did not get his own way.[41] For Guildford, a

marriage with Lady Jane Grey, the King's cousin, was beyond his wildest dreams and no doubt appealed to his vanity. His three elder brothers were all married, but none of them had made a match of this prestige.[42] His younger brother, Harry, had recently been either married or betrothed to Jane's cousin, Margaret Audley, but that was still no comparison to the marriage arranged for Guildford.[43] Two of his siblings had married for love (Mary and Robert), but in Guildford's case, the circumstances were very different.[44] Prior to his betrothal, it seems unlikely that Guildford had ever even had a conversation with Jane. He may have observed her during her occasional visits to court, but that was probably as far as it went. Her feelings had been made perfectly clear, and Guildford had almost certainly heard of her distaste for their marriage. He had only to look at her cool demeanour for her hostility to be evident. As of yet, Guildford had been given no opportunity to develop any feelings of his own for Jane, and her countenance was less than encouraging. Only time would tell whether he would grow to love her, and whether she in turn would see past his family connections and grow to love him too.

CHAPTER 12

The First Act of a Tragedy

G IVEN THAT JANE was the eldest daughter of one of the most important peers of the realm, her marriage should have been a cause for celebration. But considering the disappointing choice of husband that had been selected for her, neither she nor her mother were excited by what lay ahead. Frances, however, certainly felt a greater degree of enthusiasm for the marriage of her younger daughter, Katherine. It had been agreed that Katherine was to share her elder sister's wedding day, while little Mary was to be betrothed. By the same token, Jane's wedding day was destined to be a triple celebration, and she just one of three brides. Northumberland's daughter, another Katherine, was also to wed in what was expected to be a spectacular day of merrymaking. Like Jane's, these other marriages had been arranged in an attempt to bind loyalties and cement alliances for Northumberland's future plans. All of the parents involved were happy to comply, but their children had no choice.

A letter written by Northumberland explained the marital arrangements concluded that spring. Having first related that 'my Lord of Suffolk and I are thoroughly concluded upon a marriage between two of our children', he had revealed that 'the Earl of Pembroke's son shall marry another of my said Lord's daughters'.[1] The son in question was Henry Herbert, the fifteen-year-old heir of the Earl of Pembroke by his deceased wife Anne Parr, sister of Jane's beloved Queen Katherine and the Marquess of Northampton.[2] Henry Herbert was to marry Jane's twelve-year-old sister

Katherine, a match that had probably been arranged at the same time as Jane and Guildford's.[3] Of a similar age to Katherine, Henry Herbert was a dashing youngster who had academic interests on a par to Jane and had even been taught by her Italian tutor, Michelangelo Florio.[4] Moreover, it appears that he and his young bride quickly developed a fondness for one another, which was hardly surprising given that Katherine was believed to have been the beauty of her family. Meanwhile, eight-year-old Mary was to be betrothed to a distant relative, Arthur Grey, Lord Grey de Wilton.[5] At a stroke, the marital prospects of all three of the Grey sisters appeared to have been settled. The final marriage to be performed on 'the same day' was that of Henry Hastings, the heir of the Earl of Huntingdon, who 'shall marry another daughter of mine': Katherine Dudley, the Duke's youngest daughter.[6]

Plans for Jane's wedding gathered pace, for it had been agreed that there was no time to be lost. There would be no long betrothal for Jane. Her marriage was to be celebrated at Whitsuntide, and the date had already been chosen: 25 May.

Preparations for the wedding had begun immediately after the negotiations had been concluded, and every detail had been given the greatest attention. Of great importance was the attire of the bridal party, which was to be of the utmost splendour. The King, who had given his blessing to Jane's marriage, had ordered his Master of the Wardrobe, who was incidentally Northumberland's brother, Sir Andrew Dudley, to supply all of the clothes for the wedding party, and sent a warrant to that effect.[7] Detailing all of the materials that were to be gifted, it provided for the sumptuous outfits to be worn not only by Jane and Guildford, but also by those with whom they were to share their wedding day.[8] In addition, Duchess Frances was provided with a 'loose gown of black velvet embroidered', and 'a Clock set in gold and crystal garnished with six rock rubies and two table rubies [a gemstone cut so that the top appears flat, like a table]'.[9] The Duchess of Northumberland was given some fine clothes and jewels.[10] Gorgeous clothes were even provided for the Marchioness of Northampton, the probable instigator of the match.

The majority of the warrant, however, was dedicated to 'our well beloved cousin the Lady Jane', and 'the Lord Guildford Dudley'.[11] The level of splendour and opulence in Edward's generous gifts was truly magnificent, and included a variety of the finest fabrics in a blend of rich colours. Among the materials were elegant 'black silver cloth of tissue raised with roses and branches of gold', 'cloth of gold tissued with white silver', 'purple and white cloth of tissue raised with roses', and 'crimson cloth of gold branched with velvet'.[12] Purple was a colour worn only by royalty, while only those of the rank of duke or marquess were permitted to wear cloth of gold. The message was clear: this was a royal wedding, and one of the utmost significance. In addition to the gorgeous clothes, it was observed that 'The King has sent presents of rich ornaments and jewels to the bride.'[13] There was a magnificent *billement* (decorative border often used to decorate a French hood) containing 'thirteen table diamonds set in gold enamelled black', a carcanet (a chain or collar of jewels) of seventeen 'great pearls' and seventeen 'pieces of goldsmith's work enamelled black with one flower of gold enamelled white and black with a fair triangle diamond and one emerald', as well as a girdle fashioned with gold.[14] The gifts Jane received from her cousin left nobody in any doubt of her regal status.

Not only were the wedding clothes impressive, but Northumberland was also determined to ensure that the celebrations were equally remarkable. The Imperial ambassador had heard that 'they are making preparations for games and jousts', and that 'there will be very good Company'; every effort was being made to ensure that the triple wedding was as magnificent as possible.[15]

AS THE MORNING of 25 May dawned, it was a fine day: perfect for a wedding. But Jane did not have the joyous feeling of butterflies experienced by many prospective brides on their wedding day. Instead, her heart was full of dread that could not be disguised by the fine clothes she wore. Her beautiful wedding gown of royal purple with gold and silver brocade, embroidered with costly diamonds and pearls, was a far cry from the sober black and white that she usually wore.[16] Her long hair was loose as a symbol of her virginity, and she was adorned with the brilliant jewels that the King had given her. This was Jane's opportunity: her chance to shine. On that day all eyes were on her, but while some of the guests were looking at her exquisite gown and her shimmering jewels, others were looking at the girl who they were planning to make their queen.

The setting for Jane's wedding was the impressive Durham Place. The house had a history of royal connections, and had recently been acquired by Northumberland from Jane's cousin the Lady Elizabeth, much to her chagrin.[17] Situated on the Strand with sprawling gardens that stretched right down to the River Thames, it was a splendid house, and the ideal choice for a wedding.

As the array of important guests gathered in the chapel within the house ready to witness the three weddings, one guest was conspicuous by his absence. The King's health had ensured that there was no question of him attending, much to the disappointment of Jane's family. Moreover, many of the guests were those with whom Jane was only vaguely familiar – members of the King's Privy Council, and foreign ambassadors. This highlighted the fact that Jane's wedding was not for her at all, as it is unlikely that, unless she had wed the King, most of these men would have been in attendance. Though it was extravagant, majestic even, it was all for show. It was a wedding made of necessity, and with the anticipation of events that were to follow.

As Jane and the two Katherines entered the chapel with its large and elaborate windows filled with stained glass, they knew what was expected of them. It was Jane who stood out as she walked towards her groom at the altar, the purple on her gown serving to highlight her royal status. At the altar, before their families and a host of diplomatic spectators, Jane and Guildford exchanged their vows. It seems probable that Jane would have uttered something similar to the vows exchanged by her great-uncle Henry VIII and his wives, in which case she would have promised to take Guildford 'to my wedded husband, to have and to hold from this day forward, for better for worse, for richer for poorer, in sickness and in health, till death do us part, and thereto I plight thee my troth'. Perhaps she also promised to be 'bonny and buxom in bed and board'.[18] There was no love in the vows uttered, only formality. Thus, with the exchange of just a few simple words and a ring symbolic of their union, Guildford and Jane became man and wife. On Jane's side at least, there was no notion of love, though she had promised to love and obey her new husband; only duty, and an acknowledgement that their futures now lay intertwined.

Following the ceremony, the guests proceeded to the Great Hall where the celebratory banquet ensued. The Great Hall was 'stately and high, supported with lofty marble pillars. It standeth upon the Thames very pleasantly', and provided the perfect setting.[19] As early as 12 May, preparations for the entertainment had been noted, and Northumberland had written to Sir Thomas Cawarden, the Master of the Revels, whose responsibility it was to organize such merriments, to order amusements especially for the occasion.[20] Some of these were to be staged in the extensive grounds of Durham Place, which contained a blend of fine fruit trees, fishponds and views overlooking the Thames. He had requested

> [a] couple of fair masques one of men and another of women it will be anytime the better to make merry the whole company. And for that I think so many of the nobles as be here abouts will be as is and also the most part of the ambassadors I would be very glad to have the thing rich and it which hath been seldom used wherein as you shall do me great pleasure to give order with your officers and servants for the performances and accomplishments.[21]

The guests and the wedding party enjoyed a lavish array of dishes arranged across a number of courses, and drank the constant flow of wine heartily. It could almost have been a happy occasion. It certainly earned the desired admiration of contemporaries, for Robert Wingfield related that 'a most magnificent marriage was celebrated in the great palace of the bishop of Durham by the Thames; the French ambassador was present, and most of the English nobility dignified the ceremony with their attendance'.[22] Jane, it was observed, led to her table 'the French and Venetian Ambassadors' who were seated between two ladies.[23] Furthermore, several members of the Council were 'on their knees with due ceremony toward the ambassadors as would have befitted the King in a solemn procession'.[24] This was done with a clear purpose, for the Councillors, knowing what was afoot, and that Northumberland intended to open the way 'for Jane and Guildford to usurp the crown', were attempting to smooth things over and gain goodwill for their venture from abroad.[25]

The brilliance of the feast, however, was soon spoilt. For though great efforts had been made to prepare it, one of the cooks accidentally 'plucked one leaf for another' while preparing a hot salad dish.[26] The result was that 'My Lord Guildford Dudley' and 'other lords and ladies, recently fell very ill'.[27] Indeed, so serious was the food poisoning that nearly a month later on 12 June they 'are still suffering from the results'.[28] Though it was observed that 'The weddings were celebrated with great magnificence and feasting at the Duke of Northumberland's house in town', and 'with such splendour the like of which I had never seen in this kingdom', it was hardly the ending that had been anticipated as the jovial atmosphere of the diners descended into a delirium of sickness.[29]

For Jane, Guildford's temporary illness may have come as a relief, although it had already been agreed that her marriage would not be consummated immediately. According to the Imperial ambassador, the reason for this was 'because of their tender age'.[30] However, given that both Jane and Guildford were over the age of consent (the church stated that the age of consent was twelve for girls, and fourteen for boys), it seems more likely that there was another reason for the delay. This appears to be supported by the fact that Jane's sister Katherine was immediately sent to live with her husband and his family at the Earl of Pembroke's London home, Baynard's Castle. That her parents allowed Katherine to live with her husband implies that they expected the marriage to be consummated, despite Katherine being four years younger than her sister Jane.[31] Perhaps in Jane's case it was simply Guildford's inability due to his unfortunate sickness, but it is more likely that it was a calculated decision, maybe to prevent the marriage from being binding before the events of the immediate future became clearer. After all, King Edward had not yet named Jane as his heir, and should she become pregnant promptly after her wedding then it could scupper all of Northumberland's plans if he failed to do so.[32]

Once the revelries of the day had come to an end, Jane was able to bid farewell to her new husband; indeed, in the immediate aftermath it would appear that little had changed. Unusually, she had been allowed to return home with her parents to the Charterhouse, and to her studies. For the moment, Durham Place was not to be called home, and neither did she have to reside with Guildford; the nightmare of her wedding could almost be forgotten. But not for long. Jane's marriage to Guildford was 'fast bound … according to the customs of the country', and there was no going back.[33]

It is difficult to ascertain whether Guildford shared Jane's sentiments of relief, for certainly as his wedding day drew to a close he was probably in no fit state to feel anything beyond the discomfort in his gut. Some of his later behaviour towards his new wife would show him to be discourteous, pompous even, but this was almost certainly born out of immaturity. Initially, there was no time for the newlyweds to bond as they resumed their separate lives; but already they were both part of a far bigger game, for on every side 'plans and preparations are being made to strengthen and consolidate the position'.[34] Moreover, their separation was of brief duration: within a short space of time Jane was back at Durham Place – perhaps around the time that King Edward made his final alterations to his Devise – where she was forced to confront the reality of married life. Her marriage was consummated, and she now had no choice but to live alongside Guildford.

Aside from the unfortunate food poisoning incident, Jane's wedding had run as any bride would wish in all but one respect: she was not in love, and her marriage had been made of necessity. Little did she know that there was worse to come, for as an anonymous contemporary observed, 'men of intellect' within the kingdom 'judged this wedding to be the first act of a tragedy'.[35]

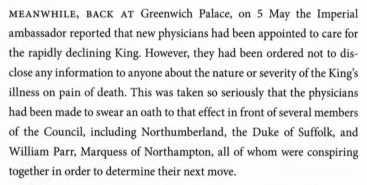

MEANWHILE, BACK AT Greenwich Palace, on 5 May the Imperial ambassador reported that new physicians had been appointed to care for the rapidly declining King. However, they had been ordered not to disclose any information to anyone about the nature or severity of the King's illness on pain of death. This was taken so seriously that the physicians had been made to swear an oath to that effect in front of several members of the Council, including Northumberland, the Duke of Suffolk, and William Parr, Marquess of Northampton, all of whom were conspiring together in order to determine their next move.

The following week, the King's physicians made a further diagnosis of a 'suppurating tumour' on the lung, though in fact Edward may have been suffering from tuberculosis or a pulmonary infection.[36] The ambassadors' reports for this period give a clear description of Edward's symptoms that reveal the gruesome extent of his suffering. The Imperial ambassador had been informed that 'he is beginning to break out in ulcers; he is vexed by a harsh, continuous cough, his body is dry and burning, his belly is swollen, he has a slow fever upon him that never leaves him'.[37] To make matters worse, rumours of the King's death were beginning to circulate, and three of his subjects who had spread whispers to that effect were punished by having 'their ears torn off' as a grisly warning to others.[38] To counteract this, 'A rumour was spread recently that the King was on the way to recovery and his illness was decreasing, to appease the people who were disturbed', but nobody was fooled.[39] He was growing weaker by the day, and if Northumberland's plan was to be successful, it was crucial that he begin to further it as quickly as possible.

The task of persuading Edward to name Jane as his successor, thus disinheriting both of his half-sisters, turned out to be remarkably easy for Northumberland. As Mary was a Catholic, the King could see the problems of allowing her to succeed, and was eager that she should not be given the opportunity to reverse all of the work he had done in the cause of religious reform. The Imperial ambassador was already aware that something was afoot, reporting that 'The Duke's and his party's designs to deprive the Lady Mary of the succession to the crown are only too plain. They are evidently resolved to resort to arms against her, with the excuse of religion, among others.'[40]

But that still left Elizabeth, and Edward was initially reluctant to exclude her. Though the restoration of both Mary and Elizabeth to their place in the line of succession had never been formally legitimized, the two sisters were extremely popular with the English people, a point that Edward completely overlooked. Once it became clear that Edward could not exclude one without also excluding the other, his thoughts turned to Jane's mother, Frances, whom he now considered as his successor. Yet Frances had been overlooked in Henry VIII's will, and she did not feature in Northumberland's plan. Even so, she still had a strong claim, and, prompted by Northumberland, Frances arrived at Greenwich Palace, and there renounced her right in the presence of the dying King. But why did she not press her own claim? It has been suggested that she avoided pursuing her right in an attempt to secure her own safety should the events of Northumberland's plan not work in Jane's favour. This is certainly possible, and Frances may have believed that should Mary succeed then she would be more likely to forgive her if she was not a central conspirator. If this was the case then, given Frances's relationship with Mary and Jane's youth, she probably realized that she would be in a stronger position to defend her daughter. After all, Frances was aware that her familial proximity to Mary stood her in good stead, and knew her well enough to understand the best way to appeal to her. But equally, any ambitions Frances may have harboured about becoming queen could have already been quashed when her uncle excluded her from the line of succession in 1546, and since that time it seems likely that all of her ambitions had been for her daughters. Northumberland realized that Frances would not be as easy as Jane to control – he had probably made it very clear that he would not support her if she chose to press her own claim, and she would be unlikely to receive support from any other quarter. This appears to be corroborated when, several months later, on 24 July the Imperial ambassadors reported to the Emperor:

Thomas Grey, brother of the Duke of Suffolk, said it seemed strange to him that the Lady Jane, and not her mother, had been chosen, and that the Duke of Northumberland thus showed that the object of his ambition was to place the crown on the head of his son, husband to the Lady Jane.[41]

Any consideration of Frances succeeding the King was now removed, and at the beginning of June, under his own auspices but with Northumberland's connivance, in his own hand Edward painfully drew up 'My Devise for the Succession', an extraordinary will in which he undertook to change the succession as laid out in the terms of Henry VIII's will. It is still debated when the Devise was first drafted, but religion was undoubtedly Edward's decisive factor in creating it.[42] The document ruled both the Ladies Mary and Elizabeth out of the succession on account that they had both previously been declared bastards, and in the case of 'lack of issue of my body', ruled that the crown ought to be inherited by his cousins of the house of Suffolk. In line with his father, Edward believed that a male heir was preferable, and at thirty-five 'our entirely beloved cousin the Lady Frances, now wife to our loving cousin and faithful counsellor Henry, Duke of Suffolk' was still young enough to have sons.[43] This was clearly Edward's first thought, for initially he willed that his successor should be 'the Lady Frances's heirs male'.[44] Should Frances fail to produce a son, then Edward decreed that the throne would go to 'the Lady Jane's heirs male', followed by any sons that Jane's younger sisters, Katherine and Mary, might have.[45]

But this was not the end of the matter. As it became clear that the King's death was fast approaching, with the encouragement of Northumberland, 'that consummate old fox', Edward made an alteration to the Devise, probably on 10 June.[46] First he removed 'the Lady Frances's heirs male', for Frances was not pregnant and therefore would not produce a son in the immediate future. Then, instead of any sons Jane might have being next in line, the King inserted two words so that his successor by the terms of his Devise read 'to the Lady Jane and her heirs male', doing the same for Jane's two sisters.[47] His alterations meant that Lady Jane Grey and her sisters could inherit the throne in their own right, but only if there were no male alternatives. As neither Jane nor her sisters had children, it was obvious who would succeed.

By the terms of Henry VIII's will, Jane was now already third in line to the throne, and after extolling her virtues – her well-known advocacy of the Protestant faith and hatred of Catholicism, as well as her vast intellectual abilities – Northumberland was easily able to persuade the King, 'then almost in his grave', that she should be his heir.[48] The King could be confident that Jane would continue his good work in religion, under the guiding hand of Northumberland. Through the amendments to the Devise, Northumberland had got what he wanted, for Jane was now heir to the throne.

On 12 June, there had already been whispers of what might be about to happen, and the Imperial ambassador had heard that

their main object will be to make shift to exclude the Princess and the Lady Elizabeth, and declare the true heir to be the Duke of Suffolk's eldest daughter, who was lately married to the Duke of Northumberland's son, for according to the late King's will the Duchess of Suffolk's legitimate heirs are appointed to succeed if the present King and the two aforesaid ladies die without issue.[49]

The terms of the Devise were not made public, but many people were already aware of Northumberland's plans and guessed that 'perhaps Northumberland and Suffolk might rule as governors or joint-protectors'.[50]

In order for the Devise to stand any chance of success, the support of Edward's Council was essential. However, among the members were those who were doubtful of its legitimacy. Henry VIII's Act of Succession had been passed in Parliament, and Edward's attempt to overturn it with a new will was technically illegal. The King was furious, and having declared that he would have his Devise put into Letters Patent to be passed in Parliament, on 15 June he demanded their obedience in the matter. Six days later, on 21 June the King ordered his Council to sign the new Devise, ratifying the changes in the succession. It was an agonizingly difficult situation, as many of them found that their loyalties were torn: while the King was alive they owed him their duty, but for many it was with a troubled conscience that they signed the Devise and they were full of foreboding for the future. Nevertheless, the King's will had been done, and had 'opened the way for Jane and Guildford to usurp the crown'.[51] Willingly or not, the Council had accepted that Jane would be queen.

All that remained was for Jane, herself utterly unaware of the happenings at Edward's court, to be informed of the King's wishes. The precise date that Jane learned that she was now heir to the throne is unclear, but given Jane's later version of events it seems likely to have been shortly after 21 June. Jane had, by this time, been married to Guildford Dudley for almost a month, and after a brief return home to the Charterhouse, had taken up residence with her husband's family at Durham Place on the Strand. The young bride was extremely distressed, however, when her new father-in-law, the Duke of Northumberland, made her aware of her cousin the King's mortal illness, and delivered some shocking news:

> *After having been openly stated that there was no hope of saving the life of the King, as the Duchess of Northumberland had promised me that I could remain with my mother, after she heard that news from her husband the Duke, who was also the first person to tell me about it, she did not allow me any more to leave my house saying that when God would be pleased to call the King to his mercy, not remaining any hope of saving his life, I had immediately to proceed to the Tower, as I had been made by his Majesty heir to the crown.*[52]

Northumberland's words had a tremendous impact on Jane, who was utterly horrified. She had always known that she had a place in the line of succession, her parents had made sure of that, but she was bewildered by the news that, at the stroke of a pen, she had gone from third in line by the terms of her great-uncle's will, to first. The news 'caught me quite unaware', and 'very deeply upset me'.[53] Though her words do not even begin to convey the emotional turmoil she must have felt, they do at least clarify her keen desire for familiarity, and the wish to remain with her own family. But even this, as she had discovered through the auspices of her mother-in-law, was to be denied her:

> *I cared little for those words and refrained not from going to my mother. So that the Duchess got angry at her and at me also saying*

that if she wanted to keep me, she would also keep my husband by herself, thinking that anyway I would go to him.[54]

Despite her protests and the best efforts of her mother, Jane was forced to remain with her husband at Durham Place. Her confusion and heightened emotions were overwhelming; she had been married against her wishes, a union that had been consummated and from which she could not escape. In addition, she had been confronted with the report that not only was her cousin the King dying, but that she had unexpectedly been made his heir. The impact that this news and unpleasant encounter with her mother-in-law had on Jane became alarmingly clear when she fell ill soon after. Though described as 'well made', Jane had never been physically robust, and though the nature of her malady is unclear, it seems likely that it was exacerbated by stress.[55] Deeply unhappy at Durham Place, Jane 'craved permission to go to Chelsea', a former royal manor which was now owned by Northumberland, and where, permission having been granted, she lay ill.[56] Her desire to remove to Chelsea may have been inspired not only by her wish to distance herself from her husband and his unpleasant family, but also by happy memories she had of the old palace. Six years earlier, Chelsea had been the home of the widowed Queen Katherine Parr, who had removed there following the death of Henry VIII. Famous for its exquisite knot gardens and boasting an assortment of fruit trees, rural Chelsea provided a serene contrast to the bustle of Durham Place just a few miles away. Jane had enjoyed Katherine's company at Chelsea on a number of occasions while she was a member of Thomas Seymour's household, but those days were long gone, and as Jane lay sick in the manor she had such fond remembrances of, it must have occurred to her that her future was now shrouded in uncertainty.

Elsewhere, news of the King's Devise was spreading, and on 4 July the Imperial ambassador reported that 'I hear for a fact that the King of England has made a will, appointing as true heir to the Crown, after his death, Suffolk's eldest daughter, who has married my Lord Guildford, son of the Duke of Northumberland. The Princess [Mary] has been expressly excluded on religious grounds.'[57] He was not the only one who had been alerted to such rumours, and the mood in the capital was now extremely tense as whispers circulated. Northumberland was doing all he could to secure the loyalty of as many of the lords as he could, by whatever means possible. According to the report of one contemporary, 'he gained over some by fear, and others by promises, and others by gifts'.[58] Despite his connivance behind closed doors, outwardly 'Northumberland is still behaving courteously towards the Princess [Mary], as if nothing were about to happen.'[59]

That same day, both Mary and Elizabeth were summoned to Greenwich, on the pretext that their presence would be a great comfort to the sick King. In reality, Northumberland had realized that in order for his strategy to succeed, he needed to secure the persons of both of the King's half-sisters. Elizabeth, always suspicious, immediately sent word that she was sick and too unwell to travel, but Mary, though extremely wary, set out from her estate at Hunsdon in Hertfordshire for Greenwich.

The King's condition was continually worsening, and after demands from his worried subjects 'he has shown himself at a window at Greenwich, where many saw him, but so thin and wasted that all men said he was doomed, and that he was only shown because the people were murmuring and saying he was already dead'.[60] To make matters worse, it was reported that 'the Duke is utterly loathed and suspected of having poisoned the King, and is only able to command obedience by terrorising the people'.[61] Unbeknown to the Londoners, Northumberland had enlisted the services of a wise woman, who administered regular doses of antidotes to the King in an attempt to keep him alive for longer while Northumberland furthered his plans.[62]

The plans seemed to be coming to fruition, for 'the Duke of Northumberland has 500 men wearing his livery, the Duke of Suffolk

300 and the other councillors numbers proportionate to their rank and importance'.[63] This had made Northumberland even more unpopular, and 'the result is that everyone is murmuring against Northumberland, saying he is a great tyrant, that he has poisoned the King, and wishes to plunge the kingdom into disturbances'.[64]

Though Northumberland had not yet been able to procure the custody of Mary and Elizabeth, in all other respects he was now ready for the King to die. And having endured much suffering, on the afternoon of 6 July, the young King's agonizing struggle finally came to an end. After whispering, 'I am faint; Lord have mercy upon me, and take my spirit,' Edward died in the arms of his childhood companion, Sir Henry Sidney.[65] The Imperial ambassador was quick to inform his master that 'King Edward departed this life, not without suspicion of poison, according to popular report.'[66] It was an excruciating and tragically early end for the boy who had shown such promise, and whose 'manner was so gracious and his countenance so modest and pleasant that he charmed observers into an exceptional love and an extraordinary devotion towards their sovereign'.[67] As the King's corpse lay lifeless at Greenwich, his death was kept a secret while Northumberland implemented the final stages of his plan. The time had come: Jane, lying sick at Chelsea, was summoned.

In spite of her weakened condition, as the sun set that evening, Jane left Chelsea for the last time. She was ordered to Syon House on the outskirts of London, and, still enfeebled by her illness, she boarded the barge that conveyed her across the rippling waters of the Thames in the company of her sister-in-law, Lady Mary Sidney. She had no idea that she was about 'to receive that which had been ordered by the King'.[68]

There are two similar versions of what happened next, recorded in the narratives of the papal envoy Giovanni Commendone, and Fra Girolamo Pollini, who may have gleaned at least some of his account from Commendone's manuscript. As the journey came to an end and the barge docked on the banks of Syon, Jane was confronted by the sight of the imposing former 'great monastery', dissolved by her great-uncle Henry VIII and transformed into a sumptuous residence and 'a beautiful palace on the Thames' that was now owned by her hated father-in-law, Northumberland.[69] It was here, too, that her great-uncle's coffin had rested on its final journey to Windsor, and here that he had sent his adulterous fifth wife, Katherine Howard, to endure a strenuous house arrest before her final, fateful journey to the Tower. Jane would have been familiar with Katherine's story, but as she alighted from her barge and made her way towards the house through the elaborate gardens filled with an array of exotic plants and sweet-smelling flowers, she could never have imagined that she too would leave Syon destined for the Tower, in circumstances that would transpire to be chillingly similar.

To her surprise, as Jane entered the unfamiliar house she discovered that there was nobody there to meet her. As she waited in the gloom of the panelled Long Gallery overlooking the river, her anxiety and feelings of uncertainty grew.[70] Some time later, Northumberland and four leading members of King Edward's Council at last joined her, but it was not until she had been 'entertained a long time' that, according to Commendone, in Jane's own words, 'they did tell me of the death of the King'.[71] Stunned, Jane's confusion was heightened by the lords around her who 'were doing me such homage, not in keeping with my position, kneeling before me, that greatly embarrassed me'.[72] Feeling uncomfortable and unsure what to do, Jane was clearly relieved by the sight of her mother, Frances, Duchess of Suffolk, who entered the Gallery at Northumberland's signal alongside Jane's mother-in-law, Jane, Duchess of Northumberland, and Elizabeth, Marchioness of Northampton, who had engineered the match between Jane and her husband.[73]

If Jane had hoped that her mother had come to rescue her from the situation in which she now found herself, she was to be sorely disappointed. The room was soon filled with the well-known faces of Jane's father and her husband, and the vaguely familiar men who had served King Edward.

With everyone gathered, Northumberland gravely reiterated the news of King Edward's death. There was a deathly silence in the room as, according to Pollini's account, he continued to inform them that on his deathbed the King had chosen to remove his 'bad sisters', the Ladies Mary and Elizabeth, from the line of succession, for 'in no manner did he wish that they should be heirs of him, and of that crown, he being able in every way to disinherit them' on the grounds of their former bastardy, and for fear that the Lady Mary would return the realm to the 'Popish faith'.[74] Giving her barely a moment to absorb his words, 'The Duke then added that I was the heir named by his Majesty, to succeed to the crown.'[75] Jane was stunned, 'stupefied and troubled'.[76] As she struggled with the enormity of Northumberland's words, her emotions, and her body, still weak from illness, gave way and she fell to the floor, weeping bitter tears. Those around her looked on in silence, unable or unwilling to comfort Jane as she was tormented by an agony of grief and shock. Commendone recounts that Jane, under pressure to compose herself, 'was unwilling to accept such a burden', and cried, 'The crown is not my right and pleases me not. The Lady Mary is the rightful heir.'[77] This was not the reply that was expected, and a mortified Northumberland replied, 'Your Grace does wrong to yourself and to your house.'[78] Finally, after being 'pressed with many arguments by the Council, the Duke and her Father, she submitted to their will', and according to Commendone managed to utter a few words through her tears:

> *I greatly bewailed myself for the death of so noble a prince, and at the same time, turned myself to God, humbly praying and beseeching him, that if what was given to me was rightly and lawfully mine, his divine Majesty would grant me such grace and spirit that I might govern it to his glory and service, and to the advantage of this realm.*[79]

Jane had no choice: through her tearful words she had accepted the crown, and she was now Queen of England. However, the late King's half-sisters and Jane's cousins, the Ladies Mary and Elizabeth, were still unaware of the King's death, and though Northumberland and the Council had accepted Jane as queen, as she and all of those around her knew, her rule was by no means assured. Her path was still shadowed in uncertainty, and she was about to embark on the most dangerous experience of her life.

CHAPTER 13

————⚬————

Long Live the Queen!

WITHIN THE PRIVACY of Syon's walls, Jane had several days to come to terms with her heightened status.[1] The day following the shock news of her accession, Northumberland had hosted 'a great banquet', attended by Jane, her family and 'all the other members of the Council', and it was here that 'The Council fixed upon their plan of action.'[2] But for all this, still no announcement had yet been made of the death of the King: nobody was aware of the fact that they had a new queen, and her name was Jane. Nevertheless, Edward's death was a badly kept secret, for rumours had been circulating and most people now believed that their King had expired; some even believed that the King's death had come at the hands of Northumberland's poisoners. Londoners were in a state of unrest and uncertainty about what would happen next, for it was obvious that something was afoot. Suspicions had been roused over Northumberland's behaviour when his liveried men had arrived in the capital the previous month, and people were saying 'that the Duke's designs are obvious, and that God wishes to chastise the kingdom'.[3] It was not long before everything became clear as events began to unfold.

Northumberland had no doubt primed Jane as to how she must now act. It was essential that she compose herself and behave like a queen, for there was no more time to be lost; though officially Jane had been queen for the last four days, it was now time for her to be openly declared and presented to her subjects.

154

About three o'clock on the afternoon of 10 July, 'Lady Jane was conveyed by water to the Tower of London, and there received as queen.'[4] This was the observation of Rowland Lea, an official of the royal mint and the probable author of *The Chronicle of Queen Jane*. Lea's valuable account explains that Jane was rowed from Syon across London in the company of her husband, parents, and 'other ladies attended by a great following' in the splendour of the royal barge that had been sent for her.[5] If she was nervous she did not show it. She was, after all, a Tudor. However, it soon became startlingly clear that she was not the Tudor the people wanted.

As Jane's barge arrived at the Tower steps and she alighted, she was at last confronted with her people. It was a beautifully sunny day, but if she had been hoping for a warm reception she was to be disappointed. Three new Imperial ambassadors from the court of the Emperor Charles V had recently arrived in order to support their colleague, Jehan Scheyfve, and as supporters of the Lady Mary, they gleefully informed their master that 'no one present showed any sign of rejoicing, and no one cried: "Long live the Queen!" except the herald who made the proclamation and a few archers who followed him'.[6] The ambassadors' reports were, unsurprisingly, biased in Mary's favour. Nevertheless, they were remarkably well informed, and on this occasion they were quite right. Even the best efforts of a crier who declared that both the Lady Mary and the Lady Elizabeth were illegitimate, and that the Lady Mary would try to revert the realm to Catholicism if she became queen, did not stir the crowd in Jane's favour, and they remained in stunned silence. This was hardly surprising, for Jane was virtually unknown in the realm. Apart from her occasional visits to court during King Edward's reign, she had not been raised in the public eye or as heir to the throne. Unlike the Ladies Mary and Elizabeth, she was not the daughter of a king, but merely a niece. Jehan Scheyfve was right when he said that the 'lady [Mary] is loved throughout the land', and though Jane inspired warmth and affection in many of those who knew her, at this moment that meant nothing.[7] Her queenship having been thrust upon her involuntarily, she was then confronted with the faces of these glum Londoners staring at her in dismay, and it must have been somewhat disconcerting – but there was no means of escape. What was more, the people understandably associated her with Northumberland, who 'is hated and loathed for a tyrant', which only served to heighten her unpopularity.[8] As Jane had emerged from the royal barge, her rich and elaborate train was carried by her mother, Frances. For her, whose claim to the throne was in terms of blood stronger than Jane's own, carrying her daughter's train must have been a rather strange experience. Moreover, the behaviour of Jane's parents drew comment from an anonymous eyewitness, who recalled how extraordinary it was to see a 'living mother and father, neither king nor queen' speak 'humbly and to serve her on their knees'.[9] However, Frances had resolved to do all she could to support her daughter, and Jane would surely have been comforted by her familiar presence among the hostile crowd.

Fortunately not all of those gathered were disappointed to see her, and as Queen Jane approached the Tower entrance, whose guns were fired in salute, she 'was received at the door by the Duke [Northumberland] who, kneeling, put the keys in her hands'.[10] The Council had also arrived to welcome her, saluting their queen on bended knees in a public display of solidarity and loyalty likely engineered to encourage the crowd to follow suit, while Guildford watched 'hat in hand', perhaps hoping that they would soon be paying him similar obeisance as the Queen's husband.[11] In an attempt to enforce Jane's new heightened status, Northumberland had decided that her arrival at the Tower ought to be as grand as possible; a magnificent display of contrived propaganda with which to convince the people of Jane's right. The Imperial ambassadors grudgingly conceded that the ceremony that followed her arrival was conducted with 'accustomed pomp', while her supporters made great displays of deference to her.[12] The Duke wanted to ensure that nobody was left in any doubt as to who was to be queen, and it was not Mary.

However, the cool reception of the people did not go unnoticed, and it worried him.

Though there are no surviving physical descriptions of Jane's features, it is clear that, at this most crucial moment in her life, appearances meant everything. Simply described as 'virtuous, wise and good looking' by the French ambassador, Antoine de Noailles, on this most important occasion Jane would have been elaborately dressed in rich materials, perhaps edged with ermine, the fur reserved for royalty, and covered with a sparkling array of jewels in order to showcase her heightened status.[13] An anonymous observer at the Tower described Jane as 'a beautiful young woman, pretty and endowed with intelligence, educated and well dressed'.[14] Furthermore, the chronicler Richard Grafton, who was undoubtedly familiar with Jane, described her as 'that fair lady whom nature had so not only beautified, but God also had endowed with singular gifts'.[15] Grafton had been the King's Printer during the reigns of both Henry VIII and Edward VI, and was a supporter of Jane's. More than that, he printed the proclamation of Jane's accession, proudly signing himself 'Printer to the Queen'.[16] Though he favoured Jane, Grafton's description is verified by other reports, so it seems probable that it is relatively accurate. Perhaps Jane had also inherited some of the features that distinguished the Tudor family: the red hair and fair skin that were evident in her great-uncle, Henry VIII, and her cousin the Lady Elizabeth. While many portraits have been claimed to represent her, in truth no authenticated likenesses of her are known to still exist.

Though she may have seen it, it is unlikely that Jane had ever visited the Tower before. Situated to the east of the city and described as 'the strongest castle in the kingdom', the Tower had, in recent years, acquired a chilling reputation as a prison, and place of torture and execution.[17] It was here that Anne Askew, that female martyr to the Protestant faith to which Jane was so devoted, had been tortured by her great-uncle's Councillors, her flesh torn and limbs stretched on the rack as she refused to recant. On the other hand, there was no doubt that, as the strongest fortress in London, the Tower was equally as capable of keeping people out as it was at detaining those within. It was for this reason that it had been chosen as Jane's base until she could be crowned at the imposing Westminster Abbey, which it was rumoured would be in 'a fortnight or more'.[18] Her path was still littered with danger, and it was by no means certain that she would be accepted as queen. But there was no turning back now, and as Jane entered the Tower's precinct, surrounded by her family and her Council, she was wrought with uncertainty as to what would happen next.

Once inside the Tower, Jane and Guildford were taken to the Royal Apartments where they were to be lodged, and which as queen she now had every right to occupy. The apartments stood next to the White Tower, overlooking a fragrant ornamental garden reserved for the monarch's use, and formed part of a lavish complex which had been refurbished by Jane's great-grandfather Henry VII, and more recently by Henry VIII just over two decades earlier.[19] However, by the time of Jane's arrival the Royal Apartments had not been used for some time, for though it was traditional for a monarch to lodge there before their coronation, as a residence the Tower had fallen out of use. Both Henry VIII and Edward VI preferred the more modern and palatial residences of Greenwich, Whitehall and Richmond – now Jane's palaces. Royal Apartments they may still have been, but the golden threads of their tapestries were starting to fade, and they were beginning to fall into a state of disrepair. In a chilling twist, the rooms had recently been used as prison quarters to house two of Henry VIII's wives, Anne Boleyn and Katherine Howard, prior to their executions. For Jane the Tower was full of reminders of her forebears, both in life and in death.

The Royal Apartments consisted of the Presence Chamber, used by the monarch to receive visitors, a dining chamber and a bedchamber, all of which had been decorated in the rich antique style so popular during the Renaissance period. Jane's parents may also have been lodged within the apartments so that they could be close to their daughter, something of a relief for Jane, especially as she was soon to discover a side to her husband's character that she did not like.

Jane was barely given time to settle into her new surroundings before she was conducted to the Presence Chamber, where her Council were waiting to greet her. She was still getting used to the displays of obeisance, her Councillors falling to their knees as she sat on the splendid throne beneath the canopy of state. The most prominent members besides Northumberland and her father were William Parr, Marquess of Northampton; Henry FitzAlan, Earl of Arundel, who was Jane's uncle by marriage; William Herbert, Earl of Pembroke; John Russell, Earl of Bedford; Francis Talbot, Earl of Shrewsbury; Sir William Paget; Francis Hastings, Earl of Huntingdon; William Paulet, Marquess of Winchester; and Thomas Cranmer, Archbishop of Canterbury.[20] With the possible exception of the Earl of Arundel and perhaps William Parr, none of these were men that Jane is likely to have known well, and despite the reverence with which they treated her, in the circumstances in which she now found herself, their behaviour may have been overwhelming. Without a moment's respite to adjust to the view from her throne, Jane was then confronted with the most tangible sign of monarchy: the Crown Jewels. The opulent sceptre of gold and the 'round ball with a cross of gold' that had been stored in the Jewel House gleamed, but were overshadowed by the splendour of the crown.[21] Though she had not asked for it, Pollini reports that the Marquess of Winchester, who was also Lord High Treasurer, presented Jane with the crown, glittering with gold and precious stones, which had been used at the coronation of her forebears for centuries, and asked her permission 'to put it on my head to try whether it really became me or no'.[22] Until this point Jane had been remarkably composed, and had done all that had been asked of her despite her ill feelings. Now, however, alarmed by the sight of the crown, and to the astonishment of everyone present, she refused to allow Winchester to place the crown on her head. The enormity of the situation finally hit her, and she panicked. 'Your Grace may take it without fear,' Winchester tried to reassure her, and after some further persuasion Jane finally tried it on.[23] In that moment, Jane, resplendent with her royal crown, appeared to all of those present to be the undoubted Queen of England. It brought her no pleasure, however, and she was greatly troubled when Winchester then proceeded to tell her that 'another also should be made, to crown my husband'.[24] Jane did not reply, but neither did she forget Winchester's comments, which she 'heard truly with a troubled mind', and caused her 'infinite grief and displeasure of heart'.[25] She had already realized that her father-in-law's intention had always been to have his son crowned alongside her, and thus to rule through them. But though she had not yet said it, Jane was absolutely determined that she would not allow this to transpire. Although she still struggled with her new role as queen, she was already beginning to make some crucial decisions as to how she would rule.

At five o'clock, shortly after Jane's arrival at the Tower and her first dramatic introduction to queenship, amid 'a great display of heralds and halberdiers [men armed with a combined spear and battleaxe]', a proclamation was made in four parts of London 'of the death of King Edward the sixth, and how he had ordained by his letters patent that the Lady Jane should be heir to the Crown of England'.[26] The people listened but remained unconvinced. Nobody wanted Jane to be queen, and they were convinced that she had cheated the King's daughters, namely Mary, of their rights. As one of the Imperial ambassadors observed, 'I was present in person when the proclamation was made, and among all the faces I saw there, not one showed any expression of joy.'[27] According to Rowland Lea, in addition to the proclamation,

> [c]riers at the street-corners published an order given under the Great
> Seal of England, which, by the new Queen's authority, declared the

Lady Mary unfitted for the Crown, as also the Lady Elizabeth. Both
ladies were declared to be bastards; and it was stated that the Lady
Mary might marry a foreigner and thus stir up trouble in the kingdom
and introduce a foreign government, and also that as she was of the
old religion she might seek to introduce popery.[28]

A printed proclamation was also prepared for distribution across the
country, declaring Jane to be the true 'Queen of England, France, and
Ireland, Defender of the Faith, and of the Church of England and Ireland
the supreme head'.[29] This made little difference, for the loyalty of the
people did not lie with Jane, and the Imperial ambassador concluded his
report to the Emperor Charles V: 'Thus your Majesty may gather the state
of feeling in England towards the Lady Mary.'[30] Mary had always been
popular, and there were still those who remembered her mother,
Katherine of Aragon, with affection. Despite the stigma of illegitimacy,
she was still considered by many to be Henry VIII's legitimate daughter
and thus Edward VI's natural successor. They were furious that the upstart
Northumberland was attempting to deprive her of what many considered
to be her birthright. For the time, however, Northumberland appeared to
hold the winning hand.

Back inside the safety of the Tower's walls, Jane was aware of the
people's hostility as she prepared herself for a lavish banquet held in her
honour that evening. As if she had not already had enough to cope with,
the already tense atmosphere became infinitely worse with the arrival
of a messenger. Thomas Hungate, 'bordering on old age', was a 'faithful
servant' of the Lady Mary, and it was from her that the message came.[31]
Unbeknown to the Council, Mary had heard of the death of her half-
brother, thus her message was a simple one: 'her demands were that they
should belatedly renounce Jane, falsely styled queen, and recognise and
welcome herself as their undoubted liege lady'.[32] As they listened, everyone in the room was 'astonished and troubled', and 'the Duchesses of

Suffolk and Northumberland, it is said, began to lament and weep'.[33] It was Hungate, however, who having 'bravely delivered' Mary's demands, immediately felt their effect on Jane's Council.[34] Turning on the ageing man, Northumberland berated him: 'Hungate, I am truly sorry that it was your lot to be so immature and thus rashly to throw yourself away in this embassy.'[35] With that, Hungate, 'second to none in his obedience and diligence' to Mary, was led away to a prison cell, while the Council deliberated over what to do.[36] Jane was now Queen of England, but there was still a long way to go. The hearts of the people were very much with the Lady Mary, as the reactions of the Londoners on that day at the Tower revealed. Besides that, Mary had already made it clear that in her eyes there was only one queen, and it was not Jane.

IN THE EARLY days of July, the Lady Mary waited anxiously for news of her half-brother King Edward's health at her manor of Hunsdon in Hertfordshire.[37] While she was there, 'she got wind of the aristocratic conspiracy aimed at her destruction', and, learning that her half-brother was close to death, consulted with her trusted and loyal advisors.[38] Though she initially set off for Greenwich Palace upon receiving the summons of the Duke of Northumberland, she was quickly warned 'by those most loyal to her' that it was a trap, and that she ought to avoid the capital at all costs.[39] Thus there was only one course of action open to her. In order 'to escape as soon as possible from the jaws of her enemies', on the day of King Edward's death she secretly fled with just a handful of her supporters.[40] Mounting her horse and spurring it on as fast as was possible, Mary and her party rode towards East Anglia where she was both popular and a great landowner. It was a wise decision. Three days later she reached her house of Kenninghall, and it was here that she received the definitive news from a medical practitioner named John Hughes – 'a weighty man worthy of belief' – that King Edward was dead.[41] What was more, her worst fears were confirmed: though the Council had accepted that England's next monarch would be a queen, it was not Mary to whom they had declared their allegiance, but her cousin Jane. An overwhelming array of emotions confronted Mary, but now was not the time for grief. Though she could have attempted to head for the coast and flee abroad, where she would surely receive sanctuary from her cousin the Emperor, at this point Mary did no such thing. Robert Wingfield reported the course of action she decided upon:

> With her usual wisdom the lady now perfectly judged the peril of her situation, but nothing daunted by her limited resources, she placed her hopes in God alone, committing, as they say, the whole ship of her safety, bows, stem, sails and all, to the winds of fortune, and firstly decided to claim the kingdom of her father and her ancestors, which was owed to her as much by hereditary right as by her father's will.[42]

Mary had decided to fight, and East Anglia provided her with the ideal base. Summoning her household, she informed them of the death of King Edward, which meant that 'the right to the Crown of England had therefore descended to her by divine and by human law', and graciously asked for 'the aid of her most faithful servants, as partners in her fortunes'.[43] Inspired by her words, her household 'cheered her to the rafters and hailed and proclaimed their dearest princess Mary as queen of England'.[44] That evening, she entrusted her servant Thomas Hungate with a letter to the Council in which she set out her intentions by demanding their allegiance:

> We require you and charge you, and every of you, that every of you, of your allegiance which you owe to God and us, and to none other, for our honour and the surety of our person, only employ yourselves, and forthwith upon receipt hereof, cause our right and title to the

Crown and government of this Realm to be proclaimed in our City of
London, and other places as to your wisdoms shall seem good.[45]

Any hopes that the Council may have held that Mary would meekly submit to her half-brother's will were now quashed, for it was certain that she would never accept her young cousin Jane as sovereign, and had decided to fight for her rights.

⎯⎯⎯⎯~⎯⎯⎯⎯

ASIDE FROM THE sobbing cries of Jane's mother and the Duchess of Northumberland, on the evening of 10 July there was silence in the Royal Apartments at the Tower, as the Council reeled from the contents of Mary's letter. Having hoped to have secured Mary's custody by now, this was the first tangible indication they had received that she would fight back, but it was too late to back down. If the Council had been hoping that Mary would meekly submit to their decision to supplant her, they were sorely mistaken. Jane made no show of emotion at the news, but inside she was in turmoil. Her mind was still disturbed by the earlier events of that day, and the Marquess of Winchester's remarks about a crown for the use of her husband had struck a particularly raw nerve. But for the moment that would have to wait, for Mary could not go unanswered: it was imperative that some form of response be sent to her cousin. Though many of the Council were greatly troubled by Mary's words, and were fearful lest she should receive foreign assistance from her cousin the Emperor, urged on by Northumberland they managed to compose a defiant reply. They informed Mary that on Edward VI's orders, Jane was now Queen of England:

For as much as our sovereign Lady Queen Jane is after the death of
our sovereign Lord Edward the sixth, a prince of most noble memory
invested and possessed with the just and right title in the Imperial

Crown of this Realm, not only by good order of old ancient laws of this Realm, but also by our late sovereign Lords Letters patent signed with his own hand.[46]

This confirmed that Jane's authority had been bestowed by the late King, but to add insult to injury they continued to remind Mary that through the actions of her father, she had been 'justly made illegitimate', and was therefore unable to inherit the crown: 'We must therefore, as of most bound duty and allegiance, assent unto her said Grace [Jane], and to none other.'[47] The words were similar to those set out in the proclamation signed by Jane, which had been read to the citizens of London earlier that day. It had begun with a resolute statement of royal authority: 'Jane, by the grace of God Queen of England, of France and of Ireland, defender of the Faith, and after Christ, principal Head on Earth of the Church of England and Ireland.'[48] After declaring in no uncertain terms the illegitimacy of the Ladies Mary and Elizabeth, Jane's proclamation had made further assertions in a bid to win the loyalty of the people:

We do therefore by these presents signify unto all our most loving, faithful, and obedient subjects, that like as we for our part shall, by God's grace, show our self a most gracious, and benign Sovereign Queen, and Lady to all our good Subjects in all their just, and lawful suits, and causes, and to the uttermost of our power shall preserve and maintain God's most holy word, Christian policy, and the good laws, customs, and liberties of these our realms and dominions: So we mistrust not, but they, and every of them will again see their parts, at all times, and in all cases show themselves unto us their natural liege Queen, and Lady, most faithful, loving, and obedient subjects, according to their bounden duties, and allegiances, whereby they shall please God, and do the thing that shall tend to their own preservations, and sureties.[49]

It was clear that Mary was expected to do the same, and quietly resign herself to the fact that she had been ousted from her place in the succession. The letter in which the Councillors now addressed her, pledging their loyalty to Queen Jane, was signed by all twenty-three of its members, headed by Thomas Cranmer, Archbishop of Canterbury. Everyone realized, though, that a mere letter was not going to be enough: action was needed too.

Jane had remained calm throughout the evening's events, for her thoughts had been elsewhere. When at last the troubled Councillors had retired for the evening and she was left alone with her husband, she took the opportunity to confront him. Having had several hours to ponder Winchester's comments, Jane now made it abundantly clear to Guildford that she had absolutely no intention of making him king. Perhaps her brutal comments were intensified by the anguish she felt upon receiving Mary's letter, and Guildford, towards whom she had few warm feelings, bore the brunt of it, but Jane was not prepared to back down. Guildford was stunned. He listened as Jane conceded that she would only allow him to take the title of her consort if she were petitioned by Parliament, but her reluctance was glaringly obvious. After all, Guildford shared none of Jane's royal blood, and any notions of becoming king had been born purely out of ambition. As a concession she offered to make her husband a duke, perhaps the Duke of Clarence. Despite any feelings of disappointment, initially Guildford appeared to comply with her wishes. However, having had time to think on the matter, Guildford was amazed by Jane's attitude. She might be queen but she was still his wife, and was duty-bound to honour and obey him. Their contemporaries certainly expected him to be Jane's consort, for in a dispatch to the Emperor the Imperial ambassadors had referred to 'the new King and Queen'.[50] Realizing that despite his best efforts he would be unable to alter her mind single-handedly, Guildford now sought someone to help fight his corner, and he did not have far to look. The Duchess of Northumberland was fiercely protective of her children, and she had never warmed to Jane. When Guildford told her of the heated words exchanged with his wife, the Duchess immediately took her son's side. According to Jane, the Duchess 'got very angry at me' and advised Guildford to shun Jane's bed in an attempt to bring her to heel – a threat that had no impact on Jane.[51] Deciding to take his mother's advice, Guildford now reacted with complete and utter outrage: not only had he been married to a girl who treated him with contempt, but now she had also resolved to deny him the title to which he believed that, as her husband, he was entitled. Guildford insisted that he would be king, but Jane refused to yield. So furious was the Duchess of Northumberland with her daughter-in-law that she took her guidance one step further, drastically urging her son to prepare to leave the Tower with her that same evening in order to force Jane to be reasonable.

Hearing of the fraught exchange between Guildford and Jane, and the schemes of his wife to depart from the Tower, the Duke of Northumberland was alarmed. It appeared that Jane was not as pliable as he had expected, and was seemingly prepared to make her opinions heard. Jane's parents and those who knew her were well aware of how stubborn she could be, but Northumberland, who barely knew her, was amazed. It had never occurred to him that Jane would not be willing to go along with his schemes; the girl had a mind of her own, and was perfectly willing to assert it. When Jane heard that Guildford and his mother were planning to leave, she immediately sent orders to prevent them from doing so. Much to their chagrin, Guildford and the Duchess had no choice but to obey Jane's commands, albeit with ill grace. Jane was nevertheless furious about the whole affair, which only served to add further to her anxiety. Equally, Guildford was determined not to give up on his visions of becoming king, and it was later observed that he had himself addressed as 'Your Grace' and 'Your Excellency', and 'sat at the head of the Council board, and was served alone'.[52] His behaviour, in such contrast to that exhibited by Jane thus far, demonstrated that he could be petulant and incredibly selfish with little regard for his wife. In Jane's mind it proved a point: Guildford was highly unsuited to kingship, and she would stand her ground.

As tempers flared, Jane prepared to spend her first night at the Tower. The day had been an overwhelming whirl of emotions, and the pressure of the situation in which she now found herself was causing her incredible stress. She was angry, forced into an unhappy marriage and a queenship that she had never sought. Jane had very little in terms of emotional support, for despite the presence of her mother, both knew what was expected of her. Yet still she had managed to make her voice heard; she had already shown that she was prepared to assert her authority and that she would not be bullied. In the coming days it would be crucial for her to continue in a similar vein, for Mary's letter had shown that she had nailed her colours to the mast. There could only be one Queen of England: Jane or Mary.

RIGHT: Mary Tudor and Charles Brandon. The marriage of Jane's maternal grandparents was a love match, and it was through Mary that Jane inherited her royal blood.

BELOW: The tomb of Jane's mother, Frances Brandon, in St Edmund's Chapel, Westminster Abbey. The nature of the relationship that Jane shared with her mother has been hotly debated for centuries.

LEFT: Lady Katherine Grey. Jane's sister was reputed to be the beauty of the family, and was married in the same ceremony as Jane and Guildford.

RIGHT: Lady Mary Grey. Jane's youngest sister was later described as a hunchback, but nevertheless travelled with and was educated alongside her sisters.

RIGHT: Jane's tutor, John Aylmer. Jane flourished under Aylmer's tutelage, and she inspired his most fervent admiration.

BELOW: The beautiful ruins of Bradgate Park in Charnwood Forest, Leicestershire. It was here that Jane spent much of her childhood in company with her sisters.

John Aylmer D.D.
Lord Bishop of London.

LEFT: Jane's great-uncle Henry VIII. The terms of the King's will dominated Jane's future.

RIGHT: Edward VI. Jane's parents had high hopes of a marriage between Jane and Edward. However, when it became clear that Edward was dying, he eventually named Jane as his heir.

RIGHT: Mary I. The relationship between Jane and her cousin Mary was tumultuous, and eventually Mary was left with no choice but to order Jane's execution.

LEFT: Jane's cousin, the Lady Elizabeth. The two girls spent time together whilst Jane was the ward of Sir Thomas Seymour, but are unlikely to have been close. Elizabeth, however, learned much from Jane's tragic example before she too wore the crown.

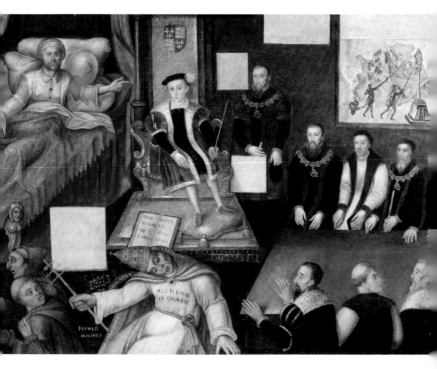

ABOVE: The deathbed of Henry VIII. The King can be seen pointing towards his successor, Edward VI, while the Pope lies crushed at his feet. Members of the Council can also be seen, several of whom were closely associated with Jane. Immediately to the right of Edward is Edward Seymour, the Lord Protector, while two figures down from him is Thomas Cranmer, Archbishop of Canterbury. To the right of the Pope is John Dudley, later Duke of Northumberland.

RIGHT: Katherine Parr. This portrait that was once believed to represent Jane in fact shows the woman to whom Jane was to grow close, and who doubtless influenced her heavily in matters of religion.

LEFT: Sir Thomas Seymour. Jane's guardian was a charismatic man of great charm. He was also greedy and dangerous, though to Jane he appears always to have been as a 'kind and loving father'.

BELOW: Sudeley Castle, Gloucestershire. Jane accompanied Katherine Parr and Sir Thomas Seymour to Sudeley in June 1548.

Durham House.

ABOVE: Durham Place. It was here that Jane was married to Guildford Dudley on 25 May 1553, and here that her father-in-law rallied Jane's forces before leaving London in July.

BELOW: Syon House. Jane was brought to Syon on 6 July 1553, where to her dismay she was informed that she was Queen of England.

My deuise for the Succession. 317

1. For lakke of issu of my body. To the L Frances heires masles, if she haue any such issu befor my death to the L Janes heires masles, To the L Katerins heires masles, To the L Maries heires masles, To the heires masles of the daughters which she shal haue hereafter. Then to the L Margets heires masles. For lakke of such issu, To theires masles of the L Janes daughters To theires masles of the L Katerins daughters and so furth til you come to the L Margets daughters heires masles.

2. If after my death theire masle be entred into 18 yere old, then he to haue the hole rule and gouernance therof.

3. But if he be under 18, then his mother to be gouuernres til he entre 18 yere old. But to doe nothing without thauise of 6 parcel of a counsel to be pointed by my last will to the nomore of 20.

4. If the mother die befor theire entre into 18 the realme to be gouuerned by the counsel Prouided that after he be 14 yere al great matters of importance be opened to him.

5. If i died without issu, and ther were none heire masle, then the L Fraunces to be gouuernres. For lakke of her the her eldest daughters and for lakke of them the L Margets to be

ABOVE: 'My Devise for the Succession'. In this extraordinary document, Edward VI sought to alter the line of succession as set out in the terms of his late father's will, making Jane his heir.

ABOVE: Framlingham Castle, Suffolk. It was from Framlingham that Mary rallied her troops and prepared to fight for her throne in July 1553.

BELOW: Though much altered due to the damage caused by the Great Fire of London, the Great Hall, Guildhall, was the scene of Jane's trial.

LEFT: The White Tower at the Tower of London. The Royal Apartments once occupied by Jane during her reign once adjoined the White Tower, the oldest part of the fortress.

BELOW: The Queen's House on Tower Green. In Jane's lifetime the house was called the Lieutenant's Lodging, and was the home of Sir John Brydges. The house in which Jane was lodged no longer stands, but once stood to the right of this.

LEFT: Carving of the name 'Jane' in the Beauchamp Tower. It has often been said that this was done by Guildford during his imprisonment in reference to his wife.

RIGHT: Jane's signature as queen adorns a warrant she issued for cloth. At some point after her brief queenship came to an end, someone has deliberately struck out the words 'the Quene'.

LEFT: Carving in the Beauchamp Tower of the Dudley arms with elements representing the brothers. The roses represent Ambrose, the oak leaves and acorns are for Robert, the honeysuckle is for Harry, and the gillyflowers are for Jane's husband, Guildford.

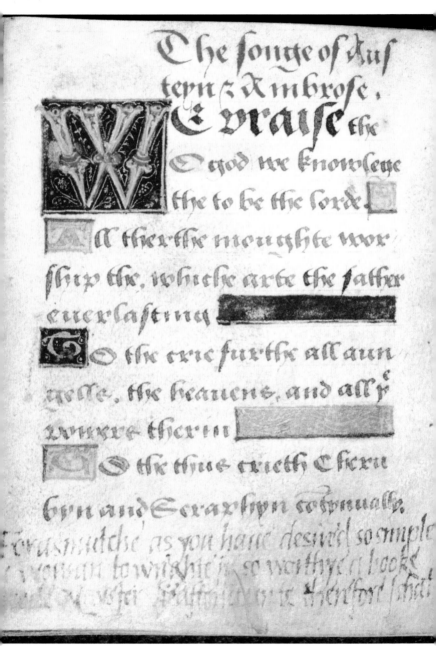

The songe of Aus
tern z Ambrose.

PRAISE the
O god we knowlege
the to be the lorde.

All therthe mowghte wor
ship the, whiche arte the father
everlastinge

To the crie furthe all aun
gelle, the heauens, and all y
power therin

To the thus crieth Cheru
byn and Seraphyn cotynually.

Forasmutche as you haue desired so simple
a woman to wrighte in so worthye a booke
good M.... lyfter Patridge or it therfore shal

ABOVE: Jane's treasured prayer book, now in the British Library. The messages Jane and Guildford inscribed for Jane's father can still be seen on the pages of her only surviving possession.

Holy arte thow Holy arte

thow Holy arte thow

Thow arte the lorde god of

hostes.

Heauen and earthe are fulfil

led wᵗ the glorie of y̅ majestye

The glorious company of y̅

apostelles praise the

The godly felowshippe of the

prophetes worship the

The faire felowshippe of mar

tere praise the.

The holy congregacion of

a frende desyre you and as a christian you
to call vpon god to cucline where harte to
la wes to quicken you in his waye and po

ABOVE: *The Execution of Lady Jane Grey* by Paul Delaroche. This iconic painting, completed in 1833, has had a profound impact on public perceptions of Jane as a tragic victim.

CHAPTER 14

Falsely Styled Queen

WITH THE RECEIPT of Mary's letter on 10 July it was imperative that action be taken; if Jane was to sit securely on her throne then it was crucial that Mary be apprehended, and quickly. More importantly, Jane's authority as queen needed to be asserted. Jane's supporters greeted her accession with delight; a Protestant Merchant Taylor named Richard Hilles, who mixed in similar circles to the Greys, was thrilled to be writing to Bullinger that 'the government of this realm has devolved upon this queen Jane, to which event may our good and gracious God grant his blessing!'[1] He joyfully believed that Jane's subjects 'shall nevertheless be able to live a godly, quiet, and tranquil life, in all peace, virtue, and righteousness; and that the pure word of God will always be sincerely preached in this realm, and the true doctrine of the gospel maintained to the great comfort of all believers who dwell here, which may the Lord Almighty grant!'[2] However, Hilles was among the minority, for it was perfectly clear that in general the people were 'discontented with the election of Jane', and at eight o'clock on the morning of 11 July, Gilbert Pott, a young man who had spoken 'seditious and traitorous words' against Jane 'was set on the pillory, and both his ears cut off'.[3] Although the example of Pott's was a singular occurrence, it was not a good start to the new reign. At this moment Jane chose to show her true strength of character. Reacting to the news that Mary 'caused herself to be proclaimed Queen in Norfolk, and is continuing to do so in the neighbouring districts, both verbally and by means of letters', she retaliated by issuing a number of proclamations, ordering her subjects to stand by her as their rightful queen, and as a contemporary observed, 'in many parts of the kingdom Jane was proclaimed two or three times over'.[4] Though the people listened, according to the papal envoy Giovanni Commendone they heard the words 'with remarkable discontent as hateful to everybody'.[5] In a warrant directed to her father's old friend William Parr, Marquess of Northampton, Jane made it clear what was expected of him:

> *You will endeavour yourself in all things to the uttermost of your power, not only to defend our just title, but also assist us in our rightful possession of this kingdom, and to disturb, repel, and resist the feigned and untrue claim of the Lady Mary bastard daughter to our great uncle Henry the Eight of famous memory.*[6]

In the battle of the female cousins, Jane and Mary proved that they had far more in common than their royal blood – they were both true Tudors through and through, determined not to give up until the bitter end.

In these first few days, there was not a moment to be spared: every second counted, and delay could be fatal. Already Northumberland had sent his son Robert to try to secure Mary's custody, as well as giving orders for 'several armed vessels to be prepared' in an attempt to protect the country should the Emperor send forces to aid Mary.[7] He had also sent his cousin Henry Dudley to France in order to try to rally foreign support from King Henri II, a move that unsurprisingly drew caustic comment from the Imperial ambassadors: 'Such a thing is the courage of a resolute tyrant, especially when he is making a desperate attempt to grasp power.'[8] But more was needed, and in London '[t]he drum is being beaten here to raise troops.'[9] Jane's father the Duke of Suffolk was naturally one of her most steadfast supporters, so who better to defend her crown than he? Henry then, it was decided, would lead Jane's forces in an attempt to capture Mary. According to Robert Wingfield, though, Henry had other ideas:

> The duke was most unhappy at being entrusted with such a weighty task, and on the virtuous and salutary advice of his wife Frances, refused the offer, using some fainting fits, or according to others, attacks of giddiness as his excuse. His daughter, the so-called queen, strongly urged him to embark on this expedition, saying with great boldness that she could have no safer defence for her majesty than her most loving father.[10]

The first part of this account seems highly plausible, for it was not the first time that Henry would plead illness as an excuse. Neither did he relish military action, as his previous experience demonstrated. Heeding his wife's advice also sounds familiar, although in truth he probably needed little persuasion. The astute Frances may have envisaged that if events did not work in their favour at this uncertain time, then Mary would be more likely to show mercy if Henry was not seen to be leading the oppositional forces. However, Jane's reaction is at odds with all other accounts, and it is more probable that she was anxious for her father to remain by her side.[11] Rowland Lea, illustrating Jane's stubbornness once more, claimed that 'the duke of Suffolk was clean dissolved by the special means of the lady Jane his daughter, who, taking the matter heavily, with weeping tears made request to the whole council that her father might tarry at home in her company'.[12] Her anxiety was understandable, and seeing that there was no question of Henry leaving the Tower, 'the council persuaded with the duke of Northumberland to take that voyage upon him'.[13] The Duke was 'the best man of war in the realm', and 'was therefore so feared, that none durst once lift up their weapons against him'.[14] Northumberland was the obvious choice, but it transpired to be a fatal mistake.

Northumberland, too, was reluctant to leave London, for he was wary that without his commanding presence the loyalties of his colleagues might be swayed towards Mary. Already reports of growing support for Mary in East Anglia were beginning to reach the capital, and the Council heard that 'the whole country of Norfolk had come to her obedience and had taken up the arms to join in her defence'.[15] Seeing that he had no other choice, however, he answered that 'since ye think it good, I and mine will go, not doubting of your fidelity to the queen's majesty, which I leave in your custody'.[16] The decision had been made, and when Jane was informed that Northumberland had been selected to lead her forces, she 'humbly thanked the duke for reserving her father at home, and beseeched him to use his diligence, whereto he answered that he would do what in him lay'.[17]

Approaching his task with the utmost seriousness, Northumberland immediately 'threw all his energies into the campaign and prepared a most excellent army', for 'he was very ready to despise the plans of a mere woman'.[18] His preparations could not have gone better, and it was observed that he had 'more than three thousand horsemen well equipped and about thirty pieces of cannon and ammunition wagons'.[19] Many of these were no doubt enticed by the promise of pay set at eight crowns a month plus expenses. Northumberland was not deterred by the news that many of the lords across the counties had pledged their allegiance to Mary, for 'there were also many who obeyed the orders of the Duke to enlist soldiers against her'.[20] As Jane's forces gathered at Durham Place, where 'he appointed all the retinue to meet', she too must have felt less anguished since the Council had appointed Northumberland as leader of her army in place of her father, and the thought of his absence probably provided some welcome relief.[21] The Duke himself, though, was still extremely apprehensive about leaving. He urged the Council to send reinforcements to him following his departure, which they agreed to do. He then made a moving speech in which he reminded his colleagues of the loyalty they owed to Jane. However, he warned them,

if ye shall violate, hoping thereby of life and promotion, neither
acquit you of the sacred and holy oath of allegiance, made freely by
you, to this virtuous lady the Queen's Highness, who, by your and
our enticement is rather by force placed thereon than by her own
seeking and request.[22]

Assured as far as was possible but full of foreboding, after dinner in
the Royal Apartments on the evening of 13 July, Northumberland
'went into the queen', and there he 'took his leave of her'.[23] He then
left the Tower with the Marquess of Northampton and 'divers other',
and headed for Durham Place, 'where that night they mustered
their company in harness, and the next day in the morning the duke
departed'.[24] They left 'with a force which amounted to some 2,000 horse
and 3,000 foot at least', and with 'twenty great pieces of artillery'.[25]
As Northumberland rode out of London with an outward display of
confidence for his expedition, his spirits were dampened when he
observed that 'the people press to see us, but not one sayeth, God speed
us'.[26] Nevertheless, he had good reason to feel optimistic about his
cause and his ability to rally more men, for 'he could animate his army
with witty persuasions'.[27]

The hearts of the Londoners may have belonged to Mary, but her
supporters were by no means convinced that she would be victorious,
and on 14 July the Imperial ambassadors told their master that 'We
therefore believe that she is weak.'[28] Indeed, the odds appeared to be
very much stacked in Jane's favour. Initially, 'they who had acknowledged her Highness as Queen were so dejected that they fully deemed
that they would be ruined on her account'.[29] Concerned for her safety,
the Imperial ambassadors wrote to the Emperor that 'We believe that
my Lady will be in his hands [Northumberland's] in four days' time
unless she has a sufficient force to resist,' for the Duke 'is strong on land
and by sea, so, as far as we can see, none of the people who are secretly

attached to the Lady Mary can or dare declare for her or rise unless they hear that she is being supported by your Majesty'.[30] The next few days would be vital.

No sooner had Northumberland left than word reached Jane that several of her lords were defecting to Mary in other counties across her realm, including John Bourchier, Earl of Bath, the Earl of Sussex, and Lord Dacre in the north. Although this was in many ways unsurprising given that all of these men had Catholic sympathies, it was still disastrous news, made infinitely worse by the fact that there was no one in London whom Jane could trust to take control of the situation. With Northumberland gone, Jane's father was now head of the Council. Henry, however, had none of the authority of Northumberland; neither did he inspire confidence. What is more, he was rattled by the news that support for Mary was growing, and 'for the fear which the Duke of Suffolk had of them of the Council, lest in the absence of Northumberland they should cause a revolution, he would not suffer them to go out of the Court, even to their own houses'.[31] They were all in this together, and Henry at least was determined that it would stay that way. Jane and her father trusted nobody within the Council, for they were all too aware that despite the assurances they had made to Northumberland, promises were easily broken. In particular, suspicion fell on the Marquess of Winchester, and as he tried to leave the Tower one evening for his London home, to his dismay he discovered that 'the gates of the Tower upon a sudden was shut, and the keys carved up to the queen Jane'.[32]

'THE DUKE OF Suffolk's daughter, who has been accepted as Queen, is at the Tower with her ladies and Council; and it is said she will not move thence nor have herself crowned for a fortnight or more.'[33] Perhaps it was with her coronation in mind that on 14 July, the day of Northumberland's departure from London, Jane's thoughts turned to one of the more pleasurable aspects of queenship. On that day, 'by our order and commandment', she instructed Sir Andrew Dudley to deliver 'unto our own hands those jewels and other things' that had once adorned her royal predecessors.[34] Jane would have learned, both from her mother and from the late Katherine Parr, of the importance of projecting the royal image of grandeur and majesty, and jewels were an integral part of that process. They were a visible symbol of wealth and status in an age in which an outward display of magnificence could leave a lasting impression on contemporaries. If Jane were to succeed in her role as queen, it was imperative that she should look the part. She had already ordered Dudley to deliver 'for our use of our silks and other stuff', including 'twenty yards of crimson velvet to cover two chairs and two close stools', as well as some Holland cloth.[35]

As the coffers of jewels arrived, there were hundreds of pieces from which Jane could choose, and she must have been dazzled by the assortment of objects and the shining gold inlaid with a variety of beautiful gemstones.[36] Not only were there brooches, including one with 'nineteen table rubies and two table diamonds and eight red rubies' surrounding a picture, but there were also bracelets, rings, 'a cross of ten diamonds and three pearls pendant', pairs of beautiful beads, buttons 'set with table rubies', and girdles. In addition, there were also clocks, aiglettes, a toothpick shaped like a fish, and even 'two glasses with ostrich feathers', and crystal handles.[37] Jane must have been particularly interested in the books that formed part of the collection, and included 'a book garnished with gold and covered with black velvet', and 'a book garnished with Acorns of Gold'.[38] She may have taken less notice of the jewels that had a romantic theme, such as the 'fair tablet with Cupid's face', 'a spoon of gold with a Cupid on the knot', and 'a heart enamelled red'.[39] This vast collection, now at Jane's disposal, formed the jewels with which she would adorn her royal person, helping to transform her image into that of a queen who was determined to make a positive impact on her people.

As if that were not enough, a further coffer containing yet more treasures arrived from the Palace of Westminster, some of which were perhaps intended for Guildford's use. Listed among them were 'A sword girdle of red silk and gold', a shirt, 'the collar and ruffles of gold', and perhaps significantly given Jane's previous declaration that she would make her husband a duke rather than king, 'A coronet for a duke, set with five roses of diamonds, six small pointed diamonds, one table emerald, six great ballasses [rubies], seven blue sapphires and thirty-eight great pearls, with a cap of crimson velvet, and a roll of powdered armyons [ermines] about the same.'[40] There were also several beautiful mufflers; one of purple velvet embroidered with pearls and 'garnished with small stones of sundry sorts, and lined with white satin', some rich hats and a 'purse of a sable skin perfumed'.[41] With so many luxury items now in her possession, Jane must have looked every inch the queen.[42]

WHILE JANE BUSIED herself with thoughts of grandeur, elsewhere in the realm support for Mary was growing each day. By 12 July Mary had reached her formidable stronghold of Framlingham Castle. As 'the strongest castle in Suffolk', Framlingham was more easily defensible than Kenninghall, with battlements that commanded views of the countryside for miles around.[43] That same day, Mary sent to the city of Norwich ordering the citizens to proclaim her queen. Initially refusing 'because they were not certain of the king's death', soon after when 'rumours both of the king's death and of her bid for the throne were spreading far and wide through Norfolk and Suffolk with incredible speed', the city not only proclaimed for Mary, 'but also sent men and weapons to aid her'.[44] At Framlingham men began flocking to her banner, determined to do all that they could to help Mary claim her rightful inheritance. From London, in an exaggerated report, the Imperial ambassadors had heard that 'Her forces are said to amount to 15,000 men', and that more and more people were 'rising against the royal authority (*royaulme*) and, more especially, against the Duke of Northumberland'.[45] Though the ambassadors also claimed that 'It seems to us there are many people in the realm who love the Lady Mary and hate the Duke and his children,' it was Northumberland who was considered to be the real villain.[46] That Jane was barely given a mention in their reports is a demonstration of the fact that she was simply viewed as a figurehead whose royal blood validated Northumberland's attempts to hold on to power. It must have come as a further boost when news reached Mary that the sailors in the fleet at Yarmouth that Northumberland had rallied had now mutinied in her favour. Mary's outward show of self-assurance and fighting spirit did much to inspire those who followed her, and encouraged others to join her cause.

As he marched towards East Anglia, however, Northumberland was still confident of success. Shortly after his departure from London his close supporter Sir John Gates followed him and more supplies were not far behind. He seemed oblivious to the fact that he was hated throughout the land, and that few men cheered or joined his ranks as he passed. So assured was he of victory that he wrote to the Council 'that within a few days he would bring her Highness captive or dead, like a rebel as she was', and 'assuredly all thought so too'.[47] Despite Northumberland's confidence, the Council were becoming increasingly concerned by the regular reports of Mary's popularity. For Jane there was no such warmth.

In a further attempt to turn the hearts of the Londoners towards Jane, on 16 July the Bishop of London, Nicholas Ridley, preached at St Paul's Cross of the death of Edward VI, and declared that the Ladies Mary and Elizabeth 'were both base born', and therefore illegitimate.[48] However, 'the people murmured sore' at his words, for their feelings towards Queen Jane had not thawed.[49] The citizens were in fact becoming more outspoken, and 'fortune was beginning to smile on sacred Mary's righteous undertaking' as 'men from all ranks of life were joining her every day'.[50] This 'wonderfully strengthened and augmented' Mary's forces: it was becoming clear that the odds were turning in her favour, and she was now rumoured to have thirty thousand men ready to fight for her.[51] Besides that, more were expected to join her, and the Imperial ambassadors believed that 'As far as we are able to ascertain, the Duke is so hated for his tyranny and ambition that there is likelihood that the Lady Mary, if she is able to hold her own in the first encounter, will give him a great deal of trouble, induce many more men to join her, and may perhaps come to the throne.'[52] So fervent were the Londoners in their loyalty to Mary, that Jane's Council were forced to take precautions:

A strong guard is being mounted round the Tower, where the Queen and the Council are, to protect her from a popular tumult; for they know that my Lady Mary is loved throughout the kingdom, and that the people are aware of their wicked complaisance in allowing the Duke to cheat her of her right.[53]

Though concealed from view behind the Tower's walls, nothing could hide Queen Jane from the people's hostility. During the six days since her proclamation, the people's antipathy to her had intensified, for many believed that she was 'falsely styled queen'.[54] The report of the Imperial ambassadors painted a realistic picture of what the atmosphere in the Tower must have been like as those inside deliberated and waited for news from Northumberland: 'it does appear that the Council are anxious, fearing that the people may rise, that my Lady's forces may grow stronger, and that the new Queen may not be accepted by the Commons'.[55] It was perhaps this that prompted Jane to issue another warrant to the Lieutenancy of Surrey in a further bid to demand support. After once more asserting the legitimacy of her claim, Jane continued:

We understand the Lady Mary doth not cease by letters in her name, provoked thereto by her adherents, enemies of this realm, to publish

and notify slanderously to divers of our subjects matter derogatory to
our title and dignity royal, with the slander of certain of our Nobility
and Council, we have thought mete to admonish and exhort you, as
our true and faithful subjects, to remain fast in your obeisance and
duty to the imperial Crown of this Realm, whereof we have justly
the possession; and not to be removed any wise from your duty by
slanderous reports or letters, dispersed abroad either by the said Lady
Mary, or by her adherents.[56]

After reiterating once more that it was by King Edward's wishes that she
had succeeded, Jane's letter ended:

Wherefore we leave to proceed further therein, being assured in the
goodness of God that your hearts shall be confirmed to owe your
duty to us your sovereign Lady, who means to preserve this Crown
of England in the royal blood, and out of the [blank] of strangers
and papists, with the defence of all you our good subjects, your lives,
lands, and goods, in our peace against the invasions and violence of
all foreign or inward enemies and rebels.[57]

Authoritatively signing her name 'Jane the Queen', Jane had done all that
she could in her attempt to assert her sovereignty and obtain the support
of her subjects.[58] Support for her cause was fading fast as people across
the land continued to declare for Mary, yet still she clung to her title.
However, Jane and her father were quickly losing any control they held
over the Council, 'who were as though prisoners in the power of Lady
Jane and the Duke of Suffolk'.[59] With every hour that passed, more news
reached them that Mary's popularity was continuing to soar, and that an
increasing number of lords across the counties were declaring for her.
From the Tower there was little else that they could do aside from issuing
proclamations in Jane's name, and punishing those who spoke against

her. One man who had written a letter addressed to Jane and the Council was thrown into the Tower, for 'it is presumed that the letter's contents were scandalous'.[60] All other hopes for the success of Jane's cause now lay in Northumberland's hands.

CHAPTER 15

Jana Non Regina

O N 17 JULY the Duke and his men approached the market town of Bury St Edmunds, where Jane's maternal grandmother lay buried in the church of St Mary's.[1] Bury was just twenty-four miles from Mary's base at Framlingham Castle, and as he marched his forces through the East Anglian countryside, Northumberland was becoming continuously aware that the mood of the capital was reflected elsewhere in the country. Everywhere he went, the Duke had 'commanded the country people to follow him, and he had fourteen large and small pieces of artillery, twelve cart-loads of pikes and spears, four of arquebuses and many more of other munitions with which to arm the men he intended to levy'.[2] Despite this impressive show of arms, the response was disappointing, and the Imperial ambassadors were of the opinion that 'For the moment she [Mary] appears to be stronger than the Duke, and every day we hear people muttering against her [Jane] and preparing to declare for her.'[3] Having reached Bury, the Duke's men, 'eager to come to a contest, had struck camp' and waited for their orders.[4] Informed of the growing size of Mary's force, Northumberland sent desperately to the Council to beg for more men, but his request fell on deaf ears. His confidence was slowly ebbing away. Feeling unready for a military confrontation and left with no other choice, the Duke and his men retreated the thirty miles from Bury to Cambridge in an attempt to raise more support. By the time they reached the city, however, 'men were abandoning him daily', and Mary was 'gaining reinforcements every hour'.[5] With most of his men now deserting, it seemed as though the decisive moment had already passed without so much as a sword being crossed. While Northumberland did not want to admit it, one thing was becoming startlingly clear: Jane's reign was about to come crashing down.

IN LONDON, 'THE Council was troubled, the people murmuring, and everything of doubtful issue'.[6] Support for Queen Jane was quickly fading away, and as she remained in the Tower, anxiously waiting for news from her father-in-law, her Councillors, whispering among themselves, agreed that her cause was lost. According to a contemporary eyewitness:

Those who remained at London, as though for the purpose of protecting Jane and retaining the city in its allegiance, begin forthwith to consult about deserting her; for which they plausibly allege, partly their fear of the people, all of whom are flocking to Mary, and partly the well-being of the kingdom, lest it should suffer from intestine [internal] war.[7]

As 'Suffolk and Jane could not hinder them', one by one Jane's Council managed to slip out of the Tower.[8] By the evening of 18 July, only Jane's parents, her husband, mother-in-law and her ladies remained by her side – those who were too helplessly entangled to walk away. Like Jane, they had no choice but to wait, hoping beyond hope that by some miracle Northumberland would triumph, and secure their safety and Jane's throne.

Less than a mile away from the Tower on the banks of the Thames stood the former royal palace of Baynard's Castle.[9] Originally a Norman structure, it was at Baynard's that Richard III had been proclaimed king in 1483. It was now the home of William Herbert, Earl of Pembroke, and it was here that Jane's younger sister Katherine had come to reside following her recent marriage to Pembroke's heir, Henry.[10] Perhaps Katherine noticed her father-in-law's anxiety and heard the voices of the troubled men, as on the morning of 19 July, following their desertion of Jane in the Tower, Pembroke and his colleagues gathered at Baynard's. They began crisis talks over the situation in which they now found themselves. They had all declared for Jane, and had all allowed themselves to become entangled in Northumberland's schemes; had they not signed Edward's Letters Patent, and the letter to Mary in which they declared their allegiance to Queen Jane? The events of the past nine days since Jane's public proclamation, however, had revealed that Jane was an unpopular choice in the country, and that the Councillors would now have to decide where their true obedience lay. For Pembroke the situation was particularly delicate, for his son's marriage to Katherine Grey and her residence at Baynard's served as tangible evidence of where his loyalties had once lain.

It was Jane's uncle, the Earl of Arundel, who first broached the subject of abandoning Jane's cause. Forgetting any sense of family loyalty, and perhaps also motivated by religious considerations, for he was an ardent Catholic, 'the chief instigator of this revolution' made an impassioned speech to his colleagues, exhorting them to abandon Jane in favour of Mary:[11]

And if by chance you should feel somehow guilty proclaiming now our Queen My Lady Mary, having acclaimed Jane only a few days ago, showing such quick change of mind, I tell you that this is no reason to hesitate, because having sinned it befits always to amend, especially when, as in the present circumstances, it means honour for your goodselves, welfare and freedom for our country, love and loyalty to his King, peace and contentment for all the people.[12]

In Arundel's eyes it was clear that supporting Jane had been a terrible mistake, and that there was only one path now open to them. After such a moving speech, and 'as almost all had only consented to this treason

183

under constraint', most of the Councillors agreed with him.[13] First among them was Pembroke, who was already planning to distance himself from Jane's family still further by suing for the annulment of his son's marriage to Katherine Grey: Katherine would be returned home, and Pembroke would be free to arrange a new advantageous match for his son.[14] Without the overbearing presence of Northumberland to urge them to remain faithful, each man in turn now took up his pen and signed his name to Mary's proclamation. All promises to the dead King Edward were forgotten, all promises to Queen Jane cast aside.

THAT SAME MORNING, Jane had awoken in the Tower as Queen of England, and was still deferred to as such by those around her. She knew that her Council had fled, but her mind was temporarily distracted from her tumultuous situation when she was asked to stand as godmother to the son of Edward Underhill. Underhill was a Tower warder, whose son was being christened that morning in the nearby church of All Hallows next to Tower Hill.[15] As godmother, Jane was given the honour of choosing the child's name. It was perhaps in a show of unity that she named her new godson 'Guildford after her husband'.[16] As was her prerogative, though, Jane did not attend the child's christening in person, and instead elected a representative. As Lady Anne Throckmorton left the Tower to attend the christening on her behalf, Jane had no forewarning of what would happen next.

At Baynard's Castle the Councillors were resolute in their decision, and before long William Cecil would be marking documents signed 'Jane the Queen' with 'Jana non Regina' (Jane not the Queen). Before making their news public, however, they approached Mary's staunchest supporters in England: the Imperial ambassadors. 'They informed them that they had decided to proclaim the Lady Mary Queen. Most of them, they said, had been compelled by force to proclaim the other,' and now wished to correct their mistake.[17] The ambassadors were delighted at the reversal of Mary's fortunes in winning their allegiance, and 'every one considers her success a miracle and the work of the Divine Will, considering how long the Duke of Northumberland had been laying his plans'.[18] Pointedly ignoring the fact that they had not yet informed Jane of the result of their discussions, the Council proceeded to Cheapside. Their blatant disregard for the girl they had recently proclaimed queen demonstrates that they had never truly been loyal to her, and that to them she had been a mere puppet in a much bigger game. Now the tide had turned, and the Council had turned with it. At Cheapside, 'big crowds had assembled', eagerly waiting to hear what the Councillors had to say.[19] As spokesman for the Council, it was Pembroke who addressed the crowds of excited Londoners. He began:

We having no good opportunity afore this time have proclaimed this day in the City of London, our sovereign lady Queen Mary to be in just and lawful possession of the imperial crown of this realm, as by the proclamation sent to you herewith more plainly shall appear.[20]

Upon hearing Mary's name, the crowds were so joyous that the Earl was unable to conclude his speech, and 'he himself who was wearing a cap of great value, covered with gold and precious stones, threw it up into the air, which use is observed when they give went to an exceptional joy'.[21] It may not have been quite the scene described by Mary's supporters, whereby people were 'leaping and dancing as though beside themselves', and there was 'such a clamour and din and press of people in the streets' as men 'ran hither and thither, bonnets flew into the air, shouts rose higher than the stars, fires were lit on all sides, and all the bells were set a-pealing', but all of the sources agree that the news of Mary's accession was greeted with jubilation.[22]

John Stow related that 'some cast money abroad and some made bonfires throughout ye whole city', while before long 'a great number of bells was heard ringing', and many of the lords proceeded to the great St Paul's Cathedral where a Te Deum was sung in celebration.[23] Even Julius Terentianus, a Protestant eyewitness, observed that,

> [a]t the proclamation of Jane they displayed nothing but grief. At the proclamation of Mary, even before she was proclaimed at London, and when the event was still doubtful, they gave such demonstrations of joy, as to spare nothing. They first of all made so much noise all the day long with clapping their hands, that it seems still to linger in my ears; they then, even the poorest of them, made voluntary subscriptions, and mutually exhorted each other to maintain the cause of Mary; lastly, at night they had a public festival, and threatened flames, hanging, the gallows and drowning, to all the gospellers.[24]

As the bells of the city's churches rang, the Imperial ambassadors triumphantly reported that 'the Lady Mary was proclaimed Queen of England amid the greatest rejoicing it is possible to imagine'.[25] England had a new queen, and to her supporters 'it seemed as if all had escaped from the evil world, and alighted in Heaven'.[26] By the same token, they considered it to be 'all the more marvellous for coming so unexpectedly'.[27]

Amid the celebrations, the Earl of Arundel and Sir William Paget set out for Framlingham to declare the joyous news to Mary, taking the great seal of England with them.[28]

The Council now took the opportunity to send 'nearly 1000 reliable men to the Tower, by various secret ways, to force the Duke of Suffolk to come out'.[29] They were concerned that Henry would resist all attempts to see reason, and would continue to fight for his daughter's cause. Determined to speak to Henry in person, the Councillors travelled the short distance to the Tower. They avoided Jane, whose authority they had never truly respected, and instead sought a meeting with Henry. As he stood in front of them, wasting no time, they informed Henry of their decision: Jane was no longer queen, news which was 'very painful to him on account of his daughter'.[30] However, realizing that without the support of his colleagues there was now nothing more that he could do, and that 'owing to the number of men who had entered the Tower, if he refused to obey, he would be taken out by force, he resolved to go'.[31] Knowing that his daughter's cause was now irretrievably lost, and that he must break the news to Jane, with a sorrowful countenance Henry proceeded to the Royal Apartments.

As Jane sat at supper that evening with Guildford and her attendants, her father appeared in the doorway. Upon entering Jane's chamber, the room fell silent, sensing in nervous apprehension that the news he brought was not good. Approaching his daughter as she sat beneath the royal canopy of state, the tension in the room heightened. Hesitating for a moment, words failed the Duke, who – the Imperial ambassadors were later assured – instead grabbed at the canopy. In a dramatic gesture, he tore down the symbol of royal majesty, ripping the golden silk as it fell to the floor. Finding his tongue, Henry delivered the final blow to Jane and the shocked diners: he told her 'that this place did no longer belong to her, having to submit to Fortune as changeable and envious of its own gifts'.[32] Allowing Jane only a moment to digest this disastrous news, Henry continued: 'you must put off your royal robes and be content with a private life'.[33] As those in the room tried to absorb the scene, all eyes were on Jane as they waited anxiously for her reply. When it came, it was calm, composed, and dignified:

I much more willingly put them off than I put them on. Out of obedience to you and my mother, I have grievously sinned and offered violence to myself. Now I do willingly and obeying the motions of my own soul relinquish the crown and endeavour to solve those faults committed by others if, at least, so great faults can be solved, by a willing and ingenuous acknowledgement of them.[34]

Everyone in the room was stunned by her declaration. Yet for Jane, her relief at the removal of the heavy burden of queenship that had been placed on her shoulders was evident, and heartfelt. She had never desired the crown, and had broken down with the emotional strain when she had been forced to wear it.

As her father's words rung in Jane's ears, the future seemed even more uncertain than it had been since that fateful evening at Syon, when Jane had been handed the poisoned chalice of queenship. She had tried her best to assert her authority, and to earn the respect and the acceptance of the English people. Ultimately, though, love for her rival had prevailed, and Jane had sunk in a world in which the support of fickle men was crucial. From the start she had been faced with an incredibly difficult task, for though she had been acknowledged as queen by the lords of the Council and referred to as such, she had never been an acceptable monarch in the eyes of the people, who championed King Henry's daughter. Allowing Northumberland to leave London, however, had been a fatal mistake. With no firm hand to steady their resolve, the Councillors had no respect for Jane's position, or the authority of her father. When they saw that the tide was turning in Mary's favour, they were easily able to extricate themselves from the affair. Combined with this was Northumberland's unpopularity throughout the kingdom, which deterred men from rallying to Jane's cause, and was seized upon by her rival to her great advantage. Besides that, Jane's supporters could not have foreseen that Mary's flight to East Anglia would be such a huge factor in her success. There she was a well-known and popular landowner, and this grounding gave her an excellent base from which to drum up further support. Her fighting spirit and determined perseverance, as well as her ingrained belief in her right to rule, were all important factors; what was more, the people of England believed in Mary's right too – they had never believed in Jane's.

Mary had won, and Jane was now at her mercy. Though her reign had in fact lasted for thirteen days, four of these had been conducted behind closed doors, and as a contemporary observed, to the public 'Thus Jane was queen for only nine days, and those most turbulent ones.'[35] She had worn the crown, and now it was irretrievably lost; but Jane did not mourn for it.

IN SPITE OF the celebrations without, inside the Tower's walls the atmosphere was one of panic as its inhabitants, like drowning rats fleeing from a sinking ship, prepared to abandon the seventeen-year-old girl who now sat under a fallen canopy in the Royal Apartments. As the people cheered enthusiastically for Queen Mary, no thought was spared for the girl who had been openly proclaimed queen in Mary's place just nine days earlier, and whose reception had been icily cold.

As the sun began to set over the city on 19 July, the jubilation of the people at the news of Queen Mary's accession showed no sign of abating. The Londoners indulged in the free wine that ran from fountains throughout the city, and soaked up the celebratory atmosphere. They were not alone, for back in the Tower, overcome with relief at the news that her thirteen-day reign was at an end and that she was Queen Jane no longer, Jane looked to her father. There was only one question on her lips: 'May I go home?' Home was the place Jane had always longed for, her only security, but her father, knowing what lay ahead and unable to bring himself to answer her truthfully, simply turned and walked away. As he left the dining chamber, the truth dawned on Jane: the Tower of London, so recently her palace, was now her prison.

~

CHAPTER 16

Shut Up in the Tower

T HE SCENE IN the Royal Apartments following the declaration of Jane's father was one of panic that spread like wildfire to those few who remained, now desperate to escape. Lady Anne Throckmorton, who had just returned to the Tower from the nearby church of All Hallows, where she had played the role of Jane's deputy, was shocked to discover that 'the Cloth of Estate was taken down, and all things defaced. A sudden change!'[1] In the midst of it all, still seated beneath the torn canopy, was Jane. Having made her acknowledgement of her abruptly altered status, 'she withdrew to a private room with her mother and other Ladies, though with deep sorrow, but bearing the ill fate with great valour and endurance'.[2] She had remained calm and composed amid the confusion that was happening around her – a reaction that was almost certainly due to shock, and uncertainty as to what was expected of her. Still, she made no attempt to try to flee from the scene of disaster that had so recently unfolded before her. To the world she was, once again, just Jane: a fallen queen.

But Jane did not find comfort in her mother's arms for long. Duke Henry soon made it clear to the Duchess Frances, and to Jane's mother-in-law, the Duchess of Northumberland, who had had no choice but to watch the recent scene, that 'they had to withdraw, recognising as Queen the one who had recently been proclaimed'.[3] There was no other option for the two Duchesses: they would have to leave, 'and so they did'.[4] The Duchess Frances, who not only shared her royal blood with the new

Queen Mary, but had until now also enjoyed a close relationship with her, realized that time was of the essence if her family were to stand any chance of survival amid the wreckage of Jane's disastrous queenship. Together with her husband, Frances prepared to flee the Tower and throw herself and her family upon the Queen's mercy: it was their only chance and their only choice.

Heartbreaking though the prospect of leaving Jane behind may have been for Frances, there was no question of Jane coming too. Within a short space of time 'the guard of the Tower and subsequently of the Lady Jane was entrusted to the Lord Warden', Sir Thomas Cheyne, who now assumed the post of jailer until he received further orders; for the moment at least, Jane would have to remain ensconced in the Tower's walls.[5]

Jane's father, Henry, hurriedly gave instructions that all of the ladies, who had, just a short time ago, waited on Jane as queen, were now free to leave the Tower if they wished. Unlike their mistress, they were given the opportunity to free themselves from the tangled web of intrigue, and to walk away from the memories of the past nine days at the Tower. With that, Jane's former ladies and her parents 'left all for their own homes, abandoning Jane'.[6] Though the future was uncertain, neither Jane, nor her mother, had any idea that they would never see one another again.

Jane's father was also worried about the plight of his daughter, and as he left the Tower, he encountered William Paulet, the Lord Treasurer, who had so recently placed the crown on Jane's unwilling head. Henry begged him, as a friend, to 'obtain the Queen's pardon to save him and his family', so concerned was he for their welfare.[7] Paulet, who considered his own situation to be equally desperate and could now only think of his own safety, nevertheless assured Henry that he would do all that he could. There was nothing further Henry could do, and with that he finally left, leaving his daughter at the Queen's mercy.

There was no sign of the Duchess Frances as Henry emerged from the Tower's walls and commanded his men to drop their weapons, 'saying that he himself was but one man'.[8] Perhaps she had hurried ahead of him, anxious to be reunited with the youngest of her three daughters, Jane's sister Mary, at the Charterhouse.[9] Maybe she had, for the time being, entrusted Henry with the task of proclaiming the family's loyalty to the new regime. Aware that in order to save both himself and his family submission to Mary was compulsory, Henry made one strident attempt to prove his new loyalty. Making his way the short distance to Tower Hill, 'that historical and blood-stained ground to the north-west of the Tower' on which traitors had been executed for centuries, Henry swallowed any remaining pride and proclaimed Mary the rightful queen in front of the assembled crowds of Londoners.[10] He had done his duty: he had accepted that Jane was queen no longer, and turning away from the Tower that still held his daughter inside, Henry left to join his family at the Charterhouse, and to wait on events.[11]

The Royal Apartments were now almost deserted. Any who remained were those for whom flight was not an option: Jane and Guildford. Similarly, despite Henry having given her earlier instructions to withdraw, as guards began to take up posts at the doors, Guildford's mother the Duchess of Northumberland had been forbidden from leaving, almost certainly by the Lord Warden, Sir Thomas Cheyne. She too could now only wait for news of her fate. It seems improbable that Jane found any solace in the arms of her husband, or of his mother; any comfort she did receive was most likely found in prayer. As evening drew in, Queen Mary's guards arrived to remove the young couple. So recently appointed to protect her person, they were now ordered to ensure that Jane remain a prisoner. Unlike her queenly predecessors Anne Boleyn and Katherine Howard, both of whom had spent their final days in the Royal Apartments, there was no question that Jane would be allowed to remain there. She was an upstart, who, though unwillingly, had tried to usurp the rightful place of Queen Mary, whose arrival at the Tower would soon be expected, and who would occupy the apartments in which Jane now stood. Neither was there any question of Jane remaining with Guildford, and though their fates inevitably lay intertwined, they were now escorted to separate prisons. For Guildford, his new lodging was in the thirteenth-century Beauchamp Tower, the walls of which were already covered with the personal carvings of those who had been unfortunate enough to be imprisoned there, and to which he would perhaps add his own memorial.[12] Jane was not far away, for she was to be lodged on Tower Green in the house of the Gentleman Gaoler Nathaniel Partridge, in whose custody she now remained to await the Queen's orders as to her future. Partridge's house lay next to the Lieutenant's Lodgings, but contrary to later accounts Jane was never actually lodged in the Lieutenant's house itself, although she may have visited it.[13] The Lieutenant of the Tower served directly under the Constable, and was responsible for the care of the Tower's prisoners. Jane and Guildford's quarters had no doubt been chosen for their proximity to the Lieutenant's Lodgings, which made them ideal locations for important prisoners.

'The other Queen has renounced all her honours, and has been shut up in the Tower with her husband and the Duke's wife, though all the rest are outside,' the Imperial ambassadors wrote to the Emperor.[14] There was no mistaking the fact that everyone in London now knew that Jane and Guildford were prisoners. The events of the past thirteen days had been overwhelming for Jane; she had gone from heir to queen in the blink of an eye, and from queen to prisoner almost as quickly. With none save Partridge and three ladies, Mistress Ellen, Mistress Tilney and Mistress Jacob, appointed to wait on her for company, Jane would have been forgiven for thinking of the past, and the steps which had brought her to such a fateful moment, and seemingly doomed conclusion.[15] She was consciously aware of who she was – a lady of the royal house of Tudor – but it was not an inheritance she had sought, or indeed, wished to pursue.

Jane's claim to the throne and the hopes that her parents had had for her were now permanently dashed as she contemplated events from her prison in the Tower – she could only watch, helpless to control the events of the future. A little over a hundred miles from the Tower, in the leafy countryside of East Anglia, lay the mighty Norman stronghold of Framlingham Castle. Though Mary had written to the Council demanding their allegiance, a week later she was still unaware of the news that Jane's claim had collapsed and that she herself had been proclaimed queen in London. Preparing for a fight, Mary was rallying her troops. On 20 July, at four o'clock in the afternoon, Mary rode out of the castle

> [t]o muster and inspect this most splendid and loyal army. While her majesty was approaching, the white horse which she was riding became rather more frisky at the unaccustomed sight of such an army drawn up in formation than her womanly hesitancy was prepared to risk, so she ordered her foot-soldiers, active and dutiful men, to lift up their hands to help their sovereign until she got ready to get down; obedient to their gentle mistress's request, they brought the queen down to the ground. Once she had got down from her horse, the good princess first gave warning in an order that no harquebusier should fire his gun, nor any archer release his arrows until her majesty had inspected her army. When this order was given, such was the respect that everyone felt for their sovereign that no harquebusier nor archer fired after her command; but the soldiers bowed low to the ground and awaited their beloved mistress's arrival with as great an obeisance as they could manage. When she came along, they offered her such reverence that I had serious doubts whether they could have given greater adoration to God if he had come down from Heaven.[16]

It was an encouraging sight, but one which would prove to be unnecessary. As she returned to the castle and the evening drew in, two men rode into the courtyard at Framlingham, and were quickly admitted to Mary's presence. One was Jane's uncle, the forty-year-old Henry FitzAlan, Earl of Arundel, 'a nobleman of much worship and among the good men of this kingdom', accompanied by his slightly older colleague, Sir William Paget.[17] Both men had been members of Jane's short-lived Council, but now that Jane's reign had collapsed, like so many others, their foremost concern was the preservation of their own lives and influence, and it was this which had hurried them to Mary's side. Finally, in the presence of the woman who they had now declared their rightful queen, they informed Mary of her proclamation in the capital, and were obliged to beg for

> [h]er pardon for the offence committed in the reception of the Lady Jane of Suffolk, and perform the ceremonies usually gone through in England when pardon has to be demanded for so heavy a crime, which are said to consist in the guilty party appearing on his knees with a dagger turned towards his stomach in recognition of his offence and submission to the penalty deserved.[18]

As Mary absorbed the news, she showed herself to be both gracious and merciful to the two men. After all, this was her moment of triumph, and it was one that she was determined to savour. She had been victorious and won her kingdom without bloodshed – she was now Queen of England.

In the days that followed, 'many nobles and knights presented themselves in the castle where the Queen was'; men who had once supported Jane, and were now eager to ingratiate themselves with Queen Mary in order to procure her forgiveness and goodwill.[19] Mary showed herself to be equally merciful, and declared that in spite of their treachery, they would be forgiven and their lives spared. But there was one for whom forgiveness was not an option – one who was still at large. Soon after his arrival at Framlingham, 'her Highness gave commission to the said Arundel to go with armed men and take order that the Duke of Northumberland and his chief partisans should be apprehended and kept in safe custody'.[20] With orders issued for Northumberland's arrest and the rest of her enemies now reconciled or imprisoned, nothing now remained but for Mary to assume her rightful place as queen in her capital city. As she began to prepare for her departure, her cousin Jane, the fallen queen, imprisoned within the Tower's walls, could only wait, and pray, that the Queen would be as merciful to her as she had been to Jane's former supporters.

QUEEN MARY WAS triumphant, and having sent the Earl of Arundel in pursuit of the Duke of Northumberland, 'as a first priority she arranged with her chaplains that they should give thanks and pour forth prayers to Almighty God, the first and sole author of this victory'.[21] Of Mary's 'humility, piety, and religion it is unnecessary to speak', so renowned was her devotion to the Catholic faith.[22] It was her faith that had seen her through some of the most trying times in her life, and a faith that she would do all that she could to restore to her land. A steadfast adherence to religion was, in fact, something Queen Mary shared with her young cousin Jane, now languishing in the Tower.

On 24 July, five days after Jane's deposition, Queen Mary departed from Framlingham Castle on the first stage of her journey to London, to take possession of her kingdom. Mary was jubilant – at the age of thirty-seven she had at last come into her rightful inheritance. While the new Queen had the adoration of her people and the unswerving devotion of those who served her, she was, nonetheless, twenty years her cousin Jane's senior. The years had not been kind to Mary, and though 'her face is well formed', she had prematurely aged.[23] She 'is of low rather than of middling stature', with auburn hair, and her voice was 'rough and loud, almost like a man's, so that when she speaks she is always heard a long way off'.[24] Nevertheless, she was 'never to be loathed for ugliness', and more importantly, 'she shows herself to have been born of truly royal lineage'.[25] In the Tower, news that the Queen was journeying to London reached Jane. Just seven short months ago as the year 1553 began, nobody could have envisaged the tumultuous events that had led to Jane's rise, fall and imprisonment, for there had been no indication of what lay ahead. The year's events had come as a complete surprise to those involved, for only once before had England witnessed a year of three sovereigns – and that had been disastrous.[26] Equally, never before had Jane been considered as a serious contender for the English throne, though her right had been there from the moment of her birth.

THE DUKE OF Northumberland was nowhere to be seen. On 20 July the Imperial ambassador had reported: 'I know nothing more of the Duke's movements for the moment: but he must have heard of what has happened here. He will hardly escape.'[27] Northumberland, who had ridden from London bound for East Anglia in an attempt to secure Jane's throne by apprehending Mary just days earlier, had indeed heard of what had happened. No sooner had his wearied horse arrived in the city of Cambridge, than it became clear from the cool response of the citizens and Mary's evident popularity that his visions of power, and all of his hopes, were to come to nothing – and worse.

On the same day as the Imperial ambassador's letter, Northumberland received word from the Council in London that Mary had been proclaimed Queen of England in London. Realizing that he now had no chance of victory, he 'was so thunderstruck that he immediately ordered her Highness to be proclaimed Queen, and took down and tore with his own hands the proclamation of Jane'.[28] With no thought for the welfare of the girl whom he had so recently made every effort to proclaim queen, Northumberland proceeded to throw a hat full of gold coins into the air in the marketplace at Cambridge and 'so laughed that the tears ran down his cheeks for grief'.[29] In shock, and doubtless planning his next move, he retired for the evening with his sons to the house of John Cheke, tutor to King Edward, and 'ye same night after he was laid in his bed ye guard came and ceased upon his weapons and his body and took him in charge'.[30] Finding himself confronted by his one-time ally the Earl of Arundel, the same man who had informed Mary that she was now queen, Northumberland 'fell down on his knees and desired him to be good to him, for the love of God'.[31] He tried to reason with Arundel, arguing that 'I have done nothing but by the consent of you and all the whole council.'[32] But it was no use. 'I am sent hither by the queen's majesty, and in her name I do arrest you,' Arundel replied.[33] Though he accepted his former colleague's charge, Northumberland begged him to 'use mercy towards me, knowing the case as it is'.[34] Arundel could only reply by telling him that 'ye should have sought for mercy sooner; I must do according to my commandment'.[35]

Together with his two eldest sons, John and Ambrose, and his youngest son Harry – Guildford's brothers – and his own brother Sir Andrew Dudley, who had been captured alongside their kinsman and leader, the prisoners were taken back to London, 'guarded by about three thousand soldiers'.[36] Their destination was a foregone conclusion: the Tower, 'where he has sacrificed his victims and practiced his tyrannical immolations'.[37] Arriving on 25 July, 'one can hardly convey the size of the crowds which filled the streets to see the prisoners, so enormous that they could scarcely ride on through it'.[38] The crowd were so hostile on seeing Northumberland, this evil councillor who had tried so hard to deprive Queen Mary of her rightful inheritance, that they could not resist hurling stones and jeering at him as he passed, and 'had it not been for the strong guard of soldiers, it would not have been possible to bring Northumberland to prison alive'.[39] Though his youngest son Harry wept, Northumberland retained 'a calm countenance', and as he reached the Tower, 'his remorse and evil conscience were astonishing'.[40] Greeted at the gate to the fortress by the recently reappointed Constable, Sir John Gage, 'a man of advanced age but of great steadfastness and long experience', who was also Northumberland's brother-in-law, and the newly appointed

Lieutenant, Sir John Brydges, Northumberland and his sons were escorted to their prison lodgings.[41] Shortly afterwards they were joined in their imprisonment by Guildford's brother Robert.[42]

Jane, from her lodgings near Tower Green, would have been able to hear the commotion of the hostile crowd outside, and see the party of prisoners pass as Guildford's brothers were taken to join him in the Beauchamp Tower, while Northumberland was lodged in St Thomas's Tower.[43] It must have been a pitiful sight: the fallen Duke, so recently the most powerful man in England, captured alongside his four sons – all young, all handsome – and returned to the very fortress that Northumberland had left just days ago, full of hope for the future. His fate was already sealed, but for his sons, and for Jane, there was no telling what the future might hold. It was still all to play for, and the wheel of fortune remained undecided.

CHAPTER 17

Jane of Suffolk Deserved Death

A S QUEEN MARY approached London, her adoring subjects flocking to see her along the way, she broke her journey at her Palace of Beaulieu. She may have recollected with sadness unpleasant memories of the visit made to her by her teenage cousin at Beaulieu almost four years earlier. For the moment, however, there was little time to dwell on this, for at two o'clock on the morning of 30 July, a visitor arrived at the Palace, desperately seeking an audience with the Queen: Frances had come to beg for the lives of her family.

Despite the fact that Frances and her husband had fled the Tower for the Charterhouse, it was not long before Queen Mary's officers had clattered into the courtyard. On 28 July, Henry was arrested and returned to the Tower. There, whether feigned or in truth, he 'was taken ill', and was reported to be 'in such case as no man judgeth he can live'.[1] Frances, realizing that the task of saving her family now lay in her hands, immediately set off to beg the Queen for mercy in person.

Despite the awkward circumstances in which they now found themselves, Mary had no qualms about meeting with Frances. The two were, after all, cousins, and cousins who had been reasonably close before the disastrous sequence of events that had so recently taken place. The two women now came face-to-face within the Royal Apartments at Beaulieu, and Frances began her appeal. She told Mary that she had come to 'intercede for her most unfortunate husband – of whom (for shame!) much must be said in a more appropriate place – and obtain his liberty on parole from the most merciful queen'.[2] Henry was not to blame, Frances told the Queen, for the fault lay solely at Northumberland's door. The Imperial ambassadors reported that Frances claimed that

> [h]er husband had been the victim of an attempt to poison him, and that the Duke of Northumberland had done it. She then prayed for her husband's release from the Tower, where he had been imprisoned two days previously. We have also heard that an apothecary, on learning that the Duke of Northumberland had been taken, went and drowned himself.[3]

Frances's accusations of poison caught Mary's attention, and she immediately demanded proof of the poison attempt. But she also hated Northumberland vehemently, and was probably all too willing to believe Frances's claims. As to freeing Henry from the Tower, having heard that 'his sickness was getting worse' and concerned lest he should die, 'she freely conceded this, won over by cousinly affection, by her entreaties and by her own merciful nature'.[4] However, she insisted that he remain under house arrest at the Charterhouse, and could be returned to the Tower at any time. Mary's forgiveness suggests more than cousinly affection, for after all, Frances's daughter Jane had attempted to wear the crown that Mary believed was rightfully hers, an act of high treason. It indicates that she truly believed that Frances and her family had played no willing part in the events of the past few months; in essence, Mary rightly believed that Northumberland was the instigator, and for that he would be punished.

Thus far, Frances's mission had proven to be successful, due in part to her persuasive charms, bolstered by her familial links with the Queen and Mary's desire to be merciful. But what of Jane, who like her father, lay incarcerated in the Tower? No contemporary source makes any reference to Frances interceding with Queen Mary on behalf of her eldest daughter during her audience at Beaulieu. Such an omission has always been taken as a demonstration of a lack of maternal feeling on Frances's part, but this is not necessarily the case. The comment that Henry had made to his daughter at the Tower that she must 'be content with a private life' following her deposition suggests that he believed that Mary would be merciful to her, and Frances probably shared this belief. Alternatively, Mary may have already made it clear that she would spare Jane on account of her tender age, and comments made by the Imperial ambassadors in their report of 16 August confirm that Mary had informed them that 'she could not be induced to consent that she [Jane] should die'.[5] Whatever the circumstances, Frances was able to leave Beaulieu with some relief and a great measure of success: she had an assurance that her husband's life would be spared, and probably some intimation that Jane would also be allowed to live.

The Queen was true to her word, and the day after she met with Frances she ordered Henry's release from the Tower. He immediately returned home to join his wife and younger daughters at the Charterhouse, there to commence his house arrest.[6] Given his crime, he was fortunate. For Jane, there was no such swift end to her imprisonment, and she remained incarcerated in the Tower. Moreover, the conditions of her captivity were relatively strict, and it was observed that she and Guildford 'receive sour treatment, somewhat different to that meted out to them during their eight [sic] days' reign'.[7] The young couple had been forbidden from meeting with one another, and were being kept in close confinement. Jane's parents, realizing how fortunate they were to be alive and free, but aware that they were by no means out of danger, lay low while events unfolded, and trusted to the Queen's mercy on behalf of their daughter.

Frances was not the only one who had rushed to approach Queen Mary directly. A short distance behind, the Duchess of Northumberland, who had been 'let out of prison sooner than was expected', made her way to Beaulieu, desperate to persuade the Queen, 'to move her to compassion towards her children' and her husband.[8] She came to within five miles of the Palace when word reached her that 'the Queen ordered her to return to London, and refused to give her audience'.[9] It was a crushing blow for the Duchess, and one that communicated Queen Mary's firm resolution to destroy her husband. Bitterly disappointed, the Duchess had no choice but to turn back. But even then, determined to be her husband's champion and the only person to speak in his defence, the desperate woman wrote to Lady Paget. In her letter to the wife of William, one of Jane's former Councillors who had now ingratiated himself with Mary, the Duchess begged Lady Paget to urge her husband to try to intercede with the Queen on behalf of her sons, 'although I do not so much care for them as for their father who was to me and my mind the most best gentleman that ever living woman was matched'.[10] The marriage of Guildford's parents was a love match, and theirs had been a happy family. But despite the Duchess's grovelling pleas, it was on the verge of collapse, for, as she would soon discover, her words could not save her husband.

ON 3 AUGUST, Queen Mary made her state entry into London 'and took possession of her kingdom'.[11] With her came 'a large escort of infantry and cavalry, to the number of 12,000 men', and many of those who had hurried to dance attendance on their new queen, all 'arrayed sumptuously'.[12] The new Queen 'was in rich apparel, her gown of purple velvet French fashion, with sleeves of the same', and she was dripping in rich jewels.[13] Her half-sister the Lady Elizabeth, who had written a congratulatory note upon hearing of her accession, and was determined to share in her glory, accompanied Mary. A 'great number of ladies after them', and many of the same lords who, just a few short weeks previously had declared for Jane joined them.[14] Among them was Jane's uncle, the Earl of Arundel, who rode before the Queen, 'bearing the sword in his hand'.[15] Mary had readily forgiven this 'sorry crew of scoundrels' when they had admitted their mistake and begged her pardon, and they now revelled

in her triumph.[16] Her subjects 'with general and marvellous rejoicings' cheered the Queen rapturously; they were overjoyed that she had at last received her rightful inheritance.[17] That same evening, at seven o' clock, she arrived to take up residence at the Tower 'where all her prisoners were in confinement; and there was such a discharge of ordnance, that the like has not been heard there these many years'.[18] As she arrived, four prisoners 'met the queens grace at the Tower gate, and there they kneeling down saluted her grace, and she came unto them and kissed them and said, "These are my prisoners."'[19] Jane, however, was not among them. The prisoners were Stephen Gardiner, Bishop of Winchester; the old Duke of Norfolk; the Duchess of Somerset, the wife of the executed Lord Protector; and Edward Courtenay, all of whom had been imprisoned through the auspices of Henry VIII or Edward VI.[20] Moved to compassion, 'in her incomparable goodness she not only gave them liberty but also restored their original honours and positions'.[21] Several other prisoners were released shortly afterwards, and 'This most notable example of mercy did much to win her subjects' affections.'[22] The Tower was being emptied of its prisoners in a sign of goodwill and reconciliation for the start of the new reign, but this did not extend to everyone.

From her room in the Tower, Jane had heard the rapturous celebrations of the Londoners as Queen Mary made her entry into the city, a reception that differed so greatly from her own. She knew that Mary had arrived at the Tower, had freed many of those who had been locked within the fortress's walls for years – but not her. Though the Queen was now residing in the same fortress, Jane realized that she would be deprived of a personal audience with her, and instead took up her pen. She had always been a scholar of astonishing ability, but the letter that she wrote now would be the most important of her life. She was writing her version of events; she was writing for her life. Sadly, the original letter has not survived, but it was probably very similar to a declaration that Commendone and Pollini reported that Jane made just months later, in which she acknowledged her guilt in the circumstances in which she found herself:

> *Although my fault be such that, but for the goodness and clemency of the queen, I can have no hope of finding pardon, nor in craving forgiveness, having given ear to those who at that time appeared, not only to myself, but also to a great part of this realm, to be wise, and now have manifested themselves the contrary, not only to my and their great detriment, but with the common disgrace and blame of all, they having with such shameful boldness made so blameable and dishonourable an attempt to give others that which was not theirs, neither did it become me to accept (wherefore rightly and justly am I ashamed to ask pardon for such a crime), nevertheless, I trust in God that as now I know and confess my want of prudence, for which I deserve heavy punishment, except for the very great mercy of your majesty, I can still on many grounds conceive hope of your infinite clemency, it being known that the error imputed to me has not been altogether caused by myself. Because, although my fault may be great, and I confess it to be so, nevertheless I am charged and esteemed guilty more than I have deserved.*[23]

Jane's remorse was evident, but she could not stress enough that 'no one can ever say either that I sought it as my own, or that I was pleased with it or ever accepted it'.[24] The crown had been forced upon her, and she had been left with no option but to comply. Jane continued to place the blame for events squarely at Northumberland's door, stressing 'thus in truth I was deceived by the duke and the council, and ill treated by my husband and his mother'.[25] Clearly she harboured no warm feelings either for Guildford or his family. As if that was not damning enough, in sentiments that echoed those of her mother, Jane continued to level an accusation of poison against her parents-in-law: 'I know for certain that, twice during this time, poison was given to me, first in the house of the duchess of Northumberland, and afterwards here in the Tower, as I have the best and most certain testimony, besides that since that time all my hair has fallen off.'[26] Her evidence for this claim is unclear, but it seems certain that in the first instance she was referring to the illness she had experienced following her marriage. Preposterous though such a claim was, given that Northumberland had needed Jane in order to validate his authority, it served as further fuel to blacken his name.[27] More puzzling is the claim that she had lost her hair, but if that were partially true then this was perhaps due to the stress of the past few months.[28] Having done all she could to exonerate herself in the eyes of the Queen by playing to her strength of the written word, Jane may have ended her letter with a powerful statement similar to that which she later made: 'And all these things I have wished to say for the witness of my innocence and the disburdening of my conscience.'[29]

Others, including Jane's mother, had probably been made aware by now that Mary's intention was to spare Jane. This may also have been communicated to Jane, in which case she had good reason to be hopeful that her letter would receive a favourable response from the Queen, and that she too would be granted the same mercy and freedom given to others. Mary was certainly sympathetic to Jane's situation, and though she soon removed from the Tower to Richmond Palace without seeing her cousin, Jane was not forgotten. By 13 August it seems clear that Mary had received Jane's letter, and that she had accepted her version of events. During their audience with her that day, the Imperial ambassadors reported that though the Queen made it clear that 'she had not pardoned anybody yet', and there were many who whispered in the Queen's ear that 'Jane of Suffolk deserved death according to English law', Mary, conscious of their familial bonds and Jane's tender age, could not bring herself to execute her cousin.[30] It was evident that Mary believed in Jane's innocence, for in words that almost echoed those in Jane's letter, the ambassadors informed their master that Jane knew nothing of the plans in which she had become helplessly entangled, 'nor was she ever a party nor did she ever give her consent to the Duke's intrigues and plots'.[31] This seems to indicate that Mary had indeed received Jane's account, and she was firm in her decision to be merciful. The Queen's conscience, the ambassadors continued, 'would not permit her to have her put to death', despite the fact that she had been warned by the use of an example from Roman history that it would be better to put Jane to death, 'because of the scandal and danger that might have followed'.[32] Jane's life, it seemed, was safe. If Jane herself was not aware of this at this time then it seems likely that she would have received some indication shortly afterwards. Furthermore, Mary appeared to have decided on her ultimate fate, and had assured the Imperial ambassadors that 'before setting the Lady Jane at liberty she would take the greatest possible care for the future'.[33] The taste of future freedom was tantalizing, but for the time being, Jane was going nowhere.

By contrast, for Jane's father-in-law Northumberland, there was not a moment to be wasted. The date of his trial was set: on the morning of 18 August he left the Tower, destined for Westminster. He was to be tried alongside his eldest son, John, and William Parr, 'Marquis of Northampton, who was generally held to be one of the guiltiest'.[34] The fact that a trial for Jane was not arranged at the same time is indicative of Mary's plans to forgive Jane, for had she wished to rid herself of her cousin then she had legitimate grounds to do so. The Imperial ambassadors had warned her that 'even were she [Jane] married to an inferior, yet the title she had borne, though in itself insufficiently proved, yet had had some semblance of foundation, and thus might be revived again to trouble the succession to the Crown', advice that Mary ignored.[35] Jane was almost certainly aware that her father-in-law's day of judgement had arrived, but her feelings towards him had not mellowed. Westminster Hall was the setting for high-profile trials, and was also the location for

the banquet that traditionally took place following a monarch's coronation. For Northumberland, this proved to be a cruel twist of fate; had his
schemes succeeded he would no doubt have revelled in presiding over
Jane's coronation celebrations – now the hall would witness his astonishingly rapid demise, of which there was no question.

As the fallen Duke arrived at the hall, with 'a good and intrepid countenance, full of humility and gravity', he was confronted by the site of his
peers, many of whom 'a few days ago he had commanded at his leisure'.[36]
His former colleagues now 'beheld him with a severe aspect, and the
greatest courtesy shown him of any was a slight touch of the cap'.[37] The
trial was presided over by the eighty-year-old Thomas Howard, Duke of
Norfolk, as Lord High Steward, 'an old man with one foot in the grave'.[38]
Recently released and restored from the Tower by the good graces of
Queen Mary, Norfolk provided a tangible example of how fortune's wheel
could swiftly turn.

Standing at the bar, Northumberland 'used great reverence towards
the judges, and protesting his faith and obedience to the queen's majesty,
whom he confessed grievously to have offended', claimed that he had no
wish to speak in his defence, but declared that he had acted merely on
King Edward's instructions.[39] He did, however, declare 'his earnest repent-
ance', and 'then he fell on his knees and appealed to the Queen for mercy,
saying that all he had done was by the advice, consent and command of
the Council'.[40] It was not enough.

The verdict was a foregone conclusion: Northumberland was guilty of
high treason, and must die. When the sentence was pronounced, 'he asked
the Court to mitigate the punishment and the form of the execution and
also to be merciful towards his sons, as their fault was due to their youth
and ignorance in obeying him'.[41] According to the nineteenth-century
antiquarian Nicholas Harris Nicolas, he also took the opportunity to
declare that 'Lady Jane herself was so far from aspiring to the Crown, "that
she was by enticement and force made to accept it"'.[42] No contemporary

source makes any reference to such an assertion, however, and it seems more probable that the Duke's concerns were for the welfare of his own children. Jane was not his problem. Having done all that he could to exonerate his sons from blame, his only thoughts were for himself, as he further requested 'the appointment of a religious and learned man, with whom he could discharge his conscience before death'.[43]

Northumberland's son John and the Marquess of Northampton were both condemned beside him, and the three men were returned to the Tower, there to await execution: Northumberland's day of reckoning had been scheduled for 21 August. Jane, meanwhile, though informed of her father-in-law's impending death, was more concerned by the reports that reached her in regard to his religion. For Northumberland had been serious in his desire to meet with men of learning, and through them had made a momentous decision: to abandon the Protestant faith – the faith for which all of his actions had striven to retain – and embrace the old religion of Catholicism that had once been so loathsome to him. His motivation was evident, and in a last-ditch attempt to try and earn a reprieve from the Queen, on the morning of Monday 21 August,

> [i]t was appointed the duke with other should have suffered, and all the guard were at the Tower; but howsoever it chanced he did not; but he desired to hear mass, and to receive the sacrament, according to the old accustomed manner. So about 9 of the clock the altar in the chapel was arrayed. And each thing prepared for the purpose; then Mr Gage went and fetched the Duke.[44]

'The lady Jane looking through the window saw the duke and the rest going to the church' as they proceeded to the Chapel of St John in the White Tower.[45] The Duke's conversion was a wonderful piece of propaganda for the new Marian regime, already intent on reversion to the old religion, and they played it for all it was worth.

Jane's disgust at Northumberland's abandonment of Protestantism and her general hatred of him were unsurprising. For most of her short life she had found herself at the centre of plots engineered by ambitious men eager for power, and as a result she had learned not to trust them. The will of her great-uncle, Henry VIII, had transformed her position and heightened her importance in the vicious circle of Tudor politics, and Northumberland had not been the first to notice it. After all, Jane had previously been used as a pawn in the power games of Sir Thomas Seymour – a strategy that had almost resulted in disaster.

As Jane absorbed the news of her father-in-law's religious betrayal, she had time to consider his decision, but it remained utterly incomprehensible to her. Her feelings towards those who converted were made plain in a letter that she later wrote to her first tutor, Dr Harding, upon hearing that he too had reverted to Rome: 'And wilt thou honour a detestable idol, invented by Romish popes, and the abominable college of crafty cardinals?'[46] 'Fight manfully, come life, come death: the quarrel is God's, and undoubtedly the victory is ours', Jane had urged Harding.[47] In her mind it was evident that she believed that her faith was her salvation, and that she could not understand those who thought otherwise – even those on the point of death. She believed that conversion to Catholicism led to nothing but the damnation of the soul, and eternal doom. It was a fate she believed that her father-in-law was about to come face-to-face with.

Jane understood Northumberland's motivation for converting, later telling Rowland Lea that 'he hoped for life by his turning', and acknowledging that 'though other men be of that opinion, I am utterly not'.[48] It was a choice that she herself could never imagine making. She believed that the Duke's hope was even more incredulous given his crime, for as she told Lea, 'what man is there living, I pray you, although he had been innocent, that would hope of life in that case; being in the field against the queen in person as general, and after his taking, so hated and evil spoken of by the commons?'[49] She was quite right.

ON THAT SUMMER morning, 22 August, from her room in Master Partridge's lodgings, Jane would have been able to hear, maybe even see, the guards as they marched towards St Thomas's Tower, there to lead the fallen Duke of Northumberland from his prison. His scheming, plotting, ruthless ambition, and ultimate betrayal of the Protestant faith had all culminated in this. He had been hopeful that his conversion to Catholicism would save him, but it did not. His actions had merely delayed his end by a single day.[50] Northumberland was led out from the Tower for the final time 'under a strong guard', amid the vast and hostile crowd that had gathered to witness his final moments, and his death.[51] Indeed, 'the whole town of London concurred to attend to the spectacle', and Jane, as well as the Duke's incarcerated sons, would almost certainly have heard the noise and commotion from the rowdy Londoners who were baying for his blood.[52] Behind him came Sir John Gates and Sir Thomas Palmer, his former supporters who, like Northumberland, had been condemned to die.[53] Northumberland was the first to mount the scaffold; the same scaffold that, in an ironic twist of fate, 'was first put up for his father, who lost his head at the same place and on the same day forty-five years ago, for similar crimes and ambition'.[54]

Perhaps he was still hoping for the sight of a messenger bringing a last-minute reprieve from the Queen. If this was his hope, then it was in vain. Nevertheless, with just moments to live, his last words were spent on professing his devotion to the Catholic Church to which he had so recently converted, and advising the people to obey the Queen, 'whom I have intolerably offended'.[55] Unsurprisingly, he made no mention of Jane, or of his wife and children. Having uttered his final words he knelt down on the straw. Simon Renard, one of the Imperial ambassadors who became close to Queen Mary, rather exuberantly reported that after making the sign of the cross, '[Northumberland's] head was cut off in the presence of over fifty thousand people' who clamoured in approval as his severed head was held up by the executioner.[56]

From her room, Jane would have been able to hear the deafening roar of the assembled crowd as her father-in-law's head was struck from his body. But to Jane's mind his punishment had only just begun, for in consequence of his abandonment of Protestantism, he was now destined to burn in the raging flames of Hell. She was unperturbed; for her, death at the hands of the headsman's axe was a fate with which she was already chillingly familiar: four years earlier her guardian, Sir Thomas Seymour, had lost his head at the same site on which Northumberland had drawn his last breath.

Though Northumberland's widow was distraught at the loss of her husband, and his children too doubtless mourned him, his violent death did not mellow Jane's feelings towards him.[57] On Tuesday 29 August, Northumberland had been dead for a week. That same evening, Rowland Lea paid a visit to his friend Master Partridge in the Tower. As he arrived at Partridge's house near Tower Green to dine with his friend and his wife, he discovered that Partridge's charge, Lady Jane, was also joining them. Jane had already placed herself at the head of the table as her rank demanded, and was accompanied by one of her ladies and her manservant.[58] Lea recalled that Jane, perhaps eager to restore an element of normality to the situation, insisted that he and Partridge 'put on our caps', and 'once or twice drunk to me and bade me heartily welcome'.[59] Jane, it seems, was enjoying the company, and in the long days of her lonely imprisonment, human communication was more precious to her than ever. As she chatted, in a peak of gratitude towards her royal cousin she cried, 'the queen's grace is a merciful princess; I beseech God she may long continue and send his bountiful grace upon her'. [60] This confirms that Jane had been informed of the Queen's intentions to spare her life, and perhaps one day her freedom. Her relief at the mercy shown to her by Mary was genuine, and heartfelt. As the conversation continued, the

subject fell upon 'matters of religion'.[61] On 18 August Mary had issued
a proclamation in which she claimed that she would make no attempt to
enforce Catholicism on her people until Parliament met, but Jane knew
that 'the Queen is so Catholic that it is held for certain that her Highness
will have no regard to heretical knaves', and was therefore wary of Mary's
ultimate intentions.[62] Perhaps with this in mind Jane continued to enquire
as to what had been preached at St Paul's Cross recently.[63] 'I pray you,' she
asked, 'have they mass in London?' Lea replied that 'in some places' the
Mass, so closely associated with Catholicism and banned by King Edward,
had indeed been restored.[64] Jane answered that she was not so surprised
by that, as by the conversion of Northumberland to that faith. 'Perchance
he thereby hoped to have had his pardon,' Lea responded. On hearing this,
Jane's feelings spilled over into angry words and she made no attempt to
hide her fury. 'Pardon? Woe worth him!' she exclaimed. 'He hath brought
me and our stock [family] in most miserable calamity and misery by his
exceeding ambition.'[65] Even his death had not mellowed Jane's feelings
towards her father-in-law, and the intensity of her dislike became clear as
she continued:

> *Like as his life was wicked and full of dissimulation, so was his end
> thereafter. I pray God, I, nor no friend of mine, die so. Should I, who
> (am) young and in my few years, forsake my faith for the love of
> life? Nay, God forbid! Much more he should not, whose fatal course,
> although he had lived his just number of years, could not have long
> continued.*[66]

The message was simple: in Jane's mind, her father-in-law had risked his
immortal soul for the preservation of his earthly body. It was unforgivable
in the eyes of God, for as she continued, '"Whoso denieth him before men,
he will not know him in his Father's kingdom."'[67] Her words, spoken
with such conviction, astonished her fellow diners; here was a girl aged

seventeen who proclaimed that her devotion to her faith was so profound that she would rather die than forsake it. More than that, she abhorred anyone who was not prepared to do the same, and was becoming increasingly intolerant of those with opposing religious views. For Jane, her religion was her life, and Northumberland's betrayal was, in her eyes, an abominable mistake from which there could be no redemption. If ever the opportunity arose, she was determined to show as much dedication to her religious beliefs as her idols had done.

Though, at present, death seemed like an unlikely conclusion for Jane, Mary was still under immense pressure to have both her and Guildford executed. Thus far she had spared their lives, but Jane was still referred to as 'the usurper'.[68] It remained to be seen whether Jane would escape from the Tower's clutches alive.

CHAPTER 18

Justice is an Excellent Virtue

'ALTHOUGH THE QUEEN'S clemency is worthy of praise, yet it will be well that she take care not to exercise it so as to prejudice the establishment of her reign.'[1] The Queen's cousin, the Emperor Charles V, admired Mary's leniency in sparing the lives of most of those who had been involved in the summer coup, but he knew that there were limits.[2] Nevertheless, Mary had executed the Duke of Northumberland, and was beginning to act against those whose religious beliefs were in contrast to her own. New prisoners were still arriving at the Tower, all of them believed to be Protestant heretics. Bishop Hugh Latimer had been brought to the Tower, 'there to remain a close prisoner', closely followed by the Archbishop of Canterbury, Thomas Cranmer, who was lodged 'where the duke of Northumberland lie before his death'.[3] With the support of her cousin the Emperor, Mary had even taken the first steps towards restoring Catholicism to her realm. They had been subtle at first: on 9 August 'the Queen held an obsequy for the King [Edward VI] within the church in the Tower, her Grace being present, and had a solemn dirge sung in Latin', while the following day, Mass had been held there, for which 'the Catholics showed additional joy, and the heretics great dejection'.[4] The Mass had been 'utterly disowned' by Mary's half-brother – and Jane too, who almost certainly heard, if not saw the Queen entering the chapel from her room near Tower Green, would have been horrified.[5] By 1 September the Protestant Bishop John Hooper was writing from his prison that 'The altars are again set up throughout the kingdom; private

215

masses are frequently celebrated in many quarters; the true worship of God, true invocation, the right use of the sacraments, are all done away with.'[6] It was clear which way the wind was blowing. However, even the Pope had urged Mary to tread carefully, for though many of the English people had found the religious reforms of Edward VI too stringent, they were also fearful of change.

Though wildly different in both character and tastes, Jane and Mary shared a common bond aside from the royal blood which flowed in their veins: their religious devotion was unswerving, and the dominant factor in both of their lives. For Mary, the situation was heartbreaking. Jane's mother, Frances, had been a close childhood companion. Frances, like her husband and her daughter, was a Protestant, though perhaps not as fervent in her faith as her husband and eldest daughter. Despite the fact that she and Mary were on opposing sides of the religious fence, to all appearances their differing beliefs had never driven a wedge between the cousins. Frances was a seasoned courtier, and as such was well skilled in the art of diplomacy. It seems likely, therefore, that when she was in the company of her childhood friend, the two women tactfully avoided conversing on the subject of religion. After all, there were many at court who managed to maintain friendships with people who held differing religious beliefs, and Mary had also been friendly with Jane's step-grandmother, Katherine Willoughby. But it was quite different with Jane, for though Mary had tried her best with the teenager, and had done her utmost to be affectionate, the relationship was not a harmonious one. The age gap between them meant that to Jane, Mary was probably more like an aunt than a cousin. Mary may have been twenty years Jane's senior, but it was not age that lay at the heart of the matter; the reason for the distance between the two cousins was perfectly simple: religion.

QUEEN MARY WAS determined to stamp out the religious changes established by her predecessor, and return England to the folds of the

Catholic Church in Rome. Despite her declaration that she would do nothing until Parliament met, the Mass for King Edward's soul had been just the first step. Already, however, Mary's moves towards religious change caused 'prolonged trouble', for many of her people 'took it very ill that their factious religion should be destroyed', and were against the idea of England falling once again under the authority of the Pope.[7] When she realized that 'the minds of men were dizzy from the sudden alteration in religion', though set on her course, for the moment Mary turned her attention elsewhere. In an attempt to distract her subjects by giving them a cause to relive the joy they felt at her succession, Mary set a date for her coronation.[8]

On 1 October, Mary achieved what Jane never had: she became the first Queen Regnant of England to be crowned in Westminster Abbey. Four days after the coronation, the first Parliament of Mary's reign met at Westminster. Immediately the Act of Repeal was passed, which dissolved all of the religious laws passed by Edward VI. Mary was intent on the destruction of the Protestant nation that the boy king had been determined to build, and that Jane would have continued to strengthen. At the same time, the marriage of her parents was declared to be lawful and valid, thus confirming Mary's own legitimacy. She was furious, however, when Jane's father Henry, to whom she had been so bountiful, continued to try her patience. The precise nature of his complaint is unclear, but it is probable that he had voiced opinions about his abhorrence for Catholicism that it was wisest to keep quiet about, for Renard reported that 'the Duke of Suffolk is doing bad work in connection with religion, and the Queen is angry with him for his manner of abusing her clemency and good nature'.[9] Henry's timing was certainly poor, and continued to place Jane's future in jeopardy. He had clearly learned nothing from the example of Guildford's mother, the Duchess of Northumberland, whom it had been observed 'is doing her utmost to secure a pardon for her children; so far we have not heard that the Queen has taken any resolve'.[10]

Before her coronation had even taken place, though, Mary, whose authority had suffered due to her clemency that 'people have come to judge her actions so freely that they go so far as to laugh', had made a momentous and agonizing decision regarding Jane's future.[11] Thus far she had been merciful, and perhaps in an attempt to neutralize the perceived threat that Jane's royal blood caused and avoid having to give orders for her execution, on 4 November Mary sought another way out. Renard informed the Emperor that 'the Duke of Suffolk's children have been found to be bastards, because he had been betrothed *per verba de presenti* to the Earl of Arundel's sister before taking the Lady Frances to wife'.[12] Henry's previous betrothal had been well known, but this was the first occasion on which the validity of his marriage to Jane's mother had ever been questioned.

The issue was still the subject of talk on 28 November, when Renard recalled a conversation he had shared with the Queen in relation to her possible successors. According to Renard, the possible candidates were Mary, Queen of Scots, 'the Lady Frances, wife of the Duke of Suffolk, who would also have a claim if the Queen of Scotland were excluded as having been born abroad', and the Lady Elizabeth.[13] That Frances was considered a potential successor at this point is testimony not only to her relationship with Queen Mary, but also to the fact that she was considered to have a strong claim, despite being overlooked in Henry VIII's will. Ultimately, however, it was acknowledged that Mary, Queen of Scots, had the best claim, for 'the marriage of the said Frances with the Duke of Suffolk had been rather a concubinage than a marriage' on account of Henry's previous betrothal.[14] In other words, the marriage of Jane's parents was considered to be invalid and their daughters illegitimate, rendering any claim they had to the throne void. Whatever the motivation behind the issue, no further mention was ever made on the subject – certainly no Act of Parliament ever officially declared the Suffolks' marriage illegitimate. However, it may have played some part in shaping Henry's actions in the coming months.

Still under pressure to do more to punish Jane, Mary decided that justice must be seen to have taken its course. She had therefore resolved that Jane, together with her husband and his four brothers, must be 'tried and sentenced to receive capital punishment for the crimes they have committed'.[15] It is clear that Mary had no wish to see her young cousin die, and the trial may therefore have been intended as no more than a formality, after which Jane could resume her imprisonment. After all, it was a queen's prerogative to show mercy, and it was one that Mary intended to use.

It is unclear precisely when Jane was informed that she was to face this most harrowing ordeal, or how she reacted. After all, Mary had indicated that she would be given her life, and in time her liberty, thus the thought of standing trial, though not wholly unexpected, may still have come as something of a shock. As Jane contemplated the chilling prospect of her trial and what lay ahead, she would have been all too aware that in the past she had caused Mary so much humiliation and annoyance. But Mary had a kind heart and had refused the advice of her Councillors, several of whom had urged her to take Jane's life in order to secure her own safety. As Jane now faced a perilous trial, her only hope of survival lay in Mary's previous inclination to clemency. Nevertheless, she was well aware that many of those who stood trial did not survive the consequences. The stage had been set.

THERE WAS A chill in the air on the morning of Monday 13 November, which did not stem purely from the winter weather or the breeze that came from the Thames. Jane was dressed from head to toe in black, unintentionally reflecting the solemnity of the occasion. Her 'black gown of cloth' was covered with a velvet-lined cape to protect against the weather; 'a French hood, all black, with a black billement', and 'a black velvet book hanging before her', emphasized Jane's image as a sober Protestant gentlewoman. On this day all eyes would fall on Jane as she finally received judgement for the crimes of which she had been accused – it was the day of her trial.[16] Within the precincts of the Tower that morning, Jane was reunited with Guildford. It was almost certainly the first time that the young couple had seen one another since their imprisonment, but there was no time to talk had they wished to, for they were not alone. It had been determined that two of Guildford's brothers, Ambrose and Harry, as well as Thomas Cranmer, would join them.[17] It would prove to be a humiliatingly public occasion.

The setting for the scene of justice had been chosen carefully. Not for Jane the same Westminster Hall that had seen the condemnation of her father-in-law and that was frequently chosen for peers of the realm, but instead the infinitely closer Guildhall. Traditionally, Guildhall had been the long-established headquarters for the administration of the government of the City of London, and it was therefore an appropriate location for the trial of one who had tried to establish her own government in the city. Moreover, it was an acknowledgement of the fact that the men tried alongside Jane were commoners, and that she was also to be treated as such. The Great Hall in Guildhall had been prepared for the day's events. In days long past the hall had hosted a number of joyous occasions. It had once been the setting for the entertainment of Jane's ancestors King Henry V and his Queen, Katherine of Valois, by the Mayor of London, Dick Whittington, whose escutcheons were blazoned on to the windows. But on this day, there were no echoes of that revelry, only the memories of those who had been condemned, and of those whose fates were as of yet undecided.

As the guards gathered within the Tower precincts ready to escort their charges, the sombre party were 'led out of the Tower on foot, to be arraigned, to Guildhall, with the axe before them' as was traditional in treason trials.[18] The blade of the axe was turned away from the five accused in the smallest gesture that they were not yet condemned. According to

Florio, who may have been there to witness it first-hand, there were 400 halberdiers on duty, but nobody made a sound as the prisoners were all led separately from their prison.[19] The Constable of the Tower, Sir John Gage, was responsible for escorting the prisoners, and ensuring that they arrived 'safe and sound' at their destination: Cranmer came first, followed by Guildford, and then Jane.[20] She was accompanied by 'her two gentlewomen following her', while Ambrose and Harry came behind.[21] Aside from Cranmer, who was sixty-four, all of the prisoners were in the first flush of youth, and made for a truly tragic sight.

They all walked the single mile from the Tower to Guildhall, crowds lining the way to stare in what had been a planned attempt at humiliation. As they passed through the narrow streets of London, the axe in front of them, the Londoners who had recently proved themselves so hostile to Jane's queenship watched. Jane was now deposed, and as they looked upon her, the citizens may have felt pity. She was, after all, only a girl, and one who was frail in body, if not in spirit, from the months of imprisonment.[22] Jane seems to have barely noticed the crowds, for her mind had become lost in the 'book in her hand open', which she read from as she made her journey.[23] Jane's piety would never leave her, for even now, when she had every reason for her mind to be focused elsewhere, her thoughts were on God and her faith. This was how she wanted to be seen by the people – and remembered.

The walk was over all too quickly, and soon the sight of the imposing fifteenth-century façade with its pointed turrets and the statues of Christ and four noble and pious ladies came into view.[24] Perhaps for a moment, Jane's thoughts turned to others who had stood trial in the same building: the lovers of her great-uncle's treacherous fifth wife, Queen Katherine Howard; Henry Howard, Earl of Surrey, condemned for treason and the last man of Henry VIII's reign to be executed; and more poignantly for Jane, the young female Protestant martyr, Anne Askew. All had been condemned, and all had received the death penalty as a result of their crimes. But for Jane, the circumstances were different, for until now 'the Queen full of bounty and mercy' had indicated that she would live, and she would still have been hopeful that this was the case.[25] As Jane entered the gloomy stone walls she walked past the statue of Jesus Christ, and an assortment of other imposing statues of those who had associations with Guildhall in times long gone.

The accused were led up the steps to the Great Hall, the largest room in the building at 152 feet long, with walls that were five feet thick. Displaying a floor paved with Purbeck stone, a high vaulted ceiling and large windows, the hall was an imposing sight. Jane would also have recognized the statues of Gog and Magog, the two giants, traditional guardians of the City of London, which adorned the room to which she was led.[26]

Silence had been called as Jane and the four men were led into the room, the axe still carried alongside them. The trial was a public occasion, and though no mention is made of the number of people present, it almost certainly numbered over a thousand.[27] The gallery was packed with spectators, watching and listening in eager anticipation. At the opposite end of the hall, facing Jane and the accused men, were those who had been appointed by the Queen 'to hear and examine them and any one of them, and force them to respond, and to trial, terminate and adjudged them to the due end'.[28] The hall had probably been set up in a similar fashion to that at Westminster for the trial of Northumberland, where it was observed that there was a stage, 'very majestic and richly tapestried, and in the midst of it a rich canopy, and under this a bench with rich cushions, and carpets at its foot'.[29]

The familiar face of the old Duke of Norfolk stood out to Jane. As Earl Marshal holding 'a long white wand', Mary's 'most beloved kinsman and counsellor' had presided over numerous trials over the years, including that of his own niece Anne Boleyn, and had once more been called upon to ensure that justice prevailed alongside 'his said fellow Justices'.[30] Another prominent gentleman, the Lord Mayor of London, Mary's 'beloved and faithful' Thomas White, was in his sixties, and alongside him sat fourteen others – a mixture of lords and commoners, who had been appointed by the Queen 'with full and sufficient power and authority and a special mandate to receive and investigate' the accused.[31] Among them were Edward Stanley, Earl of Derby; Henry Radcliffe, Earl of Sussex; John Bourchier, Earl of Bath; and eleven knights, including Mary's Chief Justice, Sir Richard Morgan. Significantly, they were all Catholic in sympathy, and furthermore, almost all of them were men who had come to Mary's aid during the tumultuous events of July.[32] They had received their orders from the Queen two days earlier, orders to which they had been instructed to 'apply yourself diligently', and Mary had assured her trusted panel that she had 'the utmost faith in your fidelity'; she believed that they would ensure that justice was done, for 'justice is an excellent virtue'.[33] The judges were all conscious of the severity of the case for they had all lived through, though not participated in, the recent doomed days of Jane's reign. And as men of experience they were surely already aware of the outcome of the day's proceedings. Jane, Guildford, his brothers, and Cranmer all 'stand indicted of various acts of high treason committed and perpetrated by them' – there were no higher charges in the land, and Mary had stipulated that 'when the truth has been thereby discovered and adjudged, then you should render it in this respect according to the laws, statutes, customs and ordinances of our kingdom of England, and proceed, pass sentence and judgement' against the accused.[34] The 'truth' of the matter was that all of those who sat in judgement knew that they would that day be delivering a guilty verdict. Be that as it may, the sight of the accused may have caused some pause. Ambrose was in his early twenties, but Jane and Guildford had yet to reach the third decade of their lives, and Guildford's brother Harry was younger still.[35] Jane in particular, dressed from head to toe in penitent black, cut a striking figure. She was a woman alone among men; it was a scenario that she had experienced time and again throughout the short course of her life, and one that she was now used to. Nevertheless she was seventeen years old, and was standing trial for her life. Jane was well accustomed to being used as an instrument in the games of older men, but never before had the consequences been so critical.

As Norfolk sat on the chair of estate indicating that he was in overall charge of the proceedings, the accused were 'led to the bar here in their own persons' by Sir John Gage.[36] All of the accused were forced to stand – Jane was not to be granted the same courtesy of rank that had been accorded to Anne Boleyn, who had been allowed to sit during her trial. Jane was the second Queen of England to stand trial for her life, but the manner in which it was conducted made it abundantly clear that she was not to be tried or treated as such – she was quite simply Jane Dudley, wife of Guildford, and was referred to in this way throughout the proceedings.[37]

Under the gaze of the spectators, a hush descended as the charges against the accused were read out. This was the first occasion on which Jane and those alongside her had heard the full extent of the crimes of which they stood accused, and it made for harrowing listening. By 'falsely and treacherously' raising 'Jane Dudley, wife of the same Guildford Dudley' to the 'position, title and power of the Queen of this kingdom of England' they had attempted to 'deprive their due mistress, the Queen [Mary], their supreme ruler, of her royal status, title, order and power of her kingdom of England, and destroy the Queen herself with finality'.[38] The charges were grave, not least for the venom with which they were read out. Though they had yet to make their plea and hear their judgement, already they were told that they were 'traitors and rebels against the most illustrious ruler, Mary'.[39] They were berated as the court heard how Jane and Guildford had entered the Tower on 10 July and 'then took possession of it falsely and treacherously, and against the said Queen and her will forcibly held it', before 'the same Jane then and there falsely and treacherously assumed and took up for herself the title and power of the Queen of this kingdom of England'.[40] In a move to further demonstrate

Jane's role in the matter, the court heard how she had 'signed various writings in her own hand by the following words in English: Jane the Queen'.[41] In addition, Guildford was accused of 'falsely and treacherously helping, aiding, abetting and assisting the said Jane, against his due diligence, and against the peace of the Queen, her crown and dignity'.[42] There was barely time for Jane and those in the hall to absorb fully the severity of the charges against them before the defendants were expected to make their pleas. No witnesses were brought against them, neither was there anyone to speak in their defence; in cases of treason this was strictly prohibited. There was not even an opportunity for the accused to speak in their own defence, and in any case they had been given no opportunity to prepare one.

As those on the judging panel listened, and the spectators strained to hear, the accused were asked to deliver their pleas. Jane was given a brief respite, for it was Cranmer whom the court addressed first. However, he caused an outcry when he said 'that he is no respect culpable' of the crimes of which he was accused.[43] While certain members of the panel retired to 'speak among themselves' regarding his claim, the rest of those in the hall waited in anxious anticipation. The atmosphere was unbearably tense, but they were not kept waiting for long. When the panel returned, certain 'pieces of evidence' were 'given here in the court publicly and openly' against Cranmer. Whatever the 'evidence' was, it did the trick; Cranmer changed his plea. He admitted that he 'is guilty as charged', and 'expressly acknowledged those acts of treason'.[44]

Cranmer had admitted his sins, and now all eyes turned to Jane and Guildford. Would they too acknowledge their crimes? Those in the court waited in suspense to hear how Jane and Guildford would plea. They stood together on charges of high treason: charges that, if they were found guilty of them, could have terrifying consequences for both. Just six months earlier, the couple had stood side by side at the marital altar. Never in their worst nightmares could they have predicted how drastically, and how quickly, circumstances would change for them.

As Jane and Guildford stood on trial for their lives, they were both in the same dire peril. In just a matter of months they had been married and given the briefest taste of eminence, only for it to be snatched away. This had resulted in imprisonment, and a trial for crimes of which they were primarily innocent. In spite of all this, Jane barely knew the husband who stood by her side. Those in the courtroom now listened as she and Guildford delivered their pleas: guilty, or not guilty?

THERE WAS SILENCE in the courtroom; the atmosphere was tense as everyone waited. Then, 'the said Guildford Dudley and Jane his wife, Ambrose Dudley and Henry Dudley charged with each and every one of the said acts of treason' were 'asked how they wish to acquit themselves'.[45] This was the moment: the evidence against Jane and the Dudley brothers was compelling, but with Cranmer's turncoat example before them, there was no telling how they would plead. In addition, Jane had already made it clear to the Queen that 'although I accepted that of which I was not worth, I never sought it'.[46] The judges and the spectators waited, and one by one, in a courageous and brave declaration that sealed their fates by the terms of the law, all four defendants

> [s]aid that they cannot deny that they themselves supported the acts of high treason being carried out by themselves, and are each charged above in the said form, are guilty, and each expressly acknowledged these acts of treason, and each therefore placed themselves at the mercy of the Queen.[47]

Jane had pleaded guilty. Despite her protestations to Mary that she had been manipulated, Jane had also acknowledged that she 'should not have accepted' the crown, and that she considered this to be such 'a crime' that she was ashamed to be 'begging to be pardoned'.[48] That she did so confirms that, in her eyes, she was guilty in deed if not in thought. As she uttered the words, along with Guildford and his brothers, she knew that there could only be one outcome, and one verdict. 'Each of them has individually' and resignedly 'acknowledged the said acts of treason of which they were individually charged', and so they waited, knowing but not yet hearing what the judgement cast upon them would be.[49] It must have been a painful admission for Jane, for none of the events of the summer had been of her own making, yet it was she who was forced to face the consequences. There was no eluding the terror of the situation in which Jane and Guildford now found themselves. Thus far, the most testing day of Jane's life had been her wedding day, but it was nothing compared to this.

'Guildford Dudley and Jane his wife', Cranmer, Ambrose, and Harry 'have expressly acknowledged the said acts of treason of which they were individually charged above, and each of them has individually expressly acknowledged them according to due form of law'.[50] They had admitted their guilt, and as such, knew that the result was inevitable: 'indictment and execution'.[51] It had been a foregone conclusion, for in her earlier instructions to the judging panel, Queen Mary had asserted that once the truth had been discovered, 'their execution should be ordered to take place, and you should do, exercise and carry out each and every other thing that is pertinent and required in this respect'.[52]

Those who observed may have watched for signs of distress, but there were none. There was barely time for breath, either for the guilty party or for the spectators, before the Duke of Norfolk read out their brutal sentence. The men heard their fates first. Guildford, his brothers and Cranmer were informed that

> [e]ach of them should so be dragged, and there hung and each of them hung, and laid out rotting on the ground, and their interior organs

should be brought outside their stomachs, and as these rot they should be burned. And their heads should be cut off, and their bodies, and those of any of them, should be divided into four quarters, and their heads and quarters should be placed where the Queen wishes them to be assigned.[53]

The appalling violence of the sentence was sickening, but it was not over. Jane's turn was next, and in the same manner that he had done for his niece Anne Boleyn, Norfolk now read her punishment aloud to the court:

The said Jane be led off by the said Constable [Sir John Gage] of the said Tower of London to the prison of the said Queen within the same Tower, and then on the order of the Queen herself led to Tower Hill and there burned, or the head cut off, as it will then please the Queen.[54]

Jane and Guildford 'were there condemned to death' in what must have been a terrifying experience for the two young teenagers.[55] But rather than being paralysed with fear, Jane showed no emotion when she heard the full extent of her sentence, and retained her composure and calm demeanour. Perhaps because she hoped that Queen Mary would show mercy; perhaps because she was in shock; or perhaps because she had prepared herself and was able to keep her feelings within. As the axe blade slowly turned towards the four men and Jane in a sign that they had all been condemned, the outcome of the day's proceedings may have dawned on her: she had been found guilty of high treason, and she was a condemned traitor. All of her royal blood, all of her meticulous scholarly studies, had been in vain, for even if she were granted a reprieve, what hope did the future now hold for her? The stigma of treason would stick, and she would always be a target for dissenters. There was nothing more to be said, and nothing that could be done – shockwaves resonated around the Great Hall at Guildhall as Lady Jane Grey became the youngest woman of her time to be condemned for high treason: a sentence of death loomed and the axe was poised, ready to fall.

CHAPTER 19

Fear Not for Any Pain

G OSSIP WAS CIRCULATING in the city. People whispered in the inns and stews, for it was thought that the Lady Jane Grey, lately Queen Jane, must surely die. She had been condemned at Guildhall alongside her husband; it was only a matter of time. Following their trial, Jane and Guildford, together with the three men found guilty beside them, had been led out from the Great Hall of Guildhall, back through the streets of the city to the Tower once more. This time, the blade of the axe was turned towards them in a chilling display for the citizens, who could see the penalty for traitors.

However, no date had yet been set for the executions and it was possible that it might never be. Despite the annoyance caused by Jane's father and Queen Mary's formal instructions to Jane's judges, she appeared to be true to her original promise of mercy. Renard had heard that 'when execution is to take place is uncertain, for though the Queen is truly irritated against the Duke of Suffolk, it is believed that Jane will not die'.[1] Jane, Guildford, his brothers and Cranmer all resumed their separate imprisonment, and their daily lives as Tower prisoners continued.[2] On the surface, little had changed.

Jane's future had, for many months, seemed racked with anxious uncertainty, but following the court's verdict one thing was now certain: she was a convicted traitor, and no matter what clemency Mary showed her, it was a permanent taint on her name. More alarmingly, now that Jane had been pronounced guilty, all it took was one wrong move in the future and the Queen could order her execution. The axe may have been suspended, but it still hung indefinitely and hauntingly above her.

------⁘------

DURING THE DARK days of her imprisonment, disturbing news reached Jane. Her first tutor, Dr Thomas Harding, who had also once been a chaplain at Bradgate, had chosen, following in the footsteps of Jane's father-in-law, the occasion of Queen Mary's accession to distance himself from the faith he had professed all of his life. Much to Jane's revulsion, Harding had converted to Catholicism.[3] According to Foxe, when Jane was informed,

> [b]eing not a little aggrieved, and most of all lamenting the dangerous state of his soul, in sliding so away for fear from the way of truth, writeth her mind unto him in a sharp and vehement letter: which, as it appeareth to proceed of an earnest and zealous heart, so would God it might take such effect with him, as to reduce him to repentance, and to take better hold again for the health and wealth of his own soul.[4]

Jane took up her pen, and wrote to Harding in such a harsh manner that centuries later the Victorians were convinced that the letter must be a forgery, so far distant was it from the image of the gentle and tragic heroine whom they revered. Jane's words were indeed shocking: 'I cannot but marvel at thee, and lament thy case,' Jane began,

> which seemed sometime to be the lively member of Christ, but now the deformed imp of the devil; sometime the beautiful temple of God, but now the stinking and filthy kennel of Satan; sometime the unspotted spouse of Christ, but now the unshamefaced paramour of antichrist; sometime my faithful brother, but now a stranger and apostate; sometime a stout Christian soldier, but now a cowardly runaway.[5]

Jane was appalled that her former co-religionist had turned his back on what she perceived to be the true faith. Likewise, she was amazed at the level of hypocrisy her former family chaplain was demonstrating. 'Wherefore past thou instructed others to be strong in Christ, when thou thyself dost now so shamefully shrink, and so horribly abuse the testament and law of the Lord?' she berated him.

In what was undoubtedly a reflection of her own state of mind and emotions at this time, as she clung to her faith for strength, she asked Harding,

> Why dost thou now show thyself most weak, when indeed thou oughtest to be most strong? The strength of a fort is unknown before the assault, but thou yieldest thy hold before any battery be made. O wretched and unhappy man, what art thou, but dust and ashes?

In an attempt to convince the chaplain of his mistake, and echoing sentiments that she herself would later emulate, Jane reminded him of 'the saying of Christ in his gospel: Whosoever seeketh to save his life, shall lose it: but whosoever will lose his life for my sake, shall find it. And in the same place, whosoever loveth father or mother above me, is not meet for me.'[6] These were powerful words, and Jane's letter ended with a final petition to him to show strength: 'Be constant, be constant; fear not for any pain: Christ hath redeemed thee, and heaven is thy gain.'[7] Her words to Harding were more than a reassurance to the chaplain: they are an insight into her own devotion to her faith.

Though the authenticity of the letter has been questioned, it is undoubtedly genuine. In his message to Bullinger in March 1554, John Banks referred to Jane's letter 'to a certain apostate, to bring him back to Christ the Lord', and enclosed a copy.[8] The words reveal the extent of Jane's belief and show how her faith had shaped her life. It was with sincerity that Banks continued to inform Bullinger, 'your excellence may perceive that the pains which you have taken to enlighten that family and incite them to the love of godliness have not been ill bestowed'.[9] Jane's words to Harding had been brutal, but were a reflection of the fact that despite her youth, she would never renounce her faith for hope of earthly life. Her beliefs, as she would soon prove, were unshakeable. She believed unswervingly in 'the shield of faith'.[10]

--------⁂--------

IT SEEMS LIKELY that it was Jane's condemnation that prompted her father to take drastic action in an attempt to win Queen Mary's favour, for just four days after her trial, Renard made an astonishing revelation: 'The Duke of Suffolk has made his confession as to religion.'[11] Henry had, apparently, forsaken everything in which he had so steadfastly believed and promoted. His devotion to Protestantism had been as celebrated as Jane's, but not, so it appeared, as enduring. His actions directly contradicted the opinion of Northumberland's former chaplain, John Hooper, who had once noted that Henry was 'pious, good, and brave, and distinguished in the cause of Christ'.[12] Nevertheless, his outward show of conformity to the Catholic faith appeared to have the desired effect, for Queen Mary, thrilled at this apparent reconciliation with the old religion, immediately 'reinstated him by means of a general pardon'.[13] His actions also had direct consequences for Jane, for in the same report Renard related, 'As for Jane, I am told that her life is safe, though several people are trying to encompass her death.'[14] However, it would soon become strikingly clear that Henry's protestations in terms of religion were only surface deep. Perhaps Queen Mary hoped that Jane would follow her father's example, but though she almost certainly heard of her father's momentous decision, Jane remained silent. Instead she waited, anxious to see whether her unlikely champion Queen Mary would spare her. As each day in the Tower brought her no closer to freedom, there was nothing else for Jane to do to distract herself from the enormity of her situation but to immerse herself in one of the few things that brought her any pleasure: her studies.

The high expectations once placed on Jane's young shoulders now seemed a world away as she sat reading her books in her Tower lodgings. According to Florio, much of her time was occupied by reading from the pages of her Bible, 'the sacred books'.[15] This familiar pastime no doubt brought comfort to her, and perhaps restored an element of stability to her otherwise frightening situation. John Foxe would later write,

> *If her fortune had been as good as was her bringing up, joined with finesse of wit: undoubtedly she might have seemed comparable, not only to the house of the Vespasian's, Sempronian's, and mother of the Grachie's, yea, to any other women beside that desired high praise for their singular learning: but also to the university men, which have taken many degrees of the schools.*[16]

Though Jane was not forgotten, her father's shock revelation in regards to religion meant that her fate was no longer a current priority for the Queen. Almost immediately after Mary's succession, thoughts had turned to her marriage. At thirty-seven, she was considered old to be making a first marriage by contemporary standards, especially as she was also eager to produce children: Catholic heirs to reign long after her. Several potential candidates were suggested, including the recently freed Edward Courtenay, and of particular interest to Jane, her paternal uncle, Thomas Grey. It was observed that Thomas 'so outshines Courtenay that Courtenay dares not show himself when the other is present', and despite the earlier behaviour of his brother he was held in high favour by Mary.[17] Desperate to win back Queen Mary's favour, Henry and his former ally the Earl of Huntingdon were, according to Renard, 'professing undying loyalty and saying that she may marry whom she pleases, for they will maintain, honour and obey her choice'.[18]

However, it became clear that Mary had no intention of marrying within her realm, for she cherished hopes of marriage with another: 'it was soon learned that the Queen was inclining in favour of the Prince'.[19] The Prince in question was the son of Mary's cousin the Emperor Charles V, Philip of Spain. As the nephew of Katherine of Aragon, Charles had been Mary's mother's most steadfast champion during the trying days of her annulment case. Similarly, Mary had at one time been betrothed to her royal cousin, and it had always been the dearest wish of Mary's mother that her daughter should marry into her Spanish family. Since the death of Katherine of Aragon, Mary too had shared a close relationship with the Emperor, despite the fact that she had only met him once in childhood. She too cherished a wish to marry a Spaniard, and though Charles was unavailable, his son was not. At twenty-six, Philip was eleven years Mary's junior, but when his magnificent portrait, completed by the famous Italian artist Titian, was sent to her in September, she soon fell in love with it. She wrote to her cousin the Emperor gushing that 'I was glad to receive because of my affection for the person represented.'[20] Her feelings towards the comely likeness, with its piercing blue eyes, brown beard and moustache, and slightly protruding lower lip that was typical of his family, were already intense. However, Mary's personal feelings of desire were of little concern to her subjects. The idea of the Queen marrying a Spaniard was extremely unpopular, for many feared that Philip would attempt to embroil England in foreign wars, while others were afraid that as an ardent Catholic like Mary, England would once more be overwhelmed and enveloped further into the clutches of the Catholic Church and the Pope in Rome. Though Mary was undoubtedly popular, by the time of her succession people had accepted the break from the Church of Rome and sovereign authority in England, and were fearful of change. With a Spanish prince by her side, there was apprehension that Mary would be persuaded to retract her promise not to force Catholicism on her people, and that papal authority would be restored.

Mary, though, chose to follow her heart and her faith, and ignoring the concerns of her people, she resolved to pursue the marriage. Accordingly, the terms were sent from Spain for the approval of the Queen and her Council, but there were whispers of dissension from those who were unhappy, for it 'caused dissatisfaction in many quarters as it was shown shortly afterwards'.[21] Though Jane was in the Tower, she almost certainly heard of the Queen's plans for matrimony to a foreign Catholic prince. Like Mary's subjects, she was probably appalled by Mary's choice, but her own situation demanded her undivided attention. She had been through a lot, but it seemed likely that she would survive the dangerous web of intrigue in which she had become hopelessly entangled. Despite the chilling outcome of her trial, the fact that Mary had made no attempt to implement her sentence may have convinced Jane to hope that her life was safe, and thus at present she perhaps gave little thought to the Queen's marriage. Little did she know that it would prove to have far-reaching, and permanent consequences for her.

---ᴖᴖᴖᴖ---

Liberty of the Tower

A S THE DAYS passed by and November turned into December, 'the day of Christmas as celebrated in our lands was approaching', and the conditions of Jane's imprisonment in the Tower were relaxed.[1] Sir John Brydges had been appointed Lieutenant of the Tower in August with his brother Thomas to assist him, and already Sir John had become extremely fond of Jane.[2] To outward appearances this was surprising, for Sir John was an ardent Catholic whom Jane's supporters had, in the past, tried unsuccessfully to rally to her cause. However, he was a kindly man, in his early sixties, and quickly discovered that he liked and admired his young ward. Sir John visited Jane in her rooms, and she too may have been invited to the Lieutenant's Lodgings, which were close to her own. While in her company, Sir John encouraged Jane to look positively towards the future and to hope for a pardon and freedom; though inwardly this was what she had every reason to expect, to the Lieutenant she simply replied that her mind was occupied only by thoughts of heaven.[3] Nevertheless, she was heartened by 'all hope of life'.[4]

On 17 December Sir John received instructions from the Council,

[w]illing him at convenient times by his discretion to suffer the late Duke of Northumberland's children to have the liberty of walk within the garden of the Tower, and also to minister the like favour to the Lady Jane and Doctor Cranmer, upon suggestion that divers of them be and have been evil at ease in their bodies for want of air.[5]

It is unsurprising that several months of close confinement had taken their toll among the prisoners. It is unclear if Jane specifically was suffering, but given that she had fallen ill on previous occasions, perhaps exacerbated by stress, it is certainly likely. Sir John implemented his orders immediately, and the following day Rowland Lea noted that 'the lady Jane had the liberty of the Tower, so that she might walk in the queen's garden and on the hill'.[6] This taste of freedom must have been exhilarating for Jane, but even as she walked on Tower Hill the sight of the Tower loomed large, a constant reminder that she was still a prisoner. Perhaps, as she stood close to the site where her father-in-law had lost his head, she was reminded that she too had been condemned to die on that same spot.

Guildford and his brother Robert had been moved to apartments in the Bell Tower, possibly due to the fact that apartments had recently become available there; with the four Dudley brothers lodging in the Beauchamp Tower, it had become somewhat cramped. Although there is no evidence that Guildford met with his wife during this time, given that the conditions of their confinement were improving it is perhaps possible. Jane had certainly been permitted the occasional visitor besides the kindly Lieutenant; according to Florio she was visited by 'noblewomen'.[7] The identities of these women are sadly unknown; one of them may have been her mother Frances, who had undoubtedly been concerned for her daughter's welfare. If this was the case, though, then it seems likely that Florio would have named her. More probable is that the 'noblewomen' were the wives of Sir John Brydges and his brother, for Sir John's wife was distantly related to Jane.[8]

If Jane's husband were among her visitors then their meetings would most certainly have been supervised. For Jane and Guildford there were to be none of the opportunities granted to his brothers John, Ambrose and Robert, whose wives were permitted to visit them in their prison quarters for private trysts.[9] Even if permission to meet had been granted, it is possible that Jane chose not to see her husband. After all, relations between them were hardly close, and she would later deny Guildford his request of a final meeting. Whether Jane communicated with her husband or not, Guildford could probably see her from a distance, for he too had been granted some leniency in his confinement. Lea observed that Guildford and Robert were given 'the liberty of the leads [flat lead roof] in the Bell Tower', allowing them to see beyond the Tower's menacing walls.[10]

Having been allowed these small freedoms, it must have felt like it was only a matter of time before it became a reality, especially as those incarcerated alongside them were beginning to be released. A few days before Christmas, William Parr, Marquess of Northampton, who had been tried and condemned beside Northumberland, 'had his pardon, and was delivered out of the Tower'.[11] Northampton was living proof that those who had been judged to die could evade execution. Yet freedom still eluded Jane and Guildford, and as the city of London began its celebrations for Christmas, it showed no signs of materializing.

Queen Mary's court had removed to the splendid Richmond Palace for the festive season, where there were many reasons to be joyous. Foremost among them was that with God's help Mary had triumphed over her enemies, and was now reigning supreme over her kingdom. On 15 December a proclamation for the re-establishment of the Mass was made: the true religion of Catholicism would be restored throughout the land. It was observed that 'all the services began again in Latin in all the churches through the Queen's dominions by Act of Parliament', and placards announcing the religious changes were posted across the country.[12] It took some time for these to infiltrate across the whole country, but in London Renard reported that generally 'there seem to be no signs of protest, such as were feared'.[13] There was, however, no news as of yet from the rest of the country, and when it came it was not good.

The Queen, though, was 'utterly delighted to embrace a Spanish marriage' with Prince Philip, and preparations were now well underway.[14] The Emperor had written to the Queen assuring her that marriage with his son 'will be instrumental in God's service, and of great profit to our realms and dominions'.[15] For Mary, the future was full of promise and hope:

> *Moreover, since this most honourable sovereign had no desire to conceal the betrothal, she caused Winchester [Stephen Gardiner, Bishop of Winchester], the Chancellor of England, to proclaim it throughout the realm, so that everyone might rejoice with their sovereign at this, the most splendid royal match since the Norman Conquest.*[16]

However, such joy was not shared among her subjects, for Renard had heard that 'the country-nobility and people are as hostile to the alliance as they are to the old religion'.[17] Despite Renard's claim that London seemed content with the changes, some 'heretics' in the city had already 'torn down' the placards posted in several places, and as a result 'ten or twelve of them were seized and two hanged'.[18] Though Jane's father claimed that he would support the Queen in her choice of a husband, Renard had heard rumours that Jane's paternal uncles, Lord Thomas and Lord John Grey, 'are conspiring to prevent his Highness from landing, though the only argument they have left against the alliance is that the Spanish will wish to govern'.[19] They were not alone, for the Queen had been warned that 'attacks, verbal and written, were being made against the Spaniards and the alliance in terms that rang with revolt'.[20] Nevertheless, Renard was still hopeful that 'his Highness may enter the realm in safety', but as a precautionary measure he advised the Emperor that it would be 'very opportune to make a few gifts of money in order to win over persons who might become dangerous'.[21] To make matters worse, 'every day that passed was revealing signs of a rebellious spirit in the country against the Act of Parliament on religion'.[22] The policies of Mary's reign, though still in their infancy, were already proving to be unpopular.

More alarming for Jane, perhaps, was the news that the Lady Elizabeth, the cousin she had so praised for her religious modesty, appeared to be outwardly conforming to the Catholic faith. Retiring from court for Christmas, Elizabeth, who 'makes a show of her great satisfaction with the Queen', had entreated Queen Mary to send her 'ornaments for her chapel: copes, chasubles, chalices, crosses, patens and other similar objects', and the Queen had graciously done so, 'as it was for God's service and Elizabeth wished to bear witness to the religion she had declared she meant to follow'.[23] In spite of this, Mary was suspicious of her half-sister, and Renard claimed that she 'recalls trouble and unpleasantness before and since her accession, unrest and disagreeable occurrences to which Elizabeth has given rise. There is no persuading her that Elizabeth will not bring about some great evil unless she is dealt with.'[24]

It is probable that this news was relayed to Jane, who would surely have been horrified. From a distance, Elizabeth had witnessed the events of Jane's downfall unfold. Aware that her half-sister was surrounded by those who spoke against her, perhaps the same who had whispered about Jane, Elizabeth was intent on self-preservation and avoiding the same prison that Jane now occupied. Before Elizabeth left court, she had urged the Queen 'not to believe anyone who spread evil reports of her without doing her the honour to let her know and give her a chance of proving the false and malicious nature of such slanders, that were only designed to harm her'.[25] Despite Elizabeth's protestations, Queen Mary was wary, and her young half-sister was probably wise to her having given orders for spies 'to watch what takes place in her house'.[26]

Christmas in the Tower proved to be a sombre one for Jane. No doubt Master Partridge and his wife tried their best to make the most of the occasion, while Jane also had her three ladies for company. She had remained optimistic throughout the days of her imprisonment, but at this time of year, when families were supposed to be together to share in the season of peace and goodwill, Jane must have yearned in her heart for the familiar surroundings of home. The company of her parents, the annoying chatter of her younger sisters, and the sermons once preached by James Haddon in the family chapel would all have been a most welcome distraction from her situation. At the Charterhouse, too, where Jane's family were residing over Christmas, Jane was conspicuous by her absence. There seemed to be little cause for celebration, for though the Grey family had emerged largely unscathed from the cataclysm of the summer, Jane was still not home. The Christmas of 1553 was filled with none of the laughter and revelry that the family had once enjoyed at this most holy time of year – those days were long gone.

At Richmond Palace, Queen Mary celebrated the season with a heightened sense of fervour. She anticipated that she would soon be wed to a handsome husband, 'a prince ripe in age and estate, worthy of her pleasant embraces', and that together she and Philip could build a strong, Catholic dynasty to rule across Europe in future generations.[27] She was blissfully unaware that anything was wrong. Underneath the surface of revelry, however, opposition to Mary's policies was already beginning to simmer. Jane's father may outwardly have claimed that he was content for the Queen to marry where she would, but his true feelings were very different. What is more, he was not alone. For while Christmas was celebrated at Richmond Palace in hopeful expectation for the future, Henry was embarking on an expedition that not only highlighted his own stupidity, but also put the lives of his family in grave danger. As Jane languished in the Tower, like Mary, she was unaware that plans were already afoot that would test the loyalty of Mary's subjects, and would seal Jane's fate.

NEW YEAR WAS then, as now, a time of fresh starts and anticipation. As the new year of 1554 began, Jane's hopes for the future may have been high, for once Queen Mary was married and the security of her throne and faith assured, surely she would be released?[28] On 2 January there was 'a great peal of guns in the Tower', as the Emperor's envoys 'landed at Tower wharf', having arrived in England to finalize the negotiations for Mary's marriage to Prince Philip.[29] Jane heard the guns sound, and though she may have been hopeful of the personal consequences for herself once the marriage was concluded, privately she likely shared the thoughts of the Queen's subjects on her choice of groom. The previous day the retinue of the Spanish envoy arrived in the capital, and 'the boys pelted at them with snowballs', then, as the envoy himself made his way through the streets of London to the Palace of Westminster, 'the people, nothing rejoicing, held down their heads sorrowfully'.[30] It was not an auspicious start.

Upriver at Sheen, while the Christmas and New Year celebrations had been underway, Henry Grey had been busy. But it was not thoughts of masques and feasts that had occupied his mind: it was rebellion. Thus far, Henry had been fortunate that through his wife's intervention with the Queen, and Mary's good graces, his family had been allowed to slip into a life of peaceful obscurity, with the hope that their daughter would later be returned to them. But this was not enough for Henry, and always naïve by nature, he showed himself to be 'ungrateful for the favour he had received and the pardon he had obtained from his sovereign after Northumberland's sedition'.[31] Unbeknown to the Queen, Henry had been engaged in secret communication with Sir Thomas Wyatt, 'a young man disposed to every kind of mischief and an experienced soldier'.[32] Wyatt was fiercely anti-Spanish, and was one of several 'demented fellows', that 'made the prospect of this wedding an excuse for rebellion'.[33] Henry, equally vehement in his distaste for a Spanish king in England, carelessly allowed himself to be drawn into the plots of 'secret treachery'.[34] Not only was Henry riled by the prospect of Mary's marriage to a Spaniard, but he was also motivated by religious factors. Despite Henry's outward display of conformity to Catholicism, James Haddon was at pains to assure Bullinger that this was not where his heart lay: 'The duke himself holds to the true God, and I hope by God's help will fully retain his opinions about true religion, in opposition to the devil, whose agents are striving with all their might to lead his lordship astray.'[35] Henry's eldest daughter was still a Tower prisoner under sentence of death, and he himself was disgruntled by the fact that although he was foremost among the leading peers of the realm, he had been excluded from a place in Mary's government. His expectations, given the seriousness of the events of the past months, were preposterous. Besides that, he had been incredibly fortunate to avoid both forfeiture and execution – he had walked away almost completely unscathed. He also chose to involve his younger brothers and his half-brother George in this new treason, thereby demonstrating the lengths to which the family were prepared to go in their efforts to support one another. As Henry exchanged letters with Wyatt and his co-conspirators in order to discuss plans, Henry cannot have failed to have been aware of the risks involved. He knew that he was placing his family in grave danger, and more pertinently, that his actions were putting Jane in mortal peril.

WITHIN THE SERENITY of the Kent countryside, at Allington Castle, Sir Thomas Wyatt and his colleagues planned their move. First and foremost, the marriage of Queen Mary to Philip of Spain must be avoided at all costs, but there was also another objective. Though she had only been queen for a matter of months, Mary had already begun her efforts to transform England into a Catholic realm ruled by the Pope once more, much to the dismay of her people who were widely in favour of sovereign authority. Perhaps it was time to replace her, and with someone whose aversion to Catholicism was as strong as that of many of the English people. Clearly Lady Jane Grey was not a popular choice, for her queenship had already been tried and resulted in dismal failure. But what of Queen Mary's half-sister, the Lady Elizabeth? She was young, and she was popular. Outwardly she may have had to conform to the Queen's religious policies, but there was no doubting where her heart really lay in matters of conscience. Moreover, if Elizabeth became queen she could then be married to Edward Courtenay. Not only was Courtenay an Englishman and a Protestant, but he was a marital candidate with royal blood who had been rejected by Mary, and whom the conspirators chose to involve in their plans.[36] As a Protestant, it was only natural that the leaders of the conspiracy should look to Elizabeth as the focal point for opposition to Mary and the Spanish marriage.

Wyatt's strategy consisted of a three-pronged attack. From his base in Kent, Wyatt was confident that he could raise a substantial force, while his colleague Sir Peter Carew would do the same in the south-west. Meanwhile, Henry Grey was a great landholder in the Midlands, so it was only natural that he should be responsible for rallying troops there, with the assistance of Sir James Croft, who had previously lent his support to Jane's accession. If the plan were to stand any chance of success, it was crucial that the conspirators move swiftly, as plans for the Queen's marriage were already quickly developing.

On 9 January Renard reported that 'the ambassadors have finally concluded the marriage articles and treaties'.[37] In what was no doubt an attempt to calm fears, a passage was inserted into the marriage contract whereby it was made clear that Philip would not be given any authority above that of the Queen, and that he would merely 'assist his consort in the task of government, saving always the kingdom's laws, privileges and customs'.[38] The Queen had demanded that her Council support her marriage, and had called upon them all to sign their approval. There had, however, already been rumours of what was being plotted elsewhere in the realm, and alerted to the suspicious behaviour of Sir Peter Carew, the Council sent a summons, ordering him to court. Twice refusing to obey, Carew 'declared himself openly a rebel, thereby plainly showing the evil intentions in his mind'.[39] As a result, 'the Council have issued orders to the officers to seize him bodily and take him prisoner to the Tower of

London. During the last few days six or seven nobles and commoners have been arrested.'[40] Carew, however, managed to evade capture and slipped away to France.[41] When Wyatt heard that Carew's treachery had been discovered, he immediately began to gather men in Kent, 'stirring up strife in that whole part of the Country and preparing to march swiftly on London'.[42]

Until now, Henry's name had not been mentioned in connection with any of the rebels. When the Queen, though, was informed of Wyatt's plans, she 'decided to send against the said Wyatt the Duke of Suffolk with troops'.[43] Perhaps she thought that this would provide Henry with the perfect opportunity to redeem himself and to prove his loyalty, but she was to be mistaken. On the morning of 25 January, one of the Queen's messengers arrived at the Charterhouse to summon Henry to court, there to receive the Queen's orders. Henry was already outside, on the verge of leaving home in order to rally the Midlands and 'levy some soldiers' when he spotted the Queen's messenger riding into the courtyard.[44] As 'a man who had not a clear conscience', for a few moments panic probably spread throughout his body and his heart may have beat a little faster as he waited for the message in anxious anticipation: had he been discovered?[45] Calming whatever nerves he may have felt, he managed to retain his composure as the messenger relayed to him the Queen's request that he should repair to court. 'Marry,' he began, 'I was coming to see Her Grace. Ye may well see that I am booted and spurred ready to ride; and I will but break my fast to go,' he replied steadily.[46] If he had any second thoughts about the plot, now would have been the time to abandon them. But Henry did not. Dismissing the messenger to receive refreshments in the Charterhouse kitchens, Henry mounted his horse. Perhaps as he bade farewell to his wife and his two younger daughters that morning, Frances made an attempt to persuade him to desist from his plans, for later evidence suggests that she did not approve of her husband's plots, and was probably also deeply concerned about the effect they would have on Jane.[47] Henry, however, was set on his course, and as he rode out of the Charterhouse that morning with no intention of travelling to court, he must have been aware that there was a chance that he would never see his wife or daughters again. His path was now fraught with danger and uncertainty. In the Tower, though Jane did not know it, her future was about to be determined by the actions of her father; it was do or die.[48]

CHAPTER 21

The Permanent Ruin of the Ancient House of Grey

G UILDHALL WAS ONCE more the setting, but the circumstances were very different. This time a queen was not on trial; a queen was begging for the support of her subjects to help her keep her throne. Standing tall, Queen Mary 'with her sceptre in her hand in token of love and peace', rallied her subjects to stand firm against the traitor Wyatt who was marching towards the capital; to stay true to their anointed queen, and if needs be, to fight on her behalf.[1] It was Thursday 1 February, at two o'clock in the afternoon, and the Queen, accompanied by her Council and her guard, 'spoke to the people, and said that the objects she had ever had in view since coming to the throne were to administer justice, keep order and protect the people's peace and tranquillity'.[2] All that Mary had striven for was now under threat, and for a time she may have felt a flicker of the uncertainty experienced by Jane as she waited to learn whether or not her subjects would rally to support her. Renard informed his master that as 'Wyatt was nearing London', and as Mary stood with her people before her, she

> wished to hear from her people whether they meant to behave like good subjects and defend her against this rebel, for if they did, she was minded to live and die with them and strain every nerve in their cause; for this time their fortunes, goods, honour, personal safety, wives and children were in the balance. If they bore themselves like

*good subjects she would be bound to stand by them, for they would
deserve the care of their sovereign lady. And thus, with befitting
persuasions, she urged them to take up arms.[3]*

The Queen's words had the desired effect: 'So elegant and eloquent was
her speech, that all the people cried out loudly that they would live and die
in her service, and that Wyatt was a traitor; and they all threw up their caps
to show their goodwill.'[4] Despite the unpopularity of Mary's proposed
marriage and some of her religious policies, she had thus far retained the
love of her people, who were still committed to her and believed in her
right to rule. They were determined to fight off the approaching rebels,
and to fight for their queen. It was a loyal spirit that they had never
displayed for Jane.

The rain poured in London as the Queen began to muster her troops.
The Londoners were unsettled when they heard that '3000 well-armed
rebels were daily drawing nearer to London, and indeed were within one
league of the town', while the Queen 'was without the means of resistance'.[5]
Uneasy about whom she could trust, 'The Queen summoned Elizabeth'
to court from her estate at Ashridge, determined to have her half-sister
where she could keep an eye on her.[6] However, 'Elizabeth is very ill', or
so she claimed, and was unable to make the journey.[7] Distracted by the
potential threat posed by Wyatt and his rebels, for the time being Mary
allowed Elizabeth's pleas of illness to pass her by, and Elizabeth remained
where she was. As a precautionary measure more spies were placed in
her household, and like Jane, Elizabeth could only watch, wait and see
how events unfolded. It is doubtful if we will ever know the full extent of
Elizabeth's complicity in the plot. That she knew of the rebels' plans there
can be no doubt, but she was too clever to allow herself to be implicated
in anything that might lead to her own downfall, and Wyatt would later
exonerate her from blame.[8]

WITH ANY FEIGNED sentiments of loyalty for Queen Mary now vanished, Henry Grey rode for the Midlands with his brothers in tow. They were determined to rally as many men as they could in the cause of rebellion, and their confidence was high. Henry would later claim that his brother Thomas had persuaded him to flee rather than to come to court as the Queen had commanded, while the Imperial ambassadors had heard that 'the French ambassador had caused the Duke of Suffolk to fly by telling him that unless he did so the Council would have him arrested'.[9] Meanwhile, the day after Henry's departure, Thomas Wyatt issued a proclamation to the people of Kent urging them to join him. It proved to be successful, and thus it was with a force that numbered around 4,000 men that he began to march towards London.

When Queen Mary was informed that Henry had not only disobeyed her summons but had abused her clemency by attempting to incite her people to rebel with the support of his brothers, she was furious. A letter was swiftly issued in her name, declaring that 'the Duke of Suffolk and his brothers (Lord John and Lord Thomas Grey) with others, forgetting their allegiance to God and us, and the great mercy the duke lately received, conspired to stir our subjects to rebel against us and the laws lately made by Parliament'.[10] They were also guilty of 'spreading false rumours that the prince and Spaniards intended to conquer this realm'.[11] The Queen appealed to her subjects to help her in apprehending these rebels. There was one who immediately answered the call and came to her aid.

Francis Hastings, Earl of Huntingdon, 'who is a mortal enemy of the Duke of Suffolk, has implored the Queen to be allowed to go forth against him and put a stop to his proceedings; and permission has been given to him together with the requisite powers'.[12] Just months earlier, Huntingdon's heir had been married to Northumberland's daughter alongside Jane and Guildford. His sudden enthusiasm to apprehend Henry therefore seemed perplexing. According to Renard, it was motivated by two factors: first and foremost, having previously thrown himself wholeheartedly into supporting Northumberland's scheme, Huntingdon was eager to rehabilitate himself in the eyes of Queen Mary, and saw the mission as an ideal means of achieving this. Also, as with Henry, many of Huntingdon's lands were in Leicestershire, and if Henry were removed Huntingdon would reign supreme in the county. The Queen immediately accepted Huntingdon's offer, and he set off in hot pursuit of the treacherous Duke.

By now panic had begun to spread through the capital, as word reached the citizens of the rebellion and the anticipated arrival of Wyatt and his men. Hurried preparations were made to protect the city, and in the Tower the faithful Sir John Brydges ensured that the artillery was ready and 'made great preparation of defence'.[13] Jane had heard of what was afoot, and was left in no doubt of her father's treachery. Was this the moment that her heart sank as she realized that his actions could be the death of her? For unless the rebellion were successful all hopes of liberty – of resuming a normal life with her family – were permanently dashed. By the same token, it was not only Jane's liberty that was at risk, but her life too. Her fate had yet to be determined, and she had no choice over her own destiny, for it lay in the hands of others. It always had done.

IN THE TOWER, Jane witnessed the spreading panic but was helpless to do anything other than wait for news. No doubt she absorbed herself in prayer, but for whom was she praying? Perhaps for her father, for by now most people knew that 'the Duke of Suffolk and his brothers, Lord Thomas and Lord John (Grey), have gone off to the Duke's house some forty miles hence and have been proclaimed traitors'.[14] The Earl of Huntingdon and his men closely followed them. Huntingdon was determined to punish Henry for his shocking betrayal, thereby ingratiating himself in Queen Mary's favour. He quickly discovered that Henry had left a hot trail, and unbeknown to those in London, Huntingdon had soon 'routed the Duke of Suffolk, taken all his men prisoners, seized all his money and baggage, and forced him to fly with his two brothers accompanied only by five horse'.[15] It was believed that 'the Duke is making for Scotland. The people would not rise for him, and it is hoped that he will soon be a prisoner or forced to leave the realm.'[16] It was a terrifying situation for Jane; her father had been deemed a traitor, his cause was hopeless, and if he were apprehended, death seemed a certainty for them both. To make things worse, another of Henry's servants had been 'caught and hanged', and had been discovered to be 'carrying a placard issued by the Duke to be published all over the country, to the effect that there were 12,000 Spaniards at Calais and as many more in the West Country, all ready to conquer England'.[17] His traitorous intent was clear, and traitors were not pardoned twice. What is more, association had already tainted Jane.

On 3 February, to the alarm of Queen Mary, Wyatt's forces had reached Southwark. There was panic in the city as nobody really understood his true intentions: initially the Queen had dispatched the elderly Duke of Norfolk with 'infantry, artillery and ammunitions' in an attempt to deal with Wyatt, but this had failed when many of Norfolk's men had defected to Wyatt's cause, and the Duke himself had been captured.[18] Shortly afterwards, he was released, and beat a hasty retreat back to court. The Queen had then sent desperately to ask Wyatt for his terms, and to inform him that 'by raising a force against the Queen, he was committing treason and throwing the realm into disorder'.[19] Undeterred, Wyatt sent word of his demands: 'He wished to have London Tower in his hands, and also the Queen in order to furnish her with a better Council than her present one. He also wanted three or four Councillors, whom he meant to punish, and he intended to restore religion to its recent condition.'[20] No mention had been made of Jane, who languished in the very Tower Wyatt wished to occupy, confirming that she had no place in Wyatt's plans. When his terms had been unsurprisingly indignantly rejected, Wyatt and his forces continued in their descent on the capital. However, at Southwark the true loyalties of the Londoners were revealed. Mary's forces stationed at London Bridge and led by the Lieutenant of the Tower, Sir John Brydges, thwarted the rebels' attempts to penetrate further into the city by damaging the city's bridges, thereby preventing them from crossing the river. So steadfast was Sir John in his loyalty to Mary, he had even threatened to fire on his own forces if necessary.

By no means discouraged, Wyatt and his men withdrew from Southwark and managed to cross the Thames to the south-west of the city. As they marched through Charing Cross, along the Strand towards the Tower, Jane would have been aware of the high tension and alarm as she waited anxiously in her prison. As Renard observed fearfully, 'If London rose the Tower would be lost, the heretics would throw religious affairs into confusion and kill the priests, Elizabeth would be proclaimed Queen, irremediable harm would be the result.'[21]

When the rebels reached Ludgate on the morning of 7 February, they came to a standstill as they found the gate to be heavily fortified under the command of the Lord Admiral, William Howard, and closed against them. Wyatt and his supporters, 'not thinking the Queen's forces to be so strong, and expecting the conspirators and heretics to rise like desperate men in his support', had completely misjudged the mood of the country, for though many people were opposed to the Spanish marriage, they were still loyal to Queen Mary.[22] It was this that prevailed as the Londoners began to repel the rebels from Ludgate and prevent them from travelling further east. Surprised and dismayed by the fighting spirit of the citizens, who it had been hoped would flock to the rebel banner, support for Wyatt began to melt away, with many of his followers choosing this moment to desert him. In addition, the Queen's Commander, the Earl of Pembroke, and Lord Clinton had followed Wyatt towards Ludgate and had cut down many of his supporters along the way.

With no choice but to abandon his plans, Wyatt and his remaining followers retreated to Temple Bar, their cause lost. The rebellion had been a dismal failure, and Queen Mary, once more victorious over her enemies, had triumphed. Although the Queen's Council had taken the rebellion seriously and had been fearful for the Queen's safety, the Wyatt Rebellion would come to be seen as a poorly organized attack. The lack of secrecy among the conspirators, and action taken by the government to try to minimize the threat, ensured that it was quickly discovered. If the Londoners had risen in support of Wyatt then it may have stood some chance of success, but though they loathed the idea of a Spanish marriage, they ultimately still loved their English queen.

As '"Te deum" was sung in the Queen's Chapel for joy of the said victory', Wyatt and his remaining supporters were rounded up and arrested.[23] Among those who were imprisoned was Sir John Harington, who had been previously entangled in the Seymour scandal. Harington claimed only to have carried a letter to the Lady Elizabeth from Jane's father, but the authorities were convinced that he was guilty of more.[24] A terrible fate awaited those who had supported him, as 'A large number of the prisoners, up to 200 were hanged, and it was an awful sight to notice through every street in London gallows and dead men.'[25] While his comrades suffered death, Wyatt was predictably taken to the Tower, 'a worthy and extremely fitting place for his wickedness and for wicked men'.[26] As he was brought in at five o'clock on the same evening as his failed attempt to pass through Ludgate, perhaps Jane watched as Sir John Brydges grabbed him by the collar 'in most rigorous manner', and berated him: 'Oh! Thou villain and unhappy traitor!'[27] He did not end there, and added that if it was not for the fact that 'the law must justly pass upon thee, I would strike thee through with my dagger', as he moved one hand to his sheath and shook Wyatt vigorously.[28]

Wyatt's end was a fait accompli, but as of yet no mention had been made of Jane, or of her father, whom she may have believed was still at large.[29] However, the odds were not good, for though Jane had been innocent of any complicity, it was clear to all that her father could not be trusted: would Jane pay the price for his treachery?

———◦◦◦———

INSIDE A HOLLOW tree on his Warwickshire estate of Astley, on which he had once played as a child, Henry Grey was hiding from Queen Mary's authorities. He had tried his best to rally troops in the Midlands but to no avail, and what was more, in desperation 'he started again to proclaim his daughter as Queen'.[30] Perhaps this was his intention all along, but there was nothing more to be done, and 'having lost all hopes of any success', Henry had 'directed everyone to look after his own salvation, waiting for more favourable times when he could carry out his plans'.[31] His brother Thomas fled towards the Welsh border, while his half-brother George also attempted to escape. Henry and his youngest brother John, aware that they were being pursued, approached a labourer who worked on the Astley estate and persuaded the man to help hide them in the park. The winter winds, however, were still swirling, and Henry, 'having remained almost two days without food, and frozen to death, had left the tree' for a short time.[32] Little did he know that the labourer, hearing of Queen Mary's damning proclamation naming him a traitor, and knowing that the Earl of Huntingdon was closing in, 'changed his mind' and, hoping to be gener-ously rewarded, 'went to see the Earl disclosing him the hiding place of the Duke'.[33] Huntingdon was thrilled to receive this news, and on 2 February he proceeded to Astley in order to apprehend his target. For Henry, time had run out and there was nowhere left to hide. Having returned to the tree, he was discovered there by one of Huntingdon's dogs, while his youngest brother John was found beneath a pile of hay.[34] Before long Thomas and George were apprehended too. This time, there would be no more chances.

Delighted to have apprehended his one-time ally, Huntingdon imme-diately arrested the two brothers in the Queen's name, and under guard conducted them to the nearby city of Coventry.[35] He wrote triumphantly to the Sheriff of Rutland that 'by the providence of god the Duke of Suffolk and the Lord John his brother are this day apprehended and in my custody', which news was 'a wondrous good beginning' in Renard's view.[36] Imprisoned with no chance of escape, and with a heavy heart, 'The Duke of Suffolk has written out with his own hand and signed his confession.'[37] Unfortunately the confession no longer survives, but Renard related that rather than displaying remorse for his behaviour, in the document Henry 'owns that irritation at his arrest, the small esteem in which the Council held him', as well as his conversations with his fellow conspirators Carew and Crofts, 'who had plotted, together with many others, to set the Lady Elizabeth on the throne, moved him to leave the Queen's party and join the rebels'.[38] He also claimed that his brother Thomas 'specially strove to persuade him, and also tried to win over Pembroke, who refused to listen'.[39]

Henry made no mention of Jane, the daughter whom he had betrayed in the most appalling manner. She was doubtless informed of his capture, and with that news vanished her last hopes of freedom. It seems that Henry still hoped for a reprieve, for Renard had learned that 'he implores mercy, not justice'.[40] As he left Coventry with his brother, escorted by 300 horses and destined for London, there to join his daughter in prison, there was no doubt that Henry's actions had had disastrous consequences both for himself, and more poignantly for Jane. Renard confirmed that Queen Mary 'is resolved to let justice have its course, as her clemency has already been abused, and allow their heads to be cut off'.[41] Though Jane's fate had yet to be announced, it was clear that Henry's reckless stupidity had led to 'the permanent ruin of the ancient house of Grey of Dorset'.[42] It was as if the events of the previous summer were repeating themselves once more.

QUEEN MARY HAD made a decision. Agonizing though it had been for her, she now realized that while Jane lived, she could potentially form a focal point for future dissenters. She had done all that she could in order to preserve the life of the young girl, but she could do no more. Even after Wyatt's treachery had been discovered, 'the Queen was already considering to have her reprieved, but, judging that such an action might give rise to new riots, the Council ruled it out and sentenced her to death'.[43] Moreover, 'Renard in the closet, and Gardiner in the pulpit, alike told her that she must show no more mercy.'[44] Thanks to the actions of her father, the death sentence handed to Jane at Guildhall would have to become a reality. As the seventeenth-century historian Sir Richard Baker put it:

> *The Fathers have eaten sour grapes, and the children's teeth are set on edge: the innocent Lady must suffer for her Father's fault; for if her Father the Duke of Suffolk, had not this second time made shipwreck of his loyalty, his Daughter perhaps had never tasted the salt-waters of the Queen's displeasure.*[45]

The actions of her father had effectively signed Jane's death warrant. More specifically, it was his cries for Jane's restoration as he rode through Warwickshire that 'determined the queen to sacrifice her to her own safety'.[46] It is unclear precisely when Mary made this decision, but Jane was probably informed that she was to die on the evening of 7 February, the same evening on which Wyatt arrived at the Tower.[47] The hour of her death was fast approaching, and as she heard this news, 'Jane, as she had long expected it, received the message with great resolution.'[48] Once more, Jane demonstrated the outer strength and dignity that she had shown at her trial, for what is clear is that she drew admiration from all of those who came into contact with her. The reality, however, was that Jane was seventeen years old and through no fault of her own she would never again see her home, her family or her beloved tutor.

Jane's thoughts turned to her end, and she was determined to show courage and die steadfast in the faith that she had adhered to for all of her short life. She learned that her execution had been scheduled for 9 February: there was little time to be had, though Jane was about to be faced with one final challenge.

CHAPTER 22

Bound by Indissoluble Ties

O
N THE MORNING of 8 February, a visitor arrived at the Tower. He was here, he said, to see the Lady Jane, by order of the Queen. As he was led through the Tower precincts and conducted to the house of Nathaniel Partridge, the sight of the young girl who had necessitated his visit confronted him. For Jane the arrival of a visitor provided a mixture of welcome relief at having somebody to talk to, and impatience when she was informed of the reason. Her visitor was Dr John Feckenham, Queen Mary's personal chaplain. A priest was designed to offer comfort to the needy, but in Jane's case it provided no such thing. For Feckenham had been sent with a very specific task – and if he was successful, he believed that it could save Jane's immortal soul.

Though Queen Mary had resigned herself to the fact that she had no choice but to take the lives of Jane and her husband, her mind was still uneasy. For she was acutely aware that unless the couple abandoned their Protestant faith, in her mind their souls would be eternally tormented within the fires of Hell. She could not save Jane's life, but she could at least attempt to save her soul. Thus when Feckenham arrived at the Tower, 'after some words of ceremony, he began to desire to do as much as he was himself ordered'.[1] It is unlikely that Jane had ever met Feckenham before, for though he too was a learned man, he was as staunch a Catholic as Jane was Protestant, and had spent much of King Edward's reign as a prisoner in the Tower for his beliefs. His feelings at returning there now must have brought back unpleasant reminders of his imprisonment. But perhaps Feckenham more than any other had an understanding of how Jane felt, caged and alone, and this may have increased his empathy for her. Nevertheless, he had not been sent merely to commiserate with Jane on her fate. As this 'clever and crafty papist' began his attempt to 'free her from that superstition in which she had grown up, so that when dying her body, the soul would not be lost', though Jane 'listened to him considerately', she replied that he had come too late, for her end was fast approaching, and she had not enough time to consider such things now.[2] She had been born and raised a Protestant; it was a faith in which she had been nurtured by some of the most influential theologians of her day, and she was not prepared to abandon it now. But neither was Feckenham ready to give up so easily, and believing himself to be able to return Jane to the folds of the Catholic Church, he left the Tower convinced that he might be able to achieve his objective. All that was needed was a little more time, and the only person with the power to necessitate this was the Queen. Keen to fulfil his task, Feckenham approached his mistress, and informing her that he felt hopeful of swaying Jane, asked that 'a new lease of life should be granted to her so that she might have time to get converted'.[3]

Mary was delighted by Feckenham's news; perhaps some good might arise from the situation after all, and she graciously agreed to postpone both Jane and Guildford's executions by three days. Little did Mary and Feckenham know that Jane's belief in her faith had deeper roots than they could ever have anticipated, and that she was prepared to stand her ground come what may.

Relieved that Queen Mary had so readily agreed to delay Jane's execution, Feckenham returned to the Tower once more. In high hopes of a positive outcome, he informed Jane that 'the Queen had granted her three more days of life to enable her to amend her errors and therefore she should prepare herself to that for the weal of her soul'.[4] But Jane was alarmed when she heard Feckenham's words, and was at pains to assure him that she had already resigned herself to her fate:

> *She had taken leave from all earthly matters so that she did not even think of the fear of death and that she had prepared patiently to accept it in the way in which the Queen would be served to command; it was quite true that it would be painful to her flesh as mortal thing, but her soul was happy to abandon this darkness and ascend to the eternal light, as she was confident, putting her trust in God's mercy alone.*[5]

Her reaction was extraordinary. Her father-in-law had done all he could in an attempt to evade death, but Jane it appeared, positively welcomed it. Her declaration was admirable, and surely masked her inner feelings of terror. So thought Feckenham, for perhaps she could yet be persuaded to relinquish her faith? Thus, he began to debate with Jane on that very question, and was amazed by her response. 'What is then required of a Christian man?' Feckenham asked her. Jane replied simply and with confidence, 'That he should believe in God the Father, the Son, and the Holy Ghost, three persons and one God.'[6] The differences in their religious beliefs were highlighted when the chaplain questioned Jane as to how many Sacraments there were. 'Two,' Jane answered, 'the one the sacrament of baptism, and the other the sacrament of the Lord's supper.'[7] Appalled, Feckenham told her that she was wrong, for there were in fact seven Sacraments. But Jane did not back down. 'By what Scripture find you that?' she replied defiantly. 'Well, we will talk of that hereafter: but what is signified by your two sacraments?' Feckenham probed. Jane was ready with her answer:

> *By the sacrament of baptism I am washed with water and regenerated by the Spirit, and that washing is a token to me that I am the child of God. The sacrament of the Lord's supper, offered unto me, is a sure*

> *seal and testimony that I am, by the blood of Christ, which he shed for me on the cross, made partaker of the everlasting kingdom.*[8]

Jane had proven that not only was she more than capable of holding her own against a man of differing beliefs, but also that she was indeed worthy of her scholarly reputation. She was 'very learned in matters of the Bible', and she did not stop there.[9] Each question that Feckenham fired at her she responded to fully, and it became clear that she would not renounce the faith in whose cause she so steadfastly answered.

Feckenham had tried his utmost, but 'he had great difficulty in trying to convince her'.[10] Nevertheless, according to Foxe he tried one last time. 'You ground your faith upon such authors as say and unsay both in a breath; and not upon the church, to whom ye ought to give credit.'

'No,' Jane responded,

> *I ground my faith on God's word, and not upon the church. For if the church be a good church, the faith of the church must be tried by God's word; and not God's word by the church, neither yet my faith. Shall I believe the church because of antiquity, or shall I give credit to that church which taketh away from me the half part of the Lord's supper, and will not any man receive it in both kinds? Which things, if they deny to us, then deny they to us part of our salvation. And I say, that it is an evil church, and not the spouse of Christ, but the spouse of the devil, that altereth the Lord's supper, and both taketh from it, and addeth to it. To that church, say I, God will add plagues; and from that church will he take their part out of the book of life. Do they learn that of St Paul, when he ministered to the Corinthians in both kinds? Shall I believe this church? God forbid!*[11]

Jane was triumphant: she had stood her ground and fought for her beliefs. Her faith had withstood the scrutiny and questioning, and now as the hour of her death drew nearer, she was determined that she would die for her faith, another female martyr to the Protestant cause.[12]

Even Feckenham, though saddened by his failure to turn Jane's heart, could not help but be impressed by her fortitude. Indeed, he felt an admiration for her that he had never expected to feel, and decided that 'with kind zeal and charity' he would not abandon her until the end.[13] Jane too, found that not only had her debate with the Queen's Chaplain been stimulating, but that she also quite liked Feckenham. Be that as it may, she was determined to have the last word, and as Feckenham stood to leave he turned to Jane, telling her that he was sorry for her, for 'I am sure,' he began, that 'we two shall never meet'. With a steadfast countenance Jane agreed: 'true it is', she said, 'that we shall never meet, except God turn your heart; for I am sure, unless you repent and turn to God, you are in an evil case. And I pray God, in the bowels of his mercy, to send you his Holy Spirit; for he hath given you his great gift of utterance, if it pleased him also to open the eyes of your heart.'[14]

Exhilarated by her final declaration and confident of finding eternal glory, Jane was now left alone with her thoughts. She hoped that her conversations with Feckenham might be circulated after her death, high-lighting her desire to be seen as a martyr. The next days would be her last: a time for reflection, contemplation and composition. A time to prepare herself to die.

EACH SECOND THAT passed brought Jane closer to death. The date that had been fixed upon was 12 February, and preparations were already well underway. Guildford was to die on the same day, on the same scaffold on Tower Hill on which his father had so recently lost his life. But there was to be no such public spectacle for Jane, for it had been decided that she would die within the confines of the Tower, away from the curious eyes of the city folk. Through her mercy, Queen Mary had been gracious

enough to commute the full horrors of their sentences to simple decap-
itation. Despite the Queen's clemency it was still a fearful prospect,
which before long would become a conclusive reality. All of those
imprisoned in the Tower would have heard the hammer of nails on
wood as the scaffold on which Jane was to be executed was erected, and
all would have known that her cause was now hopeless. From her rooms,
Jane could even see the scaffold just a short distance away, yet she
remained unfazed.

As she prepared herself for what lay ahead amid the noise of the
Tower, Jane's thoughts turned to her family. On 10 February her father,
himself now a prisoner, had arrived at the Tower. He was reported to
be in distress, possibly exacerbated by the fact that he had recently
been 'very sick with colic and stone', while her mother and her two
younger sisters now faced an uncertain future tainted by their father's
treason.[15] As Jane was shortly to remind her sister Katherine, 'if God
had prospered him [Henry], you should have inherited his lands'.[16] It
had been six months since Jane had seen her parents, perhaps longer
since she had seen her sisters; none of them could have envisaged that
the girl who had shown such promise would soon have her life taken
from her in the most brutal manner and undeserved circumstances.
Jane knew that she would never see her family or her home again, and
in an attempt to comfort them she began to write. She was aware that
her words in the last letters she ever wrote would serve as a final testimony to the strength with which she met her end, and so she resolved
to make them count.

Her sister Katherine had always been frivolous, and as the eldest of her
sisters, it was important to Jane that she should offer her guidance. She
decided to send Katherine her copy of the New Testament in Greek, and
chose to accompany it with a stern lesson in morality. 'I have here sent
you, good sister Katharine, a book, which, although it be not outwardly
trimmed with gold, yet inwardly it is more worth than precious stones,'

Jane began.[17] Such sentiments indicate the low value that Jane placed on material objects, and demonstrate once again her belief that what lay within 'shall bring you to an immortal and everlasting life'. Jane saw it as her duty to guide her thirteen-year-old sister, and exhorted her to pay heed to the words of the book, for 'It shall teach you to live, and learn you to die.' In what was perhaps a sad hint at her own situation, she warned Katherine not to trust that 'the tenderness of your age shall lengthen your life; for as soon (if God call) goeth the young as the old'. As if to reassure her sister, however, Jane urged 'as touching my death, rejoice as I do, good sister, that I shall be delivered of this corruption, and put on incorruption. For I am assured, that I shall, for losing of a mortal life, win an immortal life.' Though the book no longer survives, Jane's message was ultimately an account of how she had prepared for her end: 'die in the true Christian faith, from the which (in God's name) I exhort you, that you never swerve, neither for hope of life, nor for fear of death'.[18]

Despite the impersonal tone, it is clear that Jane had a genuine desire to instruct her sister. She had clung to her faith so devotedly, and perhaps she realized that, like her conversation with Feckenham, this letter too would be circulated among her co-religionists after her death, as indeed it was. Jane's thoughts also turned to her mother. No letter to Frances survives, and this has often been taken as evidence that the relationship between mother and daughter was a fraught one. However, according to the account of Jane's Italian tutor Michelangelo Florio, Jane did indeed write to her mother during her final hours.[19] If this is true, then the fate of the letter is a mystery. Perhaps it was destroyed by Frances, in which case she must have had a good reason for doing so. She may have found the reminder of her daughter's situation too unbearable to contemplate, or perhaps in view of the new reign, deemed it wise to burn it. Equally mysterious is the contents of the supposed letter, but it may have been designed by Jane to offer some comfort to her mother in a similar manner to the words she would write to her father.

Elsewhere in the Tower, Jane's father languished in his room.[20] He had been informed that his daughter would die; yet he was forbidden from meeting with her, and denied the opportunity of a final farewell. Nevertheless, he was most certainly in Jane's thoughts, and she took the opportunity of leaving him one final message. In 1570 a letter appeared in the second edition of Foxe's *Acts and Monuments* which pertained to be written by Jane, in which she berated her father. According to Foxe, Jane admonished Henry because 'it hath pleased God to hasten my death by you, by whom my life should rather have been lengthened', before steadfastly declaring that 'I may account myself blessed, that washing my hands with the innocency of my fact, my guiltless blood may cry before the Lord, Mercy to the innocent!'[21]

There is good reason to believe, though, that this letter is a fake. In the aftermath of Jane's death, John Banks informed Bullinger that 'it may be seen how her truly admirable mind was illuminated by the light of God's word, by two letters, one of which she herself wrote to the lady Katherine, her sister, a most noble virgin, to inspire her with a love of the sacred writings, and the other to a certain apostate [Harding]'.[22] No mention was ever made of such a letter to Jane's father, and as Banks confirms, Jane's considerations at this time were primarily religious.

In fact, as Jane's final hours drew to a close, her thoughts for her father were far from so admonishing. Opening the prayer book that was one of her greatest treasures, Jane began to write a few short words of comfort to her father, almost certainly to be shown to him following her death.[23] Starting beneath the words 'keep me waking least the slumber of death come upon me', Jane wrote:

> *The lord comfort your grace and that in his word wherein all creatures only are to be comforted and though it hath pleased god to take away two of your children yet think not I most humbly beseech your grace that you have lost them but trust that we by losing this mortal life*

have won an immortal life and I for my part as I have honoured your
grace in this life will pray for you in another life. Your graces humble
daughter, Jane Dudley.[24]

Jane had almost certainly selected the pages on which she wrote with care,
and she may have been struck by the poignancy of the words that stared
out at her: 'Oh Lord, be not far: O my strength, hasten thee to come and
help me. Deliver my life from the death stroke.'[25] How apt they were at this
time – never before had they held so much meaning. Her words would,
she hoped, be a comfort to her father, who was doubtless suffering in his
mind at the affliction that he had brought upon his family. Jane, however,
had forgiven him, and had shown herself to be his obedient daughter even
as the hour of her death drew near.

Moreover, by some collusion with their jailer, Jane's prayer book was
passed to Guildford. Like Jane, he too took the opportunity to write to his
father-in-law beneath words that were full of equal meaning: 'Tarry not
for I am even at the point of death': 'Your loving and obedient son wisheth
unto your grace long life in this world with as much joy and comfort, as
did I wished to myself, and in the world to come joy everlasting. Your
most humble son to his death, G Dudley.'[26] The courage demonstrated
in the words of the two teenagers was staggering, and it was clear that
they had both reconciled themselves with the inevitable. Jane, at least,
was confident that she was about to leave one world for another that was
infinitely more desirable.

Jane's confidence was seemingly more than that of her husband, for
though Guildford too had refused to convert to Catholicism, he did request
a final meeting with his wife on the eve of their execution. According to
the account of the papal envoy Giovanni Commendone, 'before dying he
wished to embrace and kiss her for the last time, wherefore he begged her
to allow him to pay her a visit'.[27] This suggests that he had developed some
kind of feelings towards his wife, however small, or perhaps wished to beg

for her forgiveness for the petulant behaviour he had once demonstrated towards her. But Jane, perhaps not wishing to distress either of them any further than necessary, refused to see him:

> *She let him answer that if their meeting could have been a means of consolation to their souls, she would have been very glad to see him, but as their meeting would only tend to increase their misery and pain, it was better to put it off for the time being, as they would meet shortly elsewhere and live bound by indissoluble ties.*[28]

Whatever her personal feelings of distaste towards him may have been, Jane believed that she and Guildford would soon be reunited in an everlasting paradise; one in which there would be nobody who could use them as pawns for their ruthless ambitions; one in which they would be free to be themselves.

Jane had left her final words to those she loved. She now turned her attention to posterity, and began to compose a final statement 'wishing to account to the World' for her actions. She asserted that it was her 'lack of prudence for which I deserve the greatest punishment', and most of all, 'although I accepted that of which I was not worth, I never sought it'.[29]

She had done all that she could to acquit herself in the eyes of future generations. Now her remaining thoughts were only for herself, and for her own salvation. She had composed a prayer, and on her last night of life on earth, prayer was all that she could think of:

> *O Lord, thou God and Father of my life, hear me, poor and desolate woman, which flieth unto thee only, in all troubles and miseries. O merciful Saviour, craving thy mercy and help, without the which so little hope of deliverance is left, that I may utterly despair of any liberty.*

Jane further urged that God should be 'unto me a strong tower of defence', and give her the strength to face her ordeal with bravery:

I beseech thee, with thy armour, that I may stand fast, above all things taking to me the shield of faith, wherewith I may be able to quench all the fiery darts of the wicked; and taking the helmet of salvation, and the sword of the Spirit, which is thy most holy word.[30]

It was a sad and desperate plea, and one that was shortly to be answered.

CHAPTER 23

I am Come Hither to Die

THE MORNING OF 12 February was a cold and crisp one, the last that Jane and Guildford would ever experience. As Jane carefully prepared herself that morning, there was one final spectacle to endure. It had been arranged that Guildford would die first, and as he was led from his prison at around ten o'clock in the morning, from her window Jane watched as he passed. She had never wanted to marry Guildford, and she had been unhappy with his behaviour, but now, as their end approached, the harsh reality of their entwined fates hit home. They were both youths, both betrayed by Guildford's father, and both had been callously manipulated. They had stood side by side on trial for their lives, and received the chilling news of their condemnation and ultimate impending death sentences together. Moreover, they had resisted the attempted persuasions of Feckenham to convert, and they had both remained true to their faith.[1] It was their faith that they believed would ultimately save them as they left this mortal life for the next.

As Guildford was led from the Tower, passing through its historic precincts one last time, for a moment he seems to have been gripped by fear. Noticing some noblemen with whom he was familiar, as he passed he 'took by the hand Sir Anthony Browne, Master John Throckmorton, and many other gentlemen, praying them to pray for him'.[2] They were helpless to do anything more for him, and Guildford was forced to continue his journey. Accompanied by the guards and Sir John Brydges, Guildford was delivered into the custody of the Sheriff of London, Thomas Offley,

270

who was responsible for the smooth running of what followed. Guildford walked the short distance to Tower Hill. The scaffold lay ahead of him: it was the same spot on which his father and his grandfather before him had died. With his death, three generations of his family would have been executed as traitors; would his brothers, who still lay in the Tower, suffer too when he was gone? Guildford made no protest as he mounted the scaffold, where he was quite alone save for the executioner who would shortly end his life. He simply 'kneeled down and said his prayers; then holding up his eyes and hands to God many times; and at last, after he had desired the people to pray for him, he laid himself along, and his head upon the block'.[3] The axe fell, and with one stroke Guildford's head was severed from his body. Grafton related that it was a travesty that Guildford 'as an innocent suffered execution, whom god had endowed with such virtues', and that even those who had never seen him prior to his end 'did with lamentable tears bewail his death'.[4] Carelessly, 'his carcass thrown into a cart, and his head in a cloth, he was brought into the chapel within the Tower', where he was unceremoniously buried close to his father.[5] Now it was Jane's turn.

MINUTES HAD PASSED since Guildford was led from the Tower. With only moments left before she too would be conducted from her rooms, Jane was confronted with the gruesome reality of what awaited her. As Guildford's bloodied and broken body was carried back into the Tower, Jane, 'whose lodging was in Partridge's house, did see his dead carcass taken out of the cart, as well as she did see him before alive going to his death'.[6] The final living image she had of her husband had been shattered. For a moment her calm deserted her as she cried out, 'Oh Guildford, Guildford!' bewailing the bitterness of death.[7] She quickly composed herself, however, and Rowland Lea observed that the young girl was 'nothing at all abashed, neither with fear of her own death, which then approached, neither with the sight of the dead carcass of her husband when he was brought in to the chapel'.[8]

Shortly afterwards, Sir John Brydges arrived at Master Partridge's house. He was greatly troubled by the duty he was obliged to perform that day: he had already witnessed the death of one youngster, and now another one must inevitably follow. Sir John had become fond of his courageous young charge, and in 'his great affection towards her' he had begged for a keepsake with which to remember Jane by.[9] She had only one thing left to her that she could give. Her tiny prayer book in which she had inscribed her farewell message to her father would be his, she promised him, when she no longer had need of it. At his request, she had written a final message to him too:

> Forasmuch as you have desired so simple a woman to write in so worthy a book, good master lieutenant, therefore I shall as a friend desire you and as a Christian require you to call upon god to incline your heart to his laws, to quicken you in his way, and not to take the word of truth utterly out of your mouth, how still to die that by death you may purchase eternal life and remembrance how the end of Mathusael [Methuselah] who as we read in the Scriptures was the longest lived that was of a man, died at the last, for as the Preacher sayeth there is a time to be born and a time to die and the day of death is better than the day of our birth. Yours as the lord knoweth as a friend, Jane Dudley.[10]

It was clear that Jane wanted to be remembered by the manner of her death, and her conduct in her final moments was, therefore, of critical importance.

'By this time was there a scaffold made upon the green over against the White Tower, for the said lady Jane to die upon.'[11] Now was the time, and escorted by the kindly Sir John and Mistresses Tilney and Ellen, Jane left her prison lodgings for the final time. Rowland Lea reported that, *[t]he lieutenant leading her, in the same gown wherein she was arraigned. Her countenance nothing abashed, neither her eyes anything moistened with tears, although her two gentlewomen, Mistress Elizabeth Tilney and Mistress Ellen wonderfully wept, with a book in her hand, whereon she prayed all the way til she came to the said scaffold.*[12]

The scaffold was just steps away from her room, and there was barely time for Jane to glance at her prayer book, which she clasped to her, determined to take as much comfort from it as she could. Perhaps her father, from his Tower prison, saw his daughter as she made her final journey, for he would certainly have known of what was about to happen – the consequences of his reckless actions. With remarkable composure, Jane managed to put one foot in front of the other as she walked, but seconds later the journey was over: 'After these things thus declared, it remaineth now, coming to the end of this virtuous lady, next to infer the manner of her execution, with the words and behaviour of her at the time of her death.'[13]

Jane reached the scaffold, where Dr Feckenham was waiting for her. He had asked to be there during her final moments, and had been true to his word. It was too late now, he realized, to open Jane's eyes to conversion, and so he would not make any such attempt. He was not there to offer spiritual comfort, but instead, in a strange way, as a friend. Commendone noted that as Jane

[a]rrived near the scaffold, she turned towards those who stood by to see her die, and greeted them all asking them to take her death as witness of her innocence. Taking then by the hand the theologian who had accompanied her to the spot without ever abandoning her even if it had been of no avail, she embraced him and told him to go and that God may reward him; she also thanked him for having kept

her company, letting him know that during those few days she was
more bored by him than frightened by the shadow of death.[14]

In another time and another place Jane's words to Feckenham may have
been humorous, but there was nothing jovial about the occasion. Turning
away from him, Jane mounted the few small steps and stood on the scaffold. In front of her Jane was faced with a chilling sight, for there stood the
executioner: the man who had been paid to end her life. He was dressed in
black, and his face was covered. But his identity was not important. It was
here on this scaffold that her life would end, and here that Jane had her
chance to make it count. There had been other times in her life when she
had shed tears for things that she could not change, but now would not be
one of them. At the moment of her death she would be remembered for
her strength, and her bravery.

Jane stood on the recently erected scaffold, and looked out upon the
faces of those who had gathered to watch.[15] They had come to see her
die. Their faces betrayed their sadness at the spectacle they were about
to witness, but Jane was determined not to show fear. This was her
moment, her chance to make her mark on posterity, and to be remembered. She turned to the people, clinging to her tiny prayer book, and
prepared to speak. She had rehearsed the words in her head, her final
statement to the cruel world into which she had been born, and was
shortly to leave:

Good people, I am come hither to die, and by a law I am condemned
to the same. The fact, indeed, against the Queen's highness was
unlawful, and the consenting thereunto by me: but touching the
procurement and desire thereof by me or on my behalf, I do wash
my hands thereof in innocency, before God, and the face of you, good
Christian people, this day.[16]

She paused for a brief moment and wrung her hands, composing her thoughts before continuing:

I pray you all, good Christian people, to bear me witness that I die a true Christian woman, and that I look to be saved by none other mean, but only by the mercy of God in the merits of the blood of his only son Jesus Christ: and I confess, when I did know the word of God I neglected the same, loved myself and the world, and therefore this plague or punishment is happily and worthily happened unto me for my sins: and yet I thank God of his goodness that he hath thus given me a time and respect to repent. And now, good people, while I am alive, I pray you to assist me with your prayers.[17]

It was a confirmation of all that she had believed in, all that she held to be true. Jane had made her final declaration to the world; those were the words that she would be remembered for. There was no more that she could do.

Kneeling down Jane opened her prayer book. There were several other people on the scaffold, but Jane turned to Feckenham, who had remained true to his promise not to abandon her until the bitter end. 'Shall I read this psalm?' she asked him. 'Yea,' he replied simply.[18] 'Have mercy upon me, O God,' she began, before reciting Psalm 51 in English, one of the psalms for the penitent, 'asking people to join her in raising prayers to the Almighty.'[19] Her air of dignity and calm never left her as she read the psalm 'in most devout manner, to the end'.[20] When she had uttered the final words, Jane stood up, handing her gloves and her handkerchief to Mistress Tilney, and her precious book with its farewell messages to Thomas Brydges, the Lieutenant's brother.

She had done all that she could to prepare her soul for death; now all that remained was to prepare her body. As she began to untie the laces of her black gown, the headsman went to help her. But Jane was determined that he ought not to touch her until it was necessary, and repulsed, she 'desired him to let her alone', instead turning towards the familiar faces of Mistress Tilney and Mistress Ellen, 'who helped her off therewith'.[21] As she 'loosened her hair' one final time, she was handed 'a fair handkerchief to knit about her eyes', but before she could do so, 'the hangman kneeled down, and asked her forgiveness, whom she forgave most willingly'.[22] He then 'willed her to stand upon the straw: which doing, she saw the block'.[23] In this moment the shocking brutality of what was about to happen seems finally to have dawned on Jane: it was on this block, here and now, that she would die. Whatever her inner turmoil may have been, it remained hidden, but glimpses of it were apparent in her words as she simply begged the executioner, 'I pray you dispatch me quickly.'[24] She wanted it to be over, and kneeling down, turned to the headsman once more. 'Will you take it off before I lay me down?'[25] Perhaps her thoughts had been drawn to Anne Boleyn, whose head had been removed with a swift stroke of a French headsman's sword without the use of a block. 'No, madam,' he answered. With that, Jane's final sights of the Tower, of those around her, and of the block, disappeared as she 'tied the kerchief about her eyes'.[26]

Now blind, Jane felt for the block with her hands, but to her alarm found that it was just out of her reach. For a brief flash her composure completely deserted her as she cried out desperately, 'What shall I do? Where is it?'[27] It was a pitiful sight as Jane's hands snatched at the cold air, and moved by compassion one of those on the scaffold, perhaps Thomas Brydges, guided her hands to rest on the wooden block. Jane composed herself once more, determined to make a courageous end. She 'laid her head down upon the block, and stretched forth her body', knowing that she would never rise from it. There was time for just a few more words, and as an indication that she was now ready, Jane cried, 'Lord Jesus, into thy hands I commend my spirit!'[28] The headsman raised his axe; seconds later it fell and severed Jane's head in a single stroke: 'And so she ended.'[29] Lady Jane Grey, 'the innocent victim of the sins of others', was no more.[30]

Those who had gathered around the scaffold heard the sickening thud of the axe as it sliced into Jane's flesh, and were forced to witness a sea of red as the scaffold became drenched in 'an abundance of blood'.[31] Though saddened, they could walk away from the scene of devastation, but there was one final indignity for this young girl who had lost her life at the age of seventeen. Her body, broken by the executioner's axe, lay on the blood-soaked scaffold for several hours before it was at last removed. The reason for the delay is unclear; perhaps there was doubt over Jane's final resting place in the chapel. Jane's remains were at last taken for burial in the Chapel of St Peter ad Vincula. The precise location of her grave is unclear, but presumably she was laid to rest beside her husband, her hated father-in-law, and her queenly predecessors, Anne Boleyn and Katherine Howard, beneath the chancel pavement. No memorial was ever erected to her, a fact that caused astonishment to one of Jane's Victorian admirers: 'it is equally extraordinary that no monument of so celebrated a character, or of her husband should exist'.[32] However, at the time in which Jane died it was not extraordinary at all. Aside from those who knew her, and despite the claim that Jane's death 'appeared hapless and bloody not only to the English people but also to all men of all nations', in the grand scheme of European politics Jane was almost forgotten, and her death elicited no more than a simple line or two in ambassadors' reports.[33] Nevertheless, one contemporary noted that her execution was met

[w]ith great sorrow of the people, testifying their compassion for the iniquity of her lot, especially when it became known to everybody that the girl, born to a misery beyond tears, had faced death with far greater gallantry than it might be expected from her sex and the natural weakness of her age.[34]

A later tale emerged that Jane's body was secretly removed from the Tower and brought to Bradgate Park, where it was interred in the parish church. This is almost certainly complete fabrication, and is not based on any evidence. In 1876, on the orders of Queen Victoria, the Chapel of St Peter ad Vincula underwent restoration, and during this time many of the remains of the prominent persons buried within were uncovered. During the course of the work, the floor began to collapse and the digging in the chancel had to be abandoned, by which time the remains of neither Jane, nor Guildford, had been discovered. This is why Jane was sadly not afforded one of the beautiful marble stones that others buried in the chancel were. Nevertheless, Jane's body was assumed to be there, and thus a slab was placed at the foot of the chancel that stated that she and others were believed to be buried nearby. There are no grounds to assume that this was not the case, and though we lack the conclusive evidence that Jane's skeleton would have provided, she almost certainly still rests in St Peter ad Vincula today. The Victorian historian Thomas Babington Macaulay accurately summarized Jane's final resting place:

In truth there is no sadder spot on the earth than that little cemetery. Death is there associated, not, as in Westminster Abbey and Saint Paul's, with genius and virtue, with public veneration and with imperishable renown; not, as in our humblest churches and churchyards, with everything that is most endearing in social and domestic charities; but with whatever is darkest in human nature and in human destiny, with the savage triumph of implacable enemies, with the inconstancy, the ingratitude, the cowardice of friends, with all the miseries of fallen greatness and of blighted fame.[35]

She had spent the last months of her life as a prisoner in the Tower, and never emerged alive from its precincts. Moreover, even death could not free Jane from its walls, and she has, thus far, spent more than 460 years buried within. It is hardly surprising, therefore, that her ghost has reportedly been sighted on a number of occasions.[36] Her poignant associations with her prison are as persistent as her memory, which over the centuries has inspired both sympathy and admiration.

CHAPTER 24

God and Posterity Will Show Me Favour

N O SOONER HAD the axe fallen than Jane was being revered as a Protestant martyr by those who had known her. In many contemporary accounts, however, her end was barely worthy of note. The day after Jane's execution, Renard simply informed his master that 'Jane of Suffolk was yesterday executed, whilst her husband, Guildford, suffered in public.'[1] Her admirers, though, were determined that she ought to be remembered. As historian Hester Chapman put it, 'The remarkable character and dramatic martyrdom of Lady Jane Grey made her as famous in her own generation as she is today.'[2] Grafton wrote that most people believed that Jane was killed because of her father's crimes, 'rather than for any guilt or fault that was in her', and 'great pity was it, for the casting away of that fair lady'.[3] Similarly, John Stow related that Jane's death was 'the more hastened for fear of further troubles and stir for her title, like as her father had attempted', while Commendone praised her as she had 'submitted the neck to the axe with more than manly courage'.[4]

A month after Jane's death, John Banks was writing to Heinrich Bullinger, whom Jane had so much revered, lamenting her death. Jane, he said,

> [w]as truly admirable not so much by reason of her incredible attainments in literature, by which in the seventeenth year of her age she excelled all other ladies, as by reason of the remarkable firmness

with which, though a young girl, she surpassed men in maintaining
the cause of Christ; insomuch that she could neither be defeated by
any contrivances which the papists imagined against her, nor be
deceived by any of their artifices.[5]

He continued to explain that Jane had 'persevered in this confession of faith even to the last'.[6] What was more, it was not only Jane who had been affected, but her whole family were 'now overthrown and almost extinct, on account of their saving profession of our Saviour, and the cause of the gospel'.[7] This certainly appeared to be the case, for on the same day as Jane's execution Renard informed the Emperor that 'Jane of Suffolk and Guildford, her husband, were to be beheaded, and the whole house of Suffolk would be obliterated by the execution of the three brothers now prisoners, whose death, as they were heretics, would contribute to the firm re-establishment of religion.'[8] However, Banks continued to assert that 'yet all godly and truly Christian persons have not so much reason to mourn over the ruin of a family so illustrious, as to rejoice that the latest action of her life was terminated in bearing testimony to the name of Jesus'.[9]

Those who knew Jane were determined to remember her as a pious girl who had been slain for her faith. It was an idea of which Jane herself would have approved, and which she had been only too keen to promote as her end drew near. As Jane had hoped, word of her debates with Dr Feckenham soon spread, and although it is unclear how, her former family chaplain James Haddon was soon writing to Bullinger of it: 'But as to what regards the lady Jane herself, and what is said in her name, (as for instance, her exhortations to a certain apostate, and her discourse with Feckenham,) I believe, and partly know, that it is true, and did really proceed from herself.'[10] Banks had already sent Bullinger a transcript of the conversation in which Jane expressed 'her opinion with much learning and ingenuity', as well as a copy of the letters Jane wrote to her sister

Katherine and Harding, with the belief that they seemed 'worthy of being universally known'.[11] However, Haddon begged Bullinger not to make Jane's words public at that time, and they remained under wraps. Nevertheless, her memory inspired the deepest admiration among the men Jane had once looked up to, who were impressed by her heartfelt religious devotion.

John Foxe was undoubtedly the most famous of Jane's contemporaries to capitalize on this image. In the pages of his *Acts and Monuments*, more famously known as *The Book of Martyrs*, which was first published in 1563, nine years after Jane's death, Jane is immortalized, together with her husband, as 'two innocents in comparison of them that sat upon them. For they did but ignorantly accept that which the others had willingly devised, and by open proclamation consented to take from others and give to them.'[12] Foxe also claimed that Jane had inscribed a pretty verse in Latin into the walls of her cell in the Tower using a pin:

> *Non aliena putes homini quæ obtingere possunt,*
> *Sors hodierna mihi, tunc erit illa tibi.*
> *Jane Dudley.*
> *Deo iuuante, nil nocet liuor malus:*
> *Et non iuuante, nil iuuat labor grauis.*
> *Post tenebras spero lucem.*[13]

Translated into English the words read:

> *Do never think it strange,*
> *Though now I have misfortune.*
> *For if that fortune change,*
> *The same to thee may happen.*
> *Jane Dudley.*
> *If God do help thee,*

> *Hate shall not hurt thee;*
> *If God do fail thee,*
> *Then shall not labour prevail thee.*

If this was the case then Jane's words have since disappeared, and it is unclear how Foxe came to know of them. Foxe went on to relate the harrowing tale that Sir Richard Morgan, 'who gave the sentence of condemnation against her, shortly after he had condemned her, fell mad, and in his raving cried out continually to have Lady Jane taken away from him; and so ended his life'.[14] Although no other reports exist to back this up, the circumstances surrounding Morgan's death are somewhat mysterious, and it is possible that he died insane. Foxe's story continued to be repeated and circulated, serving to fuel the flames and highlight the terrible consequences of those who had had a hand in Jane's fall. Finally, he chose to include two short epitaphs written by John Parkhurst, the very same who had once written about Katherine Parr, in which he revered Jane as a martyr who had been cruelly slain.

Jane's story quickly gathered momentum in the popular imagination. In 1562 another contemporary, George Cavendish, wrote a poem in which the ghost of Jane placed the blame for her fate solely at her father's door:

> *My sorrows are treble and full of double woe,*
> *To remember the tragedy, and woeful case,*
> *That to my father, my husband, and me also*
> *Is happened, through folly and lack of grace;*
> *It causeth the tears to run down my face,*
> *And to lament your misfortune and mine,*
> *By such blind folly to fall into ruin.*[15]

It is possible that Cavendish knew Jane; he was certainly familiar with some of those who featured in her story, and thus did not have to look far to find inspiration for his tragic poem.

Tragedy was destined to become the common theme as the popularity of Jane's story took hold over the centuries. Shortly after Cavendish, Sir Thomas Chaloner's elegy was published in 1579. Chaloner certainly knew many of those who were close to Jane, including her great-uncle, Nicholas Wotton, and it is not implausible that he had also met the heroine of his piece, entitled *A lament on the death of that most eminent heroine, Lady Jane Grey, daughter of Henry, Duke of Suffolk who was smitten with the axe and died in most steadfast spirit.*[16] Chaloner's elegy was incredibly sympathetic to Jane's plight, and accused Queen Mary of lacking in compassion towards her cousin: 'Should not a lady once cultivated herself have been moved by another so cultivated as Jane?'[17] Chaloner was relentless in his praise for Jane's looks and her learning, and continually labelled Mary as the villain of the piece. Chaloner and Cavendish were just two among many who attempted to capture the tragedy of Jane's story through poetry, the works becoming increasingly more pitiful in tone. In 1762, George Keate's *An Epistle from Lady Jane Grey to Lord Guilford Dudley* stressed not only the relationship between Jane and her husband, but also Jane's determination to die for her beliefs:

> Let the Clouds gather, let the Storm
>   advance,
> Unmov'd, its bursting Horrors I'll
>   defy,
> And steady to my Faith a Martyr
>   die.[18]

Jane's supposedly loving relationship with Guildford added a further strand to her appeal. As well as providing a muse for poets, she also inspired playwrights to take up their pen and cast their heroine on to the stage of the theatre. At the beginning of the seventeenth century Jane was the subject of a play by the famous John Webster and Thomas Dekker, and although, sadly, the script no longer survives, it capitalized on the notion that Jane was deeply in love with her husband. It is probable that the play formed part of the playwright duo's *The Famous History of Sir Thomas Wyatt*, which was first published in 1607, and in which Jane and Guildford feature heavily. The idea of Jane and Guildford as star-crossed lovers was taken one step further in the 1690s when John Banks's *Innocent Usurper: or, the Death of Lady Jane Grey* was published. The play not only grossly embellished the relationship between Jane and Guildford, but also depicted Guildford threatening suicide unless Jane accepted the crown. However, in the aftermath of the Glorious Revolution, which witnessed the deposition of a monarch, James II, the play never made the stage, and was banned for political reasons. The following century, another tragedy about Jane's life emerged, this time by Nicholas Rowe. *Lady Jane Grey: A Tragedy in Five Acts* was first staged at Drury Lane in 1715. Dedicated to the Princess of Wales, Caroline (later Queen Caroline, wife of George II), the play was successful for its day both on stage and in print.[19] The Epilogue of the play neatly summed up the essence:

> *The palms of virtue heroes oft' have worn,*
> *Those wreaths to-night a female brow adorn.*
> *The destin'd saint, unfortunately brave,*
> *Sunk with those altars which she strove to save.*[20]

By the nineteenth century Jane's story had gathered extraordinary momentum, exacerbated by the creation of a painting that now hangs in the National Gallery. Paul Delaroche's iconic *The Execution of Lady Jane Grey* still has an overwhelming impact on modern interpretations of Jane. Exhibited in Paris's Salon in 1834, the year after its completion, the painting caused a stir, not least because of the memories it triggered in the minds of the French of their own Revolution and the executions of the French royal family.[21] A portrayal of Jane's final moments, the painting depicts a blindfolded Jane being guided towards the block by Sir John Brydges – poetic licence on Delaroche's part. The executioner looks on unperturbed, while two women (presumably Mistresses Tilney and Ellen) are tormented by grief. The painting is not historically accurate by any means, as is highlighted by the fact that the artist has portrayed Jane's execution as taking place inside a building. This doubtless served to intensify the dark image of the Tower as a gloomy prison. Significantly, Jane is depicted dressed in white, which not only distinguishes her as the central figure in the painting, but is perhaps also intended to represent her innocence. Delaroche painted a number of famous historical scenes, including *The Death of Queen Elizabeth* and *Cromwell gazing at the body of Charles I*, but his image of Jane has sparked enduring admiration and a powerful torrent of sympathy. What is more, Delaroche was not alone, for between 1827 and 1877 twenty-four paintings on the subject of Jane were displayed at the Royal Academy, a testament to the popularity of her story. However, as with Delaroche's, all of these depictions were based on romantic sensibilities and tragic ideals rather than historical accuracy. Nevertheless, it is the Delaroche image that still inspires its audience, and as Roy Strong asserts, its success 'is due to the artist's oft-used trick of bringing the main action of the picture almost out of the canvas, directly towards the onlooker'.[22]

Jane has also been the subject of two operas, and a number of historical novels. This is a trend that continues to this day, and seems sure to endure into the future. Jane featured in William Harrison Ainsworth's fourth novel, *The Tower of London*, released in 1840. Though she is not the main character of the book, she is characterized in a highly emotional manner that played up to every other portrayal of Jane as a tragic heroine. Two decades later in Agnes Strickland's *Lives of the Tudor Princesses*, Strickland described Jane in suitably glowing terms: 'Lady Jane Grey is without doubt the most noble character of the royal Tudor lineage. She was endowed with every attribute that is lovely in domestic life, while her piety, learning, courage and virtue qualified her to give lustre to a crown.'[23] Though novel-istic in tone, Strickland's work was intended to be a work of non-fiction, demonstrating the appeal that Jane held to writers of various genres.

In the twentieth century the dramatic 1986 film *Lady Jane*, written by David Edgar and directed by Trevor Nunn, has had an extraordinary effect on popular perceptions of Jane. It was the third film about her story, and certainly the most powerful.[24] The film exacerbates many of the traditional assumptions of her story: that she was badly treated by cruel parents who forced her into marriage; that the match between Jane, played by Helena Bonham Carter, and Guildford, whose part was taken by Cary Elwes, grew into a love story; and that Queen Mary offered Jane her life if she would convert to Catholicism. The film has therefore done much to embed these ideas as facts into popular consciousness. What comes across most strongly, however, is the idea of Jane and Guildford as innocent teenagers manipulated by ambitious parents – it is a powerful, and largely accurate image.

Many of the places that Jane knew have sadly disappeared, or have been altered as architectural fashions have changed through the passages of time. However, there are two sites with which Jane had particularly strong associations and at which she is still remembered. The magnificent ruins of Jane's childhood home, Bradgate Park, are still largely associated with Jane and her family, and bear testament to the splendour in which Jane was raised. The landscape at Bradgate is largely unchanged, and just as breathtaking as it must have been nearly 500 years ago. Among the ruins, with an element of imagination it is not difficult to conjure the young Jane reading her books in the hall, or walking with her sisters in the beautifully ornate gardens of the house, which was once one of the most spectacular in the country.

At the Tower of London, Jane is still commemorated as one of its most tragic inmates. Her story is told by the Yeoman Warders to the hordes of visitors who flock to the Tower each year, though many of the tangible reminders of Jane's tale have long since vanished. The Royal Apartments that Jane once occupied have been demolished, and the site on which she lost her life is unmarked.[25] The only reminder of Jane in the chapel is the Victorian slab which lists her as one of those whose remains rest there. Similarly, no evidence of the rooms in which Jane spent her imprisonment survive, though the buildings which held her husband and others arrested in connection with the events of the summer of 1553 can still be seen. Perhaps most poignant of all are the two carvings of the name 'Jane' that still survive in the upper chamber of the Beauchamp Tower in which Guildford was once held. Whether they refer to Jane or not, they are nevertheless a persistent reminder of her story, and of her fatal associations with the Tower.

Jane has also lent her name to modern-day buildings, as well as the Lady Jane Grey School in her home county of Leicestershire, which provides a different kind of testimony to her enduring appeal. Over the centuries her story has inspired writers, artists and playwrights, to name but a few, and the examples discussed cover just a fraction of the material that has been produced since her execution. In the days following her death and most certainly today, Jane is undoubtedly spoken about more than she ever was in her own lifetime.

What precisely is it about Jane and her story that has captured popular imagination, and continues to fascinate to this day? Her age and the fact that she met a violent death are certainly important, as is that she was most certainly a victim convicted for the sins of others. But there is something more than that. It is a sense of intrigue. Though her life was short, Jane had demonstrated that she was remarkably intelligent, and given the chance she could have been a woman of exceptional ability who achieved extraordinary things. Furthermore, she had a determined spirit, and could not and would not be swayed into renouncing her beliefs.

Had she been given the opportunity to live a life in which she was free to be herself – without the events of 1553 which saw her unwillingly raised to the throne and then swiftly deposed – there is no telling what she might have accomplished. By contrast, had Jane succeeded in retaining her throne it is interesting to consider what might have happened, and how she would have ruled. Undoubtedly the religious reforms implemented during the reign of Edward VI would have continued with Jane's wholehearted support, further consolidating the foundations of Protestantism in England. Perhaps they might have become even more radical, and it could have been Jane who was remembered for the burning of religious 'heretics', rather than her cousin Mary. It is possible that Jane and Guildford would have had children, and thus that she may have founded a line of kings and queens. We will never know what Jane could have accomplished had her life not been cut short, and it is perhaps this that makes her one of history's most fascinating 'what ifs?' However, Jane's life was not her own, and was ultimately dominated by her blood. As her example demonstrates, royal blood could be a curse. Though she has made her mark on the pages of English history, it is in many respects for the wrong reasons. Jane is chiefly remembered as a pitiful victim who was ruthlessly manipulated, when the reasons for her recognition should lie elsewhere. Today, we ought to remember her in the way in which she wanted to be commemorated by posterity: as a girl who was so steadfast in her religious faith that she was prepared to die for it; a heroine who believed in immortality, and that her soul would live on. As she was preparing her final messages for those she loved, and writing her farewell statement accounting for her behaviour to the world, her thoughts also turned to how she would be remembered, and she penned three short epigrams in three of the languages in which she was fluent: Latin, Greek and English. It seems fitting, therefore, that the last words, and the most enduring, ought to be Jane's:

[Latin] *If Justice is done with my body, my soul will find mercy in God.*

[Greek] *Death will give pain to my body for its sins, but the soul will be justified before God.*

[English] *If my faults deserve punishment, my youth at least, and my imprudence were worthy of excuse; God and posterity will show me favour.*[26]

Epilogue

⸻⸻⸺ꞏꝏꞏ⸺⸻⸻

HE TRAGEDY OF Jane's short life was at an end, but it marked only the beginning of the disaster that would engulf her family. Five days after Jane's execution, her father Henry was tried and found guilty of treason at Westminster Hall.[1] On 23 February, just eleven days after the death of his daughter, Henry also fell victim to the headsman's axe and was executed on Tower Hill.[2] Like his daughter, at his end he professed his devotion as a Protestant, and a contemporary acknowledged that 'by this faith he supported himself, and in this faith he at length ended his life'.[3] Soon after, Jane's uncle, Thomas Grey, was also executed. Through the intervention of Jane's mother, her youngest uncle John Grey was spared, as was her half-uncle, George Medley.[4] All four of Guildford's brothers who were imprisoned alongside him were also released, much to their mother's relief. Robert in particular managed to rise to incredible heights and bask in royal favour: in fact, he came closer to becoming king than his younger brother Guildford ever had.[5]

Jane's mother Frances was now a widow at the age of thirty-six with two young daughters to support. It is a testament to the strength of her relationship with Queen Mary that she was granted the manors of Groby, Bardon, Astley, Beaumanor, and the great park at Loughborough for her lifetime, though Bradgate Park was confiscated and not restored to the Grey family until long after her death.[6] It may have been confidence in her relationship with the Queen that encouraged Frances to take her fate into her own hands. On 9 March, less than a month after Jane's death and precisely a fortnight after the execution of her husband, Frances married for a second time. Her husband was a member of her household, the thirty-four-year-old Adrian Stokes. Initially the marriage was kept a secret, but when it became public it met with the approval of Queen Mary. Mary appears to have been grateful to Frances; by marrying a commoner, Frances had effectively neutralized any threat she may have been deemed to pose via her status as a royal widow. To quote the rule of the heralds: 'if a noble woman marries a commoner, she ceases to be noble', and though Frances continued to be referred to as the Duchess of Suffolk, her title was now of little matter. The marriage was a happy one, and Adrian proved to be a loving stepfather to Jane's sisters, Katherine and Mary. Furthermore, on 16 July 1555, her thirty-eighth birthday, Frances gave birth to her final child, a daughter named Elizabeth. Sadly the child died on 7 February the following year, the second daughter that Frances had lost.

On the same day as Jane's execution, her cousin the Lady Elizabeth began her journey to London, there to be interrogated for her role in the Wyatt Rebellion. She was committed to the Tower on 18 March, where she was poignantly reminded of Jane when she saw that the scaffold on which she had lost her life still stood. In contrast to her cousin's stay, however, Elizabeth's occupancy of the Tower was destined to be of short duration; no evidence being found against her, she survived her term of imprisonment and was later freed. Nevertheless, as time would reveal, she had learned valuable lessons from Jane's example, and never forgot the fate of her young cousin.

In July 1554, Queen Mary married the Spanish Prince Philip, but sadly the marriage brought her none of the happiness she so desired. Having suffered with two phantom pregnancies, she died childless and sorrowful on 17 November 1558. Her twenty-five-year-old half-sister Elizabeth succeeded her. Mary had treated Jane's younger sisters with kindness, taking Katherine into her household as one of her ladies, but Elizabeth was to show no such generosity. Her dislike for the family was soon made abundantly clear.

Her first marriage having been annulled, Katherine Grey fell hopelessly in love with Edward Seymour, Earl of Hertford, the son of the executed Lord Protector, and the man once spoken of as a potential suitor for Jane. Through his mother, Anne Stanhope, Duchess of Somerset, who was descended from Edward III, Edward had a trickle of royal blood in his veins.[7] The couple hoped to marry, and Katherine sought her mother's intercession to secure Queen Elizabeth's permission. Frances began a letter to the Queen, one that was sadly left unfinished. Before it could be completed Frances succumbed to an illness, and died aged forty-two on 21 November 1559. She was given a royal funeral in Westminster Abbey, the first royal funeral to be conducted according to Protestant rites, and a splendid tomb was erected to her memory in St Edmund's Chapel. Her death left Katherine without a champion, and feeling that there was no other choice, Katherine and Edward married clandestinely in December 1560. There was only one witness to the marriage, Edward's sister Lady Jane Seymour, who died soon afterwards. Katherine quickly became pregnant, and once her condition became obvious she chose to confide in her mother's old friend, Bess of Hardwick, who berated Katherine for unwillingly involving her. Once Queen Elizabeth discovered the truth her rage knew no bounds; she was incensed that the couple would dare to wed without seeking her permission – permission that would almost certainly have been denied due to the royal blood that flowed in the veins of both Katherine and Edward. Many people considered Katherine to be Elizabeth's heir, causing the Queen further outrage. The couple were thrown into the Tower, the place that had so many unhappy associations for Katherine.

The Queen's dislike of her cousin Katherine was intensified when, still imprisoned, Katherine gave birth to a son, named Edward. The little boy was separated from his mother, much to her sorrow. The Queen refused to release Katherine and her husband, and in 1562 their marriage was annulled as Katherine had lost her marriage certificate, and the only witness to the wedding was dead. However, this did not dampen the couple's ardour for one another, and the Queen's wrath was further increased when through the connivance of a sympathetic jailer they were able to meet and conceive another child. To prevent any further meetings that might lead to more children, Katherine was removed from the Tower following the birth of a second son named Thomas, and sent to live with her uncle, Lord John Grey. She was later transferred to the custody of Sir William Petre in November 1564. As it became clear that the prospects of being reunited with her husband and children were slim, Katherine gave up hope and slowly wasted away. She died aged twenty-seven in January 1568 at Cockfield Hall in Suffolk, and was buried in nearby Yoxley Churchyard. There have been suggestions that she died of anorexia, but her symptoms also coincide with those experienced by sufferers of tuberculosis, and it was probably this that killed her. Her remains were later moved to Salisbury Cathedral by her grandson, where the magnificent double tomb she shares with the husband she loved so dearly can still be seen to this day.

Following Katherine's death her husband Edward was released from the Tower, and fought for many years to have his marriage declared good and valid. Finally, in 1606, three years after Queen Elizabeth's death, the marriage was legitimized and Katherine and Edward's two sons could claim to have been born within wedlock.

Her younger sister Mary had clearly learned little from Katherine's example. She too fell in love. The object of her desire, though, was not one with a claim to the throne, but the Queen's Serjeant Porter, the widowed Thomas Keyes, who had several children. Perhaps she had thought that in choosing a man beneath her social standing, as her mother had done, she would be safe. If this was her belief then she was sadly mistaken. Mary, too, married in secret in 1565, and one of the witnesses at her wedding was her cousin Margaret Willoughby, to whom she was close. However, when the marriage was discovered, once more Queen Elizabeth was furious at her cousin's presumption to marry without seeking her consent – and to a commoner. Keyes was imprisoned in the common jail of the Fleet, while

Mary was sent first to Chequers, then into the custody of her stepfather Adrian, and later to her step-grandmother, Katherine Willoughby. Like her sister, Mary was never allowed to live with her husband, and tragically never saw him again. Though Keyes was released in 1569, his health had been drastically affected by the conditions of his imprisonment, and he died shortly afterwards. Mary begged for permission to look after her husband's orphaned children but was refused. Despite a brief period of rehabilitation at court, she died in poverty on 20 April 1578, at the age of thirty-three. She was buried in her mother's tomb in Westminster Abbey.

It appeared that all of the scheming of 1553 had been for nothing, for both Mary and Elizabeth, whom Edward's 'Devise' had sought to exclude, came to wear the crown. While Mary's reign ended in misery and is remembered for the cruel burnings of nearly 300 Protestant heretics, many modern historians have celebrated Elizabeth as one of England's greatest monarchs. Her forty-five-year reign, though, did witness the imprisonment, torture and executions of many Catholics, primarily as a result of Pope Pius V's bull of 1570. This absolved Elizabeth's subjects of their loyalty to her, meaning that many Catholics were subsequently viewed with suspicion and were at greater risk of persecution.

For many years Elizabeth enjoyed a close relationship with Robert Dudley – so close that it was rumoured the couple would marry. They never did, for Elizabeth was determined to reign supreme, married only to her people, but there is little doubt that Robert won her heart – in a way that his brother Guildford had never won Jane's. Elizabeth soon swept aside the religious changes implemented by Mary, and unlike her father and her half-brother, she styled herself Supreme Governor of the Church of England, a decision that would have met with Jane's approval. Though Jane's courage has echoed down through the centuries, her life was ultimately taken from her for nothing. Her inheritance and her title of queen had determined her doom: she had been forced to wear a crown of blood.

~~~

The Queen Without a Face: Portraits of Lady Jane Grey

IT IS REMARKABLE that for someone of Jane's fame, no authenticated likenesses of her exist. She was, after all, a member of the royal family – the great-niece of Henry VIII, and a queen in her own right. On the other hand, it does not seem strange at all. Jane was queen for just thirteen days – thirteen turbulent and uncertain days at that, when commissioning a portrait of her would have been low on the list of priorities. Moreover, the fact that no physical descriptions of Jane – her hair colour, her features and her height – survive makes it very difficult to identify or dismiss images purported to be her. Nevertheless, we know that Jane sat for her portrait on at least one occasion, as her mother's friend Bess of Hardwick owned a likeness of her, which she kept at her magnificent home, Hardwick Hall. Unfortunately, the whereabouts of the portrait is now unknown – it may have been lost, destroyed, or misidentified in the same way that many Tudor portraits have been over the centuries.

The female miniaturist Levina Teerlinc painted members of Jane's family – her sister Katherine, her cousin Elizabeth, Katherine Parr, possibly even her mother.[1] Indeed, one of Teerlinc's miniatures has, in the past, been identified as Jane, almost certainly incorrectly.[2] That is not, however, to say that Jane was not painted by Teerlinc, but if she was then the likeness probably no longer survives.

Over the centuries many likenesses have been claimed to represent Jane. The most famous is the full-length portrait painted by the mysterious

'Master John' that now hangs in the National Portrait Gallery. For many years after the Gallery acquired the painting in 1965 it was accepted as an unquestionable image of Jane, until it was reidentified in 1996. Historian Susan James made a convincing case that the portrait was in fact of Katherine Parr, based on its provenance and the items of jewellery that the sitter wears, which can be identified in Katherine's surviving jewel inventories.[3] Most notable among these is the distinctive crown brooch that Katherine wears at her breast, a piece that was commissioned by her. Even if Jane had borrowed these pieces from Katherine for the purpose of having her portrait painted, as has been suggested, there is still good evidence for identifying the sitter as Katherine. The portrait was painted in either 1544 or 1545, probably in order to celebrate Katherine's success as Regent of England while her husband, Henry VIII, was campaigning in France. At this time Jane would have been either eight or nine years old – an impossible age for the lady in the portrait. As J. Stephan Edwards highlights in his study of portraiture relating to Jane, for many centuries the portrait was identified as Katherine, and formed part of the collection of Glendon Hall, the one-time home of Katherine's cousins, the Lane family.[4]

The 'Master John' portrait is not the first of Katherine to be misidentified as Jane. At least three other images that at one time were believed to have portrayed Jane have now been proven to be of Katherine, all of which were loosely based on the 'Master John' portrait.[5] This is probably also true of another portrait in the collection of the National Portrait Gallery, known as 'The Streatham Portrait' due to its provenance.[6] The portrait was actually inscribed with the words 'Lady Jane', and after careful research by the Gallery was indeed believed to represent Jane. However, as Edwards suggests, there are many similarities between this portrait and others of Katherine Parr, most notably the jewels worn by the sitter.[7] Furthermore, dendrochronology dates the portrait to 1594 at the very earliest, so even if it were of Jane, it could not have been a contemporary likeness. As Edwards argues convincingly, the portrait is more likely to represent Katherine, and has been altered in order to make it appear to be Jane, hence the inscription.

It is interesting that so many of Katherine Parr's portraits have become confusedly associated with Jane – something that Jane would perhaps have been rather flattered by given her admiration for Katherine. But Katherine is not the only one of Jane's contemporaries with whom portraits have become confused. The portrait at Syon labelled as Jane, and of which at least five similar copies survive, almost certainly depicts her cousin, the future Elizabeth I, or as Edwards has argued, perhaps her sister Katherine. Many of the images associated with Jane can be discounted easily, and have only been identified as her in the centuries following her death when her reputation and the popularity of her story increased.

During her short term as queen, Jane in fact did not even reign long enough for her image to be struck on to any official currency, or even a seal. That Jane remains the queen without a face, however, does not detract from her ability to inspire fascination in her story – one that has, thus far, lasted for over 400 years.

Jane's Debate with Dr John Feckenham

HERE IS THE full transcript of the debate that took place between Jane and Dr Feckenham in the days before her execution. The conversation was referred to by several of Jane's contemporaries, but this version comes directly from Foxe's *Acts and Monuments.*

Feckenham: Madam, I lament your heavy case; and yet I doubt not, but that you bear out this sorrow of yours with a constant and patient mind.

Jane: You are welcome unto me, sir, if your coming be to give Christian exhortation. And as for my heavy case, I thank God, I do so little lament it, that rather I account the same for a more manifest declaration of God's favour toward me, than ever he showed me at any time before. And therefore there is no cause why either you, or others which bear me good will, should lament or be grieved with this my case, being a thing so profitable for my soul's health.

Feckenham: I am here come to you at this present, sent from the queen and her council, to instruct you in the true doctrine of the right faith: although I have so great confidence in you, that I shall have, I trust, little need to travail with you much therein.

Jane: Forsooth, I heartily thank the queen's Highness, which is not unmindful of her humble subject: and I hope, likewise, that you no less will do your duty therein both truly and faithfully, according to that you were sent for.

Feckenham: What is then required of a Christian man?

Jane: That he should believe in God the Father, the Son, and the Holy Ghost, three persons and one God.

Feckenham: What? Is there nothing else to be required or looked for in a Christian, but to believe in him?

Jane: Yes, we must love him with all our heart, with all our soul, and with all our mind, and our neighbour as ourself.

Feckenham: Why? Then faith justifieth not, nor saveth not.

Jane: Yes verily, faith, as Paul saith, only justifieth.

Feckenham: Why? St Paul saith, if I have all faith without love, it is nothing.

Jane: True it is; for how can I love him whom I trust not, or how can I trust him whom I love not? Faith and love go both together, and yet love is comprehended in faith.

Feckenham: How shall we love our neighbour?

Jane: To love our neighbour is to feed the hungry, to clothe the naked, and to give drink to the thirsty, and to do to him as we would do to ourselves.

Feckenham: Why? Then it is necessary unto salvation to do good works also, and it is not sufficient only to believe.

Jane: I deny that, and I affirm that faith only saveth: but it is meet for a Christian, in token that he followeth his Master Christ, to do good works; yet may we not say that they profit to our salvation. For when we have done all, yet we be unprofitable servants, and faith only in Christ's blood saveth us.

Feckenham: How many sacraments are there?

Jane: Two: the one the sacrament of baptism, and the other the sacrament of the Lord's supper.

Feckenham: No, there are seven.

Jane: By what Scripture find you that?

Feckenham: Well, we will talk of that hereafter. But what is signified by your two sacraments?

Jane: By the sacrament of baptism I am washed with water and regenerated by the Spirit, and that washing is a token to me that I am the child of God. The sacrament of the Lord's supper, offered unto me, is a sure seal and testimony that I am, by the blood of Christ, which he shed for me on the cross, made partaker of the everlasting kingdom.

Feckenham: Why? What do you receive in that sacrament? Do you not receive the very body and blood of Christ?

Jane: No surely, I do not so believe. I think that at the supper I neither receive flesh nor blood, but bread and wine: which bread when it is broken, and the wine when it is drunken, put me in remembrance how that for my sins the body of Christ was broken, and his blood shed on the cross; and with that bread and wine I receive the benefits that come by the breaking of his body, and shedding of his blood, for our sins on the cross.

Feckenham: Why, doth not Christ speak these words, take, eat, this is my body? Require you any plainer words? Doth he not say, it is his body?

Jane: I grant he saith so; and so he saith, I am the vine, I am the door; but he is never the more for that the door or the vine. Doth not St Paul say, He calleth things that are not, as though they were? God forbid that I should say, that I eat the very natural body and blood of Christ: for then either I should pluck away my redemption, or else there were two bodies, or two Christs. One body was tormented on the cross, and if they did eat another

301

body, then had he two bodies: or if his body were eaten, then was it not broken upon the cross; or if it were broken upon the cross, it was not eaten of his disciples.

Feckenham: Why, is it not as possible that Christ, by his power, could make his body both to be eaten and broken, and to be born of a virgin, as to walk upon the sea, having a body, and other suchlike miracles as he wrought by his power only?

Jane: Yes verily, if God would have done at his supper any miracle, he might have done so: but I say, that then he minded no work nor miracle, but only to break his body and shed his blood on the cross for our sins. But I pray you to answer me to this one question: Where was Christ when he said, Take, eat, this is my body? Was he not at the table, when he said so? He was at that time alive, and suffered not till the next day. What took he, but bread? What brake he, but bread? And what gave he, but bread? Look, what he took, he brake: and look, what he brake, he gave: and look, what he gave, they did eat: and yet all this while he himself was alive, and at supper before his disciples, or else they were deceived.

Feckenham: You ground your faith upon such authors as say and unsay both in a breath; and not upon the church, to whom ye ought to give credit.

Jane: No, I ground my faith on God's word, and not upon the church. For if the church be a good church, the faith of the church must be tried by God's word; and not God's word by the church, neither yet my faith. Shall I believe the church because of antiquity, or shall I give credit to the church that taketh away from me the half part of the Lord's Supper, and will not let any man receive it in both kinds? Which things, if they deny to us, then deny they to us part of our salvation. And I say, that it is an evil church, and not the spouse of Christ, but the spouse of the devil, that altereth the Lord's supper, and both taketh from it, and addeth to it. To that church, say I, God will add plagues; and from that church will he take their part out of the book of life. Do they learn that of St Paul, when he ministered to the Corinthians in both kinds? Shall I believe this church? God forbid!

Feckenham: That was done for a good intent of the church, to avoid a heresy that sprang on it.

Jane: Why, shall the church alter God's will and ordinance, for good intent? How did King Saul? The Lord God defend!

With these and such-like persuasions he would have had her lean to the church, but it would not be. There were many more things whereof they reasoned, but these were the chiefest.

After this, Feckenham took his leave, saying, that he was sorry for her: 'For I am sure,' quoth he, 'that we two shall never meet.'

Jane: True it is that we shall never meet, except God turn your heart; for I am assured, unless you repent and turn to God, you are in an evil case. And I pray God, in the bowels of his mercy, to send you his Holy Spirit; for he hath given you his great gift of utterance, if it pleased him also to open the eyes of your heart.

———— ✺ ————

Following in Jane's Footsteps: Places to Visit

MANY OF THE places that Jane would have been familiar with have sadly vanished, or are much changed. However, the settings for some of the most dramatic scenes of her life still exist. As you stand amid the beautiful ruins of Bradgate Park, or in the Chapel of St Peter ad Vincula within the Tower of London, to name but two, it is possible to get a real sense of Jane, and to imagine her at some of the happiest moments of her life, and some of the most tragic.

Bradgate Park, Leicestershire

The magnificent remains of Jane's childhood home still stand among the largely unchanged spectacular landscape of the parkland at Bradgate. The outline of the elegant gardens can still be seen, as can parts of the brickwork of the Great Hall. The only part of the building to survive partially intact, though much altered since Jane's day, is the Chapel. It still houses the tomb of one of Jane's cousins – Sir Henry Grey – the son of her uncle John Grey and his wife, Anne Windsor.

Excavations by the University of Leicester are currently taking place in order to try to unearth some of Bradgate's secrets, so that we may in the future discover more about its splendid past. Nearby, the little church of All Saints in which Jane and her family may have worshipped can still be visited. It features a stained-glass window donated in 1915 with a figure that is thought to be Jane, portrayed as a saint (though Jane was never made a saint).

Astley Castle, Warwickshire

It is unlikely that Jane spent much time at Astley Castle, but nevertheless it has a claim to be listed among the places associated with her. It was in the park at Astley that Jane's father and uncle were discovered hiding following their disastrous involvement in the Wyatt Rebellion. The ruined castle has now been turned into modern holiday accommodation, but the imprint of the gardens can still be seen. Next to the castle stands the church of St Mary the Virgin, in which several of Jane's ancestors lie buried, including her paternal great-grandparents, and her paternal grandfather.

Chelsea Old Church, London

It is possible that Jane visited Chelsea Old Church during her visits to Katherine Parr at the palace that once stood nearby. A modern plaque now marks the spot that the palace occupied. Even if Jane did not visit the church, it remains of interest to those in search of Jane. The tomb of her mother-in-law, Jane Dudley, Duchess of Northumberland, can still be seen. Although much damaged, the tomb bears the brass plaque that lists the names of her sons, and the cavity that once held their effigies. On the opposite side of the tomb, the brass bearing the names and images of the Duchess and her daughters still survives.

Sudeley Castle, Gloucestershire

Much of Sudeley Castle was destroyed following a siege by the Parliamentarian forces during the Civil War in the seventeenth century, and the castle as it stands today is largely the work of the Victorian restoration.

However, fragments survive that Jane would have been familiar with during her brief stay at Sudeley in the summer of 1548. Most of the apartments once occupied by Katherine Parr have vanished, save for an outer chamber that Jane perhaps entered en route to Katherine's inner rooms. There are also several items of interest relating to Katherine Parr on display in the castle, and portraits of many of Jane's contemporaries.

Similarly, the church of St Mary that stands in the grounds was largely destroyed during the Civil War, but the Victorian tomb of Katherine Parr can still be seen. There is also a Victorian stained-glass window representing Jane – rather fitting given that she once played the role of Chief Mourner at Katherine's funeral in the church.

Tilty, Essex

Tilty Abbey has sadly long since vanished. However, next to the church car park the remaining stonework of the house in which Jane once spent a Christmas full of revelry and merriment can still be seen.

The beautiful church of St Mary the Virgin is well worth a visit. The medieval beams are still visible, and the brass commemorating the resting place of Jane's half-uncle, George Medley, and his wife Mary Danet lies on the floor of the chancel, north of the altar. It bears the following inscription:

> *Here under lyeth buried with his wife Mary, George Medley of*
> *Tilty in the county of Essex, Esquire. Which deceased the one*
> *and twentieth day of May in the year of our Lord God one*
> *thousand five hundredth threescore and two and in the four and*
> *fiftieth year of his age.*

Syon Park, Greater London

Robert Adam remodelled much of the Syon with which Jane would have been familiar in the eighteenth century. However, the exterior of the house remains largely Tudor, and the structure of the Long Gallery in which, traditionally, Jane was offered the crown still survives. Syon also houses a wonderful collection of portraits of some of the people who feature in Jane's story, notably her sister Katherine holding her son, the nephew that Jane never met. There is also a portrait labelled as Jane, but in fact it depicts her cousin, the Lady Elizabeth.

Guildhall, London

The impressive fifteenth-century façade of the building in which Jane was tried confronts visitors to Guildhall today. The Great Hall, the scene of the trial, has altered since Jane's day. This is due to damage to the hall during the Great Fire of London. Nevertheless, it is still possible to get a sense of the terror that Jane must have felt while standing in the imposingly large space, listening to the charges against her, and her ultimately devastating sentence.

The Tower of London

The Tower needs no introduction, and is undoubtedly the most notorious of the surviving buildings associated with Jane. The Royal Apartments no longer survive, but many of the buildings in which Jane and her family were imprisoned remain. Notably, the Beauchamp Tower, with its many inscriptions, can be visited, including the beautiful memorial to Guildford and his brothers and the two famous 'Jane' carvings.

Many visitors are oblivious to the fact that as they walk behind the White Tower, they are crossing the same spot on which Jane died.

Finally, the Chapel of St Peter ad Vincula in which Jane is buried can still be visited. The Victorian slab that commemorated Jane was replaced in the 1970s.

NOTES AND REFERENCES

The following abbreviations are used in the Notes and References:

CSPD   Calendar of State Papers Domestic

CSPS   Calendar of State Papers Spanish

CSPV   Calendar of State Papers Venetian

L&P   Letters & Papers, Foreign and Domestic, of the Reign of Henry VIII

SP   State Papers

TNA   The National Archives

Introduction

1 J. Foxe, *Acts and Monuments*, ed. Rev. S. Reed, VI (London, 1838), p. 1605.

2 Ibid.

3 As Leanda de Lisle has highlighted, Spinola's 'description' was an invention of the nineteenth-century antiquarian, Richard Davey. Battista Spinola was, however, a real person.

4 Eric Ives has suggested that 'Rowland' was actually a mistake, and that the author's real name was Richard.

5 R. Wingfield, *Vita Mariae Angliae Reginae*, trans. D. MacCulloch, Camden Miscellany XXVIII, 4th series, XXIX (London, 1984), p. 245.

6 E. Baldwin, *Life of Lady Jane Grey and her Husband* (London, 1824), p. 3.

Chapter 1: A Time to be Born and a Time to Die

1 Harley MS 2342.

2 H. Robinson (ed.), *Original Letters Relative to the English Reformation* (Cambridge, 1846), p. 7.

3 L&P, XII (890).

4 As it transpired, Frances, her husband and her mother-in-law were all banned from attending the christening, as the King was alarmed by reports that they had been residing at Croydon Palace, where 'three or four persons a day are dying of the plague there, and two persons are sick in my Lady's house'. Despite their protestations that this was not the case, the King was taking no chances with the health of his precious male heir, and they were ordered to stay away. It was also observed that at that time Frances

had been in the company of her friend Dorothy Howard, Lady Derby, and although it is unclear how long the two women had been together, if Frances had given birth to her first child that autumn she would have spent several weeks in seclusion prior to and after the birth. Lady Derby was the half-sister of the Duke of Norfolk and the wife of Edward Stanley, Earl of Derby. She was about four years older than Frances, and this is the only reference to a possible friendship between the two women. They may have been in residence at Lady Derby's London home, Derby House, close to St Paul's Cathedral.

5 If this was the case it is still difficult to pinpoint with precision exactly when Jane was born. At the funeral of Katherine of Aragon in January 1536, the role of Chief Mourner was played by Jane's maternal aunt, Eleanor Brandon. Jane's mother was not present, and had she been so, the role of Chief Mourner would have naturally been assigned to her, as the elder of the two sisters. It is possible that her absence could be explained by the fact that she was pregnant with Jane and unable to travel to fulfil the role. However, the fact that Jane was named as a compliment to Jane Seymour suggests that the very earliest that she could have been born was at the end of May, when Jane Seymour became queen.

6 Robinson (ed.), *Original Letters*, p. 276.

7 A date in 1537 appears to contradict all of the other evidence. Equally, the assertion of Roger Ascham, the tutor of Jane's cousin Elizabeth, that Jane was about fifteen years old in 1550, placing her birthdate at some time in 1535, defies all other accounts.

8 Robinson (ed.), *Original Letters*, p. 276.

9 Ibid. In April 1550, the German scholar John of Ulm, who met and admired Jane, guessed that her age at that time was about fourteen, which coincides with a birthdate in 1536.

10 M. Florio, *Historia de la vita e de la morte de l'illustriss. Signora Giovanna Graia gia regina eletta e publicata in Inghilterra e de la cose accadute in quell Regno dopo la morte del Re Edoardo VI* (Middelburg, 1607), p. 68; see J.S. Edwards, 'A Further Note on the Date of Birth of Lady Jane Grey', *Notes and Queries*, 55 (2008), pp. 146–8. Sir Thomas Chaloner's *Elegy* to Jane, published in 1579, also suggests that Jane was in her eighteenth year at the time of her death.

11 Following the death of Bradgate's owner, the 2nd Earl of Stamford in 1719, the family ceased to live there. The house then fell into a state of disrepair, and it is now a ruin.

12 E. Ives, *Lady Jane Grey: A Tudor Mystery* (Chichester, 2011), p. 36; J. Stevenson and A. Squires, *Bradgate Park: Childhood Home of Lady Jane Grey* (Newtown Linford, 1994), p. 22.

13 Cited in B.L. Beer, *Tudor England Observed: The World of John Stow* (Stroud, 1998), p. 23.

14 The other possibility is that Jane was born at Suffolk Place, the London residence of her paternal grandfather, Charles Brandon. This was not the original Suffolk Place that once occupied a site in Southwark, for on 4 February 1536 the Southwark house was exchanged with the King for Norwich Place on the Strand. The house in Southwark was demolished in 1557. Rather confusingly, Norwich Place then became known as Suffolk Place, and it is possible that Jane was born here, although her grandfather appears to have rarely used the house.

15 The Dorset House owned by the Grey family is not to be confused with the Dorset House that later occupied a site just off Fleet Street. This second Dorset House was

formerly the London residence of the Bishops of Salisbury, and was called Salisbury House. It was acquired by Richard Sackville in 1564, and following the creation of his son Thomas as Earl of Dorset in 1604, it was renamed Dorset House. The house was burned down during the Great Fire of London in 1666, and was not rebuilt. However, the names of several streets in the area indicate where it once stood, namely Salisbury Court and Dorset Rise.

16 Birthing stools had been in use in Italy since ancient times, and the idea had gradually spread to the rest of Europe.

17 Wingfield, *Vita Mariae*, p. 245.

18 There is also a sketch in the Royal Collection labelled 'The Duchess of Suffolk' that may represent Frances. Equally, it may also show her stepmother, Katherine Willoughby.

19 Charles Brandon's father, William Brandon, had been standard-bearer to Henry Tudor at the Battle of Bosworth in 1485. He had fought bravely, but in the thick of the battle he had been cut down and killed by none other than Richard III himself. His death left his wife Elizabeth Bruyn a widow with two young children to support. Although the exact date of Charles's birth is unknown, it is thought that he was born in 1484, and had an older sister, Anne. At the death of his father, however, Charles appears to have spent some time living with his paternal grandparents, and his uncle Sir Thomas Brandon. It was under Sir Thomas's influence that Henry VII later found the young Charles a place in the royal household, where he quickly became a firm favourite of the King's son, Prince Henry (later Henry VIII). Charles was created Duke of Suffolk in 1514.

20 L&P, I (3151). This was not the first occasion on which Charles Brandon had caused a stir. In around 1505 he had become pre-contracted to Anne, the sister of Sir Anthony Browne, who had formerly served Henry VIII's mother, Elizabeth of York. In the sixteenth century a pre-contract was tantamount to marriage, an arrangement whereby a couple agreed to marry followed by sexual intercourse. In 1506, however, Charles unchivalrously abandoned Anne Browne shortly after she had given birth to a daughter, named Anne, in order to make a more advantageous marriage to the rich, forty-three-year-old Margaret Mortimer, who was also Anne Browne's aunt. After Charles had made a large profit from the sale of many of her lands, the marriage was annulled in 1508 at his behest, on the grounds of consanguinity. An outraged Margaret Mortimer made her feelings clear when she declared the annulment of her marriage to be invalid. As if this were not bad enough, Charles then returned to the humiliated Anne Browne, who promptly forgave him and married him, the wedding taking place in Stepney Church. The marriage was short-lived, and though another daughter, Mary, was born in 1510, Anne died shortly after. In 1513 Charles was once more betrothed, this time to his nine-year-old ward, Elizabeth Grey, the daughter and sole heiress of Viscount Lisle (Charles was twenty-nine). The marriage never took place, however, and thus Charles's marriage to Mary Tudor was his third.

21 L&P, II (3489). Eleanor was probably born around 1519/20. Her name may have been chosen as a compliment to the sister of the Holy Roman Emperor Charles V, Eleanor, Queen of Portugal and later Queen of France.

22 There is no record of the elder Henry's death, and he and his younger brother have often been confused as being the same person. However, this was clearly not the case, as on 1 September 1533 the younger Henry was described as then being ten years old, and may have been just short of his eleventh birthday. Both boys were created Earl of Lincoln by their uncle the King in separate ceremonies. A sculpture of the younger

Henry, in which he bears a marked resemblance to his father, can be seen at Wingfield College, of which his parents were patrons, while a portrait once thought to represent Edward VI is now also believed to be Henry.

23 L&P, II (3489).

24 Francis was the successor of Mary's first husband, Louis XII. He had also had some connivance in the Suffolks' marriage.

25 Neither Katherine nor Mary were present at Frances's christening, but representatives were sent on their behalf. This practice was common, and the representatives chosen were Lady Boleyn (aunt of the famous Anne), and Lady Elizabeth Grey. Lady Elizabeth was a sister of the 2nd Marquess, and was therefore the aunt of Jane's father.

26 Westhorpe Hall was demolished in 1785, and a residential home now stands on the site it once occupied. A few small fragments from the house still remain, including a bridge decorated with terracotta, the Duke's heraldic badge, and a pediment bearing the Duchess's arms which was used to decorate a nearby farmhouse. The parish church of St Margaret in the village still contains the royal box that the family would have occupied when they visited. The family also owned Castle Rising, Henham Hall, Wingfield Castle, Donnington Castle and Ewelme Manor.

27 S.J. Gunn and P.G. Lindley, 'Charles Brandon's Westhorpe: An Early Tudor Courtyard House in Suffolk', *Royal Archaeological Institute*, 145 (1988), p. 274.

28 E. Sadlack (ed.), *The French Queen's Letters* (New York, 2011), p. 122.

29 Anne and Mary's mother was Anne Browne, who died in 1511. Following her mother's death, the younger Anne had been sent abroad to serve in the household of Margaret of Austria, a friend of Charles Brandon's. Soon after his marriage to Mary Tudor, however, Brandon wrote to Margaret requesting the return of his daughter, claiming that 'the Queen [Mary] has so entreated and prayed me to have her in spite of anything I could say to the contrary'. It is unclear where the younger Mary was at this time, but it seems clear that both girls went to live with their father and stepmother at Westhorpe. In later life both sisters fell out with their father to such an extent that it caused a permanent rift, which may also have extended to their half-sister, Frances.

30 Despite the long-standing belief that Frances and Henry were married in May 1533, the month before Mary Tudor's death, the account of her funeral confirms that this was not the case. Frances was referred to as Lady Frances, not as Henry Grey's wife, which she undoubtedly would have been had she been married at this time.

31 Robinson (ed.), *Original Letters*, pp. 406–7.

32 Ibid.

33 A. Squires, *The Greys* (Hale, 2002), p. 9.

34 Thomas was created Marquess of Dorset by his stepfather, Edward IV, in 1475. The youngest son, Sir Richard Grey, was executed at Pontefract Castle on 25 June 1483 on the orders of Richard III.

35 Thomas had first been married to Eleanor, the daughter of Oliver St John of Lydiard Tregoze in Wiltshire. It was an excellent match for Thomas, as Oliver St John was the stepfather of Lady Margaret Beaufort. This brought Thomas into close contact with the royal family; however, almost nothing is known of Eleanor or the marriage. It may have taken place around 1500, but produced no children. By 1509 Eleanor was dead, for that same year Thomas married Margaret Wotton. Margaret was the widow of William Medley, by whom she had a son, George, and the daughter of Sir Robert Wootton of Boughton Malherbe in Kent and his wife Anne Belknap. Margaret had served in the

household of Elizabeth of York, where she appears in the Queen's surviving Privy Purse Expenses.

36 Astley Castle had been the family's main seat since the fifteenth century. It had been built by the Astley family, but had come into the possession of the Greys in 1420 through the marriage of Joan Astley to Reginald Grey, 3rd Baron Grey de Ruthyn. It was a fortified castle that also provided comfortable accommodation. However, by the twentieth century, the castle had fallen into a bad state of disrepair following the Second World War, and it was restored in the 1950s as a hotel.

37 Thomas Grey was never as close to the King as Brandon; however, he was still a member of his inner circle. He was a Knight of the Garter, a Privy Councillor and a Gentleman of the Privy Chamber, and was entrusted by the King on several important missions. He had escorted Mary Tudor to France for her marriage to Louis XII in 1514, and both he and his wife had attended the ceremony. Much later he was also called upon by the King to give evidence to the effect that Katherine of Aragon's marriage to Prince Arthur had been consummated, in order to help his divorce suit.

38 Richmond had been ennobled on 18 June 1525 at Bridewell Palace, with both Frances's father and Henry's father playing significant roles in the ceremony. Henry's father bore the sword, and it was in this same ceremony that Frances's younger brother Henry was created Earl of Lincoln.

39 This was not the first occasion on which a royal household had been established at Sheriff Hutton. In 1484, Richard III had chosen Sheriff Hutton as the home of his nephews, the Earl of Warwick and John de la Pole. The following year, Edward IV's daughters had also been sent to Sheriff Hutton to await the outcome of Henry Tudor's invasion. Little of the castle remains today.

40 Leland, cited in J. Chandler, *John Leland's Itinerary: Travels in Tudor England* (Stroud, 1993), p. 543.

41 Sir William Parr of Horton was the uncle of Katherine Parr. He had a track record of impeccable loyalty to Henry VIII, and had fought for the King during his campaign in France in 1513. As a result of this, he was knighted by the King in the cathedral at Tournai on 25 September 1513.

42 Thomas and his brothers may have been educated at Magdalen College School, Oxford, where Thomas Wolsey, later Cardinal Wolsey, was their tutor. This is certainly possible, as the 1st Marquess of Dorset was an early patron of Wolsey's.

43 By January 1513 Palsgrave had been appointed as Princess Mary's tutor, and following her marriage to Louis XII he accompanied her to France. However, when Mary's English attendants were dismissed, Palsgrave travelled to Louvain before returning to England in 1517.

44 L&P, XIII (732).

45 The 2nd Marquess was laid to rest in the church at Astley alongside his parents. Nearly eighty years after his death, his vault was opened and his body was found to be well preserved. It was noted that he had been five foot eight inches tall and had yellow hair. It has not been disturbed since.

46 G. Howard, *Lady Jane Grey and her Times* (London, 1822), p. 36.

47 CSPS, IV (635).

48 L&P, V (340).

49 CSPS, IV (33).

50 R. Holinshed, *Holinshed's Chronicles of England, Scotland and Ireland*, 6 vols (London, 1807), p. 25.

51 Ibid. Little is known of Holinshed's life with certainty.
52 Ibid.
53 L&P, XIII (732).
54 L&P, VII (153).
55 Several versions of a portrait of Margaret survive, all based on a sketch by Hans Holbein now in the Royal Collection.
56 L&P, VI (300).
57 Dulcie M. Ashdown claims that Henry and Frances were betrothed when they were twelve years old, an assertion that is impossible. Not only had Henry been previously betrothed to Katherine FitzAlan, but Frances's father had also hoped to arrange a marriage for his daughter with the Earl of Surrey, heir to the Duke of Norfolk. These negotiations came to nothing, as Suffolk could not produce a sufficient dowry.
58 This marriage took place sometime between September and 19 November 1532, the first occasion on which Katherine is named as the wife of Lord Maltravers.
59 L&P, V (1557).
60 Ibid.
61 Ibid.
62 Ibid.
63 As such contracts were considered to be binding, refutation of them was relatively uncommon.
64 L&P, V (1557).
65 L&P, VII (153).
66 L&P, VI (293).
67 The nature of her illness has never been satisfactorily established, and her only symptom, which may or may not be linked, was referred to in a letter of her husband's in 1520. Apologizing for his absence from court, Suffolk explained that 'the Queen has had several physicians for her disease in her side, and cannot yet perfectly recover her health'. Mary was buried in the abbey at Bury St Edmunds. Following the dissolution of the monasteries, her remains were removed to the nearby St Mary's Church.
68 Suffolk Place does seem to be the likeliest setting, as members of the royal family and the nobility were often married in London, and Frances's father rarely left the capital during this period.
69 L&P, VII (153). In the letter Margaret complained to Cromwell that the Duke of Suffolk was asking for money to help support the couple, Henry then being at court, and 'my lady his wife being in the country; or else she and her train to be with us'.
70 There is no evidence that the King was present. However, it has been claimed that he attended the wedding of Frances's sister, Eleanor, in 1535, and he certainly attended that of their cousin Lady Margaret Douglas in 1544. It seems possible, therefore, that he may also have attended Frances's wedding.
71 Frances was often referred to in this way on ceremonial occasions during this period, such as at New Year and at the time of Jane Seymour's funeral.
72 Perhaps one of the most famous examples is that of Thomas Howard, Duke of Norfolk, and Elizabeth Stafford. The couple became estranged when the Duke took a mistress, Bess Holland, and his wife wrote on more than one occasion of the abuse she suffered at his hands. They eventually separated, and Elizabeth was one of those that gave evidence against her husband when he was attainted for treason in January 1547.
73 P. Heylyn, *Ecclesia Restaurata, or the history of the Reformation of the Church of England* (London, 1674), p. 148.

74 A. Strickland, *The Tudor Princesses* (London, 1868), p. 94.

75 Harley MS 2342, f. 78v.

76 Ibid., ff. 78r–79r.

77 It is of course possible that Frances suffered miscarriages in between the births of her children that have gone unrecorded.

78 L&P, XII (890).

79 Jane's mother, Frances, Prince Edward, and the Princesses Mary and Elizabeth were all christened three days after their births.

80 L&P, II (3489).

81 As Antonia Fraser highlights, the term 'wet nurse' was first adopted in 1620. Prior to that, women who fulfilled this role were referred to simply as 'nurses'. A. Fraser, *The Weaker Vessel: Woman's Lot in Seventeenth-century England* (London, 1984), p. 77.

82 Alternatively, there are instances where wet nurses had a child that had succumbed to illness, leaving the mother still producing milk.

83 There is no evidence to prove that Margaret Wotton had any hand in Jane's upbringing, but it is certainly possible. The relationship between Margaret and her son was strained, so this may also have affected Margaret's relationship with Frances, and in turn her granddaughter Jane.

Chapter 2: Rejoiced All True Hearts

1   R. Porter, *London: A Social History* (London, 2000), p. 45.

2   Wynkyn de Worde was William Caxton's successor.

3   CSPS, XI, p. 32.

4   Three of the seven children born to Henry VII and Elizabeth of York died young, as did both of Jane's maternal uncles, the sons of her grandmother Mary Tudor, both of whom were named Henry Brandon.

5   CSPV, I (942).

6   L&P, I (17).

7   Throughout the course of their marriage Katherine had three sons, two of whom were stillborn, and one who died young.

8   Henry's only acknowledged illegitimate child was Henry Fitzroy, his son by Bessie Blount. He may also have had two illegitimate daughters, one of which was born to Anne Boleyn's sister, Mary.

9   CSPV, II (1010).

10 Charles was the son of Philip 'the Handsome' of Burgundy, and his wife, Juana of Castile. Juana was Katherine of Aragon's eldest sister, and was nicknamed 'the Mad' due to her unstable behaviour.

11 Prince Arthur died in 1502 at Ludlow Castle.

12 Claude was the daughter of Louis XII, Mary Tudor's first husband, by his second wife, Anne of Brittany. She suffered from scoliosis, which made her appear hunchbacked, but nevertheless she provided her husband, Francis I, with seven children, five of whom survived infancy.

13 William Tyndale's *The Obedience of a Christian Man*, and *The Supplication of Beggars* by Simon Fish are two examples.

14 CSPV, VI (884).

15 CSPV, IV (761).

16 Thomas Cranmer was an enthusiastic advocate of religious reform, and later stood trial alongside Jane. By 1529 he had found favour with the Boleyn family, and took up residence in the household of Sir Thomas Boleyn. He began producing arguments for the annulment of the King's marriage, and encouraged him to question papal authority.

17 On 29 May, Henry and Frances's father, the Duke of Suffolk, were among the gentlemen who escorted Anne to the Tower in accordance with the tradition that she should stay there prior to her coronation. The following day Henry was made a Knight of the Bath, and played an active role in the coronation celebrations, as did his future father-in-law. Henry's mother also attended the coronation, travelling in the same chariot as the Dowager Duchess of Norfolk, the Queen's step-grandmother.

18 L&P, VI (1111).

19 L&P, VI (1540). Henry's mother visited Mary on two separate occasions. First at Knole on 17 March, before returning on 15 April with her daughters.

20 Katherine Willoughby was the heiress of William Willoughby, 11th Baron Willoughby de Eresby, and his wife, Maria de Salinas, a Spanish maid of honour and close friend of Katherine of Aragon. The Willoughby family were neighbours of the Suffolk's, their main residence of Parham Old Hall being about twenty-five miles from Westhorpe. It was here that their daughter Katherine was born on 22 March 1519, their only surviving child, two sons having died in infancy. Following her father's death in 1526, Katherine became Baroness Willoughby in her own right, and was made a ward of the King.

21 L&P, VI (1069).

22 L&P, XII (958).

23 Henry was born on 18 September 1535. This date was confirmed at the time of his father's death on 22 August 1545, when he was reported then to be nine years, eleven months and six days old. Charles was born on an unspecified date in either 1537 or 1538.

24 Henry Brandon died on 1 March 1534.

25 L&P, X (141).

26 L&P, X (1047). Sir John Russell also attended Henry VIII's wedding to Jane Seymour. In 1547, Edward VI granted Sir John Woburn Abbey in Bedfordshire, and in 1550 he was created Earl of Bedford. Sir John's descendants, the Dukes of Bedford, still reside in Woburn Abbey today. Sir John came to be closely involved in the events of Jane's story.

27 Anne even managed to alienate members of her own family, chiefly her maternal uncle, the Duke of Norfolk.

28 *The Statutes of the Realm*, III (London, 1963), 28 Hen. VIII, c. 7.

29 Ibid.

30 Richmond was buried in St Michael's Church, Framlingham, where his tomb can still be seen.

31 Eleanor may have been married in June 1535 – she was certainly married by January 1536. Her descendant, Lady Anne Clifford, later wrote that Eleanor was married in the presence of the King. Her marriage was an extremely happy one, and in her only surviving letter Eleanor referred to her husband as 'dear heart'. Though she and her husband spent some time at court, following her marriage Eleanor spent most of her time at her husband's Yorkshire homes of Skipton Castle and Brougham Castle. At Skipton, her father-in-law built a gallery and a new tower in her honour.

32 Eleanor's son, Henry, died in infancy, as did a later son named Charles.

33 L&P, XII (1186).

34 Ibid.

35 Ibid.

36 Although the rebels had little opportunity to do much damage at Skipton, a letter from the Earl to the King on 31 October reveals the extent of the havoc they were able to wreak on his other estates. A distressed Cumberland complained that the rebels had 'spoiled my houses at Bardon and Carleton, which were so strong as to take three days in breaking. They have stolen my money and destroyed my evidences, and yet threaten to slay me and my servants.'

37 L&P, XI (1005).

38 Sir Francis Bigod was a former ward of Cardinal Wolsey. An ardent evangelical, he was initially opposed to the Pilgrimage of Grace. He was, however, opposed to royal intervention in the church. Following the disbandment of the rebels in December 1536, Bigod doubted the King's intentions, and it was thus in an attempt to ensure that the King's promises were carried out that he instigated the second rebellion.

39 Bigod was captured on 10 February 1537. He was condemned, and hanged at Tyburn on 2 June.

40 L&P, XII (889).

41 L&P, XII (922).

42 L&P, XII (905).

43 L&P, XII (971).

44 L&P, XII (972); L&P, XII (1260).

45 L&P, XII (1105).

Chapter 3: Anyone More Deserving of Respect

1 Bradgate was made of brick rather than stone, which made it warmer than traditional castles.

2 The family continued to use Astley on occasion, as well as their London residence, Dorset House.

3 L&P, XIII (1237).

4 Ibid.

5 Sir Richard Clement of Ightham Mote was married to the widowed Anne Grey, Margaret's sister-in-law. Anne had first been married to Sir John Grey, the brother of Margaret's husband, Thomas.

6 The date of Margaret's death in 1541 is unknown, as is her place of burial. It seems reasonable to assume that she was laid to rest beside her second husband in the church at Astley. Despite a temporary reconciliation, by March 1539 Margaret was so incensed by her son's behaviour that she urged Cromwell: 'let him no longer receive the revenues of those lands which be liable to the wills of my late husband and my lady Cecil, my lord's mother (Cecily Bonville); for he pays no debts, either to the King or to any other, and I am called upon for them every term. Now in my old age I would live in peace.'

7 Robinson (ed.), *Original Letters*, p. 281.

8 Ibid., p. 282.

9 H. Chapman, *Lady Jane Grey* (Boston, 1962), p. 17.

10 Howard, *Lady Jane Grey and her Times*, p. 104.

11 Ibid.

12 On the same day as the wedding, the King's chief advisor Thomas Cromwell, who had been the prime mover behind the Cleves marriage, was executed.

13 According to tradition, Katherine was born at Dorset House. As with her elder sister, her precise date of birth is unknown. At some time the same year, Frances's sister Eleanor also gave birth to a daughter, named Margaret. Margaret was the only one of Eleanor's three children to survive infancy.

14 Mary is thought to have been born in April 1545, at Bradgate Park.

15 In later life she is known to have owned dogs and a pet monkey.

16 M. Bateson (ed.), *Records of the Borough of Leicester* (London, 1899–1905), p. 63.

17 CSPS, I (315). The precise nature of Mary's physical disability has never been determined, and nearly five hundred years later it is almost impossible to do so satisfactorily. However, it is possible that she was suffering from kyphosis. Her portrait gives only the slight impression of a hunchback, and that may have been caused by her voluminous clothing, although this may also have helped to conceal it. If Mary did indeed have kyphosis, it would been an extremely painful condition for the young girl, and would probably have greatly impacted on her daily life.

18 Chapman, *Lady Jane Grey*, p. 24.

19 Frances's only child by her second husband was born on 16 July 1555.

20 Robinson (ed.), *Original Letters*, p. 4.

21 M.A.E. Wood, *Letters of Royal and Illustrious Ladies of Great Britain, from the commencement of the twelfth century to the close of the reign of Queen Mary*, III (London, 1846), p. 245.

22 Elizabeth was William's second wife, and though the couple had been having an affair since 1543, it was not until 1547 that they were secretly married. There were complications, however, due to the slow pace of divorce proceedings from William's first wife, Anne Bourchier, and it was not until 1551 that the couple's marriage was legalized.

23 Jane is believed to have visited Katherine Willoughby at her home in the Barbican with her mother and sisters on several occasions during Katherine's widowhood.

24 Elizabeth Grey had been married to Thomas Audley, the Lord Chancellor. Audley had died in 1544, and his widow had since remarried. A miniature of Lady Audley by Hans Holbein stills survives in the Royal Collection, and may have been painted to commemorate her marriage to Lord Audley. Audley House still survives, although much altered, and is known today as Audley End House, in the care of English Heritage.

25 Margaret was later married, first to Lord Harry Dudley, younger brother of Jane's husband, Guildford. When Harry was killed at the siege of St Quentin in 1557, Margaret later took as her second husband Thomas Howard, 4th Duke of Norfolk. The couple had four children, but sadly Margaret became ill soon after the birth of her son, Lord William Howard. She died in 1564, aged just twenty-three or twenty-four, and was buried in St John the Baptist's Church, Norwich.

26 It does seem plausible that Jane spent some time with her maternal grandfather, Charles Brandon, during her youth. It is unlikely, however, that she saw much of her aunt Eleanor and her family, for Eleanor spent much of her time in distant Yorkshire. Relations between Frances's elder two half-sisters, Anne and Mary, and the rest of the family appear to have been cool.

27 Most notably Hardwick Hall and Chatsworth. For the ambitious Bess this was not enough, and with the connivance of Lady Margaret Douglas, the daughter of Henry VIII's sister Queen Margaret of Scotland, she married her daughter, Elizabeth, to Margaret's younger son, Charles, who had royal blood flowing in his veins. Their

daughter, Arbella, would later become a potential contender for the English throne, but that was all in the future.

28 Frances held Bess in high regard, and rewarded her good service with a ring, which Bess treasured all of her life. Jewellery was the ultimate sign of favour, even more so than monetary gifts.

29 Sir William was the Treasurer of the King's Chamber, and would have known Jane's parents well from court.

30 The Cavendish's first son, Henry, was named after Jane's father.

31 Sadly we have no idea exactly how much the debts amounted to, but the fact that it was noted by several of their contemporaries suggests that they may have been significant.

32 See Bateson (ed.), *Records of the Borough of Leicester*.

33 Ibid.

34 CSPV, VI (884).

35 H. Bullinger, *The Decades of Henry Bullinger*, ed. T. Harding (Cambridge, 1852), p. 528.

36 Robinson (ed.), *Original Letters*, p. 3. The book arrived in England in the spring of 1551.

37 Harding seems to have joined the Grey household at the beginning of the 1540s.

38 T. Becon, 'The jewel of joy', *The catechism of Thomas Becon ... with other pieces written by him in the reign of King Edward the sixth*, ed. J. Ayre, III, Parker Society (London, 1844), p. 424; Aylmer was consecrated in 1577.

39 Robinson (ed.), *Original Letters*, p. 277.

40 Ibid.

41 Cited in E. Read, *Catherine Duchess of Suffolk* (London, 1962), p. 29.

42 L&P, I (5203).

43 Jane may also have learned to play the virginals.

44 G.F. Commendone, *The Accession, Coronation and Marriage of Mary Tudor*, ed. C.V. Malfatti (Barcelona, 1956), pp. 44–5.

45 The other one was dedicated to Henry Herbert, later 2nd Earl of Pembroke and nephew of Katherine Parr. Henry was briefly married to Jane's younger sister, Katherine, in 1553.

46 Chaloner, *De Republica*, p. 298. According to Chaloner, Jane also knew some Chaldean.

47 Florio, *Historia*, p. 26; this was in December 1550.

48 This presentation copy survives in the Bodleian Library, Oxford. Elizabeth later made a New Year's gift of the translation in three languages of Katherine Parr's own book, *Prayers or Meditations*, to her father, Henry VIII.

49 H. Ellis (ed.), *Original Letters Illustrative of English History*, II (London, 1825), p. 430.

Chapter 4: The Imperial Crown

1 L&P, XIX (273). Jane's grandfather the Duke of Suffolk also accompanied the expedition, providing 700 men, as did her uncle by marriage, Henry Clifford, now Earl of Cumberland.

2 Suffolk had attended a meeting of the Privy Council on 19 August, but three days later he died, probably of heart failure. His wife and his daughters, Frances and Eleanor, were by his side at the end and deeply mourned his passing. There are claims that his grandchildren, including Jane, were also present, but this is highly unlikely. They were, after all, still very young.

3 PROB 11/31/456.

4 No monument was ever erected to his memory, and a stone slab in the south quire aisle now marks his resting place. Suffolk did not request to be buried beside his third wife Mary, Jane's maternal grandmother, who was buried in Bury St Edmunds, and instead probably intended that he should be laid to rest beside his fourth wife, Katherine Willoughby.

5 Margaret's first marriage to James IV of Scotland had produced James V. The second marriage of James V to Marie de Guise led to the birth of Mary, Queen of Scots, in 1542. Mary became Queen of Scots when she was just six days old, following the death of her father (possibly of a fever) on 14 December 1542. In December 1543, Henry VIII instigated the conflict known as 'The Rough Wooing', which was essentially an attempt to force the Scots to marry their infant queen to Henry's heir, Prince Edward. The conflict dragged on until March 1551, and the marriage never came to fruition. The child born of Margaret's second tumultuous marriage to Archibald Douglas was Lady Margaret Douglas.

6 L&P, XXI (634).

7 Both Frances and Eleanor had been the recipients of New Year's gifts from their uncle. In addition, Frances, and possibly Eleanor too, had visited the King at court numerous times, and been present on official occasions.

8 Sadly, Eleanor died at Brougham Castle in September 1547. Her only surviving letter, though precisely dated, may have been written in the months preceding her death, as it describes her ill health: 'I have been very sick and at this present my water is very red, whereby I suppose I have the jaundice and the ague both, for I have none abide [no appetite for] meat and I have such pains in my side and towards my back as I had at Brougham, where it began with me first. Wherefore I desire you to help me to a physician and that this bearer may bring him with him, for now in the beginning I trust I may have good remedy, and the longer it is delayed, the worse it will be.' A definitive diagnosis is impossible, but it is plausible that she was suffering from pancreatic cancer. Eleanor's husband was devastated by her death. She was laid to rest in the church of Holy Trinity at Skipton, where her remains were disturbed in the seventeenth century, and her skeleton was found to be 'very tall and large boned'.

9 Henry Grey was nominated as a Knight of the Garter on many occasions throughout the reign of Henry VIII, but each time the King chose an alternative candidate.

10 CSPS, IX, p. 7.

11 CSPS, IX, p. 20.

12 CSPS, IX, pp. 19–20.

13 L&P, XXI, Part II (756). The other person named specifically by Chapuys was the Earl of Warwick (later the Duke of Northumberland), Jane's future father-in-law.

14 The day before the coronation, the King had processed through the streets from the Tower to the city, Henry proudly bearing the sword of state. During the ceremony itself he carried the sceptre, while at the banquet that followed he was honoured as Lord High Constable. In the British Museum there survives a medal that was made to commemorate Edward's coronation, the first coronation medal to be produced in England.

15 The book can be viewed via the Royal Collection website, www.royalcollection.org.uk, catalogue number 1047357.

16 Foxe, *Acts and Monuments*, VI, p. 689.

17 In 1546 the King took great offence when Katherine took the liberty of expressing

some of her radical religious views to her husband. Through the influence of some of the conservatives at court, a warrant was drawn up for her arrest, but fortunately for Katherine she was reconciled with her husband before it could be put into effect.

18 The Act was repealed in the Parliament of 1547, the first of Edward's reign.

19 Robinson (ed.), *Original Letters*, pp. 406–7.

20 Ibid., p. 3.

Chapter 5: A Loving and Kind Father

1 Harington studied the composition of music under the great Thomas Tallis, and he was also a gifted poet.

2 CSPD, VI (182).

3 S. Haynes (ed.), *A Collection of State Papers Relating to the Affairs in the Reigns of King Henry VIII, King Edward VI, Queen Mary and Queen Elizabeth From the Year 1542 to 1570* (London, 1740), p. 82.

4 Ibid., p. 105. Seymour also made similar statements to Harington and William Parr.

5 CSPD, VI (182).

6 Ibid.

7 CSPD, V (157).

8 Katherine had first been married to Sir Edward Burgh in 1529, when she was seventeen. Following his death in 1533, the following year Katherine had taken as her second husband John Neville, Lord Latimer. Almost twenty years Katherine's senior, Latimer had been twice widowed and had two children from his first marriage. Latimer died on 2 March 1543, and on 12 July the same year Katherine married for a third time, her groom being Henry VIII.

9 Dent-Brocklehurst MS. The other time Katherine was at liberty to which she referred was the interlude between the death of her second husband, Lord Latimer, and her marriage to Henry VIII.

10 CSPS, IX, p. 340.

11 Lansdowne MS 1236, f. 26.

12 J. Strype, *Annals of the Reformation: Ecclesiastical Memorials*, II (Oxford, 1820–40), pp. 208–9.

13 CSPS, IX, p. 123. Precisely when Jane met Katherine Parr for the first time is unknown, but it seems possible, if not likely, that she had met her before Katherine's marriage to Thomas Seymour. Jane's parents were frequently at court during Katherine's queenship, so it is possible that on one of these occasions Jane was introduced to Katherine. However, there is no truth in the story that Jane served as one of Katherine's ladies. The confusion was caused during the Victorian period when Foxe's reference to Katherine's cousin Lady Lane was mistaken for Lady Jane.

14 Another of Katherine's dower properties was Hanworth on the outskirts of London, but there is no evidence that Jane ever visited the house.

15 CSPV, VI (884). This report was made in 1557, shortly before Elizabeth turned twenty-four.

16 PROB 11/68/664. This was taken at Beaumanor. No mention was ever made of Frances being part of the Queen's inner circle in the same manner as her stepmother Katherine Willoughby, which suggests that though the two women were on friendly terms, they were probably not overly close.

17 In the first year of her queenship, Katherine is known to have ordered a staggering 117 pairs of shoes. She also ordered new jewels on a regular basis, and her jewel inventories reveal the extent of the splendour with which she chose to adorn herself. Moreover, she was particularly fond of perfume, and also took milk baths.

18 Katherine's first book, *Prayers or Meditations*, published in 1545, was the first book to be written by a Queen of England and published under her own name. It proved to be extremely successful.

19 CSPV, VI (884).

20 Ibid.

21 Haynes (ed.), *State Papers*, p. 99.

22 On one occasion, Kate Ashley confessed that Katherine joined the Admiral in Elizabeth's bedchamber, and 'she and the Lord Admiral tickled the Lady Elizabeth in the bed'. Haynes (ed.), *State Papers*, p. 99.

23 Ibid., p. 95.

24 TNA, SP 10/2 f. 84.

25 Haynes (ed.), *State Papers*, p. 78.

Chapter 6: A Second Court of Right

1 At thirty-six, Katherine was considered old by contemporary standards to be pregnant with her first child.

2 Though the history of Sudeley stems back to the reign of Ethelred the Unready, in the sixteenth century most of the structure of the castle dated to the 1440s, when it was built by Ralph Boteler, a staunch Lancastrian and supporter of Henry VI. Sudeley was confiscated from Boteler when Edward IV became king, and Edward granted the castle to his younger brother, Richard, Duke of Gloucester (later Richard III), but Richard later returned Sudeley to the Crown in exchange for Richmond Castle in Yorkshire. It remained Crown property until Edward VI granted it to Sir Thomas Seymour in 1547.

3 The work is purported to have cost him approximately £1,000 (£340,000).

4 This line comes from a later poem. Cited in J. Mueller (ed.), *Katherine Parr: Complete Works and Correspondence* (Chicago, 2011), p. 188.

5 Haynes (ed.), *State Papers*, p. 82.

6 CSPS, IX, p. 19.

7 Some of these jewels had been her own personal property prior to her marriage to Henry VIII, and included bequests from her mother. Several letters from Katherine to her husband survive in which she berates the Lord Protector and his wife; on one occasion she claimed to be so enraged by the Protector that she could have bitten him!

8 CSPD, VI (182).

9 Haynes (ed.), *State Papers*, p. 75.

10 Ibid.

11 Mueller (ed.), *Katherine Parr*, p. 192.

12 Coverdale completed his translation in Antwerp, and Coverdale's Bible was printed in 1535.

13 Mueller (ed.), *Katherine Parr*, p. 174.

14 Additional MS 46348, f. 216.

15 Cited in Mueller (ed.), *Katherine Parr*, p. 169.

16 TNA, SP 10/5/2, fol. 3.

17 J. Parkhurst, *Ludicra sive Epigrammata Juvenilia* (London, 1573), pp. 153–4.
18 Ibid.
19 Katherine Parr had watched Henry VIII's funeral from a box above St George's Chapel, Windsor.
20 Parkhurst, *Ludicra*, pp. 153–4.
21 Ibid.
22 Ibid.
23 Ibid.
24 From the original account of Katherine's funeral it is difficult to ascertain precisely how many people attended. There were certainly in excess of fifty, probably over a hundred.
25 Parkhurst, *Ludicra*, pp. 153–4.
26 Ibid.
27 Ibid.
28 Ibid.
29 Ibid.
30 Haynes (ed.), *State Papers*, p. 77.
31 Ibid., p. 77; p. 78.
32 Ibid., p. 78.
33 This is the prayer book now in the collection of the British Library. Mueller argues that the book belonged to Katherine Parr and was written in her hand. This has since been disputed, and it is more likely that the words were written by a professional scribe. It is possible that the prayer book belonged to Katherine, and that it may have come into Jane's possession at the time of her death – given to her either by the late Queen, or perhaps by Seymour. However, it is unclear exactly when Jane came to own the prayer book, and it is therefore equally likely that it was given to her by someone else.
34 Richard Taverner was a Reformer, but following the accession of Mary I he wrote *An Oration Gratulatory* by means of congratulating her upon her accession. He remained in the background for the entirety of Mary's reign, and only resumed preaching during the reign of Elizabeth I.
35 Gifts of books were not unusual among those who held a particular interest in them. Lady Mildred Cecil would later make Jane a gift of a book, or perhaps it was even given to her by her parents.

Chapter 7: Ruled and Framed Towards Virtue

1 Haynes (ed.), *State Papers*, p. 72.
2 Ibid.
3 Ibid.
4 Ibid., pp. 75–7.
5 CSPS, IX, p. 20.
6 Haynes (ed.), *State Papers*, p. 78.
7 Ibid.
8 Ibid., p. 79.
9 Unfortunately the letter Seymour wrote to Jane does not survive, but judging from her reply he had been characteristically charming.
10 CSPD, V (5).

11 One or both of Jane's parents may even have dictated her letter; they almost certainly read it prior to it being sent.

12 CSPD, V (6).

13 Despite his condemnation, Sharington's life was spared. He was restored to Edward VI's favour, and died of natural causes in November 1553.

14 CSPD, VI (182).

15 Haynes (ed.), *State Papers*, p. 82.

16 Ibid.

17 Accounts differ as to where Lady Mary Seymour spent the first six months of her life. She may have been at Seymour Place; other sources place her in the care of her uncle, the Lord Protector. However, given that relations between her father and uncle were difficult, it seems more likely that she remained in her father's household, at Seymour Place.

18 Born in around 1478, Margaret was the daughter of Sir Henry Wentworth and Anne Saye. She had married Sir John Seymour of Wulfhall in Wiltshire in 1494, and the couple had nine children. Of these, Edward, the Lord Protector, was the eldest surviving son, followed by Henry, who, though serving at court, did not share the ambitions of his brothers. Thomas, the Lord Admiral, was the third surviving son. Thomas was followed by Jane, Henry VIII's third wife. Jane's birth was followed by three daughters and a son. Margaret died in 1550.

19 CSPS, IX, p. 332.

20 Ibid.

21 Parts of Henry's testimony have been cited throughout the chapter.

22 CSPD, VI (182).

23 Ibid.

24 CSPS, IX, p. 349.

25 Ibid.

26 Ibid.

27 Strype, *Ecclesiastical Memorials*, pp. 198–9. In 1550 Latimer joined the household of Jane's step-grandmother, Katherine Willoughby, Duchess of Suffolk, as her chaplain.

28 The fate of Lady Mary Seymour has never been established with absolute certainty, but it is probable that she died when she was around two years old. Katherine Willoughby was dismayed by the arrival of the child in her household, and wrote to the Council complaining of the expense of maintaining her in the style which, as a daughter of the Queen Dowager, was expected. In January 1550, an Act of Parliament meant that Mary was able to inherit property that belonged to her father, but no claim was ever made on her behalf, and nothing more is heard of her. Moreover, a poem written by Katherine's chaplain John Parkhurst in *Ludicra sive Epigrammata Juvenilia* almost certainly refers to Mary's death as a youngster.

29 CSPD, VI (189).

Chapter 8: She Did Never Love Her After

1 Foxe, *Acts and Monuments*, VI, p. 1430.

2 Mary, Queen of Scots, was married to the future Francis II of France in 1558. Following his premature death and her return to Scotland, in 1565 she was married to the son of Lady Margaret Douglas, Henry, Lord Darnley. Finally, following Darnley's murder,

Mary married James Hepburn, Earl of Bothwell, in 1567. Princess Elisabeth was married in 1559 to Philip of Spain. Philip was married first to Jane's cousin Queen Mary, but took Elisabeth as his second wife the year after Mary's death.

3 Haynes (ed.), *State Papers*, p. 74.

4 J. North, *England's Boy King* (Welwyn Garden City, 2005), p. 71.

5 Guildford had also been a close friend of Jane's maternal grandfather, the Duke of Suffolk. His first wife, and mother of his daughter, was Eleanor West.

6 Dudley had served under the Duke of Suffolk in France in 1523, and in Boulogne in 1544 among other military posts. He was also an accomplished jouster.

7 Consequences included spells of imprisonment, and loss of income and position.

8 Henry VIII left Hunsdon, Beaulieu and Kenninghall to Mary in his will.

9 Not only did Edward forbid Mary from celebrating the Mass, but members of her household were also arrested over their religious obstinacy.

10 CSPS, X, p. 5.

11 HMC *Middleton* (1911), pp. 520–1.

12 Cited in A. Weir, *Henry VIII: King and Court* (London, 2001), p. 58.

13 Margaret Wotton's acquisition of the property was clearly questionable, for shortly after obtaining the lease she had written to Cromwell, 'it does not a little trouble me to hear that you should think this abbey of Tilty is impaired by me. This is some sinister report.' George Medley was the son of Jane's paternal grandmother, Margaret, Marchioness of Dorset, by her first husband, William Medley.

14 The date of this visit has often been confused and placed in the winter of 1551, but this is incorrect. George Medley's wife was Mary Dannet. A brass commemorating George and Mary can still be seen in St Mary's Church, Tilty. Unfortunately, only one small fragment of stone still survives from the former abbey in which Jane and her family spent their Christmas celebrations.

15 George Medley and Mary Dannet had three sons, Henry, Thomas, and William, and two daughters, Elizabeth and Mary.

16 It is possible that Jane's father and his two brothers were by their sister's side at the time of her death on 3 January 1548 at Wollaton Hall in Nottinghamshire, for they were listed in the family accounts as being present at the house on that day. HMC *Middleton*, p. 395.

17 HMC *Middleton*, p. 520.

18 Thomas Grey did, however, have an illegitimate daughter named Margaret, but her mother is unknown. Margaret later married Sir John Astley, Elizabeth I's Master of the Jewels. Mary Browne was the daughter of Sir Anthony Browne of Cowdray Park, and his wife Alice Gage. Sir Anthony was the half-brother of Charles Brandon's second wife, Anne Browne. John and Mary had four sons and two daughters. Later, three more daughters were born to them.

19 It seems probable that Frances was named as a compliment to Jane's mother. Frances was later married to the brother of Lady Mildred Cecil, William Cooke.

20 HMC *Middleton*, p. 520.

21 Beaulieu translates as 'beautiful one'. The name Beaulieu, however, seems to have gone out of use eventually and it was more frequently referred to as New Hall. The palace still stands, but though some of its Tudor fabric survives, it is much altered. Today it is New Hall School, a Catholic boarding school for boys and girls.

22 HMC *Middleton*, p. 520.

23 Elizabeth's household was also established separately from Edward's court, and she had little contact with her half-sister.

24 The coat of arms of Henry VIII that once adorned the gatehouse can still be seen in the Chapel at New Hall School. One of the original stone dragons that once stood on the roof also survives.

25 The inventories for the years 1542–6 survive. Jane's aunt, Eleanor Clifford, had received a gold tablet and a pair of bracelets. As well as revealing the nature of Mary's jewels and the gifts she made, they also list the gifts and jewels she received in return. By comparison to the gifts Mary made to her cousin Frances, those that she received in return were somewhat paltry, a reflection, perhaps, of Frances's difficult financial circumstances.

26 F. Madden (ed.), *Privy Purse Expenses of the Princess Mary* (London, 1831), p. 197.

27 Ibid., p. 199.

28 The stained-glass window still survives and can be seen in St Margaret's Church, Westminster.

29 Evangelicals based their faith on what was contained in the Bible, in which Mary featured very little.

30 Foxe, *Acts and Monuments*, VI, p. 1746. It is possible that the story is apocryphal, but it does sound in keeping with Jane's character.

31 Ibid.

32 Ibid.

33 Two years later, in 1551, Edward VI introduced a law that stated that everybody had to walk to church on Christmas Day. It is a law that survives to this day.

34 HMC *Middleton*, p. 521.

35 Wassail was hot mulled cider, and wassailing was a toast made in the hope that the harvest of the fruit trees would be plentiful.

36 De Vere's ancestors had employed similar troupes of actors since the fourteenth century.

37 Today the game is more commonly known as Blind Man's Bluff.

38 Robinson (ed.), *Original Letters*, p. 286.

39 Ibid.

40 HMC *Middleton*, pp. 520–1.

41 Madden (ed.), *The Privy Purse Expenses of the Princess Mary*, p. 96.

42 HMS *Middleton* reveals regular payments that demonstrate that Jane's father and uncles moved regularly between the family homes. The family of Jane's mother was extremely limited. Both of her brothers had died in childhood, and her sister Eleanor, Countess of Cumberland, had died in 1547. Eleanor had produced one surviving child, a daughter, Lady Margaret Clifford, who was the same age as Katherine Grey. Following Eleanor's death, however, her husband, Henry, Earl of Cumberland, had remarried, and it appears that from then on Jane's family had little to do with them. Frances's stepmother, Katherine Willoughby, Dowager Duchess of Suffolk, was still alive, and to all appearances she seems to have remained on friendly terms with Jane's mother, and probably saw Jane and her family on occasion. Moreover, she shared similar radical religious beliefs to Jane, and had been a close friend of Katherine Parr. Her two sons by Frances's father, however, had both died in 1551. She would later remarry, taking as her second husband Richard Bertie, by whom she had two children.

Chapter 9: I Think Myself in Hell

1 CSPS, X, p. 7.
2 Ibid. The claim that the Marquess of Northampton had two wives is based on the fact that his first marriage to Anne Bourchier had been annulled in 1543, and his second marriage to Elizabeth Brooke was declared to be valid and invalid on several occasions. Little wonder that it led to confusion among his contemporaries.
3 Ibid.
4 R. Ascham, *The Schoolmaster* (London, 1570), pp. 35–6.
5 Ibid.
6 Ibid.
7 Edward VI had a whipping boy named Barnaby Fitzpatrick, whose role it was to take any punishment inflicted upon Edward during childhood. During the days of the Lady Mary's estrangement from her father, Eustace Chapuys reported that the Duke of Norfolk had claimed that if Mary were his daughter, 'he would beat her to death, or strike her head against the wall until he made it as soft as a boiled apple'.
8 G.R. Rosso claimed that Jane was beaten by her father when she initially refused to marry Guildford Dudley, while Ziletti's *Lettere* states that 'the father subdued her by beatings', and other accounts also support this claim. However, other sources concur with Commendone in supposing that Jane was threatened verbally rather than physically.
9 Ibid.
10 Ascham, *Works*, p. 75.
11 Ascham, *The Schoolmaster*, pp. 35–6.
12 See F. Watson (ed.), *Vives and the Renascence Education of Women* (London, 1912), p. 133.
13 Robinson (ed.), *Original Letters*, p. 430.
14 Chapman, *Lady Jane Grey*, p. 19; R. Davey, *The Nine Days' Queen: Lady Jane Grey and her Times*, ed. M. Hume (London, 1909), p. 21.
15 Wingfield, *Vita Mariae*, p. 286.
16 Robinson (ed.), *Original Letters*, p. 280.
17 Ives, *Lady Jane Grey*, pp. 53–4.
18 Robinson (ed.), *Original Letters*, p. 276.
19 W.K. Jordan (ed.), *The Chronicle and Political Papers of King Edward VI* (London, 1966), p. 53.
20 CSPS, X, p. 262.
21 CSPD, VI (73).
22 Robinson (ed.), *Original Letters*, p. 7.
23 CSPD, VI (74).
24 Ibid.
25 CSPD, VI (75).
26 Robinson (ed.), *Original Letters*, p. 305.
27 Ibid., p. 10.
28 Ibid. The wording and tone of Jane's first surviving letter to Bullinger, dated 1551, suggests that it was the first occasion on which she had written to him.
29 Ibid., p. 276.
30 Ibid., p. 279.
31 Ibid.

32 Ibid., p. 276.

33 Ibid.

34 Though this is the first of the surviving letters, it is clear that Jane had received at least one letter from Bullinger prior to this, though whether she had also written before is uncertain.

35 Robinson (ed.), *Original Letters*, p. 276.

36 Ibid., pp. 4–5.

37 Ibid., p. 5.

38 When Bucer died, he left half of his books to Archbishop Cranmer, and half to Katherine Willoughby. His manuscript collection was left to Edward VI.

39 Walter was a fellow of King's College, Cambridge, from 1536 to 1552.

40 Martin Bucer died in Cambridge on 28 February 1551. Though there is no evidence that Jane ever met Bucer, it seems highly likely that she did, given the tone in which she wrote about him. Furthermore, the two mixed in the same circles, and were certainly in London at the same time on at least one occasion.

41 Robinson (ed.), *Original Letters*, p. 5.

42 Ibid., p. 6.

43 Ibid., p. 7.

44 Ibid., p. 6.

45 Ibid., pp. 406–7.

46 Henry Grey had paid for John of Ulm to be educated at Oxford.

47 Robinson (ed.), *Original Letters*, p. 276.

48 John of Ulm, as cited in G. Lloyd Jones, *The Discovery of Hebrew in Tudor England: A Third Language* (Manchester, 1983), p. 241.

49 Ibid.

50 Robinson (ed.), *Original Letters*, p. 7.

51 Cited in Lloyd Jones, *The Discovery of Hebrew*, pp. 241–2.

52 Ibid.

53 Robinson (ed.), *Original Letters*, p. 8.

54 None of Bullinger's letters to Jane survive.

55 Robinson (ed.), *Original Letters*, p. 9.

56 Ibid., p. 10.

57 Ibid., p. 305.

58 Jordan (ed.), *The Chronicle and Political Papers of King Edward VI*, p. 75.

59 In March 1551 the Imperial ambassador reported that 'my Lord of Warwick has been trying his utmost to marry his daughter to the Duke of Suffolk, and my Lord of Somerset has also been endeavouring to obtain the Duke for his. The Duke's widowed mother, however, has refused both matches on the ground that her son is too young, only fifteen or sixteen years old, and in order to avoid his being worked upon she has managed to obtain the King's and Council's leave to take him away from Court for a time.'

60 The palace at Buckden had at one time been the residence of the disgraced Katherine of Aragon, following her separation from Henry VIII.

61 The brothers were buried together at Buckden.

62 Wood, *Royal and Illustrious Ladies of Great Britain*, I (London, 1846), p. 254.

63 CSPS, X, p. 341.

Chapter 10: Godly Instruction

1 J.G. Nichols (ed.), *The Chronicle of the Grey Friars of London*, Camden Society Old Series, LIII (London, 1852), p. 72.
2 J.G. Nichols (ed.), *The Diary of Henry Machyn, Citizen and Merchant-Taylor of London (1550–1563)*, Camden Society (London, 1848), p. 11.
3 Ascham, *Works*, pp. 239–40.
4 Ascham did not return to England until 1553, after Mary's accession.
5 A. de Guaras, *The Accession of Queen Mary*, ed. and trans. R. Garnett (London, 1892), p. 100.
6 J. Aylmer, *An harborowe for faithfull and trewe subjectes agaynst the late blowne Blaste concerninge the government of wemen* (Strasbourg, 1559), pp. 194–5.
7 Robinson (ed.), *Original Letters*, pp. 278–9.
8 It has frequently been stated that the lady to whom Jane spoke was Mistress Ellen, but in Aylmer's original text the lady is unnamed.
9 Aylmer, *An harborowe*, pp. 195–6.
10 Ibid.
11 Ibid.
12 Ibid.
13 CSPS, X, p. 392.
14 Jordan (ed.), *The Political Papers of King Edward VI*, p. 94.
15 Ibid.
16 J.G. Nichols (ed.), *The Literary Remains of King Edward VI* (London, 1851), p. 390.
17 J. Stow, *The Annales of England* (London, 1592), p. 494.
18 Chapman, *Lady Jane Grey*, p. 88. Chapman cites Agnes Strickland as her source, but Strickland gives no clue as to where the story came from. It is not referred to by any contemporary source so we may assume that it was a later invention.
19 At a similar time to the Suffolks' inheritance of the Charterhouse, Edward VI granted Henry the Minory House close to the Tower. It had at one time been the Convent of the Little Sister of St Francis, and at the beginning of the sixteenth century it had been the home of several women who had good reason to know about the fate of the Princes in the Tower. In 1553, however, Henry gave this to his brothers, Thomas and John, and his half-brother George Medley. Sir John Harington was also given use of the house. All four men appear to have used it at some time.
20 Robinson (ed.), *Original Letters*, p. 8.
21 Mildred was the daughter of Sir Anthony Cooke, and came from a family noted for their academic pursuits. Mildred and her four sisters were supposedly educated at home, where four of them became celebrated for their intellect. At some point, Mildred's sister Anne served in the household of Jane's cousin, the Lady Mary.
22 Ascham, *Works*, pp. 183–4.
23 Eric Ives highlights that in at least one of his letters to Cecil, Henry addressed him as 'cousin'.
24 The exact date of the letter is unknown, but it almost certainly dates from 1552.
25 TNA EXT 9/51 from SP 10/15, No. 79 ii.
26 It seems probable that Jane would have replied to this kind gesture, but if she did then sadly her response has not survived.
27 Three books were dedicated to Mildred in her lifetime. She was a great collector of books, and presented several to various educational institutions. More than thirty of her books still survive, seventeen of which are in the collection at Hatfield House.

28 Today he is often referred to as Saint Basil the Great.
29 J. Stow, *A Summarie of Englyshe Chronicles* (London, 1565), p. 292.
30 CSPD, XIV, pp. 42–4.
31 Ibid.
32 Robinson (ed.), *Original Letters*, p. 447.

Chapter 11: A Comely, Virtuous and Goodly Gentleman

1 Stow, *Annales*, p. 296.
2 J. Stow, *Two London Chronicles*, ed. C.L. Kingsford, Camden Miscellany (London, 1910), p. 296.
3 The Imperial ambassador first referred to Edward's illness on 17 February, though he was unsure at that time how serious it was.
4 Wingfield, *Vita Mariae*, p. 244.
5 Ibid., p. 250.
6 Ibid., p. 249.
7 Archbishop Cranmer had been married twice, having taken his second wife in 1532. The marriage was initially kept secret.
8 Ellis (ed.), *Original Letters*, p. 141.
9 CSPS, XI, p. 8.
10 CSPS, XI, p. 9.
11 Ibid.
12 Ibid.
13 CSPS, XI, p. 19.
14 Ibid.
15 Commendone, *Accession*, p. 4.
16 CSPS, XI, p. 17.
17 CSPS, XI, p. 46. In the same report, the ambassador claimed that 'It is said that if the Duke of Northumberland felt himself well supported, he would find means to marry his eldest son, the Earl of Warwick, to the Lady Elizabeth, after causing him to divorce his wife, daughter of the late Duke of Somerset; or else that he might find it expedient to get rid of his own wife and marry the said Elizabeth himself, and claim the crown for the house of Warwick as descendants of the House of Lancaster.' There is no further evidence that Northumberland made moves towards either of these things.
18 CSPS, XI, p. 35.
19 Ibid.
20 Ibid.
21 Wingfield, *Vita Mariae*, p. 244.
22 CSPS, XI, p. 35.
23 Wingfield, *Vita Mariae*, p. 245.
24 Ibid.
25 Jane had not been Northumberland's first choice of a wife for his son. He had initially set his sights on securing Jane's cousin, Lady Margaret Clifford, as a bride for Guildford. The match had the approval of the King, but it came to nothing when Margaret's father, the Earl of Cumberland, refused to allow the marriage. At one time it was also reported that Margaret would marry Northumberland's brother, Sir Andrew Dudley, but this also came to nothing. The reason for the refusal of Margaret's father to a marriage

with Guildford is unclear, but perhaps he simply did not wish to ally himself with Northumberland so closely. On 7 February 1554, Lady Margaret was married to Henry Stanley, Lord Strange, heir of the Earl of Derby.

26 CSPS, XI, p. 169.
27 Strype, *Ecclesiastical Memorials*, p. 347. King Edward provided the Marchioness of Northampton with new clothes for Jane and Guildford's wedding – the only non-family member to be mentioned specifically by name, which indicates that she had played some role in organizing the marriage.
28 Commendone, *Accession*, p. 5.
29 CSPS, XI, p. 36.
30 G. Ziletti, *Lettere di Principi, le quali si scrivono o da principi, o a principi, o ragionano di principi*, III (Venice, 1577), f. 222.
31 Wingfield, *Vita Mariae*, p. 245.
32 Cited in Lloyd Jones, *The Discovery of Hebrew in Tudor England*, p. 242.
33 Ziletti, *Lettere*, f. 222.
34 The only example was that of the Empress Matilda, daughter of Henry I. Though nominated as her father's heir, following Henry's death in 1135 the throne was seized by Matilda's cousin, Stephen of Blois. A power struggle ensued and civil war erupted in England. Matilda managed to capture Stephen at Lincoln in 1141, and then controlled the country. However, her perceived arrogance alienated her supporters, and she was driven away from London before her coronation could take place. Stephen was restored, but Matilda did not give up. From then on, however, all of her efforts were on behalf of her son, who by the terms of the Treaty of Wallingford, succeeded as Henry II following Stephen's death in 1154.
35 Commendone, *Accession*, p. 5.
36 Ibid.
37 R. Grafton, *An Abridgement of the Chronicles of England* (London, 1564), f. 159; Guildford's date of birth is not recorded, but given the approximate years of the births of his siblings, it has been estimated that his was in around 1535.
38 The ruins of Dudley Castle still survive, today as part of a zoo. Northumberland was granted the castle in 1546, and undertook a grand programme of rebuilding in the 1540s; Ely Place had been the London residence of the Bishops of Ely since the thirteenth century; Warwick Castle was granted to Northumberland in 1547; on his mother's tomb, Guildford's name is spelt Gilford, and in other contemporary sources it appears as both Guilford and Guildford. Guildford was one of thirteen children, eight of which were boys. However, five of his siblings died in childhood (Thomas, Charles, Margaret, Katherine and Temperance), and his elder brother Henry, as noted above, was killed in 1544.
39 HMC Pepys, pp. 1–2.
40 Of Guildford's brothers, John and Robert were certainly well educated, so it seems probable that Guildford was afforded the same attention.
41 Sadly, no likenesses of Guildford survive. A bronze bearing the kneeling effigies of Guildford and his brothers once adorned the tomb of his mother in Chelsea Old Church, but was unfortunately destroyed. The effigy of Guildford's sisters kneeling beside their mother, however, can still be seen.
42 John had married Anne Seymour, eldest daughter of the Lord Protector, in 1550. Ambrose had been married first to Anne Whorwood, but following her death in 1552 had later married for a second time. This time his bride was Elizabeth Tailboys.

Following Elizabeth's death in 1563, Ambrose took as his third wife Anne Russell, daughter of the Earl of Bedford and a maid of honour to Elizabeth I. A day after the wedding of his elder brother John, Robert was married to Amy Robsart, who died in mysterious circumstances in 1560.

43 Margaret Audley was the sole surviving child of Thomas Audley and his wife, Lady Elizabeth Grey, Jane's paternal aunt. It is unclear precisely when Margaret's marriage to Harry Dudley was arranged or performed, but it seems likely that it was organized at a similar time to Jane and Guildford's in order to bind the two families closer. Margaret was born in 1540, making her thirteen in 1553. As the legal age of cohabitation was twelve for girls and fourteen for boys, the marriage cannot have been performed any earlier than 1552. It had certainly taken place by the summer of 1553. As mentioned above, it is likely that Harry was born around 1538/9.

44 Mary was happily married to Henry Sidney. Similarly, Robert and Amy Robsart had probably married for love.

Chapter 12: The First Act of a Tragedy

1 Surrey History Centre, MS 6729/9/113.

2 Anne Parr died in February 1552 and was buried in Old St Paul's Cathedral.

3 The first reference to the match was made on 12 May, so presumably it had been arranged shortly before, probably at the same time as the arrangements for Jane's marriage.

4 Henry Herbert was the dedicatee of Florio's second grammar book.

5 Grey had been born in 1536, and was thus nine years older than Mary. He was a distant cousin of Jane's father.

6 Surrey History Centre, MS 6729/9/113. Although Katherine Dudley's date of birth is not recorded, it is possible that she was the youngest of the three brides, and may even have been younger than twelve years old.

7 As a result of his brother's influence with the King, Sir Andrew Dudley had also benefited. In 1551 he had been appointed Keeper of the King's Jewels at the Palace of Westminster.

8 Jane's sister and Katherine Dudley were gifted costly fabrics for their wedding dresses. Interestingly, some of the jewels and material listed in the warrant had once been the property of the executed Lord Protector and his wife.

9 New College Library, Oxford, MS 328, f. 29.

10 Ibid. The Duchess was also given a clock, and 'one piece of unicorn horn'.

11 Ibid.

12 Ibid.

13 Ibid.; CSPS, XI, p. 40.

14 New College Library, Oxford, MS 328, ff. 38–40.

15 CSPS, XI, p. 40; Surrey History Centre, MS 6729/9/113.

16 Black and white were considered sober colours for virtuous Protestant maidens such as Jane.

17 Durham Place has long since vanished, and today the Royal Society of Arts occupies part of the site on which it once stood.

18 Vows similar to this were exchanged between Henry VIII and Katherine Parr at their wedding on 12 July 1543. L&P, XVIII (873).

19 J. Norden, *Speculi Britannioæ Pars* as cited in G.H. Gater and E.P. Wheeler (eds), *Survey of London*, XVIII (London, 1937), pp. 84–98.

20 CSPS, XI, p. 40.

21 Surrey History Centre, MS 6729/9/113.

22 Wingfield, *Vita Mariae*, p. 245.

23 Ziletti, *Lettere*, f. 222.

24 Ibid.

25 Ibid.

26 CSPS, XI, p. 53.

27 Ibid.

28 Ibid.

29 Ibid., p. 46; Ziletti, *Lettere*, f. 222.

30 CSPS, XI, p. 47.

31 It later became clear that on the orders of the Earl of Pembroke, the marriage had not been consummated. This was a precautionary measure on Pembroke's part, so that if Northumberland's ploy were not successful it would be easy to extricate himself by having his son's marriage annulled on the grounds of non-consummation.

32 It ought to be remembered that, initially, Edward declared that the throne should pass to Jane's 'heirs male'. It was only when it became apparent that Jane was not pregnant that Edward altered the Devise in her favour.

33 CSPS, XI, p. 47.

34 CSPS, XI, p. 40.

35 Ziletti, *Lettere*, f. 222.

36 CSPS, XI, p. 40.

37 Ibid.

38 Ibid.

39 Ibid.

40 CSPS, XI, p. 46.

41 CSPS, XI, p. 40.

42 It is probable that the Devise was first drafted in April.

43 Inner Temple, Petyt MS 538.47, f. 317.

44 Ibid.

45 Ibid.

46 Wingfield, *Vita Mariae*, p. 246.

47 Inner Temple, Petyt MS 538.47, f. 317.

48 Wingfield, *Vita Mariae*, p. 246.

49 CSPS, XI, p. 55.

50 Ibid.

51 Ziletti, *Lettere*, f. 222.

52 Commendone, *Accession*, p. 45.

53 Ibid.

54 Ibid.

55 R.A. de Vertot and C. Villaret (eds), *Ambassades de Meisseurs de Noailles en Angleterre*, II (Paris, 1763), p. 57.

56 Commendone, *Accession*, p. 45.

57 CSPS, XI, p. 69.

58 De Guaras, *Accession*, p. 87.

59 CSPS, XI, p. 70.

60 Ibid.
61 CSPS, XI, p. 53.
62 The precise nature of what was administered to Edward is unclear, but whatever it was may have done more harm than good.
63 CSPS, XI, p. 71.
64 Ibid.
65 Cited in C. Skidmore, *Edward VI: The Lost King of England* (London, 2007), p. 258.
66 Ibid., p. 106.
67 Wingfield, *Vita Mariae*, pp. 249–50.
68 Lady Mary Sidney was the eldest daughter of the Duke of Northumberland. In 1551 she married Sir Henry Sidney, who had been by Edward VI's side at the time of his death; Commendone, *Accession*, pp. 45–6. Syon had probably been chosen because its distance from the centre of London ensured a greater degree of privacy for the scene that was to take place.
69 Ziletti, *Lettere*, f. 221.
70 I have been unable to find any contemporary evidence that confirms that it was in Syon's Long Gallery that Jane was offered the crown; the theory rests on a tradition. The Long Gallery was remodelled during the eighteenth century by Robert Adam, but still retains its original structure.
71 Commendone, *Accession*, p. 46.
72 Ibid.
73 Evidence discussed later strongly suggests that it was the Marchioness of Northampton who first proposed the idea of a marriage between Jane and Guildford Dudley.
74 G. Pollini, *L'Historia Ecclesiastica della Rivoluzion d'Inghilterra* (Rome, 1594), p. 355.
75 Ibid.
76 Ibid.
77 Commendone, *Accession*, p. 7
78 Vertot and Villaret (eds), *Ambassades*, p. 211.
79 Commendone, *Accession*, p. 7.

Chapter 13: Long Live the Queen!

1 Presumably Jane remained at Syon from 6 to 10 July, as no mention is made in contemporary sources of her being moved elsewhere.
2 CSPS, XI, p. 106.
3 CSPS, XI, p. 67.
4 J.G. Nichols (ed.), *The Chronicle of Queen Jane and Two Years of Queen Mary*, Camden Society (London, 1850), p. 3.
5 CSPS, XI, p. 106.
6 Jehan de Montmorency, Jacques de Marnix and Simon Renard had recently arrived in England to support Jehan Scheyfve in his role as ambassador; CSPS, XI, p. 80.
7 CSPS, XI, p. 45.
8 CSPS, XI, p. 50.
9 Ziletti, *Lettere*, f. 222.
10 Commendone, *Accession*, p. 8.
11 Ziletti, *Lettere*, f. 223.
12 Ibid.

13 Vertot and Villaret (eds), *Ambassades*, p. 57.

14 Ziletti, *Lettere*, f. 222.

15 Grafton, *Abridgement*, f. 159.

16 Following the accession of Mary I, Grafton was excluded from the general pardon and lost his position as the royal printer.

17 Wingfield, *Vita Mariae*, p. 271.

18 CSPS, XI, p. 83. The Imperial ambassadors reported on 11 July that Jane would not leave the Tower until such time as she was crowned.

19 The Royal Apartments have long since vanished, having been demolished in the eighteenth century.

20 Henry FitzAlan had been married to Jane's paternal aunt, Katherine Grey. Following Katherine's death in 1542, three years later in 1545 FitzAlan had taken as his second wife Mary Arundell, who had served in the households of Jane Seymour, Anne of Cleves and the Lady Mary.

21 Society of Antiquaries MS 129, f. 7.

22 Pollini, *L'Historia*, p. 357. There were several crowns in the royal collection at this time, and it is unclear precisely which crown was used. It may have been the small crown made for Edward VI, which contained diamonds, rubies, sapphires and emeralds.

23 Ibid.

24 Ibid.

25 Ibid.

26 De Guaras, *Accession*, p. 88; Nichols (ed.), *The Chronicle of Queen Jane*, p. 5.

27 CSPS, XI, p. 106.

28 Nichols (ed.), *The Chronicle of Queen Jane*, p. 5.

29 C. Wriothesley, *A chronicle of England during the reigns of the Tudors, from A.D. 1485 to 1559*, ed. W.D. Hamilton (London, 1877), p. 86.

30 CSPS, XI, p. 80.

31 Wingfield, *Vita Mariae*, pp. 252–3.

32 Ibid., p. 253.

33 CSPS, XI, pp. 82–3.

34 Wingfield, *Vita Mariae*, p. 253.

35 Ibid.

36 Ibid., p. 252.

37 Originally a fifteenth-century manor house, Hunsdon was later owned by Henry VIII. Edward VI spent much of his childhood there, and during his reign it was to become a favourite residence of Mary's. Much of the old house has now vanished, and it was largely rebuilt in the eighteenth century.

38 Wingfield, *Vita Mariae*, p. 251.

39 Ibid.

40 Ibid.

41 Ibid.

42 Ibid.

43 Ibid., p. 252.

44 Ibid., p. 252.

45 Foxe, *Acts and Monuments*, VI, p. 1430.

46 Ibid.

47 Ibid., p. 1431; H. Nicolas, *Memoirs and Remains of Lady Jane Grey* (London, 1832), p. 49.

48 Commendone, *Accession*, pp. 8–9.
49 W. Cobbett (ed.), *A Complete Collection of State Trials and Proceedings for High Treason and Other Crimes and Misdemeanours from the Earliest Period to the Present Time*, I (London, 1809), p. 739.
50 CSPS, XI, p. 78.
51 Commendone, *Accession*, p. 48.
52 CSPS, XI, p. 113.

Chapter 14: Falsely Styled Queen

1 Robinson (ed.), *Original Letters*, p. 274.
2 Ibid.
3 Commendone, *Accession*, p. 8; Wriothesley, *Chronicle*, p. 86; Nichols (ed.), *Diary of Henry Machyn*, p. 36.
4 CSPS, XI, p. 82; De Guaras, *Accession*, p. 91.
5 Commendone, *Accession*, p. 8.
6 Cited in Ellis (ed.), *Original Letters*, p. 185.
7 Robert Dudley had actually departed from London in order to apprehend Mary on 7 July, the day after King Edward's death; Commendone, *Accession*, p. 13.
8 CSPS, XI, p. 94. Henry Dudley was also a relative of Jane's, for his mother Cecily was the sister of Jane's paternal grandfather, Thomas Grey, 2nd Marquess of Dorset. He was later arrested and sent to the Tower on Mary's orders, but was released.
9 CSPS, XI, p. 87.
10 Wingfield, *Vita Mariae*, pp. 261–2.
11 Frances may have told Wingfield that Jane wished her father to fight on her behalf in order to portray Jane as a strong queen – an image that would have been distorted if it had been known that, in actual fact, Jane forbade him from leaving.
12 Nichols (ed.), *The Chronicle of Queen Jane*, p. 7. Given what we know of Jane's behaviour on learning that the burden of monarchy was now hers, when she was overcome with weeping and seems to have found comfort in the presence of her mother, this seems more likely.
13 Ibid.
14 Ibid.
15 Commendone, *Accession*, p. 8.
16 Nichols (ed.), *The Chronicle of Queen Jane*, p. 7. His reference to 'I and mine' refers to his sons, for though Robert had already left London and Guildford would remain in the Tower, John, Ambrose and Harry accompanied their father on his expedition.
17 Nichols (ed.), *The Chronicle of Queen Jane*, p. 7.
18 Wingfield, *Vita Mariae*, p. 262.
19 De Guaras, *Accession*, p. 91.
20 Commendone, *Accession*, p. 13.
21 Nichols (ed.), *The Chronicle of Queen Jane*, p. 7.
22 Ibid., pp. 7–8.
23 Ibid., p. 8.
24 Ibid.
25 CSPS, XI, p. 107; CSPS, XI, p. 103.
26 Nichols (ed.), *The Chronicle of Queen Jane*, p. 8.

27 Ibid., p. 7.

28 CSPS, XI, p. 89.

29 De Guaras, *Accession*, p. 90.

30 CSPS, XI, pp. 88–9.

31 De Guaras, *Accession*, p. 92.

32 Nichols (ed.), *The Chronicle of Queen Jane*, p. 9.

33 CSPS, XI, p. 83.

34 New College Library, Oxford, MS 328, ff. 38–40.

35 Ibid., f. 36. Holland cloth is a type of linen used to cover furniture. It was frequently imported from Europe, but more specifically the Netherlands.

36 The inventory in New College Library, Oxford, lists in excess of six hundred individual pieces.

37 New College Library, Oxford, MS 328, ff. 38–40. A girdle was a kind of belt; aiglettes were a type of metal tag through which laces and ribbons could be passed through to adjoin to clothes, which became increasingly more elaborate and decorative; glass was a term used for a mirror.

38 Ibid. It is tempting to speculate that the book covered with black velvet is the same that hung from Jane's girdle on the day of her trial, but this cannot be proven. Moreover, the jewels were crown property, so presumably it must have been relinquished by her following her deposition.

39 Ibid.

40 HMS Salisbury, I (1883), p. 129.

41 Ibid., pp. 128–9.

42 All of these items were crown property, which entitled Jane to use them. They were never owned by her personally.

43 Wingfield, *Vita Mariae*, p. 255.

44 Ibid., p. 253; Nichols (ed.), *The Chronicle of Queen Jane*, p. 8.

45 CSPS, XI, p. 86. The figure of 15,000 is probably an error, and should have read 1,500; CSPS, XI, p. 91.

46 CSPS, XI, p. 87.

47 De Guaras, *Accession*, p. 92.

48 Stow, *Two London Chronicles*, p. 27.

49 Wriothesley, *Chronicle*, p. 88.

50 Wingfield, *Vita Mariae*, pp. 254–5.

51 Ibid.

52 CSPS, XI, p. 91.

53 CSPS, XI, pp. 91–2.

54 Wingfield, *Vita Mariae*, p. 253.

55 CSPS, XI, p. 91.

56 Ellis (ed.), *Original Letters*, pp. 186–7.

57 Ibid., pp. 187–8.

58 Ibid.

59 De Guaras, *Accession*, p. 95.

60 CSPS, XI, p. 92.

Chapter 15: Jana Non Regina

1 Today a marble slab marks her resting place.
2 CSPS, XI, p. 107.
3 Ibid., p. 94.
4 Wingfield, *Vita Mariae*, p. 261.
5 Ibid., p. 263.
6 CSPS, XI, p. 103.
7 Robinson (ed.), *Original Letters*, p. 366.
8 De Guaras, *Accession*, p. 95.
9 The Castle was destroyed during the Great Fire of London in 1666. It was never rebuilt.
10 Baynard's Castle was granted to Pembroke in 1551.
11 Arundel was a Catholic, and though uncle by marriage to Jane, there is no record of him and his family spending any time with Jane and other family members in a similar manner to the Christmas celebrations at Tilty in 1549. This is not to say that they did not spend time together, but Arundel's children, Jane's cousins, were also being raised as Catholics, so perhaps the religious differences between them meant that they naturally did not see much of one another. Nichols (ed.), *The Chronicle of Queen Jane*, p. 11.
12 Commendone, *Accession*, p. 17.
13 De Guaras, *Accession*, p. 95.
14 In an act of desperation, both Katherine and her groom claimed that their marriage had been consummated, but to no avail. The marriage was annulled, and Katherine was returned home.
15 Jane's father and the Earl of Pembroke were chosen as godfathers, though neither attended the christening.
16 From 'The examination and imprisonment of Edward Underhill', in A.F. Pollard (ed.), *Tudor Tracts* (New York, 1964), p. 181.
17 CSPS, XI, pp. 107–8.
18 Ibid., p. 105.
19 Commendone, *Accession*, p. 20.
20 P.L. Hughes and J.F. Larkin (eds), *Tudor Royal Proclamations* (London, 1964), p. 3.
21 Commendone, *Accession*, p. 20.
22 De Guaras, *Accession*, p. 96; CSPS, XI, p. 108.
23 Stow, *Two London Chronicles*, p. 27.
24 Robinson (ed.), *Original Letters*, p. 368.
25 CSPS, XI, p. 96.
26 De Guaras, *Accession*, p. 96.
27 CSPS, XI, p. 108.
28 Commendone, *Accession*, p. 20.
29 Ibid., p. 19. The figure of 1,000 men is a gross exaggeration, and was almost certainly a mistake.
30 Ibid.
31 Ibid. According to another contemporary, Henry was threatened with death if he refused to comply.
32 Ibid.
33 Cited in Chapman, *Lady Jane Grey*, p. 146.
34 Ibid.
35 Robinson (ed.), *Original Letters*, p. 367.

Chapter 16: Shut Up in the Tower

1 Pollard (ed.), *Tudor Tracts*, p. 181.

2 Commendone, *Accession*, p. 19.

3 Ibid., p. 21. Commendone relates that Henry was joined in the Tower by several of the lords, who jointly explained that the ladies would have to withdraw.

4 Ibid.

5 Ibid. None of the contemporary sources explicitly name Cheyne (sometimes called Cheney); however, on balance of probability, as Lord Warden of the Cinque Ports he is likely to have been the Lord Warden to whom Commendone referred. Cheyne was a favoured courtier under Henry VIII and Edward VI, but the Imperial ambassador believed that he was against Northumberland's plan to make Jane queen. Nevertheless, he was among the councillors who had signed the letter to Mary from the Tower declaring Jane to be the rightful queen, but on 19 July he was one of the first to switch his allegiance to Mary. He may have proceeded to the Tower from Baynard's Castle, there to guard Jane.

6 Commendone, *Accession*, p. 21.

7 CSPS, XI, p. 114.

8 Nichols (ed.), *The Chronicle of Queen Jane*, p. 11.

9 Frances's daughter Katherine returned to the Charterhouse shortly afterwards.

10 W. Thornbury, 'The neighbourhood of the Tower: Introduction', in *Old and New London*, II (London, 1878), p. 95. Among those who had been executed on Tower Hill were Thomas More, the five men accused of adultery with Anne Boleyn, Thomas Cromwell, and Edward Seymour, Duke of Somerset.

11 Though Jane's parents had been allowed to leave the Tower, giving the appearance that they carelessly abandoned Jane to her fate, in truth they did no such thing. They simply had no other choice, for not only had her mother been ordered to withdraw, but they also no doubt realized that they had more hope of obtaining mercy for both themselves and their daughter if they were at liberty to do so.

12 Among the graffiti carvings at this time were those of Thomas Abel, Chaplain to Katherine of Aragon, who was later hung, drawn and quartered for his opposition to Henry VIII. Two carvings that spell out the name 'Jane' can still be seen in the Beauchamp Tower, and these have been traditionally attributed to Guildford. However, there is no evidence to prove that this was the case, and even if Guildford were responsible, the name is equally likely to refer to his mother, also named Jane. Another carving in the Beauchamp Tower certainly refers to Guildford and his brothers. This is the ornate inscription depicting Guildford and the four brothers who were incarcerated alongside him, and it has been suggested that this may have been the work of a professional carver employed by their father. Equally, it may have been the work of Guildford and/or all or any one of his brothers.

13 Today, the Lieutenant's Lodging is called Queen's House. Dendrochronology has confirmed that the house was built in 1540 and replaced another building that stood on the same site. Prisoners were certainly imprisoned and interrogated there, but there is no evidence that this was the case with Jane. One of the earliest prisoners to be held there was Jane's second cousin Lady Margaret Douglas, for whom graffiti dated 1566 still survives.

14 CSPS, XI, p. 109.

15 The precise identity of these three women has never been definitively proven. Leanda de Lisle has suggested that 'Ellen' may have been a misspelling of the surnamed 'Allen'. This is entirely possible, but it does not bring us any closer to her identity. Similarly,

John Stow refers to her as Mistress 'Helen'. There is no truth in the story that Mistress Ellen was Jane's nurse. Mistress Tilney was almost certainly the younger sister of Katherine Howard, Elizabeth. The identity of Mistress Jacob is a mystery.

16 Wingfield, *Vita Mariae*, p. 265.

17 De Guaras, *Accession*, p. 98.

18 CSPS, XI, p. 112.

19 De Guaras, *Accession*, p. 98.

20 Ibid., p. 99.

21 Wingfield, *Vita Mariae*, p. 268.

22 CSPV, VI (884).

23 Ibid.

24 Ibid.

25 Ibid.

26 The year in question was 1483, which witnessed the untimely death of Edward IV and the deposition of his son, Edward V, by the Duke of Gloucester, who usurped the throne as Richard III. Edward V and his younger brother became the two Princes in the Tower, and were never seen again.

27 CSPS, XI, p. 109.

28 De Guaras, *Accession*, p. 97.

29 Foxe, *Acts and Monuments*, VI, p. 2087.

30 Stow, *Two London Chronicles*, p. 28; Sir John Cheke was also arrested and imprisoned in the Tower, but was released in September.

31 Nichols (ed.), *The Chronicle of Queen Jane*, p. 10.

32 Ibid.

33 Ibid.

34 Ibid.

35 Ibid.

36 De Guaras, *Accession*, p. 99. Three thousand is almost certainly a huge exaggeration.

37 CSPS, XI, p. 112.

38 Wingfield, *Vita Mariae*, p. 268.

39 De Guaras, *Accession*, p. 99.

40 CSPS, XI, p. 120.

41 Wingfield, *Vita Mariae*, p. 268. Sir John Gage had been Constable of the Tower since 1540, but had been suspended in his role for his failure to support Northumberland's coup. He was married to Philippa Guildford, the younger half-sister of Northumberland's wife Jane, by their father's second marriage.

42 Robert was captured in King's Lynn, where he had proclaimed Jane queen.

43 It is improbable that all of the Dudley brothers were imprisoned in the Beauchamp Tower at the same time for the duration of their imprisonment. They appear to have been separated at some point, but whether this was always the case or implemented at a later date is unclear. The carved signature of Robert Dudley can still be seen in the lower chamber of the Beauchamp Tower.

Chapter 17: Jane of Suffolk Deserved Death

1 Commendone, *Accession*, p. 38; Nichols (ed.), *The Chronicle of Queen Jane*, p. 13.

2 Wingfield, *Vitae Mariae*, p. 271.

3 CSPS, XI, p. 133.

4 Commendone, *Accession*, p. 38; Wingfield, *Vita Mariae*, p. 271.

5 CSPS, XI, p. 168.

6 According to the Imperial ambassador, Simon Renard, a fine of £20,000 (£4 million) was inflicted on Henry, which was later remitted. Renard, however, is the only source that mentions this, and given the fact that none of the other lords who had supported Jane's accession were fined, it seems unlikely that Henry was singled out, despite his relationship with Jane.

7 CSPS, XI, p. 113. The reference to the 'eight days' reign' is an error on the part of the ambassador.

8 CSPS, XI, p. 125.

9 Ibid.

10 Cited in S.J. Gunn, 'A Letter of Jane, Duchess of Northumberland, in 1553', *English Historical Review*, CXIV (1999), pp. 1267–71.

11 CSPS, XI, p. 150.

12 Commendone, *Accession*, p. 24; De Guaras, *Accession*, p. 100.

13 Wriothesley, *Chronicle*, p. 93.

14 Ibid., p. 94.

15 Nichols (ed.), *The Chronicle of Queen Jane*, p. 12.

16 Wingfield, *Vita Mariae*, p. 274.

17 Commendone, *Accession*, p. 24.

18 De Guaras, *Accession*, p. 100.

19 Nichols (ed.), *The Chronicle of Queen Jane*, p. 12.

20 The Catholic Gardiner had held great influence during the reign of Henry VIII, but following the King's death he opposed the religious changes implemented by Edward VI, leading to his imprisonment. Thomas Howard, 3rd Duke of Norfolk, was the uncle to both Anne Boleyn and Katherine Howard. Imprisoned for treason at the end of the reign of Henry VIII and under sentence of death, Norfolk was only saved by the death of the King, which took place in the early hours of the morning that his sentence was due to be carried out. Though saved from death, he remained in the Tower for the entirety of Edward VI's reign. Anne Stanhope, Duchess of Somerset, had been arrested alongside her husband, the Lord Protector Somerset, in the latter half of 1551. Edward Courtenay had been imprisoned in the Tower since childhood, sent there with his father by Henry VIII. Edward's father, Henry Courtenay, was executed in 1539 for complicity in the Exeter Conspiracy, and though Edward was not involved, as a great-grandson of Edward IV (his paternal grandmother was Edward's daughter, Katherine of York) he was considered too dangerous to release. He remained in the Tower until his release in 1553.

21 Wingfield, *Vita Mariae*, pp. 271–2.

22 Ibid., p. 272.

23 Two similar versions of Jane's account now survive. This version is cited by Pollini, *L'Historia*, p. 355.

24 Pollini, *L'Historia*, p. 355.

25 Ibid.

26 Ibid.

27 Unsurprisingly, I have been unable to find any evidence that Jane was poisoned. It seems probable, however, that Jane was laying the blame for the illness she experienced following her marriage at the Duke and Duchess of Northumberland's door.

28 More than 450 years on, a diagnosis is almost impossible to ascertain with any certainty, but it is perhaps possible that Jane had suffered from some form of alopecia exacerbated by stress, and that she had mistaken this as a sure indication that she had been poisoned.

29 Pollini, *L'Historia*, p. 355.

30 CSPS, XI, p. 168.

31 Ibid.

32 Ibid. The example given to Mary was that of the Roman Emperor Theodosius, 'who caused Maximus and Victor, his son, to be put to death notwithstanding his tender age, because Maximus had arbitrarily attributed to himself the title of Emperor with the intention of transmitting it to his son'. Maximus had usurped the throne of Emperor Gratian, and was later overthrown by Theodosius.

33 CSPS, XI, p. 169.

34 CSPS, XI, p. 168.

35 CSPS, XI, p. 169.

36 De Guaras, *Accession*, p. 102.

37 Ibid.

38 Wingfield, *Vita Mariae*, p. 272.

39 Nichols (ed.), *The Chronicle of Queen Jane*, p. 14.

40 CSPS, XI, p. 183.

41 Commendone, *Accession*, p. 26.

42 Nicolas, *Memoirs*, p. 71.

43 Commendone, *Accession*, p. 26.

44 Nichols (ed.), *The Chronicle of Queen Jane*, p. 15.

45 Ibid., p. 16.

46 Foxe, *Acts and Monuments*, X, p. 1620.

47 Ibid.

48 Nichols (ed.), *The Chronicle of Queen Jane*, p. 20.

49 Ibid.

50 Northumberland did not give up hope of a reprieve until the very end. The night before his execution, he wrote to his former colleague the Earl of Arundel begging for his intercession with Queen Mary: 'Alas my good lord, is my crime so heinous as no redemption but my blood can wash away the spots thereof?'

51 De Guaras, *Accession*, p. 105.

52 Commendone, *Accession*, p. 27.

53 Sir John Gates had been arrested with Northumberland at Cambridge. Sir Thomas Palmer was also an adherent of Northumberland's. Northumberland, Gates and Palmer were the only three men to be immediately punished as a result of the events of the summer of 1553.

54 CSPS, XI, p. 186. Northumberland's father, Edmund Dudley, had been a minister of Henry VII's. He and his colleague, Sir Richard Empson, were deeply unpopular for their financial policies, and as a result, following the death of Henry VII in 1509, both men were arrested and sent to the Tower. Though the charge was treason, the real reason lay in their financial actions. Both men were executed on Tower Hill on 17 August 1510.

55 Several versions of Northumberland's scaffold speech survive. This is cited by Commendone, *Accession*, p. 28.

56 CSPS, XI, p. 210. Northumberland's headless body was brought back to the Tower, where he was interred in the Chapel of St Peter ad Vincula, 'at the high altar' according

to *The Chronicle of Queen Jane*. What were thought to be his remains were discovered when the Chapel underwent restoration during the reign of Queen Victoria.

57 Jane Dudley still mourned her husband at the time of her death in 1555, and referred to him on several occasions in her will. She was buried in Chelsea Old Church.

58 The identity of the manservant is unknown.

59 Nichols (ed.), *The Chronicle of Queen Jane*, p. 19.

60 Ibid.

61 Ibid.

62 De Guaras, *Accession*, p. 112.

63 St Paul's Cross once stood in the grounds of Old St Paul's Cathedral, and was an open-air pulpit used for preaching.

64 Nichols (ed.), *The Chronicle of Queen Jane*, p. 19.

65 Ibid.

66 Ibid., p. 20.

67 Ibid.

68 Wingfield, *Vita Mariae*, p. 273.

Chapter 18: Justice is an Excellent Virtue

1 CSPS, XI, p. 232.

2 Charles V was the son of Philip the Fair, the son of the Emperor Maximilian. Charles's mother was Juana, the daughter of Ferdinand of Aragon and Isabella of Castile, and sister of Mary's mother, Katherine of Aragon.

3 Nichols (ed.), *The Chronicle of Queen Jane*, p. 21. Described as 'the gate against the water-gate', this was St Thomas's Tower.

4 Wriothesley, *Chronicle*, p. 96; De Guaras, *Accession*, p. 101.

5 Wingfield, *Vita Mariae*, p. 272.

6 Robinson (ed.), *Original Letters*, p. 100. John Hooper was Bishop of Gloucester and Worcester during the reign of Edward VI. In 1555 he was burned at the stake for heresy in Gloucester.

7 Wingfield, *Vita Mariae*, p. 272.

8 Ibid., p. 273.

9 CSPS, XI, p. 332.

10 CSPS, XI, p. 280.

11 CSPS, XI, p. 241. This is the first reference in contemporary accounts to the notion of Jane standing trial.

12 CSPS, XI, p. 334.

13 CSPS, XI, p. 393.

14 Ibid.

15 CSPS, XI, p. 241.

16 Nichols (ed.), *The Chronicle of Queen Jane*, p. 25.

17 Guildford's eldest brother John had been tried alongside their father, and his brother Robert was tried separately on 22 January 1554. This was because it was decided that his main act of treason had been taking up arms alongside his father in Cambridge, rather than any of his actions in London. Therefore a London jury had no authority to try him: a Norfolk jury had to be first appointed, hence the reason for the delay.

NOTES AND REFERENCES

18 Nichols (ed.), *The Chronicle of Queen Jane*, p. 24. Traditionally, it is always referred to as Guildhall rather than 'the' Guildhall.
19 Florio, *Historia*, p. 61.
20 TNA, KB 8/23.
21 Nichols (ed.), *The Chronicle of Queen Jane*, p. 24.
22 A note made by the Privy Council the following month indicates that Jane's health had suffered as a result of her imprisonment.
23 Nichols (ed.), *The Chronicle of Queen Jane*, p. 25.
24 Part of the original façade was destroyed, and now dates from the eighteenth century. Stow believed that two of the statues were of the Empress Matilda and Philippa of Hainault.
25 Commendone, *Accession*, p. 30.
26 The original statues were destroyed during the Great Fire of London, and the present ones date from 1953.
27 In 1536, the Imperial ambassador Eustace Chapuys, though not present, had heard that over two thousand people attended Anne Boleyn's trial.
28 TNA, KB 8/23.
29 De Guaras, *Accession*, p. 101.
30 Ibid., p. 102; TNA, KB 8/23.
31 TNA, KB 8/23.
32 The knights were Sir Robert Rochester, Sir Edward Hastings, Sir Nicholas Hare, Sir Richard Southwell, Sir Edward Waldegrave, Sir Henry Bedingfield, Sir David Broke, Sir Edward Saunders, Sir Thomas Moyle and Sir Robert Broke.
33 TNA, KB 8/23.
34 Ibid.
35 Harry's date of birth is unknown, and the only certainty is that he was younger than Guildford. At the time of his trial he was at least fourteen, probably fifteen, which places his birthdate at some time around 1538/9. He is not to be confused with his elder brother, also called Harry (Henry). The elder Harry had died in 1544 during the siege of Boulogne.
36 TNA, KB 8/23.
37 Anne Boleyn was the first Queen of England to stand trial, and Katherine Howard was condemned without trial; TNA, KB 8/23.
38 Ibid.
39 Ibid.
40 Ibid.
41 Ibid.
42 Ibid.
43 Ibid.
44 Ibid.
45 TNA, KB 8/23.
46 Commendone, *Accession*, p. 45.
47 TNA, KB 8/23.
48 Commendone, *Accession*, p. 45.
49 TNA, KB 8/23.
50 Ibid.
51 Ibid.
52 Ibid.

53 Ibid.
54 Ibid.
55 CSPS, XI, p. 359.

Chapter 19: Fear Not for Any Pain

1   CSPS, XI, p. 359.
2   Cranmer was burned at the stake for heresy at Oxford on 21 March 1556 – not before he had renounced his Protestant faith, a decision that he later recanted.
3   This probably took place in November 1553.
4   Foxe, *Acts and Monuments*, X, p. 1620.
5   Ibid.
6   Ibid., pp. 1620–1.
7   Ibid.
8   Robinson (ed.), *Original Letters*, p. 304.
9   Ibid.
10 Ibid.
11 CSPS, XI, p. 366.
12 Robinson (ed.), *Original Letters*, p. 77.
13 CSPS, XI, p. 366. There is no evidence that Henry underwent an official conversion ceremony similar to the one Northumberland participated in before his execution. It is more probable that it was an outward show of conformity in order to protect his daughter and the rest of his family.
14 Ibid.
15 Florio, *Historia*, p. 62.
16 Foxe, *Acts and Monuments*, X, p. 1605. Vespasian was a Roman Emperor, responsible for endowing schools and libraries; Sempronia were a Roman family of great prestige; the Gracchus brothers, Tiberius and Gaius, were elected Roman officials who attempted to aid the poor by the proposal of a land redistribution system. However, both brothers were assassinated.
17 CSPS, XI, p. 306.
18 CSPS, XI, p. 366.
19 Commendone, *Accession*, p. 38.
20 CSPS, XI, p. 408.
21 Commendone, *Accession*, p. 38.

Chapter 20: Liberty of the Tower

1   Wingfield, *Vita Mariae*, p. 278.
2   On 8 April 1554, Sir John was created Baron Chandos, and was granted Sudeley Castle, where Jane spent the summer of 1548 in the company of Sir Thomas Seymour and Katherine Parr. He died there in April 1557, and was buried in the church.
3   Florio, *Historia*, p. 62.
4   Ibid.
5   J.R. Dasent et al. (eds), *Acts of the Privy Council*, IV (London, 1890–1907), p. 379.
6   Nichols (ed.), *The Chronicle of Queen Jane*, p. 25.

7 Florio, *Historia*, p. 62.
8 Sir John's wife was Elizabeth Grey, daughter of Edmund Grey, Baron de Wilton, who came from another branch of Jane's family. The precise identity of Thomas's wife is unclear; she was known simply as Anne.
9 If Jane and Guildford did meet, they would have been supervised in order to prevent any opportunity of Jane falling pregnant; Nichols (ed.), *The Chronicle of Queen Jane*, p. 21.
10 Ibid., p. 25.
11 Ibid.
12 Wriothesley, *Chronicle*, p. 105.
13 CSPS, XI, p. 445.
14 Wingfield, *Vita Mariae*, p. 279.
15 CSPS, XI, p. 446.
16 Wingfield, *Vita Mariae*, p. 279.
17 CSPS, XI, p. 142.
18 CSPS, XI, p. 445.
19 CSPS, XI, p. 441.
20 Ibid.
21 CSPS, XI, p. 444; CSPS, XI, p. 473.
22 CSPS, XI, pp. 439–40.
23 CSPS, XI, p. 446; CSPS, XI, p. 440.
24 CSPS, XI, p. 418.
25 Ibid.
26 CSPS, XI, p. 446.
27 Wingfield, *Vita Mariae*, p. 273.
28 It seems probable that Mary's intention was to release Jane once she had married and produced an heir.
29 Nichols (ed.), *The Chronicle of Queen Jane*, p. 25.
30 Ibid., p. 26.
31 Wingfield, *Vita Mariae*, pp. 279–80.
32 Ibid., p. 279.
33 Ibid.
34 Ibid.
35 Robinson (ed.), *Original Letters*, pp. 290–1.
36 Despite the fact that Mary had ordered Courtenay's release from the Tower and had treated him well, Courtenay was keen for a royal bride, and when Mary made it evident that she would not marry him, his hopes turned in Elizabeth's direction. Following the failure of the rebellion, Courtenay was returned to the Tower alongside Elizabeth. However, he was eventually exiled abroad, and died in Padua in 1556.
37 CSPS, XII, p. 20.
38 CSPS, XII, p. 2.
39 CSPS, XII, p. 31.
40 Ibid.
41 Carew was later captured in Flanders in 1556 and returned to England, where he was imprisoned in the Tower for a brief period before being released.
42 Commendone, *Accession*, p. 39.
43 Ibid.
44 Ibid.

45 Ibid.

46 Nichols (ed.), *The Chronicle of Queen Jane*, p. 37.

47 Always more astute than her husband and no doubt still recovering from the repercussions of Northumberland's ploy, Frances would have been all too aware of the consequences both for herself and her family should the rebellion fail, and is unlikely to have approved of Henry's participation. Moreover, she may have resented the risk that he was taking with his family's welfare, which possibly caused a rift between the couple.

48 Initially, Henry's motive appears purely to have been to object to the Queen's marriage, and it may have been for this reason that he perhaps believed that Jane's well-being would not be affected. However, he was probably aware that Wyatt and his supporters also planned to replace Mary with Elizabeth. He may have been hoping that Jane would be restored to the throne, as his later actions certainly demonstrate that he had aspirations in this quarter.

Chapter 21: The Permanent Ruin of the Ancient House of Grey

1 Nichols (ed.), *The Chronicle of the Grey Friars*, p. 86.

2 CSPS, XII, p. 79.

3 Ibid.

4 Ibid.

5 CSPS, XII, p. 69; CSPS, XII, p. 77.

6 CSPS, XII, p. 80.

7 Ibid.

8 At both his trial and on the scaffold, Wyatt claimed that Elizabeth was not involved.

9 CSPS, XII, p. 54.

10 CSPD, II, p. 24.

11 Ibid.

12 CSPS, XII, p. 55. Huntingdon had been arrested alongside Northumberland at Cambridge. Unlike Northumberland, however, he was later pardoned and released.

13 Nichols (ed.), *The Chronicle of Queen Jane*, p. 35.

14 CSPS, XII, pp. 53–4. The brothers had actually headed for Astley, which was over a hundred miles from London.

15 CSPS, XII, p. 80.

16 Ibid.

17 CSPS, XII, p. 81.

18 Commendone, *Accession*, p. 40.

19 CSPS, XII, p. 78.

20 Ibid.

21 Ibid.

22 Ibid.

23 Wriothesley, *Chronicle*, p. 111.

24 Harington was released in January 1555.

25 Commendone, *Accession*, p. 44.

26 Wingfield, *Vita Mariae*, p. 284.

27 Nichols (ed.), *The Chronicle of Queen Jane*, p. 37.

28 Ibid., p. 38.

29 Wyatt was executed on 11 April 1554.

30 Commendone, *Accession*, p. 39.

31 Ibid.

32 Ibid., p. 40.

33 Ibid.

34 CSPS, XII, p. 85. According to Eric Ives, the table and chair that Henry is supposed to have used while in his hiding place are now on display at Arbury Hall in Warwickshire.

35 The brothers were in the home of alderman Christopher Warren, where they remained for three days.

36 See D. Loades, *Two Tudor Conspiracies* (Cambridge, 1965), p. 108; CSPS, XII, p. 85.

37 CSPS, XII, p. 87.

38 Ibid.

39 Ibid.

40 Ibid.

41 Ibid.

42 Wingfield, *Vita Mariae*, p. 286.

43 Commendone, *Accession*, p. 44.

44 Cited in D.C. Bell, *Notices of the Historic Persons Buried in the Chapel of St Peter ad Vincula* (London, 1877), p. 56.

45 R. Baker, *A Chronicle of the Kings of England from the time of the Romans Government unto the Death of King James* (London, 1670), p. 458.

46 Cobbett (ed.), *State Trials*, p. 868.

47 On 8 February, Renard wrote that if Mary's commands 'were executed last Tuesday, Jane of Suffolk and her husband were to have lost their heads on that day, but I am not certain that the deed has yet been done'. The Tuesday to which he refers was 6 February, so clearly the decision to execute Jane had been taken prior to that date, perhaps at the end of January when the Queen was informed of the Duke of Suffolk's treachery. However, there was delay on two occasions, for Jane was not executed until 12 February. In Cobbett (ed.), *State Trials*, p. 868, it states that 'Two days after the taking of Wyatt a message was sent to Jane Grey and her husband to bid them prepare for death'; however, it is clear that Jane was informed prior to this. Cobbett probably confused this with the date originally set for Jane's execution, 9 February.

48 Cobbett (ed.), *State Trials*, p. 868.

Chapter 22: Bound by Indissoluble Ties

1   G.R. Rosso, *I successi d'Inghilterra dopo la morte di Odoardo Sesto, fino all giunta in quell regno del Sereniss* (Ferrara, 1560), f. 53.

2   Robinson (ed.), *Original Letters*, p. 304; Commendone, *Accession*, p. 44.

3   Commendone, *Accession*, p. 44.

4   Ibid.

5   Ibid.

6   Foxe, *Acts and Monuments*, X, p. 1618.

7   Ibid., p. 1619.

8   Ibid.

9   Commendone, *Accession*, p. 45.

10 Ibid.

11 Foxe, *Acts and Monuments*, X, p. 1619.
12 Anne Askew being the obvious previous example.
13 Commendone, *Accession*, p. 45.
14 *An Epistle of the Ladye Jane, a righte vertuous woman* (London, 1554).
15 CSPD, III (84).
16 Foxe, *Acts and Monuments*, X, pp. 1621–2.
17 Ibid., p. 1621.
18 Ibid.
19 Florio, *Historia*, p. 73.
20 It is uncertain exactly where in the Tower Henry was imprisoned.
21 Foxe, *Acts and Monuments*, X, p. 1619.
22 Robinson (ed.), *Original Letters*, p. 304.
23 It is unclear precisely when, or if in fact the message in the prayer book was shown to Henry, but it seems probable that it was intended for after Jane's death with the collusion of Sir John Brydges.
24 Harley MS 2342, ff. 78–80.
25 Ibid., f. 79.
26 Ibid., ff. 59–60.
27 Commendone, *Accession*, pp. 48–9.
28 Ibid., p. 49.
29 Ibid., p. 45.
30 Foxe, *Acts and Monuments*, X, p. 1622.

Chapter 23: I am Come Hither to Die

1   Although it is known that attempts were made to persuade Guildford to convert, it is unclear if they were made by Feckenham. However, considering his presence in the Tower in order to speak to Jane, it seems probable that he also spoke to Guildford.
2   Nichols (ed.), *The Chronicle of Queen Jane*, p. 39.
3   Ibid.
4   Grafton, *Abridgement*, f. 159.
5   Nichols (ed.), *The Chronicle of Queen Jane*, p. 39.
6   Ibid.
7   Florio, *Historia*, p. 76. Florio claims that Jane made a further impassioned comment about the couple's shared fate, but as Eric Ives highlights, this is unlikely.
8   Nichols (ed.), *The Chronicle of Queen Jane*, p. 39.
9   Commendone, *Accession*, p. 49.
10 Harley MS 2342, ff. 74–7.
11 Nichols (ed.), *The Chronicle of Queen Jane*, p. 39. Contrary to tradition, Jane was not executed on the site now marked on Tower Green, but behind the White Tower, close to the modern-day entrance to the Crown Jewels.
12 Nichols (ed.), *The Chronicle of Queen Jane*, p. 40.
13 Foxe, *Acts and Monuments*, X, p. 1622.
14 Commendone, *Accession*, p. 45.
15 Precisely how many people had gathered to witness Jane's execution is not recorded.
16 Nichols (ed.), *The Chronicle of Queen Jane*, p. 40.
17 Ibid., pp. 40–1.

18 Nichols (ed.), *The Chronicle of Queen Jane*, p. 41.
19 J.P. de Castro, 'A Diary of Events Regarding the Happenings in Connection with the Rebellion of Thomas Wyatt and others following the arrival of the Imperial Ambassadors', in Malfatti (ed.), *The Accession, Coronation and Marriage of Mary Tudor*, p. 72.
20 Nichols (ed.), *The Chronicle of Queen Jane*, p. 41.
21 Ibid.
22 Commendone, *Accession*, p. 49; Nichols (ed.), *The Chronicle of Queen Jane*, p. 41.
23 Nichols (ed.), *The Chronicle of Queen Jane*, p. 41.
24 Ibid.
25 Ibid.
26 Ibid., p. 42.
27 Ibid.
28 Ibid.
29 Ibid.
30 D. Geary (ed.), *The Letters of Lady Jane Grey* (Ilfracombe, 1951), p. 7.
31 Vertot and Villaret (eds), *Ambassades*, p. 126. This was the observation of the French ambassador, Antoine de Noailles, who may have been present.
32 Nicolas, *Memoirs*, p. 93.
33 De Castro, 'A Diary of Events', pp. 72–3.
34 Ibid., p. 72.
35 T.B. Macaulay, *The History of England from the Accession of James II* (London, 1848), pp. 628–9.
36 Jane's ghost has normally been reported on the anniversary of her death, and has been spotted as recently as 1957.

Chapter 24: God and Posterity Will Show Me Favour

1   CSPS, XII, p. 97.
2   H. Chapman, *Two Tudor Portraits: Henry Howard, Earl of Surrey and Lady Katherine Grey* (London, 1960), p. 154.
3   Grafton, *Abridgement*, f. 159.
4   Stow, *Annales*, p. 622; Commendone, *Accession*, p. 72.
5   Robinson (ed.), *Original Letters*, p. 303.
6   Ibid., pp. 303–5.
7   Ibid., p. 303.
8   CSPS, XII, p. 94.
9   Robinson (ed.), *Original Letters*, p. 303.
10 Ibid., p. 294.
11 Ibid., p. 304.
12 Foxe, *Acts and Monuments*, X, p. 1623. Later editions were published in 1570, 1576 and 1583.
13 Ibid., p. 1622.
14 Foxe, *Acts and Monuments*, X, p. 1623.
15 G. Cavendish, as cited in Wood, *Royal and Illustrious Ladies*, p. 273.
16 Nicholas Wotton was the brother of Henry Grey's mother, Margaret Wotton. Thomas Chaloner accompanied Wotton on an embassy to France in 1553. It seems improbable

that Jane was close to her great-uncle as he spent much of his time abroad on diplomatic commissions; there is certainly no record of them spending any time together; T. Chaloner, 'Deploratio acerbate necis Heroidis praestantissimae Dominae Janae Grayae Henrici Ducis Suffolchiae filiae, quae secure percussa, animo constantissimo mortem oppetiit', in *De Republica Anglorum instauranda libri decem* (London, 1579).

17 Ibid.

18 G. Keate, *An Epistle from Lady Jane Grey to Lord Guilford Dudley* (London, 1762), p. 12.

19 It played in London more than forty times, and went through numerous printed editions in quick succession.

20 N. Rowe, *Lady Jane Grey: A Tragedy in Five Acts* (London, 1782), p. 60.

21 The painting came to England in 1870 when it was acquired by an English MP, H.W. Eaton. Eaton's son bequeathed the painting to the National Gallery.

22 R. Strong, *And When Did You Last See Your Father? The Victorian Painter and British History* (London, 1978), p. 126.

23 Strickland, *Lives of the Tudor Princesses*, p. 94.

24 The other two are the silent 1923 film *Lady Jane Grey, or the Court of Intrigue* and *Tudor Rose*, released in 1936.

25 As has been mentioned previously, Jane was not executed on the official site of executions now commemorated on Tower Green.

26 Commendone, *Accession*, p. 49. Commendone is not the only writer who cites that Jane wrote these lines; Florio and Rosso also refer to them. It has been suggested that they are apocryphal, but this seems unlikely.

Epilogue

1 In an ironic twist of fate, the man who passed sentence upon him was none other than his own brother-in-law, the Earl of Arundel, the brother of Katherine FitzAlan, whom Henry had long ago repudiated in order to marry Jane's mother.

2 Henry was buried in the Chapel of St Peter ad Vincula within the Tower; however, a curious tale later emerged about the fate of his head. In the early twentieth century, Walter George Bell claimed that following Henry's execution, his head had fallen into some sawdust, and was preserved in tannin. The head was removed from the scaffold, although by whom is uncertain, and was for some time displayed as a curiosity in the Church of the Holy Trinity near the Minories. At the end of the nineteenth century, though, the church was deconsecrated, and the head was taken to nearby St Botolph's, Aldgate, where it was later discovered in a small vault near the altar. According to Bell, the head is now buried in the vestry. It is a story that is almost impossible to prove one way or the other, but it is intriguing nevertheless.

3 Robinson (ed.), *Original Letters*, p. 305.

4 Tellingly, there is no record of Frances making any attempt to intercede on behalf of her husband. She probably realized that to do so would be pointless, for Henry's treachery had sealed his fate.

5 John, Robert and Harry were released in October 1554, and Ambrose was released slightly later. Tragically, John died immediately after his release. Harry was killed in 1557 by a cannonball at the Battle of St Quentin, in which Ambrose and Robert also participated. Robert, and perhaps Ambrose too, witnessed the death of his youngest brother, an event that deeply affected him. Both Ambrose and Robert enjoyed careers

at court and rose to prominence gradually under Mary I, but more famously under Elizabeth I. Robert was proposed as a possible suitor to Elizabeth, but despite their evident closeness, a marriage never transpired. Robert married three times, and died in 1588. Ambrose died two years later. He too had married three times, but had no children. Both brothers were buried in St Mary's Church, Warwick, where their splendid tombs can still be seen.

6 James I restored Bradgate to the Grey family following his accession to the English throne in 1603.

7 Through her mother Elizabeth Bourchier, Anne Stanhope was a descendant of Thomas of Woodstock, the youngest son of Edward III.

Appendix 1: The Queen Without a Face: Portraits of Lady Jane Grey

1 There is a miniature of an unknown woman in the collection at the Victoria and Albert Museum that could possibly be Frances. Museum number: P. 48-1984.

2 This is the Yale Miniature.

3 S.E. James, 'Lady Jane Grey or Queen Kateryn Parr?' *Burlington Magazine* (1996), pp. 20–4.

4 J.S. Edwards, *A Queen of a New Invention: Portraits of Lady Jane Grey Dudley, England's 'Nine Days Queen'* (Palm Springs, 2015), p. 25.

5 One of these is now in a private collection, one belongs to the Earl of Jersey, and the other is now in the collection of Baron Hastings.

6 The portrait was acquired by the National Portrait Gallery in 2007, which purchased it from Lane Fine Art. In turn they acquired it from an anonymous owner in Streatham, hence the name.

7 Edwards, *A Queen of a New Invention*, p. 52.

Manuscript Sources

The British Library

Add MS 10617, Add MS 14024, Add MS 15215, Add 18738, Add MS 26748, Add MS 27879, Add MS 33230, Add MS 34152, Add MS 46348, Add MSS 5751, Cotton Julius F VI, Cotton Vespasian F III, Egerton 2642, Egerton MS 2986, Harley MS 2342, BM Harley MS 6286, Lansdowne MS 1236.

Inner Temple Library

Petyt MS 538.47

The National Archives

C1/1434/23-25/C89/6/4, E 101/631, E 154/2, E 154/6, E211/293, E314/80/30, E328/400, KB 8/23, LC 2/1, LR 2/118, LR 2/119, LR 2/120, PRO SC 12/37/16, PROB 11/31/456, PROB 11/68/664, SP 10/2, SP 10/5, SP 10/15.

New College Library, Oxford

MS 328

The Royal College of Arms

MS RR 21/C/I, XV

The Society of Antiquaries

MS 129

Sudeley Castle

Dent-Brocklehurst MS

Surrey History Centre

Loseley MSS 7828/2/5/3, MS 6729/3/4, MS 6729/9/113, MS Z/407/MSLb.24, MS Z/407/MSLb.503, Z 407/MSLb.504.

Primary Sources

An Epistle of the Ladye Jane, a righte vertuous woman (London, 1554).

Anstis, J., *The Register of the Most Noble Order of the Garter* (London, 1724).

Ascham, R., *The Whole Works of Roger Ascham*, ed. J.A. Giles (London, 1864–5).

Ascham, R., *The Schoolmaster*, ed. L.V. Ryan (New York, 1967).

Aylmer, J., *An harborowe for faithfull and trewe subjects, against the late blowne blaste, concerning the government of women* (London, 1559).

Bailey, E.R., *Lady Jane Grey and Other Poems* (London, 1854).

Baker, J.H. (ed.), *Reports from the Lost Notebooks of Sir James Dyer*, I (London, 1994).

Baker, R., *A Chronicle of the Kings of England from the time of the Romans Government unto the Death of King James* (London, 1670).

Banks, J., *The Innocent Usurper or, The Death of Lady Jane Gray: a Tragedy* (London, 1694).

Bateson, M. (ed.), *Records of the Borough of Leicester* (London, 1899–1905).

Becon, T., 'The jewel of joy', *The catechism of Thomas Becon ... with other pieces written by him in the reign of King Edward the sixth*, ed. J. Ayre, III, Parker Society (London, 1844).

Bell, D.C., *Notices of the Historic Persons Buried in the Chapel of St. Peter ad Vincula* (London, 1877).

Bindoff, S. (ed.), *The House of Commons, 1509–1558* (London, 1982).

Brewer, J.S., Gairdner, J., Brodie, R.H. (eds), *Letters and Papers, Foreign and Domestic, of the Reign of Henry VIII, 1509–47*, 21 vols and addenda (London, 1862–1932).

Brown, R., Cavendish Bentinck, G., Brown, H.F., Hinds, A.B., (eds), *Calendar of State Papers Relating To English Affairs in the Archives of Venice*, 38 vols (London, 1864–1947).

Bullinger, H., *The Decades of Henry Bullinger*, ed. T. Harding (Cambridge, 1852).

Burnet, G., *The History of the Reformation of the Church of England* (London, 1880).

Byrne, M. St C. (ed.), *The Lisle Letters* (Chicago, 1980).

Camden, W., *Annals of Queen Elizabeth* (London, 1688).

Cavendish, G., *Metrical Visions*, ed. A.S.G. Edwards (Columbia, 1980).

Chaloner, T., 'Deploratio acerbate necis Heroidis praestantissimae Dominae Janae Grayae Henrici Ducis Suffolchiae filiae, quae secure percussa, animo constantissimo mortem oppetiit', in *De Republica Anglorum instauranda libri decem* (London, 1579).

Clifford, H., *The Life of Jane Dormer, Duchess of Feria* (London, 1887).

Cobbett, W. (ed.), *A Complete Collection of State Trials and Proceedings for High Treason and Other Crimes and Misdemeanours from the Earliest Period to the Present Time* (London, 1809).

Commendone, G.F., *The Accession, Coronation and Marriage of Mary Tudor*, ed. C.V. Malfatti (Barcelona, 1956).

Cox, J.E., *Works of Archbishop Cranmer*, 2 vols, Parker Society (London, 1846).

Crawford, A. (ed.), *Letters of the Queens of England* (Stroud, 2002).

Dasent, J.R. et al. (eds), *Acts of the Privy Council*, 36 vols (London, 1890–1907).

Dickens, A.G. (ed.), *The Register or Chronicle of Butley Priory, Suffolk, 1510–1535* (Winchester, 1951).

Dickens, A.G. (ed.), *Clifford Letters of the Sixteenth Century* (London, 1962).

Ellis, H., *Original Letters Illustrative of English History*, First Series, Vol. II (London, 1825); Second Series, Vol. II (London, 1827); Third Series, Vol. III (London, 1826).

Epistolae Tigurinae 1531–1558, ed. H. Robinson, Parker Society (Cambridge, 1848).

Erasmus, D., *Opus Epistolarum Desiderii Erasmi Roterdami*, 12 vols, ed. P.S. Allen and H.M. and H.W. Garrod (Oxford, 1906–58).

Feuillerat, A. (ed.), *Documents Relating to the Revels at Court in the Time of King Edward VI and Queen Mary* (Louvain, 1914).

Florio, M., *Historia de la vita e de la morte de l'Illustrissima Signora Giovanna Graia, gia regina eletta a publicata d'Inghilterra* (Middelburg, 1607).

Foxe, J., *Acts and Monuments*, ed. Rev. S. Reed, VI (London, 1838).

Geary, D. (ed.), *The Letters of Lady Jane Grey* (Ilfracombe, 1951).

Godwin, F., *Annales of England* (London, 1630).

Grafton, R., *An Abridgement of the Chronicles of England* (London, 1564).

Green, M.A.E., *Letters of Royal and Illustrious Ladies of Great Britain*, 3 vols (London, 1846).

Guaras, A. de, *The Accession of Queen Mary*, ed. and trans. R. Garnett (London, 1892).

Hall, E., *Chronicle*, ed. C. Whibley (London, 1904).

Haynes, S., *A Collection of State Papers Relating to the Affairs in the Reigns of King Henry VIII, King Edward VI, Queen Mary and Queen Elizabeth from the Year 1542 to 1570* (London, 1740).

Here in this Booke ye have a godly Epistle (London, 1554?).

Heylyn, P., *Ecclesia Restaurata; or the history of the Reformation of the Church of England* (London, 1674).

HMC, *The Manuscripts of Lord Middleton*, ed. W.S. Stevenson (London, 1911).

HMC, *Calendar of the Manuscripts of the Most Honourable the Marquess of Salisbury*, I (London, 1883).

HMC Pepys, ed. E.K. Purnell (London, 1911).

Holinshed, R., *Holinshed's Chronicles of England, Scotland and Ireland*, 6 vols (London, 1807).

Hughes, P.L. and Larkin, J.F. (eds), *Tudor Royal Proclamations* (London, 1964).

Hume, M.A.S. (ed.), *Chronicle of King Henry VIII of England* (London, 1889).

Hume, M.A.S. (ed.), *Calendar of State Papers, Spain (Simancas)*, 4 vols (London, 1892–9).

Jordan, W.K. (ed.), *The Chronicle and Political Papers of King Edward VI* (London, 1966).

Keate, G., *An Epistle from Lady Jane Grey to Lord Guilford Dudley* (London, 1762).

Leland, J., *John Leland's Itinerary: Travels in Tudor England*, ed. J. Chandler (Stroud, 1993).

Luders, A. et al. (eds), *Statutes of the Realm*, 11 vols (London, 1810–28).

Macaulay, T.B., *The History of England from the Accession of James II* (London, 1848).

Madden, F. (ed.), *Privy Purse Expenses of the Princess Mary* (London, 1831).

Mitchell, M., *Lady Jane Grey: A Tragedy* (Newtown, 1925).

Nichols, J. (ed.), *A Collection of All the Wills … of the Kings and Queens of England* (New York, 1969).

Nichols, J.G. (ed.), *The Diary of Henry Machyn Citizen and Merchant-Taylor of London (1550–1563)*, Camden Society (London, 1848).

Nichols, J.G. (ed.), *The Chronicle of Queen Jane and Two Years of Queen Mary*, Camden Society (London, 1850).

Nichols, J.G. (ed.), *The Literary Remains of King Edward VI* (London, 1851).

Nichols, J.G. (ed.), *The Chronicle of the Grey Friars of London*, Camden Society Old Series, LIII (London, 1852).

Nicolas, H., *Memoirs and Remains of Lady Jane Grey* (London, 1832).

Norden, J., *Speculi Britannioœ Pars*, in G.H. Gater and E.P. Wheeler (eds), *Survey of London*, XVIII (London, 1937).

North, J. (ed.), *England's Boy King: The Diary of Edward VI 1547–1553* (Welwyn Garden City, 2005).

Orchard Halliwell, J. (ed.), *Letters of the Kings of England* (London, 1846).

Parkhurst, J., *Ludicra sive Epigrammata Juvenilia* (London, 1573).

Pollard, A.F. (ed.), *Tudor Tracts* (New York, 1964).

Pollini, G., *L'Historia Ecclesiastica della Rivoluzion d'Inghilterra, divisa in libri Quattro ne' quali si tratta di quello ch'e avvenuto in quell'isola, da che Arrigo Ottava comincio a pensare di ripudiar Cataerina … infino a quest'ultimi anni di Lisabetta* (Rome, 1594).

Robinson, H. (ed.), *Original Letters Relative to the English Reformation*, I (Cambridge, 1846–7).

Rosso, G.R., *I successi d'Inghilterra dopo la morte di Odoardo Sesto, fino all giunta in quell regno del Sereniss. Don Filippo d'Austria Principe di Spagna con Dna Maria di Lancastro, Reina di quell Regno* (Ferrara, 1560).

Rowe, N., *The Tragedy of Lady Jane Grey* (London, 1715).

Sadlack, E. (ed.), *The French Queen's Letters* (New York, 2011).

Starkey, D. (ed.), *The Inventory of King Henry VIII*, trans. P. Ward (London, 1998).

Statutes of the Realm, III (London, 1963).

Stockwell, A.H. (ed.), *The Letters of Lady Jane Grey* (Ilfracombe, 1951).

Stow, J., *A Summarie of Englyshe Chronicles* (London, 1565).

Stow, J., *The Annales of England* (London, 1592).

Stow, J., *A Survey of London*, ed. C.L. Kingsford, 2 vols (Oxford, 1908).

Stow, J., *Two London Chronicles*, ed. C.L. Kingsford, Camden Miscellany (London, 1910).

Tyler, R., Bergenroth, G.A., G. Mattingly, de Gayangos, P., Hume, M.A.S. (eds), *Calendar of State Papers, Spain*, 13 vols (London, 1862–1954).

Vertot, R.A. de and Villaret, C. (eds), *Ambassades de Meisseurs de Noailles en Angleterre*, II (Paris, 1763).

Watson, F. (ed.), *Vives and the Renascence Education of Women* (London, 1912).

Wingfield, R., 'Vitae Mariae Reginae', trans. D. MacCulloch, Camden Miscellany XXVIII, 4th series, XXIX (London, 1984).

Wriothesley, C., *A Chronicle of England during the Reigns of the Tudors, from AD 1485 to 1559*, ed. W.D. Hamilton, Camden Society (London, 1875, 1877).

Ziletti, G., *Lettere di Principi, le quali si scrivono o da principi, o ragionano di principi* (Venice, 1577).

Secondary Sources

Adams, S., 'The Dudley Clientele', in G.W. Bernard (ed.), *The Tudor Nobility* (Manchester, 1992).

Alford, S., *Kingship and Politics in the Reign of Edward VI* (Cambridge, 2002).

Alsop, J.D., 'A Regime at Sea: The Navy and the 1553 Succession Crisis', *Albion*, XXIV (1992), pp. 577–90.

Archer, I.W. (ed.), *Religion, Politics and Society in Sixteenth-Century England* (Cambridge, 2003).

Ashdown, D.M., *Tudor Cousins: Rivals for the Throne* (Stroud, 2000).

Ashelford, J., *A Visual History of Costume: The Sixteenth Century* (London, 1983).

Auerbach, E., *Tudor Artists: A Study of Painters in the Royal Service, from the Accession of Henry VIII to the Death of Elizabeth* (London, 1954).

Bailey, A., *The Succession to the English Crown* (London, 1879).

Baldwin, E., *Life of Lady Jane Grey and her Husband* (London, 1824).

Baldwin Smith, L., *A Tudor Tragedy: The Life and Times of Catherine Howard* (London, 1961).

Baldwin Smith, L., *Treason in Tudor England* (London, 2006).

Bann, S., *Paul Delaroche: History Painted* (London, 1997).

Barry, J., *The Tudor and Stuart Town 1530–1688: A Reader in English Urban History* (London and New York, 1990).

Bateson, M., *Records of the Borough of Leicester*, III (Cambridge, 1905).

Beer, B.L., *Northumberland: The Political Career of John Dudley, Earl of Warwick and Duke of Northumberland* (Kent, 1974).

Beer, B.L., *Tudor England Observed: The World of John Stow* (Stroud, 1998).

Bell, W.G., *Unknown London* (London, 1920).

Bernard, G.W., 'The Downfall of Sir Thomas Seymour', in G.W. Bernard (ed.), *The Tudor Nobility* (Manchester, 1992).

Bernard, G.W., *The Tudor Nobility* (Manchester, 1992).

Bernard, G.W., *Power and Politics in Tudor England* (London, 2000).

Bernard, G.W., *The King's Reformation* (London, 2005).

Bindoff, S., *Tudor England* (1950).

Bindoff, S., 'A Kingdom at Stake, 1553', *History Today*, III (1953), pp. 642–8.

Borman, T., *Elizabeth's Women* (London, 2009).

Borman, T., *The Story of the Tower of London* (London, 2015).

Brigden, S., *London and the Reformation* (Oxford, 1991).

Brigden, S., 'Youth and the English Reformation', in P. Marshall (ed.), *The Impact of the English Reformation 1500–1640* (London, 1997).

Brown, M.C., *Mary Tudor, Queen of France* (London, 1911).

Burnet, G., *The History of the Reformation*, 2 vols (London, 1841).

Carley, J.P., *The Books of King Henry VIII and his Wives* (London, 2004).

Carter, A., 'Mary Tudor's Wardrobe', *Costume*, XVIII (1984), pp. 9–28.

Castor, H., *She Wolves: The Women Who Ruled England Before Elizabeth* (London, 2011).

Chandler, J., *John Leland's Itinerary: Travels in Tudor England* (Stroud, 1993).

Chapman, H., *Two Tudor Portraits: Henry Howard, Earl of Surrey and Lady Katherine Grey* (London, 1960).

Chapman, H., *Lady Jane Grey* (Boston, 1962).

Chapman, H., *The Sisters of Henry VIII* (London, 1969).

Childs, J., *Henry VIII's Last Victim: The Life and Times of Henry Howard, Earl of Surrey* (London, 2006).

Cockayne, G.E., *The Complete Peerage* (London, 1932).

Colvin, H.M. et al. (eds), *The History of the King's Works* (London, 1963–82).

Cook, F., *Lady Jane Grey* (New York, 2004).

Cooper, J.P.D., *Propaganda and the Tudor State* (Clarendon, 2003).

Cooper, T., *A Guide to Tudor and Jacobean Portraits* (London, 2008).

Copinger, W.A., *The Manors of Suffolk*, 6 vols (Manchester, 1907).

Crawford, P., *Women and Religion in England 1500–1720* (London and New York, 1993).

Cross, C., *The Puritan Earl: The Life of Henry Hastings, Third Earl of Huntingdon* (London, 1966).

Dasent, J.R. (ed.), *Acts of the Privy Council of England* (London, 1890–1907).

Davey, R., *The Nine Days' Queen: Lady Jane Grey and her Times*, ed. M. Hume (London, 1909).

Davey, R., *The Sisters of Lady Jane Grey and their Wicked Grandfather* (London, 1911).

Daybell, J. (ed.), *Women and Politics in Early Modern England, 1450–1700* (Aldershot, 2004).

De Lisle, L., *The Sisters who would be Queen: The Tragedy of Mary, Katherine and Lady Jane Grey* (London, 2008).

De Lisle, L., *Tudor: The Family Story* (London, 2013).

Doran, S. (ed.), *Henry VIII: Man and Monarch* (London, 2009).

Dowling, M., *Humanism in the Age of Henry VIII* (Beckenham, 1986).

Duffy, E., *The Stripping of the Altars: Traditional Religion in England 1400–1580* (New Haven, CT, 1992).

Dugdale, W., *The Antiquities of Warwickshire* (London, 1651).

Durant, D.N., *Bess of Hardwick: Portrait of an Elizabethan Dynast* (London, 1977).

Edwards, J.S., 'On the Date of Birth of Lady Jane Grey Dudley', *Notes and Queries*, LIV (2007), pp. 240–2.

Edwards, J.S., 'A Further Note on the Date of Birth of Lady Jane Grey Dudley', *Notes and Queries*, LV (2008), pp. 146–8.

Edwards, J.S., *A Queen of a New Invention: Portraits of Lady Jane Grey Dudley, England's 'Nine Days Queen'* (Palm Springs, 2015).

Elton, G.R., *England under the Tudors* (London, 1955).

Elton, G.R., *The Tudor Constitution* (Cambridge, 1972).

Fincham, K. and Tyacke, N., *Altars Restored: The Changing Face of English Religious Worship 1547–c.1700* (Oxford, 2007).

Fisher, C., 'The Queen and the Artichoke: A Study of the portraits of Mary Tudor and Charles Brandon', *British Art Journal*, III (2002), pp. 22–7.

Fletcher, A.J. and MacCulloch, D., *Tudor Rebellions* (London, 1997).

Foister, S., *Holbein and England* (London, 2004).

Ford, F., *Mary Tudor: A Retrospective Sketch* (London, 1882).

Fraser, A., *The Weaker Vessel: Woman's Lot in Seventeenth-century England* (London, 1984).

Fraser, A., *The Six Wives of Henry VIII* (London, 1992).

Fuller, T., *The Church History of Britain* (London, 1842).

Gainey, J., *The Princess of the Mary Rose* (East Wittering, 1986).

Garrett, C., *The Marian Exiles* (London, 1966).

Goff, C., *A Woman of the Tudor Age* (London, 1930).

Graves, M.A.R., *The House of Lords in the Parliaments of Edward VI and Mary I* (Cambridge, 1981).

Grosvenor, B. (ed.), *Lost Faces: Identity and Discovery in Tudor Royal Portraiture* (London, 2007).

Gunn, S.J., *Charles Brandon, Duke of Suffolk* (Oxford, 1988).

Gunn, S.J., 'A Letter of Jane, Duchess of Northumberland, in 1553', *English Historical Review*, CXIV (1999), pp. 1267–71.

Gunn, S.J. and Lindley, P.G., 'Charles Brandon's Westhorpe: An Early Tudor Courtyard House in Suffolk', *Royal Archaeological Institute*, CXXXV (1988), pp. 272–89.

Guy, J., *Tudor England* (Oxford, 1990).

Guy, J. (ed.), *The Tudor Monarchy* (Cambridge, 1995).

Haigh, C., *English Reformations: Religion, Politics, and Society under the Tudors* (Oxford, 1993).

Hallowell Garrett, C., *The Marian Exiles* (Cambridge, 1938).

Hamilton, D.L., 'The Household of Queen Katherine Parr', PhD Thesis (Oxford, 1992).

Harbison, E.H., *Rival Ambassadors at the Court of Queen Mary* (Princeton, 1940).

Harkrider, M.F., 'Faith in a Noble Duchess, Piety, Patronage, and Kinship in the Career of Katherine Willoughby, Duchess of Suffolk, 1519–1580', PhD Thesis (University of North Carolina at Chapel Hill, 2003).

Harris, B.J., 'Power, Profit, and Passion: Mary Tudor, Charles Brandon, and the Arranged Marriage in Early Tudor England', *Feminist Studies*, XV (1989), pp. 59–88.

Harris, B.J., 'Women and Politics in Early Tudor England', *Historical Journal*, XXXIII (1990), pp. 259–81.

Harris, B.J., 'The View from My Lady's Chamber: New Perspectives on the Early Tudor Monarchy', *Huntingdon Library Quarterly*, LX (1998), pp. 215–47.

Harris, B.J., *English Aristocratic Women 1450–1550* (Oxford, 2002).

Harris, N., *Memoirs and Remains of Lady Jane Grey* (London, 1832).

Hayward, Sir J., *The Life and Reign of King Edward VI* (London, 1630).

Hayward, M. (ed.), *Dress at the Court of King Henry VIII* (Leeds, 2007).

Hickerson, M.L., *Making Women Martyrs in Tudor England* (Chippenham, 2005).

Hoak, D., 'The Coronations of Edward VI, Mary I, and Elizabeth I, and the Transformation of the Tudor Monarchy', in C.S. Knighton and R. Mortimer (eds), *Westminster Abbey Reformed* (Aldershot, 2003).

Hoak, D.E., *The King's Council in the Reign of Edward VI* (Cambridge, 1976).

Hodgett, G.A.J., *Tudor Lincolnshire* (Lincoln, 1975).

Houlbrooke, R.A., *The English Family 1450–1700* (London and New York, 1984).

Houlbrooke, R.A., *Death, Religion and Family in England 1480–1750* (Oxford, 1998).

Howard, G., *Lady Jane Grey and her Times* (London, 1822).

Hutchinson, R., *The Last Days of Henry VIII* (London, 2005).

Impey, E. and Parnell, G., *The Tower of London: The Official Illustrated History* (London, 2000).

Ives, E., *The Life and Death of Anne Boleyn* (Oxford and New York, 1986).

Ives, E., 'Tudor Dynastic Problems Revisited', *Historical Research*, LXXXI (2008).

Ives, E., *Lady Jane Grey: A Tudor Mystery* (Chichester, 2011).

Jack, S.M., 'Northumberland, Queen Jane and the Financing of the 1553 Coup', *Parergon* (1988), pp. 137–48.

Jackson, J.E., 'Wulfhall and the Seymours', *Wiltshire Archaeological and Natural History Magazine*, XV (1875), pp. 140–207.

James, M., *Society, Politics and Culture: Studies in Early Modern England* (Cambridge, 1986).

James, S., *Kateryn Parr* (Aldershot, 1999).

James, S.E., 'Lady Jane Grey or Queen Kateryn Parr?', *Burlington Magazine* (1996), pp. 20–4.

Jeffrey, K. (ed.), *Audley End* (1997).

Jordan, C., 'Women's Rule in Sixteenth-Century British Political Thought', *Renaissance Quarterly*, XXXX (1987), pp. 421–51.

Keay, A., *The Elizabethan Tower of London: The Haiward and Gascoyne Plan of 1597* (London, 2001).

Keay, A., *The Crown Jewels: The Official Illustrated History* (London, 2012).

Lacey, R., *The Life and Times of Henry VIII* (London, 1972).

Laynesmith, J., *The Last Medieval Queens* (Oxford, 2004).

Lemon, R. and Everett Green, M.A. (eds), *Calendar of State Papers Domestic: Edward, Mary and Elizabeth, 1547–80*, 8 vols (London, 1856–72).

Leslie, E., 'Lady Jane Grey', in S.C. Hall, *The Juvenile Forget Me Not: A Christmas and New Year's Gift, Or Birthday Present* (London, 1833), pp. 210–12.

Levine, C., 'Lady Jane Grey, Protestant Queen and Martyr', in M. Patterson Hannay (ed.), *Silent but for the Word: Tudor Women as Patrons, Translators, and Writers of Religious Works* (Kent, OH, 1985).

Levine, M., *The Early Elizabethan Succession Question* (California, 1966).

Levine, M., *Tudor Dynastic Problems* (London, 1973).

Lipscomb, S., *The King is Dead: The Last Will and Testament of Henry VIII* (London, 2015).

Lloyd Jones, G., *The Discovery of Hebrew in Tudor England: A Third Language* (Manchester, 1983).

Loach, J., *Parliament and the Crown in the Reign of Mary Tudor* (Oxford, 1986).

Loach, J., 'The Function of Ceremonial in the Reign of Henry VIII', *Past and Present*, CXXXXII (1994), pp. 43–68.

Loach, J., *Edward VI* (New Haven and London, 1999).

Loades, D., *Two Tudor Conspiracies* (Cambridge, 1965).

Loades, D., *The Tudor Court* (London, 1986).

Loades, D., *Mary Tudor* (Oxford and Cambridge, 1989).

Loades, D., *Politics, Censorship and the English Reformation* (London and New York, 1991).

Loades, D., *John Dudley, Duke of Northumberland* (Oxford, 1996).

Loades, D., *The Dudley Conspiracy* (Oxford, 2001).

Loades, D., *Intrigue and Treason: The Tudor Court 1547–1558* (London, 2004).

Loades, D., *Mary Rose* (Stroud, 2012).

Loades, D. (ed.), *John Foxe: An Historical Perspective* (Aldershot, 1999).

Lovell, M.S., *Bess of Hardwick: First Lady of Chatsworth* (London, 2005).

MacCulloch, D., *Suffolk and the Tudors: Politics and Religion in an English County 1500–1600* (Oxford, 1986).

MacCulloch, D., *Thomas Cranmer: A Life* (London, 1996).

MacCulloch, D., *Tudor Church Militant: Edward VI and the Protestant Reformation* (London, 1999).

MacCulloch, D., *Reformation: Europe's House Divided 1490–1700* (London, 2003).

Maclean, J., *The life of Sir Thomas Seymour* (London, 1869).

Macfarlane, A., *Marriage and Love in England 1300–1840* (Oxford, 1986).

Mack, P., 'Women and Gender in Early Modern England', *Journal of Modern History*, LXXIII (2001), pp. 379–92.

Marshall, P. (ed.), *The Impact of the English Reformation 1500–1640* (London, 1997).

Martin, J.W., *Religious Radicals in Tudor England* (London, 1989).

Matthew, D., *Lady Jane Grey: The Setting of the Reign* (Plymouth, 1972).

McConica, J.K., *English Humanists and Reformation Politics under Henry VIII and Edward VI* (Oxford, 1965).

Mears, N., 'Courts, Courtiers, and Culture in Tudor England', *Historical Journal*, XXXXVI (2003), pp. 703–22.

Mendelson, S. and Crawford, P., *Women in Early Modern England 1550–1710* (Oxford, 1998).

Mertes, K., *The English Noble Household, 1200–1600* (Oxford and New York, 1988).

Merton, C.I., 'The Women Who Served Queen Mary and Queen Elizabeth', PhD Thesis (Trinity College Cambridge, 1992).

Miller, H., *Henry VIII and the English Nobility* (Oxford, 1986).

Moorehouse, G., *The Pilgrimage of Grace* (London, 2002).

More Molyneux, J., 'Letters illustrating the reign of Queen Jane', *Archaeological Journal*, XXX (1873), pp. 273–8.

Mueller, J. (ed.), *Katherine Parr: Complete Works and Correspondence* (Chicago, 2011).

Murphy, B.A., *Bastard Prince* (Stroud, 2010).

Neville, R. (Lord Braybrooke), *The History of Audley End and Saffron Walden* (London, 1836).

Nichols, J., *The History and Antiquities of the County of Leicester*, Vol. III, Part II (Wakefield, 2002).

North, J., *England's Boy King* (Welwyn Garden City, 2005).

Page, W. (ed.), *The Victoria History of Leicester*, 5 vols (London and Oxford, 1907–64).

Perry, M., *Sisters to the King* (London, 1998).

Pettegree, A., *Foreign Protestant Communities in Sixteenth-Century London* (Oxford, 1986).

Picard, L., *Elizabeth's London* (London, 2003).

Planche, J.R., *Regal Records, or a Chronicle of the Coronations of the Queen Regnants of England* (London, 1838).

Plowden, A., *Tudor Women: Queens and Commoners* (London, 1979).

Plowden, A., *Lady Jane Grey and the House of Suffolk* (London, 1985).

Plowden, A., *Lady Jane Grey: Nine Days Queen* (Stroud, 2003).

Plowden, A., *The House of Tudor* (Stroud, 2010).

Pocock, N., *Troubles Connected with the Prayer Book of 1549*, Camden Society, XXXVII (London, 1884).

Pollard, A.F., *History of England from the Accession of Edward VI to the Death of Elizabeth (1547–1603)* (London, 1910).

Porter, L., *Mary Tudor* (London, 2007).

Porter, L., *Katherine the Queen* (London, 2010).

Porter, R., *London: A Social History* (London, 2000).

Prescott, H.F.M., *Mary Tudor* (London, 1952).

Prior, M. (ed.), *Women in English Society 1500–1800* (London and New York, 1985).

Prochaska, F., 'The Many Faces of Lady Jane Grey', *History Today*, XXXV (1985), pp. 34–40.

Read, E., *Catherine, Duchess of Suffolk* (London, 1962).

Redworth, G., *In Defence of the Church Catholic: The Life of Stephen Gardiner* (Oxford, 1990).

Reynolds, A., *In Fine Style: The Art of Tudor and Stuart Fashion* (London, 2013).

Richards, J.M., 'Mary Tudor as "Sole Queen"? Gendering Tudor Monarchy', *Historical Journal*, XXXX (1997), pp. 895–924.

Richards, J.M., '"To Promote a Woman to Beare Rule": Talking of Queens in Mid-Tudor England', *Sixteenth Century Journal*, XXVIII (1997), pp. 101–21.

Richardson, W.C., *Mary Tudor, the White Queen* (London, 1970).

Ridley, J., *Bloody Mary's Martyrs* (New York, 2001).

Routh, C.R.N., *Who's Who in Tudor England* (London, 1990).

Scarisbrick, D., *Tudor and Jacobean Jewellery* (Norwich, 1994).

Scarisbrick, J.J., *Henry VIII* (London, 1968).

Sidney, P., *Jane the Quene* (London, 1900).

Skidmore, C., *Edward VI: The Lost King of England* (London, 2007).

Slack, P., *The Impact of Plague in Tudor and Stuart England* (London, 1985).

Smith, R.S., *Sir Francis Willoughby of Wollaton Hall* (Notts, 1988).

Somerset, A., *Ladies in Waiting* (London, 1984).

Squires, A., *The Greys* (Hale, 2002).

Starkey, D., *The Reign of Henry VIII: Personalities and Politics* (London, 1985).

Starkey, D., *Elizabeth* (London, 2001).

Starkey, D., *Six Wives* (London, 2003).

Starkey, D. (ed.), *Rivals in Power* (London, 1990).

Starkey, D., Grosvenor, B. et al (eds), *Lost Faces: Identity and Discovery in Tudor Royal Portraiture* (London, 2007).

Stevenson, J. and Squires, A., *Bradgate Park: Childhood Home of Lady Jane Grey* (Newtown Linford, 1994).

Stone, J.M., *The History of Mary I* (London, 1901).

Stone, L., *The Crisis of the Aristocracy 1558–1640* (Oxford, 1965).

Stopes, C.C., *Shakespeare's Environment* (London, 1918).

Strickland, A., *The Tudor Princesses* (London, 1868).

Strickland, A., *Lives of the Queens of England* (London, 1890).

Strong, R., *Tudor and Jacobean Portraits*, 2 vols (London, 1969).

Strong, R., *And When Did You Last See Your Father? The Victorian Painter and British History* (London, 1978).

Strong, R., *Artists of the Tudor Court: The Portrait Miniature Rediscovered, 1520–1620* (London, 1983).

Strype, J., *Annals of the Reformation: Ecclesiastical Memorials* (Oxford, 1820–40).

Thornbury, W., 'The neighbourhood of the Tower: Introduction', in *Old and New London*, II (London, 1878).

Thurley, S., *Royal Palaces of Tudor England* (London, 1993).

Thurley, S., *Hampton Court: A Social and Architectural History* (London, 2003).

Tittler, R., *The Reign of Mary I* (London, 1991).

Tittler, R. and Battley, S.L., 'The Local Community and the Crown in 1553: The Accession of Mary Tudor Revisited', *BIHR*, LVII (1984), pp. 131–9.

Tuckwell, T., *New Hall and its School* (King's Lynn, 2006).

Tudor, P., 'Protestant Books in London in Mary Tudor's Reign', *London Journal*, XV (1990), pp. 19–28.

Turner, S., *History of the Reigns of Edward VI, Mary and Elizabeth* (London, 1829).

Tytler, P.F., *England under the Reigns of Edward VI and Mary* (London, 1839).

Tytler, S., *Tudor Queens and Princesses* (London, 1896).

Warnicke, R., 'Queenship: Politics and Gender in Tudor England', *History Compass*, IV (2006), pp. 203–27.

Weir, A., *Britain's Royal Families* (London, 1989).

Weir, A., *The Six Wives of Henry VIII* (London, 1991).

Weir, A., *Children of England* (London, 1996).

Weir, A., *Henry VIII: King and Court* (London, 2001).

Weir, A., *The Lady in the Tower: The Fall of Anne Boleyn* (London, 2009).

Weir, A., *Mary Boleyn* (London, 2011).

Whitelock, A., *Mary Tudor: England's First Queen* (London, 2009).

Whitelock, A. and MacCulloch, D., 'Princess Mary's Household and the Succession Crisis, July 1553', *Historical Journal*, L (2007), pp. 265–87.

Williams, P., *The Later Tudors: England 1547–1603* (Oxford, 1995).

Williams, S., *Grimsthorpe Castle* (Grimsthorpe, 2003).

Wilson, D., *The Uncrowned Kings of England: The Black Legend of the Dudley's* (London, 2005).

Wood, M.A.E, *Royal and Illustrious Ladies of Great Britain* (London, 1846).

Wyatt, M., *The Italian Encounter with Tudor England* (Cambridge, 2005).

Young, A., *Tudor and Jacobean Tournaments* (London, 1987).

ACKNOWLEDGEMENTS

THE SUPPORT I have received while writing this book has been extraordinary, and there are many people to whom I wish to express my sincerest gratitude. First, to my agent Andrew Lownie, whose excellent idea it was to write a biography of Jane.

I am incredibly grateful to everyone at Michael O'Mara Books, who have made my first experience of publishing such a delight. I would most especially like to thank my wonderful editor, Fiona Slater, for all of her brilliant insights and energy, and for pulling the book into such good shape. Also my publicist, Clara Nelson, for all of her enthusiasm, and the rest of the amazing sales team. Thanks are also due to Michael O'Mara and Hugh Barker for suggesting a new approach to the book.

There are three special ladies to whom I will be forever thankful. Alison Weir, for tirelessly championing me over the past ten years. Without Alison's belief in me I would never have made it to university to study history, let alone considered a career in writing. Tracy Borman, for her steadfast confidence in my abilities, and kind words that have given me a boost on many occasions. Sarah Gristwood, for her endless patience, enthusiasm and encouragement. You are all inspirational, and I cannot thank you enough for your friendship.

Rosa O'Neill, Dr David Butterfield, Philip Langford and his colleagues have all kindly helped with the translation and transcription of documents, and I am also grateful to Professor Diarmaid MacCulloch for allowing me to use his translation of a key document. Marilyn Roberts generously helped with the construction of family trees.

Thanks to Tony Tuckwell, who selflessly gave up his time to show

me around New Hall School, and shared his extensive knowledge with
me. Peter Tyldesley, Director of Bradgate Park, who allowed me to see
the ruins of the house out of season, and was enthusiastically informa-
tive when it came to Bradgate's history. The staff at the British Library,
the National Archives, Surrey History Centre, and New College Library,
Oxford, have been both helpful and accommodating, while Kim Gibbon,
Sean Milligan and Andrew Tongue generously allowed me to include
several of their excellent photographs.

I am fortunate to have an amazing family and friends who have always
had unwavering faith in me, but there are several who deserve special
thanks. My dear friend Kirsty Saul and Laura Montacute who took the
time to read part of the book and make helpful suggestions. Also John and
Jo Marston, who have endlessly encouraged me. Julian Alexander has,
on many occasions, given me many sound words of advice, as have Kate
Williams and Dan Jones. Thanks also to Sian Cossins, Barry Montacute,
Lesley Wilden, Peter Tomlinson, Keita Weston, David Howard and Maria
Norris. I should most especially like to pay tribute to my friend the late
David Baldwin with whom I was fortunate enough to share many conver-
sations about the Grey family.

Matthew Peters has been my sunshine; thank you for your belief in
me and for tirelessly supporting me. Special thanks go to my parents.
My mother has always inspired me to follow my dreams, and my father's
insights have been invaluable. Without their help in a multitude of ways,
I would never have been able to complete the book. To everyone who has
championed me over the years, thank you.

INDEX